Gender and Authorship in the Sidney Circle

Gender and Authorship in the Sidney Circle

Mary Ellen Lamb

THE UNIVERSITY OF WISCONSIN PRESS

The University of Wisconsin Press
114 North Murray Street
Madison, Wisconisn 53715

3 Henrietta Street
London WC2E 8LU, England

5 4 3 2 1

Printed in the United States of America

Library of Congress Cataloging-in-Publication Data
Lamb, Mary, 1946–
Gender and authorship in the Sidney circle / Mary Ellen Lamb.
308 pp. cm.
Includes bibliographical references and index.
1. Pembroke, Mary Sidney Herbert, Countess of, 1561–1621—Criticism and interpretation. 2. Wroth, Mary, Lady, ca. 1586–ca. 1640—Criticism and interpretation. 3. Sidney, Philip, Sir, 1554–1586—Friends and associates. 4. English literature—Early modern, 1500–1700—History and criticism. 5. English literature—Women authors—History and criticism. 6. Women and literature—England—History—16th century. 7. Women and literature—England—History—17th century. 8. Women in literature. I. Title.
PR2329.P2Z78 1990
821′3—dc20
ISBN 0-299-12690-0 90-50092
ISBN 0-299-12694-3 (pbk.) CIP

To my mother Irene Lamb, who is so easily pleased

Contents

Acknowledgments

This book would not have achieved whatever merits it possesses without a grant from the National Endowment for the Humanities, matched by a grant from the College of Liberal Arts at Southern Illinois University, which enabled me to spend the year 1986–7 at the Newberry Library. There I profited not only from the collections and the seminars but perhaps more especially from informal conversations with other scholars at the Newberry and in the Chicago area, who taught me more than they probably realized. Several of them generously read early portions of this book as I wrote it and some shared their work with me. I would like to thank this community of scholars and especially Rolena Adorno, Albert Ascoli, Alan Hager, David Loewenstein, Joseph Lowenstein, Judith Kegan Gardiner, Phyllis Gorfain, Clark Hulse, Gwen Kennedy, Leah Marcus, Diana Robins, Mary Beth Rose, Florence Sandler, Michael Shapiro, Richard Strier, and James Turner. In addition to the scholars I met at the Newberry, I would also like to thank Barbara Freedman, Ann Rosalind Jones, Constance Jordan, Robert Montgomery, Lee Person, Catherine Pesce, Josephine Roberts, Philip St. Clair, Iris Smith, and Gary Waller. Barbara Hanrahan of the University of Wisconsin Press and my copyeditor Carolyn Moser helped this book to reach completion.

For personal support on an almost daily basis during the time I wrote this book I owe a debt to James and Ruby Jung, as well as to Philip St. Clair and to Catherine Pesce (who deserve to be mentioned twice). I owe most special thanks to my son John Lamb, who reminds me (since I may have forgotten) that near the beginning of this project, he helped me to find my place when I was lost.

I thank the Louisiana State University Press for allowing me to quote extensively from Josephine Roberts's *The Poems of Lady Mary Wroth.* The British Library has kindly granted me permission to quote three poems from British Library Additional MS 15232; and the Newberry Library has allowed me to quote from Mary Wroth's *The Countess of Montgomery's Urania* in both its published Folio and its manuscript form. Portions of chapter one were published in an earlier draft as "The Countess of Pembroke's Patronage," in *English Literary Renaissance* 12(1982): 162–79; portions of chapter three as "The Countess of Pembroke and the Art of Dying," in

Mary Beth Rose, ed., *Women in the Middle Ages and the Renaissance: Literary and Historical Perspectives* (Syracuse: Syracuse Univ. Press, 1986), 207–26; and portions of chapter five as "Three Holograph Poems in British Additional MS 15232: A New Sidney Poet?" in *Review of English Studies* 35 (1984), 301–15. Various articles and books appeared too late for me to use them; I especially regret being unable to cite Margaret Hannay's biography of the countess of Pembroke, entitled *Philip's Phoenix,* available from Oxford University Press after this book had been copyedited.

Gender and Authorship in the Sidney Circle

Introduction

"How will you have your discourse," said she, "without you let my lips alone?"[1] With these words, Philoclea protests the prevention of her narrative by the kisses of her beloved prince Pyrocles in Sir Philip Sidney's *The Countess of Pembroke's Arcadia*. Philoclea never succeeds in telling this narrative to her amorous listener. Her written word fares no better. Written outdoors on exposed marble stone, her poem in praise of chastity is nearly erased by moisture. She responds to this loss by composing a new poem, never written down for lack of pen and ink, denigrating her smudged marks of authorship as stains on the marble's white purity. Her ready parallel between these "spots" on the stone and the "blots" created within her soul by her recently discovered sexual identity strongly implies the sexual nature of this stain.[2] These two examples of Philoclea's authorship bear several differences: one is oral, the other is written; one narrative is never told, the other is erased; one is prevented by a loved one's kisses, the other is denigrated by an internalized sense of sexual guilt. But they share a strong commonality: in both cases, Philoclea's words are pervaded by an overwhelming sexuality which precludes any sustained role for her as author.

While these scenes of a woman's attempted authorship from Sidney's *Arcadia* do not reflect practice in any simple sense, they are organized by a highly efficient discourse of gender difference that sexualized women's language to prevent, with greater or lesser success, authorship by women. The exaggerated degree of sexual power that this discourse granted to women's language exposes this sexualization as a displacement for an underlying concern for the subversive potential of women's anger. Masking the project of the containment of women within a patriarchal system, this strategy of sexualization legitimated the necessity of surveilling and controlling women's words. This strict regulation of women's language, represented as closing off sexual access to inappropriate males, also performed the even more central function of preventing women's protest against the system which contained them.[3] This discourse of gender difference created highly gendered meanings for the word *author* during the English Renaissance. At a time when authorship for men posed dilemmas between creating themselves in the images of sanctioned authorities and asserting their own independent voices, authorship for women posed an even more fundamental problem. While men struggled with choosing or adapting a voice from a range of often conflicting authorial models, cultural prohibitions purporting to contain women's sexuality threatened, in theory, to render the term *woman author* an oxymoron.[4]

The dangers of mistaking discourse for practice have recently been pointed out. Repressive statements in patriarchal treatises representing the seventeenth-century woman, for example, as silent, powerless, and utterly controlled by her husband fail to reflect what we know about the actual activities of "the patriarch's wife."[5] The Renaissance discourse of gender difference expressed a patriarchal ideal, a fervent wish sometimes existing in direct opposition to lived experience. Increasing infringements of gender rules may themselves have elicited the reassertions of the supposed bases of those rules in Scripture and natural order. Few prescriptions of behavior, including those organized by gender ideology, enforce absolute conformity or even obtain universal assent. Thus, the mere existence of writings, and even published writings, by women who were, in theory, prohibited from publicly circulating their words, demonstrates the inevitable slippage between discourse and behavior, between theory and practice.[6]

While the warning not to confuse patriarchal discourse with lived experience is aptly taken, it is equally dangerous to underestimate the effect of powerful cultural discourses. To discount these discourses is to assume the transcendental subject, unchanging through history, unaffected by gender or class; and the dangerous fallacy of this assumption has been eloquently and repeatedly demonstrated by proponents of cultural materialism.[7] There is a middle ground. Within any culture, the availability of specific discourses and the unavailability of others place restraints upon the kind of subject that can be constructed. As Foucault has demonstrated, however, even powerful discourses contain within themselves local sites of resistance.[8] Choices always exist, but choices are always limited. Thus, the Renaissance gender ideology did not succeed in preventing all Renaissance women from writing; but it exerted formative pressure upon what they wrote, how they wrote, and the ways their writings were received. The discourse of gender difference rendered women's writing different from men's.

Perhaps the most debilitating limitations placed upon potential women authors of the Renaissance proceeded from the sexualization of women's speech, even more than of their written word. The underlying project to contain women's dissent through sexualizing women's language becomes apparent in the way that marriage manuals, the juridical system, and literary works construed women's protest as sexual transgression. The attributes recommended to women in the injuction to be "chaste, silent, and obedient" were collapsed into each other, so that a fall from one implied a fall from another.[9] Thus, a married woman who would "chafe and scold" at her husband risked classification as "next to harlots, if not the same with them."[10] This classification passed into English law, so that a man who slandered a woman as a "whore" could defend himself by stating his meaning as "whore of her tonge," not "whore of her body."[11] Lisa Jardine has exposed the sexualization of the woman's tongue on the English stage as the counterpart to the man's penis, a potential source of dangerous power and of disruptive sexuality.[12] Conversely, as Margaret Ferguson has pointed out, a woman's silence signified her bodily purity.[13]

While this discourse of gender difference relied on various sources—religious, medical, legal, literary—the use of quotations from the Bible demonstrates one mechanism through which the control of women's speech was legitimated by appealing to no less an authority than God's will. One passage from Saint Paul (1. Cor. 14:34–35) prohibiting women from speaking in church and advising them to ask their questions of their husbands at home was generalized to prohibit women's speech in any public place.[14] Women's public speech, according to this model, was interpreted as a sign of disobedience to their husbands, who were by rights their sole auditors. The threat posed by the sexuality of women's untrammeled speech, already represented as a sign of disobedience to a patriarchal society, becomes apparent in another passage from Saint Paul (1 Tim. 2:11–14), which denied women any authority over men. According to these verses, women were prohibited from teaching and enjoined to a submissive silence because of the sin of Eve, who ate the apple and then persuaded Adam to eat as well.[15] Women's speech, like Eve's, was pervaded by a dangerous sexuality requiring strict containment to prevent moral damage. This Renaissance rereading of the Fall located guilt not in a human desire to possess forbidden sexual knowledge but in the failure to limit the effects of women's speech. Thus, the very authority present in the word *author* was out of the question for women.

Sometimes merging with earlier medieval or classical discourses, sometimes changing emphases to adapt to shifting cultural circumstances, this discourse of gender difference containing women's spoken words represents a complex topic of study in its own right, as a number of scholars have recently demonstrated. Analyzing the ways this discourse articulated women as property, Peter Stallybrass has examined the mechanisms by which silence came to signify chastity, as women were, in theory, to be enclosed within their houses, with their doors, their mouths, and their bodies closed off to all but their proper owners. Working primarily with conduct books, Ann Rosalind Jones has linked this repressive discourse to the projects of an upwardly mobile bourgeois class, which supplanted an earlier aristocratic discourse that had allowed women some speech albeit under perilously contradictory circumstances. Catherine Belsey has situated this silencing of women as a phase within the history of the installation of women as subjects, a project not generally accomplished until the late seventeenth century. Drawing on historical records of the use of cucking stools and public processions to punish women's speech, D. E. Underdown has posited "a crisis in gender relations" around 1600 brought on by the rise of capitalism.[16]

Work remains to be done upon the implementation of this discourse. While women whose speech was deemed inappropriate by civic or religious authorities could be ducked as scolds or even burned as witches, less juridical measures exerted their more subtle power. Primary among these was the elevation of the submissive, silent woman as an object of desire in the sixteenth century. The conduct books described by Jones played an important role in this production of this woman as a cultural ideal; so did sermons, political tracts, philosophical essays, and literature.[17] The enthusiastic endorsement of marriageable bachelors and the willing assent of young women were no doubt often elicited by the many delineations of the silent object of desire, such as this one: "There is nothing that doth so commend, avaunce, set forthe, adourne, decke, trim, and garnish a maid, as silence."[18] While the mechanisms through which this discourse operated upon actual women are difficult to document, it seems likely that the words of some unmarried women were controlled less by legal threats than by the prospect of spinsterhood. Some married women may well have guarded their words to render themselves appealing to their husbands and acceptable to their neighbors, more than from a fear of cucking. The degree to which women's silencing was a matter of cultural compulsion or of voluntary adherence can never be determined; undoubtedly their behavior was shaped both by the carrot and the stick. No doubt some women consented to their silencing in order to conform to a culturally inscribed model of desire; this is only to say that women, like men, were subject to the discourses of their day.

This containment of women's speech had obvious applications to women's writing, a potentially even more effective means of circulating women's words. There is, in fact, some evidence of the blurring of speaking and writing as distinct activities in, for example, one editor's contemptuous description of women who publish as "speaking in print like Parates with solemne countenaunces."[19] This editor's perception of the written word as conveying not only the meaning but also the voice and even the visible presence of a writer was probably possible only in a recently literate society in which writing still bore traces of orality.[20] This editor's dismissal of women writers as parrots is a reminder that alternative means of discounting women's words were available in the Renaissance. Instead of representing women writers as whores, he denies them the subjectivity necessary for authorship. As parrots, they do not "mean" their words; they merely speak what they have heard without understanding. Fears of women's authorship extended to unpublished as well as published writing, as shown by Puttenham's warning that gentlewomen who become "too precise Poets" may "with their shrewd wits, when they are maried . . . become a little too phantastical wives."[21] According to the discourse which rendered women's words innately and irremediably sexual, their circulation, in spoken or written form, beyond the household threshold could put a woman's social and marital status at risk.

In addition to the restrictions placed upon women's speech, the restrictions placed upon women's reading cannot be ignored in any attempt to understand the limitations placed upon women's authorship.[22] One obvious limitation was women's access to literacy at all. While David Cressy's figures for female illiteracy are perhaps somewhat inflated, there can be no question that fewer women were taught to read than men.[23] And the words women did read, like the words they spoke or wrote, were often constructed as sufficiently sexual to necessitate strict surveillance. The influential educator Luis Vives, for example, represents women's reading of chivalric romances as so dangerously sexual as to warrant the intervention of any sensible husband: "And verily they be but foolishe husbandes and madde, that suffer their wives to waxe more ungraciously subtyle by readinge of suche bokes."[24]

Vives's perception of women as sensual readers participates in an established tradition of associating women with misreadings, and especially with carnal misreadings, traced by Susan Noakes from the thirteenth through the eighteenth centuries.[25] In the Italian Renaissance, for example, the sensual woman reader is explicitly inscribed in the prologue of Boccaccio's popular *Decameron*, which promises to relieve its gentlewomen readers from their "amorous afflictions." According to Boccaccio's gendering of his readership, women turned to books for relief because their sedentary lives provided few alternative outlets, while men could regain composure through more active pursuits such as hunting and shooting.[26] No doubt women, as well as men, read the *Decameron* as well as chivalric romances. But the significance attached to the act of reading was filtered through gender ideology. The sexualization of women's reading is perhaps nowhere so apparent as in the way representations of Sidney's *Countess of Pembroke's Arcadia* differed depending upon the gender of the reader. As discussed below (Chapter 2), when men were represented as reading Sidney's *Arcadia*, it was usually described as a work replete with political or moral precepts; when read by women, however, it was represented as dangerously or titillatingly sexual.

Counterdiscourses arose. The humanist Richard Hyrde, for example, advanced a representation of reading as signifying chastity, rather than sexuality. In his defense of teaching women to read Latin against those who apparently feared that women would use this knowledge only to set up sexual assignations with friars, Hyrde claimed, on the contrary, that reading represents a superior form of control over women's thoughts: "Redyng and stydyeing of bokes so occupieth the mynde that it can have no leyser to muse or delyte in other fantasies[,] whan in all handy werkes that men saye be more mete for a woman the body may be busy in one place and the mynde walkyng in another while they syt sowing and spinnying with their fyngers may caste and compasse many pevysshe fantasyes in theyr myndes."[27]

This passage manipulates a long tradition according to which working with cloth signified women's chastity. In Homer's *Odyssey*, for example, Ulysses' wife Penelope had warded off suitors until her husband's return by her continual spinning. According to Livy's history of Rome, Collintinus demonstrated the chastity of his wife, Lucrece, to his fellow soldiers by spying on her late at night only to find her spinning with her maids, in pointed contrast to the licentious activities of the other soldiers' wives. For Hyrde, however, regulating women's activities is no longer sufficient; their thoughts must be monitored as well. By eliciting anxieties about the probable sexual nature of the "fantasies" women can "muse or delyte in," Hyrde empties spinning of its traditional signification to appropriate chastity for reading instead. In his representation of women as also indulging in many "pevysshe fantasyes" as they spin, Hyrde advances reading as a means of containing not only women's sexuality but also their anger.

This addition makes explicit the political project underlying the sexualization of women's language.

Hyrde's counterdiscourse did little to deny the potential of a dangerous sexuality in women's reading. Clearly, only an approved and regulated form of reading could control women's sexual or angry thoughts. Renaissance educators represented the chastity of women readers as highly contingent upon the nature of their reading, which was strictly circumscribed to exclude any works, especially chivalric narratives or books of love, that did not advance a woman's spiritual state.[28] Thus, inscriptions or representations of chaste or devout women readers did little to assuage anxieties concerning the sexual effect of the wrong sort of reading for women. Women's reading, unlike men's, shared with women's writing an exaggeratedly sexual determination, either through excess or lack of sexuality. The meanings women were described as creating through their words, the ones they read and the ones they wrote, were either replete with or devoid of sexuality; either way, these meanings were constituted in sexual terms. The words a woman read or wrote, according to these constructions, created her as a virgin or as a whore.

The restrictions placed upon works women were permitted to read severely limited what they could write. Clearly, if reading books of love was considered dangerous for their reputation, writing such books would be worse. The very point of the barrage of tracts, printed sermons, and books which enticed, advised, or threatened women to be "chaste, silent, and obedient" precluded written responses from women readers. The sanctioned authorities offered as models to male authors were not offered to women. A woman who read religious tracts or sermons was not permitted to respond by writing her own, for such writing, construed as preaching, was forbidden to women. A woman who read classical authors and church fathers could not appropriate their authority for herself, for their misogyny did not admit women imitators.[29] Perhaps most important, however, was the absence of any position as subject offered to women by most male-authored works, usually addressed to male readers.[30] Denied subjectivity as readers in most of the works they read, women were deprived of a primary source of the subjectivity necessary for them to construct themselves as authors.

But some women did write. They wrote religious and secular translations, as well as familial and personal writings, sonnets, elegies, and even pamphlets of protest.[31] Some women also read books of love, and some undoubtedly defied their husbands' authority.[32] Thus, the discourse of gender difference must not be read as a description of actual practice; it did not prevent women from writing. However, by defining writing as a highly gendered act, it confronted women writers with different and more complicated tasks than those facing men writers. The sometimes complex or even devious ways in which women created themselves as authors render visible the sites of resistance, the loopholes, the contradictions, the shiftings within gender ideology restricting women's language in the Renaissance.

Perhaps the most intense pressure exerted upon Renaissance women writers by their culture was the necessity of absolving themselves both of the motive of sexuality and of the desire to protest their containment within this patriarchal system. Several forms of writing seemed fairly innocent in these respects: private devotional works or medicinal recipes written for family members; elegies written for deceased children or parents. The necessity of defending themselves from unwelcome aspersions perhaps accounted for the most frequent form of writing undertaken by women writers in the Renaissance: translations of male-authored religious works.[33] A woman who translated a male-authored work was, presumably, less vulnerable to accusations of circulating her words inappropriately; after all, they were not, strictly speaking, her words at all. Representations like Hyrde's of the chastity and the compliance signified by women's reading of approved works no doubt also contributed to authorizing this form of women's writing. If reading a religious work kept a woman's mind from dangerous thoughts, surely translating such a work could only render her thoughts even more securely obedient and free from sexual desire.

Unfortunately, many writings by women, including many translations, have undoubtedly been lost, for relatively few works by women achieved publication. Those women who somehow managed to overcome cultural barriers against women's writing also faced "the stigma of print," a perception among the upper class that publishing—for men or for women—was unacceptably lower-class.[34] The various ploys, occasionally sincere, through which male writers circumvented prejudices against publication took on greater weight and complexity for women writers, for these strategies also served to defend women's chastity and compliance. The most frequent tactic—accusing a friend or an editor of betraying an author's writing to print—assumed special significance for women writers. For example, the apology to Anne Cooke Bacon by her editor for printing Bacon's translation of Bishop John Jewel's Latin *Apologia Ecclesiae Anglicanae* (1564) without her consent made special accommodations for her gender, representing her maidenly "modestie" which would have prevented publication, and especially her deference to his male judgement in approving her work.[35] Dedications of women's published books provide a rich and largely unexamined repository of the often brilliant verbal manuevers enabling women to be presented, or to present themselves, as writers within a culture hostile to women's speech.

In their dedications, women writers often represented themselves not only as chaste, but as powerless. This common and absolute denial by women writers of any wish to influence the wider audience implicit in the very act of publishing suggests an awareness, on some level, that beneath the discourse which sexualized their language lay a project of containment. Thus, women's dedications of their works often represented the transmission of their words beyond their domestic space as performed unwillingly, or through the agency of their husbands, or under circumstances (such as approaching death) that removed any possibility of gaining influence over an audience outside the family. Elizabeth Jocelyn's authorship of her *Mothers legacie* (1624) for the instruction of the child she feared (accurately as it turned out) she would never live to raise represents an especially interesting instance of this last strategy.[36] The "Approbation" prefacing Jocelyn's work represents her authorship as an intensely private activity: "Undauntedly looking death in the face, privatly in her Closet betweene God and her, shee wrote these pious Meditations" (A9).

Anne Cooke Bacon's dedication of her translation of the sermons of Bernadino Ochino provides only one example of the complexity of the manueverings enabling a woman's representation of herself as an author. According to her dedication, Anne Cooke Bacon translated these sermons to justify her otherwise "vaine studie in the Italian tongue" to her mother; the religious content of her translation would, she hoped, conform to her mother's "chife delight . . . in the destroying of man his glorie and exaltinge wholy the glory of God."[37] Bacon's dedication draws upon four overlapping strategies to deflect possible accusations of a desire for power or sexual satisfaction. First, she limits her "real" audience to an appropriate family member, her morally vigilant mother. Second, by creating her translation as an act of obedience to her mother, she presents her translation as firmly contained within the power structure of the family. Third, her larger project, demurely derived from her mother, of destroying "man his glorie" mitigates against her own desire to achieve glory through her ability to translate. Finally, by declaring this aim to exalt "wholy the glory of God," Bacon simultaneously voids her writing of sexuality and of a desire for earthly power.

Whatever these disclaimers, translations often embodied active political or personal designs of their women translators. In a time when religion was inextricably connected to politics, translating religious works was often a political act. Elizabeth Cooke Russell's translation of *A Way of Reconciliation Touching the True Nature and Substance of the Body and Blood of Christ in the Sacrament* (1605), for example, was apparently an attempt to solidify the Church of England by making accessible to English readers an able defense of the position concerning transubstantiation expressed in Bishop Jewel's *Apologie for the Church of England.*[38] Margaret Hannay attributes a political motive to the countess of Pembroke's translation of the Psalms, as encouragement to Queen Elizabeth to engage in the Protestant partisan policies espoused by her brother Philip.[39] Most religious works translated in the Renaissance by men or by women could profitably bear scrutiny for signs of political allegiance.

Personal motives are more difficult to discern if even more intriguing. Most interestingly, in addition to diplomatic motives accomplished in Elizabeth's translation of Marguerite de Navarre's *Le miroir de l'ame pecheresse,* Anne Prescott convincingly argues that the young Elizabeth's departures from her text to create God as a loving mother rather than a loving father reflect her sentiments concerning her own family situation.[40] Jane Lumley's schoolgirl translation of Euripedes' *Iphigenia,* a play named for a young girl sacrificed by the Greeks to gain a good wind to sail their warships to Troy, perhaps answered a need for an example of female heroism within a culture which offered few opportunities for public distinction to women.[41] This form of heroism itself was no doubt shaped by the discourse of gender difference, for a willingness to die demonstrated a woman's willingness to remove herself from the worldly sphere in which political and sexual contacts were formed. The powerful resonances of this Renaissance association of women's heroism with dying shape the countess of Pembroke's version of authorship enabling her translations discussed in Chapter 3.

Thus, however much dedications portrayed women translators as the modest mediums of the words of male authors, the act of translating opened opportunities for some limited political and personal expression. Perhaps partly because of the representations of these women translators as unassailably chaste and compliant, translating by the early seventeenth century was apparently becoming desexualized although still strongly gendered. John Florio describes his translation of Montaigne's essays as a specifically female activity, "defective . . . since all translations are reputed femalls" and therefore appropriate to dedicating to women. According to a complicated role reversal, literary "births" of original works are masculine, Florio claims, and appropriately dedicated to men.[42] Florio's association of translating (including, presumably, his own) with women shows a late accommodation of the discourse of gender difference to include women translators. It also shows the potential impact of this discourse upon male writers. The construing of writing as a gender-specific act not only limited women writers; it was also capable of introducing anxieties in male writers about their own sexual identity.

Predictably, original writings by women required even more defense than translations. Religious fervor provided one justification. Although Saint Paul's prohibition of women's speech in church was used to prevent women from writing sermons as well as from speaking them, writing private expressions of religious devotion—prayers, meditations, confessions of sin—was often permissible. Catherine Parr published two works of this kind: *Prayers or Meditacions* (1545) and *Lamentacion or complaynt of a sinner* (1547).[43] Parr avoids the authoritative tone of the preacher by using an intensely personal voice, especially in the latter work, in which she repents her "obstynate, stony, and untractable herte" (A1). Her writings exert influence upon readers through the force of her own negative example rather than through instruction or advice.

Women were forbidden to instruct men in religious matters, but alien others, such as Catholics or atheists, were fair game. The religious upheavals of the mid-sixteenth century provided many opportunities for Protestant women martyrs to speak boldly against Catholic interrogators and even to trip them up in matters of faith and doctrine. Their words, recorded in John Foxe's immensely popular *Actes and Monuments*, were circulated widely, and their defiance of the wrong sect of male religious authorities received the highest commendations. One such martyr, Anne Askew, wrote her own accounts of her ordeals, published after her death.[44] At the opposite end of the spectrum of religious protestation, but uncannily similar in form, were the witches. Becoming an alien other also created a space for women's speech. As Catherine Belsey has noted, a system of interrogation created for women a defined position, however ghastly, as speaking subjects. Their words were listened to with eager attention and meticulously recorded in writing, before these women accused of witchcraft were removed from the courtroom and burned.[45]

Finally, while women were not empowered by their church to preach, they could perceive themselves as empowered by God to prophesy. Approximately fifty pamphlets published by Lady Eleanor ouglas circulated not *her* words, but the words of the prophet peaking through her. With her manuscripts burned by her husband, and then she herself imprisoned when some of her political predictions proved accurate, her defiant version of authorship depended upon the presence of the anagram "Reveale O Daniel" within her maiden name "Eleanor Audeley."[46] The incoherence of Douglas's writings raises the possibility of madness as a mechanism by which a subject can circumvent cultural discourses. Since she wrote a number of her pamphlets in the 1640s, Davies may have also experienced the liberating effects of the time, for hers is one of several women's voices within the religious writings of the topsy-turvy mid-century. The increase in writings by women during this period suggests a temporary loosening of strictures as a result of the problematizing of hierarchies, including sexual ones, that occurred with the deposition of King Charles.[47]

Religious fervor opened up spaces for women's speech and writing within the discourse of gender difference. Opportunities apparently existed at its margins as well as within its interstices, for this discourse did not operate with uniform efficiency across classes. More work needs to be done on the juncture of class and discourse before the results are clear, but it appears that the discourse of gender difference was tempered at court by an earlier discourse receiving special currency with the publication of Sir Thomas Hoby's translation of Castiglione's *Book of the Courtier* in 1561. As Jones has noted, this aristocratic discourse allowed women some speech, within strict and confusing conditions, as a means of demonstrating their courtliness to reflect the status of their family or monarch.[48] Perhaps this discourse enabled the limited circulation of women's verse in the letters and miscellanies mentioned by Margaret Ezell.[49] As will be discussed below, manuscript verse circulated between Mary Wroth and William Herbert; Ben Jonson also read manuscript verse of Mary Wroth and the poems, now lost, of the countess of Rutland.

According to Castiglione's representation, however, most of the women in the court of Urbino were silenced; their primary function was to provide a discriminating audience for the male courtiers who were competing with each other to gain recognition for their courtliness. Despite the courtiers' elaborate theorizing about the kinds of speech permitted to women, only the duchess of Urbino herself and Emilia Pia, whom she empowered as her deputy, spoke with any regularity. The presence of their speech demonstrates the importance of political power—in their case deriving from the duchess's absent husband—as a factor enabling women's speech. The flamboyant example of Penelope Devereux Rich strongly suggests that unusual political power also eased the restrictions imposed by the discourse of gender difference in late-sixteenth-century England. Penelope Devereux Rich was the sister of the earl of Essex, who was, until his rebellion and subsequent execution, the favorite of Queen Elizabeth near the end of her reign. Perhaps the engagement of the queen's own sexuality, on some level, in the flirtatious relationship between Elizabeth and the earl worked to create Rich's relative impunity from gender ideology. Thus, instead of remaining chaste and silent in her husband's house, Penelope Rich openly managed an extramarital affair with a man named, appropriately enough, Charles Blount, Lord Mountjoy, by whom she bore several illegitimate children without incurring any obvious censure from the queen or her court.[50] While no extant poems reveal that Rich used her relative freedom to write, a perception that she was empowered as an author is revealed in the composition of at least one extended manuscript poem by another writer in her name.[51] However, such marked examples of discursive outlawry were rare. The sexuality of less well connected aristocratic women, particularly wives left on country estates, was generally organized by the discourse of gender difference. The tolerance extended to Devereux was not extended with the same generosity to Mary Wroth when she committed a similar transgression.

There is some evidence that the effect of gender restrictions was weakened in the lower classes and that a competing lower-class perception of gender and sexuality left its trace in some works produced by and for those members of the lower middle class who had access to written materials. Especially accessible to lower-class influence were popular works circulated orally as well as in print. Broadside ballads, addressed to both men and women, sometimes included scatalogical jokes and bawdy humor, and seventeenth-century "small merry books," in particular, assumed that sex was enjoyed by women as well as by men.[52] While literary evidence must not be taken at face value, it seems possible that the sexual freedom expressed in the words "jump her and thump her" in Autolycus's song for peasant maids in Shakespeare's *Winter's Tale* (4.4.195; Riverside ed.) reflected a social code competing with that of the upper or upper middle classes.[53]

Because of the paucity of written documents from these groups, any comments about the effect of these relaxed gender expectations upon women writers must be taken as speculation. But it seems accurate to say, at the least, that class must be considered as a factor strongly affecting women's authorship. Possibly a special location in class, allowing her access to literacy but not imposing strict gender restraints, enabled the author who took the name Jane Anger to write the pamphlet of protest *Her Protection for Women,* published in 1589.[54] In lieu of specific biographical information, Anger's authorship must remain an anomaly. The authorship of other such pamphlets later in the seventeenth century by women such as Rachel Speght, a minister's daugher, indicates the progressive loosening of the constraints imposed upon women.[55]

The most important factor enabling women's authorship of original works, however, was a location outside the pale, rather than at the margins of the class most affected by the discourse of gender difference. Five women authors moved, or were moved, beyond the boundaries of conventional society for a range of reasons, from royal birth, to religious affiliation, to illicit sexuality.[56] As female monarchs, Elizabeth Tudor and Mary Stuart represented anomalies within their patriarchal culture. Because of her conversion to Catholicism, Elizabeth Cary was ejected from her family by her husband to experience dire economic conditions unusual for her class. The social circumstances both of Mary Wroth and Aemelia Lanyer changed radically upon the births of their illegitimate children. It is surely no coincidence that from this group of women—all of whom led highly unconventional lives—emerged almost all of the extended, original works (as opposed to translations) written by women in sixteenth- and early-seventeenth-century England: a number of love poems, the first extant tragedy, the first extant romance, and a religious work defending, rather than accusing, Eve.

The anomalous position of queens such as Elizabeth and especially Mary Stuart undoubtedly accounts in part for their writing of original works. As Leah Marcus has pointed out, reigning queens were said to possess two bodies, one in their masculine role as monarch and another in their biological role as woman; her work on the intense cultural anxieties elicited by Queen Elizabeth's dual identity as monarch and woman provides a sharp focus upon the deployment of gender ideology.[57] Thus, the social roles of reigning queens were constructed upon two competing discourses: the expectations of them as women existed in direct conflict with their function as rulers. Since a queen's love was a matter of state, it was no doubt difficult to determine from which body, the monarch's or the woman's, the love poetry of Elizabeth and Mary proceeded.

The authorship of Elizabeth Cary, like that of Elizabeth and Mary, was empowered by a competition between two discourses which eventually carried her outside the boundaries of mainstream society.

Her duties as a wife to a strongly Protestant husband increasingly existed in direct conflict with her developing role as a witnessing Catholic. Her conversion to Catholicism, which apparently began at the age of nineteen, when she voiced her disagreements with Calvin and Hooker, did not become public until 1626, when her husband withheld all funds, her father disinherited her, and the king confined her to her rooms for six weeks. Nearly reduced to starvation, she was driven to sue her husband for support before the Privy Council in 1627. She remained desperately poor for the rest of her life.[58]

Religion provided Cary, as it had the Protestant martyrs, a justification for speech and writing. Unlike these martyrs, however, Cary lived. The shadow of death, which had assuaged cultural anxieties about any worldly influence women martyrs might have experienced from their writings (had they lived), did not provide any such excuse for Cary's translation of numerous Catholic works and saints' lives. Cary's most significant writing, *The Tragedie of Miriam, the Faire Queene of Jewry* (1613), the first extant English tragedy by a woman, was written at a time when she was leading, by any obvious standard, a conventional life, bearing eleven children and managing her husband's domestic affairs. Nevertheless, the forces which would propel her beyond the margins of her society already structure this play, in its exposition of the conflict between the protagonist's duty to her tyrannical husband Herod and her right to her own subjectivity, to speech.[59] The way that this conflict, left unresolved within the play, was to work itself out in Cary's own life connects her authorship of *the Tragedie of Miriam* and her later location beyond the pale as more than coincidence.

The extramarital sexual activities of Wroth and Lanyer apparently played formative roles in their authorship.[60] Chapter 4 will explore the centrality of Wroth's relationship with her married cousin William Herbert, who fathered at least one and probably two of her children, to the version of authorship she constructed in her lengthy romance *The Countess of Montgomery's Urania*. Wroth's exile from court has been connected to this scandalous sexual relationship, and her own father described the "shame" incurred if she had decided to raise her son in her own house.[61] More work needs to be done on Aemelia Lanyer. According to A. L. Rowse, Lanyer became the acknowledged mistress of Lord Hunsdon, lord chamberlain in Elizabeth's court, until the disgrace of her pregnancy led him to marry her off to a court musician. This marriage evidently entailed a sharp loss in status, placing her under the control of a husband who, according to her confession to the Renaissance magus Simon Forman, "dealt hardly with her" and spent her money. Forman's diary relates in ungentlemanly detail that she "for lucre's sake will be a good fellow," that on one occasion she permitted him to feel all parts of her body, and presumably engaged in intercourse with him at another time when he stayed with her all night.[62]

Rather than proceeding from competing discourses, authorship by Mary Wroth and Aemelia Lanyer interrogates the discourse of gender difference from the far side. The discourse of gender difference had itself blurred the boundary between protest and unacceptable forms of sexuality. Sexualizing women's language to contain potential political protest through the threat of social censure, this discourse, by its own logic, would seem to empower protest by women already guilty of illicit sexuality. Or, alternatively, the activities of these women may have placed them beyond the reach of this discourse, for their already soiled reputations were perhaps not significantly threatened by the addition of one more stain from writing. By whatever mechanism, the writings of Wroth and Lanyer level protests integrally related to their sexuality. Wroth's romance heroizes constant women who remain true to lovers, not necessarily to their husbands. Lanyer's *Salve Deus Rex Judaeorum* defends Eve by accusing men of the greater sin of crucifying Christ; women's sexuality, according to this model, is less guilty than men's aggression. In both cases, however, the difficulties facing even these women authors apparently limit their protests. The constant heroines of Wroth's work rarely express anger at their philandering men, and Lanyer's oddly split work contains her accusations within a conservative meditation on the stations of the cross.

One final word needs to be said about the instability of discourse itself as a means of deploying power relations. In volume 1 of his *History of Sexuality,* Michel Foucault relates the use of the vocabulary of nineteenth-century medical and juridical discourses condemning homosexuality to construct a position from which homosexuality could finally be defended.[63] Through a similar reversal, Isabella Whitney constructed a version of authorship in the 1570s by using terms from the discourse of gender difference to establish a speaking position. Ann Rosalind Jones notes Whitney's echoes from conduct books in her conventional delineations of good wives in her *Copy of a letter lately written in meeter by a yonge Gentilwoman: to her unconstant lover,* in which her woman speaker takes discursive control over the the man who jilted her by offering him generous amounts of advice from a position of pronounced moral superiority.[64] Whitney's poetry uses the very "nets and bridles" restraining women's authorship to open up a space for herself as author. But such an opportunity was rarely taken.

Thus, the discourse of gender difference was generally, but not entirely, successful in its prevention of women's authorship of original works in the sixteenth and early seventeenth centuries. This discourse operated by sexualizing speech and reading as well as women's writing, to render these activities subject to surveillance and control. The sexualization of women's words, which masked the underlying project of containment, confronted women writers with the formidable task of constructing a form of authorship absolving them from motives of sexuality and of power. The works of the women who managed to overcome this obstacle were inevitably shaped by the conditions it imposed. This discourse did not, however, operate with uniform efficiency across classes; its effects were moderated in small pockets of the upper class and probably among the lower classes. Its constraints were increasingly loosened in the early seventeenth century as England began to experience the social turmoil that would lead to the Civil War. This discourse was especially ineffective within a small group of five women located, by political, religious, or sexual identification, outside the boundaries of mainstream society. These women authored most of the original works by women in the sixteenth and early seventeenth centuries.

Mary Wroth is the only one of these five women authors who is discussed here. Instead of centering solely on women's longer original works, this book takes as its special province the various writings, ranging from translations to unpublished manuscript verse, producted by the male and female members of one extended family, the Sidneys. There are various reasons for this choice of subject. As the foregoing discussion has indicated, an understanding of women's writing in the Renaissance depends upon an understanding of their culture, and especially of the gender-specific meanings attached to the acts of reading and writing by that culture. But cultures are inevitably broad and complex, with a range of variables dependent on class, local geographical distribution, and religious affiliation, as well as gender. Focusing on the Sidney family, a cohesive social group, narrows the number of these variables to provide a manageable unit for analysis. While members of the Sidney family undoubtedly differed in opinions and concerns, their social circumstances remain more similar than those of more unrelated individuals.

As a study not only of women's writing but of the culture that shaped that writing, this book devotes its first two chapters to inscriptions of women readers and writers in works by male writers, specifically, Sir Philip Sidney and the poets aspiring to membership in the

Sidney circle. An analysis of constructions of women's reading and writing in these works provides specific information about ways women were written by male authors in this group. This focus eliminates the troublesome problem, plaguing broader studies, of a subject's knowledge of specific texts or of cultural events. While there might be some question whether the countess of Pembroke, for example, had recently perused Richard Hyrde's preface to Margaret Roper's translation from Erasmus, there can be no doubt that she was well acquainted with the works explicitly inscribing her as a character and dedicated to her by members of her circle. While scholars can dispute whether Mary Wroth would have had easy access to the approval of silent women in Thomas Becon's "New catechisme," they can assert with assurance that she was completely familiar with romantic heroines in her uncle Philip's epic romance, *The Countess of Pembroke's Arcadia*.

Finally, a study of the writings by the women in the Sidney family may provide more insights into the difficulties facing other Renaissance women writers than would a study limited to original works alone. Since as a group the women writers of the Sidney family wrote not only original works but also translations and even a fairly derivative lyric poem, they perhaps have more in common with the other Renaissance women who also wrote translations and occasionally derivative work. For this reason, a study of these women writers more nearly achieves the primary goal of this book: an understanding of the problems facing women writers in the Renaissance. My decision to write about the women of one family was based not on the brilliance of their writings, although their literary achievements remain impressive, nor is this book written as a paean to the genius of the Sidney women; such unqualified praise would reveal, in the end, a lack of respect for the individuality of works by highly intelligent women who were, however, no more infallable than other writers. An awareness of the real and knotty problems confronting women writers is best achieved by exploring limited as well as unqualified successes, and even occasional failures. In this awareness, rather than in indiscriminate enthusiasm, lies the possibility of real appreciation.

The typicality of the women in the Sidney family as writers must not, however, be overestimated. They were, after all, members of the Sidney family, and the particularity of their cultural context must also be understood. Their familial relationship with Sir Philip Sidney apparently helped to empower them as writers, for several of their extant writings point to their connection with his works. Sidney's sister, Mary, countess of Pembroke, began the major portion of her literary career by editing his works before she continued the project he had begun of translating the Psalms. The allusion to Philip Sidney's title *The Countess of Pembroke's Arcadia* in *The Countess of Montgomery's Urania* by Mary Wroth, the eldest daughter of his brother Robert, suggests the importance of her uncle's authorship as a model for her own. His daughter Elizabeth, who became the fifth countess of Rutland, wrote poetry, unfortunately no longer extant, praised by Ben Jonson as even better than her father's.[65] Finally, one of three holograph poems, most probably in a woman's hand, in a closely circulated Sidney manuscript imitates the imagery and content of Sidney's sonnets.[66]

Thus, for his sister, daughter, niece, and an anonymous poet in his family or circle, Sir Philip Sidney's name provided a competing discourse enabling authorship. They were not only women; they were Sidneys. The authority conferred by his name derived in part from the adulation bestowed upon him after his death. While his militaristic allegiance to the policies of the Continental Protestants limited his success at Queen Elizabeth's court during his life, his lavish state funeral attests to the extent his culture recognized him as its own.[67] Dying from a wound incurred in battle at the age of thirty-one, he was a war hero who gave his life mobilizing Protestant forces in the Low Countries to resist the Spanish Catholics. He was a well-read scholar, who had gained the respect of eminent Continental personages such as Hubert Languet, with whom he corresponded. He was a courteous knight, whose courtly performances at, for example, the Accession Day tilts had gained him a reputation for chivalry. If the posthumous "cult of Sidney" derived strength as propaganda for proponents of Protestant politics on the one hand and for the queen in her project of representing her court as a flowering of chivalric courtesy on the other, these only demonstrate Sidney's success in uniting often conflicting Calvinist and courtly ideologies in his own self-fashioning as a Protestant "shepherd-knight."[68]

Critics have ably detected the presence of these competing ideologies structuring Sidney's writings, from his sonnet cycle *Astrophel and Stella*, to his long chivalric romance *The Countess of Pembroke's Arcadia*.[69] Represented by their author as mere "trifles," these highly polished and elegant literary works served to affirm Sidney's courtliness and sometimes to forward his political projects.[70] But for his women relatives, they accomplished something else. Not enough has been said about the repercussions of his decision, highly unusual at the time he made it, to name his longest work after his sister. By privileging a woman as its reader, *The Countess of Pembroke's Arcadia* in its very title bestows a position as subject to a woman; it grants to her reading a determinative role in the very production of that work.

The impact of this public endowment of influential subjectivity upon a woman reader cannot be overrestimated as a force empowering Sidney's women relatives as authors. Deriving naturally from her acknowledged role as reader of her brother's writing, Mary Sidney's editing of her brother's works for publication undoubtedly played a role in her decision to publish her own translations. With the example of her aunt's writings before her, as well as with the discursive space opened by her own scandalous activities, Mary Wroth was able to write her own original works. Sidney's bestowal of subjectivity upon a woman reader in his title enabled Mary Wroth to construct her own woman reader, her sister-in-law, the countess of Montgomery, as an appropriate audience for her writing in the title of her romance, *The Countess of Montgomery's Urania.* In his *Astrophel and Stella,* too, Sidney conferred an unusual degree of subjectivity upon his inscribed woman reader Stella by writing a twenty-eight-line response for her in his eighth song. Perhaps this decision helped Wroth in the radical reformulation of the Petrarchan sonnet sequence necessary for her writing of her own *Pamphilia to Amphilanthus.* An imitation of a Sidnean sonnet by a writer of or near the Sidney family seems to show, however, that the difficulties posed to women authors by the discursive structure of the courtly love sonnet were still not entirely resolved.

The influence of a culture's representations of women readers, and particularly the way these representations offer or deny subject positions to women, plays so central a role for women writers that its discussion occupies the first two chapters of this book, which explore ways in which women readers and women writers in the Sidney family or circle were authored or inscribed in works addressed to them by men. A discussion of these representations is necessary in order to understand the complexity of the tasks confronting the women writers discussed in the last three chapters as they constructed versions of authorship which subverted, adapted, or conformed to these inscriptions of women readers and writers.

As a patron, the countess of Pembroke was invested as an especially strong form of woman reader. Chapter 1 examines how five authors inscribing the countess as a character in their poetry resolve, or attempt to resolve, the difficult problem posed by the power of her reading. Working within the discourse of gender difference, each of them constructs a subject-position for the countess that safely circumscribes her worldly influence. Nicholas Breton's "Countess of Pembroke" is an otherworldly religious mystic who abjures earthly power. Thomas Moffett's "Lady of the Plaine" contentedly raises silkworms with her daughter and her gentlewomen attendants on her country estate. The "Cynthia" and "Clorinda" of Nathaniel Baxter and Edmund Spenser, respectively, are empowered by their grief over the death of "Astrophel," or Sir Philip Sidney. Most evocatively suggesting the threat possible to the patronage relationship was Abraham Fraunce's huntress "Pembrokiana," whose attentions to a whelping bear, arguably an authorial figure, proved lethal. Even the dangerous "Pembrokiana," however, was transformed in Fraunce's later work to a demure mistress of ceremonies dutifully demurring to the knowledge of a male sage.

These inscriptions reveal a strong inverse relationship between the power of a woman's reading and the acceptability of her role as author. The writers more dependent upon the countess's patronage created bizarre subject-positions for her; they also refused to acknowledge her own writing. It took an established poet like Spenser to represent Mary Sidney as a writer, as the mournful Clorinda, author of an elegy for her brother Astrophel. Whether this elegiac form of authorship was originally invented by Spenser or by the countess, it opened a space within the discourse of gender difference by allaying anxieties about the countess's attempt to exert control over a living audience.

Among Renaissance works, Sidney's *Countess of Pembroke's Arcadia* would seem the most likely to construct a viable subject-position for women readers. Did he not claim his sister's role as reader in his title? Among Renaissance writers, Sidney would seem the most likely to transcend gender ideology. Did not his dedication of his work to his sister reveal his total lack of condescension to her, as well as his absolute respect for her intelligence? Chapter 2 demonstrates that such was not the case, at least not initially. The "fair ladies" addressed by the narrator of Sidney's unrevised *Arcadia* function as alluring bait to entrap the reader. Proceeding from their own sexual complicity, their undiscriminating compassion guides the reader to sympathize with the morally precarious actions of the royal protagonists in the first three books. The last two books, in which all addresses to "fair ladies" drop out, present a severe rereading of these actions by the judges—Divine Providence and Euarchus. This reader entrapment brings perceptions of rational (just) male readings and emotional (compassionate) female readings into direct and unresolved conflict.

While the revised *Arcadia* inscribes no woman readers, it presents a plethora of gendered narrative situations. Male protagonists tell stories to male and female audiences; but (with a few notable exceptions) women characters can tell their narratives only to women, and even then, they are usually interrupted. The poetry composed by female protagonists, usually recited in isolation, is pervaded by the same guilty sexuality characterizing the compassionate "fair ladies" to an extent unparalleled in the poetry written by male protagonists. The poetry of female characters, unlike the poetry of male characters, generally signifies not subjectivity, but erasure of self. The revised *Arcadia* introduces some radical reformulations of this discourse. By the captivity episode in book 3, the revised *Arcadia* endorses compassion as a response appropriate to men as well as women. In addition, the revised version provides a viable form of women's heroism in the ability to endure misfortune, especially domestic misfortune, reflecting domestic predicaments of women readers of the time.[71]

No matter what connections the women from the Sidney family or circle forged between their work and that of Sir Philip Sidney, the countess of Pembroke, Lady Mary Wroth, and the anonymous poet were still women and therefore subject to the discourse of gender difference. As they created themselves as authors, they navigated the treacherous waters of their culture's gender ideologies by vastly diverging routes. Chapter 3 discusses how the countess of Pembroke purified her translations from the sexual stain supposedly tainting women's writings by embedding her version of authorship within the art of dying. While her dedication of her Psalms to the spirit of her late, beloved brother Philip draws upon the elegiac version of authorship present in Spenser's inscription of her as Clorinda, her engagement with the art of dying also participated in the wider cultural practice of attempting to die well. Dying well was one of the few forms of heroism offered to women. Her own mother was written up by Holinshed as making a good death. The project of constructing a viable heroine apparently determined her choice to translate Petrarch's *Trionfo della Morte* and Garnier's *Marc Antoine,* for this choice of works apparently reflects her attempt to apply the tenets of an *arms moriendi* tract by du Plessis Mornay, which she also translated, to the specific situations of women.

The heroism of Garnier's Cleopatra and Petrarch's Laura performs the additional function of permitting an indirect expression of anger at patriarchal authority. Cleopatra's intended suicide proves not only her love for Anthony but also her defiance of Caesar; Laura's concern for her poet's soul requires her expression of coldness to moderate his ardor. As developed by Samuel Daniel under Mary Sidney's explicit influence and by Samuel Brandon within her probable proximity, the countess's constant heroine became a model for the simultaneous expression and suppression of women's rage. This use of fortitude to enable women to forge a form of heroism not only from dying well but also from conquering their own anger was implicit in the models of heroism the countess chose to translate.

Rather than purifying her version of authorship from sexuality, Lady Mary Wroth capitalized upon it. Her occasionally scandalous *roman à clef* acknowledges the sexuality permeating her writing to defend it, even to heroize it. Rather than dying well, the protagonists of her romance, *The Countess of Montgomery's Urania*, prove their heroism through their loyalty to their lovers, a loyalty sometimes at odds with their marital duties. Alluding transparently to her own sexual involvements, the topicality of her work creates her version of authorship, like the heroism of her female protagonists, as inextricably connected to her role as lover. But this heroism of the constant woman lover bears a strong resemblance to the stoic heroine of Mary Sidney's translations. If the two women set out in opposite directions as they traversed their culture's discourse of gender difference, they arrived at proximate destinations. For Wroth, the very act of authorship is grounded not only in sexuality, but also in denied anger. The narratives her heroines are finally moved to write, after long periods of loyal silence, represent in angry detail the suffering caused by the irresponsible philandering of their men even as they insist upon their infinite patience and their undiminished love for these undependable lovers.

Finally, three anonymous holograph poems provide a highly unusual opportunity to study three separate models for authorship attempted by one author. Since women were usually taught handwriting after they were taught reading and considerably after men were taught writing, this unpracticed hand strongly suggests a woman author for these poems. The nature of the manuscript makes it highly probable that the author was a member of the Sidney family or circle. Containing the most accurate extant version of various poems from the *Astrophel and Stella*, this manuscript, like other Sidney manuscripts, was closely circulated within the Sidney circle; moreover, none of the anonymous poems were copied into surviving collections. It is impossible, however, to prove absolutely the identity of the author. Thus, rather than pretending certainty, this chapter asks the reader to accept the uncertainty that is an occupational hazard accompanying the uncovering of noncanonical, marginalized writing. The alternative is to continue to ignore the evidence, necessarily slight and speculative, that remains.

Avowing the superiority of virtue to beauty, the first poem was written according to the mid-century aesthetic which C. S. Lewis has labelled "drab." The third adopts the persona of a courtly lover and the imagery of Sidney until its second section, which unexpectedly introduces the sober content and poetic technique of the first poem. This splitting apart of the third poem suggests reasons for the exclusion of women poets from the courtly sonneteers of the English Renaissance, and its rupture perhaps reveals more than the success of other women's writings about the problems encountered by women poets.

While the first and third poems mimic voices of other poets, the second poem presents a new authorial vehicle for this poet's voice: the nightingale Philomela, whose faith in love transcends the natural decay of the seasons. Sharing the stoicism of the countess's heroines and the loyalty of Wroth's, Philomela serves to elicit and to deny women's rage even more violently than the other heroines. This poet's representation of the faithful nightingale and her cheerful optimism about love depends upon the absolute suppression of the myth of origin, in which, after Philomela is raped and her tongue excised, she executes a horrible revenge before her metamorphosis into a bird. In her suppression of Philomela's anger, the anonymous poet is participating in, and probably commenting upon, a general cultural dislocution, according to which the raped and tongueless Philomela often sang sweet songs of unrequited love. This dislocution suggests the extent to which women's rage was rendered unacceptable in the Renaissance.

The sexualization of women's words—in their reading, their speech, their writing—represented a formidable obstacle to authorship which, while it did not prevent women's writing, affected what they could write. It appears, however, that the very protest which this sexualization was designed to suppress exerted perhaps an even greater formative pressure upon women's authorship in the Renaissance. While male writers pointed to women's dangerous sexuality as the primary barrier to the circulation of women's words, the versions of authorship constructed by the countess of Pembroke, Lady Mary Wroth, and the anonymous poet also reveal the centrality of rage to their writing. From their anger, however suppressed, women in the Sidney circle struggled not only into authorship but into subjectivity as well.[72]

But the problematic relationship between gender and authorship was not an issue confronting only women writers. Gender is a binary term. The masculine does not exist without the feminine; constructions of the feminine take place only in relationship to constructions of the masculine. As Elaine Showalter has pointed out, it is no longer possible to assume that masculinity is "natural, transparent, and unproblematic"; literary critics must now face the task of "defamiliarizing the masculine."[73] The Renaissance discourse of gender difference that sexualized women's language affected men's language as well. By exaggerating and politicizing the differences, real or supposed, between men and women, Renaissance gender ideology created a potential source of shame regarding the traits men shared with women through their common humanity. It created masculinity as something that could be lost, as a privilege whose terms were conditional. For this reason, reading and writing were gendered acts for men as well as for women, for Sir Philip Sidney as well as for his sister the countess of Pembroke.

If the unapproved kind of reading and writing could mark women as suspiciously sexual, inappropriate kinds of reading and writing could mark men as suspiciously effeminate. When Sir Philip Sidney, for example, addressed *The Countess of Pembroke's Arcadia* to his sister during a long idyll at her estate, he was, like his male progatonists Pyrocles and Musidorus, in retirement from the heroic activities that demonstrated a more traditional form of masculinity. The strikingly developed version of his authorship in his dedication as giving birth was more than a cliché; it is only one indication that issues of gender exerted shaping pressure on his romance, that, for him, the sword was still mightier than the pen. Similarly, the writers who inscribed the countess of Pembroke as a character confronted gender issues as they submitted their work to her patronage. Like Sidney, Abraham Fraunce constructed a version of authorship as giving birth; his version was, however, painfully bestialized as a whelping bear who, struck by the arrow of "Pembrokiana," dies as she gives birth. Thus, the first two chapters of this book analyze gender in writings by male authors to make explicit contemporary constructions of women readers and writers in works written in the Sidney circle, and to understand how gender informs versions of authorship by male as well as female writers.

Chapter 1

Pembrokiana and the Bear Whelps: Inscriptions of the Countess of Pembroke

By literally writing her into their texts, five authors reveal a range of strategies through which the countess of Pembroke was accommodated, in her roles as reader and writer, to the Renaissance discourse of gender difference. Abraham Fraunce, Nicholas Breton, Nathaniel Baxter, Thomas Moffett, and Edmund Spenser all inscribed her as a character in their poems. Their inscriptions represent attempts to hide or to bridge the contradictions posed by the strikingly public figure Mary Sidney cut as a reader and a writer to the prevailing gender ideology designed to contain women's language—reading, speech, and writing—safely within the private sphere. Revealing more about Renaissance gender ideology than they do about the countess of Pembroke, these inscriptions, in their bewildering divergence, make visible the symptomatic contradictions created by her power as a reader and writer.

As a patron, the countess of Pembroke represented an especially powerful form of reader.[1] Richard Hyrde and others who defended women's reading, for example, suggested it as a means of controlling women's thoughts, of preventing women's "pevysshe fantasyes."[2] Because she was a patron, however, Mary Sidney's reading was not only independent of patriarchal control; it was even invested with the power to demonstrate disagreement with an author's work by withholding financial favors. A recognition of the Countess's freedom to approve or to disapprove an author's efforts was acknowledged in many of the numerous published dedications or presentation poems by such authors as Gervase Babington, Barnabe Barnes, Nathaniel Baxter, Nicholas Breton, Samuel Daniel, John Davies of Hereford,

Abraham Fraunce, Thomas Howell, Aemilia Lanyer, Henry Lok, Thomas Moffett, Thomas Morley, Robert Newton, Edmund Spenser, John Taylor, and Thomas Watson.[3] By committing their work to her perusal, and by expressing this commitment in print, these authors created a public reputation for the countess as a reader.

The inscriptions of the countess in poems by Fraunce, Breton, Baxter, Moffett, and Spenser strongly suggest that women's writing required either suppression or even greater rationalizations than women's reading. The countess of Pembroke's writing, like her reading, was unusually public for a Renaissance woman. One of her occasional verses, "A Dialogue betweene two shepheards, *Thenot*, and *Piers*, in praise of *Astrea*," was apparently written for a state occasion, an expected visit by Queen Elizabeth to Wilton which never materialized.[4] Two others were included in the prefatory material to a translation of the Psalms begun by her brother Philip and continued by Mary after his death.[5] Her translation of the Psalms apparently represented more than a private devotional exercise, for an elaborate presentation copy was prepared for Queen Elizabeth. Unlike many other Renaissance women who complied, or nearly complied, with gender ideology by translating only religious works, she translated Petrarch's *Trionfo della Morte* as well as Robert Garnier's thoroughly secular *Marc Antoine*. The latter was even published during her lifetime, as was her translation of Philippe Du Plessis Mornay's *Discourse de la vie et de la mort*. Her translations of Garnier and Mornay appeared together in 1592 with her name on the title page: "Both done in English by the Countesse of Pembroke." In the absence of prefatory material, it is possible that her work was appropriated without her knowledge, but the successive publications of her translation of Mornay's treatise again in 1600 and in 1608 with her name still on the title page suggest at least her passive acquiescence by 1600.[6]

Acknowledging the countess as a writer was apparently only possible at all for those writers most secure in their vocations. Fraunce and Breton, the two writers most dependent upon her patronage, never allude to her writings, despite the fact that certainly Fraunce and perhaps Breton were present at Wilton at the very time she was translating works from Garnier and Mornay. Baxter and Moffett mention her writing in passing. Only Spenser, the most established poet of the group, represents the countess explicitly as a writer in his inscription. Spenser's representation of her as a poet provides an elegiac version of authorship much like the one she finally adopts in her own translations. Even the version of authorship constructed in

Spenser's poem and in the countess's own work is, however, strongly shaped by Renaissance gender ideology.

In their response (or refusal to respond) to Mary Sidney's authorship, these five writers are not unusual within their culture. Descriptions of her writing by other authors, as well, reveal three standard operations, also present in the inscriptions, through which her authorship is discounted. The first is denial. The absence of any mention of her writing by Fraunce and Breton represents a form of denial practiced explicitly by John Harington towards the beginning of the seventeenth century. Revealing his doubts concerning the quality of authorship possible to a woman, Harington suggests that the countess had drawn heavily upon the advice of her chaplain Gervase Babington for her translation of the Psalms: "[Gervase Babington] was sometime Chaplaine to the late Earle of *Pembroke,* whose Noble Countesse used this her Chaplaines advice, I suppose, for the translation of the Psalmes, for it was more then a womans skill to expresse sence so right as she hath done in her verse."[7] Harington's suspicions seem unfounded, for Babington left his post as chaplain at Wilton by 1581, probably long before she had begun her translation of the Psalms.[8] She was apparently still working on them in 1599, when Moffett begged her to "give rest to Sacred Writte."[9]

Sir Edward Denny employed another strategy in his distortion of countess's literary activities to fit the more permissible activity of religious translation. Like Nicholas Breton, he portrayed her interests as solely religious. In his attempts to dissuade Lady Mary Wroth from continuing her work on *The Countess of Montgomery's Urania,* Denny suppressed his knowledge of Mary Sidney's secular translations from Garnier and Petrarch, the former of which had been published. "Leave idle bookes alone," he wrote Wroth, "for wise and worthyer women have writte none. . . . Redeeme the tym with writing as large a volume of heavenly layes and holy love as you have of lascivious tales and amarous toyes . . . followe the rare, and pious example of your vertuous and learned Aunt, who translated so many godly books and especially the holy psalmes of David."[10] The chaste piety implied for Mary Sidney's translations defined by contrast the "lascivious tales and amarous toyes" which Denny accused Wroth of producing.

It seems probable, if impossible to prove, that a third strategy was to eroticize the countess's writing. John Aubrey's speculations concerning her sexual proclivities are extreme even for that compilation of notorious gossip published as *Brief Lives.* Connecting these rumors to her authorship is rendered difficult, however, by Aubrey's omission of any mention of the countess's writing. His description of "all the *Psalmes of David* translated by Sir Philip Sydney, curiously bound in crimson velvet," in the library at Wilton suppresses her role as translator even more thoroughly than Harington's unfounded suspicions.[11]

Still, Aubrey's scandalous allegations concerning the countess may well form his response to a reputation that was already soiled by literary activities. Anxieties about the sexual predilections of intelligent women inform, for example, Aubrey's assertion that Mary Sidney remained at Wilton because her father-in-law "did see that his faire and witty daughter-in-lawe would horne his sonne, and told him so" (138). Even far removed from court, the countess managed, according to Aubrey, to act upon unseemly sexual desires:

> She was very salacious, and she had a Contrivance that in the Springe of the yeare, when the Stallions were to leape the Mares, they were to be brought before such a part of the house, where she had a *vidette* (a hole to peepe out at) to looke on them and please herselfe with their Sporte; and then she would act the like sport herselfe with *her* stallions. One of her great Gallants was Crooke-back't Cecill, Earl of Salisbury. (138)

Aubrey advances her brother Philip as another of her "great Gallants": "There was so much love between him and his faire sister that I have heard old Gentlemen say that they lay together, and it was thought the first Phillip Earle of Pembroke was begot by him, but he inherited not the witt of either brother or sister" (139).

The sexualization of women's writing was a common Renaissance practice shaping representations of women's reading and patronage as well. The countess's patronage, for example, was sexualized in Abraham Fraunce's disturbing inscription of Pembrokiana shooting a phallic arrow into a pregnant bear. Women's reading, presumably including Mary Sidney's reading, was sexualized in Moffett's *Silkewormes and Their Flies,* which cast silkworms in the romantic roles of Pyramis and Thisbe, whose plights are imagined as eliciting the easy compassion of his women readers. Moreover, Moffett proposes to his women readers that their pleasure in raising silkworms will be enhanced by the opportunity to listen to the "hurring" and the "churring song" of silkworms acting out "hot *Priapus* love."[12]

The Metamorphoses of Pembrokiana

Of the five authors who inscribed the countess as a character, Abraham Fraunce provides the most information about the hopes and fears of a Renaissance author who had gained the support of a woman patron. The countess's centrality to his writing, and particularly the centrality of her wealth and status, is suggested by his inclusion of her rank and her country estate, Ivychurch, in the titles of three of the five works he dedicated to her between 1587 and 1592: *The Countess of Pembrokes Ivychurch* (1591), *The Second Part of the Countess of Pembrokes Ivychurch* (1591), and *The Third Part of the Countess of Pembrokes Ivychurch* (1592). The power of Mary Sidney's reading that had led Sir Philip Sidney to include her name in the title of his romance had derived from her relationship as sister. Fraunce's inscriptions of her as the character "Pembrokiana" strongly suggest that for him, however, her power as reader derived from her role as patron. As partial translations, Fraunce's works are, literally, readings of other authors, into which Fraunce sometimes awkwardly inserts the figure of Pembrokiana, who inspires the fervent admiration of "nymphs" and "pastors" happily residing at Ivychurch.

By localizing the writing of other authors—Torquato Tasso, Thomas Watson, and Ovid—on the countess's estate, Fraunce creates texts through which to interpret her power as patron and reader. The bizarre mixture of characters from fictional texts with representations of real-life persons at Ivychurch was no doubt intended as an elegant compliment to the countess, an elevation of her life to the status of art. But the various transformations of the countess figure as she travels through the three *Ivychurch* poems reveal the strenuousness of his attempts to cope with her authority as his patron. In *The Countess of Pembrokes Ivychurch,* a series of classical and contemporary allusions provide reason to perceive Pembrokiana's killing of a whelping bear as a model for the patronage relationship. In *The Second Part of the Countess of Pembrokes Ivychurch,* this dangerous huntress of bears becomes transformed into an admiring commemorator of a dead shepherd poet, whose work she celebrates annually. By *The Third Part of the Countess of Pembrokes Ivychurch,* her function as a moderator of Ovidian tales narrated by pastoral characters is circumscribed by the intellectual authority of the male sage Elpinus, who explicates their hidden meanings. Inconsistencies and contradictions riddling these texts finally create the countess's power over texts as not so much resolved as barely contained.

Mary Sidney's power appears to have been particularly threatening to Fraunce, perhaps because his need for patronage was so great. According to the countess's husband, Sir Philip Sidney had "bred" Fraunce up "long in Cambridge."[13] Perhaps Sidney's death cut off a source of support, for in the succeeding year Fraunce's dedication to the countess of his *Lamentations of Amyntas for the Death of Phillis* (1587) described to her his "afflicted mind and crased bodie."[14] His need for patronage apparently took precedence over the seriousness of his literary pursuits for their own sake; *Lamentations* was plagiarized even by loose Renaissance standards. He neglected to mention that this work had been originally composed in Latin by Thomas Watson until Watson called attention to this theft in his preface to *Meliboeus*, which he dedicated to the late Philip Sidney's father-in-law, Sir Francis Walsingham.[15] This plagiarism, and the generally low quality of his work in general, suggests that Fraunce's poetry may have functioned as a means to an end rather than as an end in itself. This end was probably, in part, to gain the notice of the countess's husband, the earl, who repeatedly and unsuccessfully recommended Fraunce for a position as solicitor in Wales in 1590 and 1591.[16] After his last dedication of a work to the countess in 1592, little more is heard of him. He may have been in the employ of the earl of Bridgewater. Such employment would have been no sinecure; according to a now-lost manuscript prose epistle, Fraunce wrote epithalamia for all of Bridgewater's seven daughters.[17]

In its title as well as its text, *The Countess of Pembroke's Ivychurch* creates Ivychurch as the setting for Torquato Tasso's graceful play *The Aminta*, in which a deserving shepherd wins a lovely huntress, saving her from rape by a rampaging satyr in the process. Fraunce's rewriting of Tasso's play in terms of the countess's patronage is evident in his substitution of the activities of a new character—"peareles *Pembrokiana*" (B2v), "princelike *Pembrokiana*" (E1v), "brave Lady Regent of these woods" (E2v)—for Tasso's allusions to Alphonse d'Este's patronage, which drop out entirely.[18]

The first of Fraunce's additions to the *Aminta* creates a flattering flurry of interest in Pembrokiana's personage among Tasso's characters. The female protagonist, Phyllis, breathlessly announces that Pembrokiana herself means to be present at a hunting party, "and with her owne person give grace and life to the pastime" (B2v). Arriving with "a company gallant / Of flowering damsells" carrying bows and arrows as they wait on her, Pembrokiana motivates a major event of the play, for in her desire to gain Pembrokiana's admiration, Phyllis shoots an arrow into a wolf's ear, an act which eventually leads to the false announcement of Phyllis's death and Amintas's attempted suicide:

> Soemuch wrought in her hart sweete sight of *Pembrokiana*,
> Soemuch did she desire to be praysd of *Pembrokiana*.
>
> (E1v)

The power yielded to Pembrokiana by her social inferiors as she graces their gatherings and receives their admiration resonates with the power of the patronage relationship. The countess's protégés no doubt also competed with each other to please her; they no doubt also performed as well as they could to gain her esteem. Perhaps the odd and original detail of Phyllis's shooting the wolf's ear seems to make sense in this context: the power of the real-life pastors and nymphs lay in their words.[19] The graceful image of a noble lady regent graciously receiving the rapt attentions of her pastors and nymphs seems at first an elegant tribute, a charming depiction of the respect the countess earned through her patronage. But anthropological studies suggest that asymmetrical giving outside a family structure seldom occurs without strings.[20] Thus, the mutual solidarity expressed in literature or in dedications produced within a patronage relationship may mask a less stable and less comfortable bond. Thus, it is perhaps no real surprise that Fraunce's bizarre image of Pembrokiana and the bear whelps points to a darker side of the experience of the countess's patronage.

This darker side begins with Phyllis's enthusiastic description of Pembrokiana's skillful shooting of a bear, an event original with Fraunce:

> But what a dart was that, which mightily flew from the fingers
> Of brave Lady Regent of these woods, *Pembrokiana*,
> Unto the forreine Beare, which came with greedy devowring
> Iawes to the harmeles game?
>
> (E2v)

In its description of Pembrokiana's unabashed display of her ability, this passage seems at first to glory in her power. But as the passage continues, the nature of the bear is radically revised. Implicitly male in its aggression, this greedy devourer of "harmles game" is, as it turns out, a devoted mother to her own unborn offspring. In her eloquent death speech addressed to Pembrokiana, the bear even commends her cubs to Pembrokiana's care:

> Unto her owne yong whelpes, whose groanes thus lastly
> resounded
> Whose dying howre was a birth-day
> Deaths dart, (yet sweete dart, as throwne by *Pembrokiana*)
> Make my wound more wyde, give large scope to my yong ones,
> Geve them a free passage, herself hath ge'un them a pasport.
> (E2v)

A variety of contexts present themselves as a filter through which to read this striking passage. On the most superficial level, Pembrokiana's assertion of skill has become an act of cruelty; and Phyllis's enthusiasm for her ability suddenly becomes unsettling. This qualification of an initially positive attitude about women hunters conforms to the general movement of the play, which delineates Phyllis's change from chaste huntress, scorning Amintas's affection, to a mature and receptive woman, willing and able to return his love. As the play opens, a conversation between Phyllis and her friend Daphne connects Phyllis's love of the hunt and her dislike of male attention. Phyllis informs Daphne that "hunting is my joy; with stubburne beasts to be striving, / Until I fell them downe" (A4v). Daphne replies that she, too, loved to hunt until she discovered the pleasures of love. After one night of love, she gave the goddess Cynthia back her horn and bow, and she expects that Phyllis will, too.

In this exchange, Phyllis's love of hunting is expressed as a love of competition, a desire for victory, traits that, according to the assumptions of Daphne and the play in general, are acceptable in adolescent girls but which must be someday outgrown. This main plot line puts Pembrokiana's marksmanship in a less positive light. Pembrokiana represents, in fact, all that Phyllis gives up by the end of the play. Surrounded by bow-and-arrow-bearing ladies, Pembrokiana resembles the huntress Diana, goddess of chastity, enemy to love and to sexual pleasure, asserting her dominance over stray men and beasts alike. These values are rejected when Phyllis casts herself, "face to face, mouth to mouth" (F2v), upon the prostrate Amintas near the end of the play.

Yet the prospective birth of the bear cubs still requires some explanation. The presence of bears at all becomes significant in Fraunce's adaptation, because the only animal hunted in Tasso's play was a wolf. In providing no clues as to the reason for this change, the text points outside itself for possible answers. According to the natural history current in the Renaissance, bear cubs possessed one unique feature—they were born without form until their mothers licked them into shape.[21] Interpretations of this phenomenon, particularly in emblem books, connected the bear's licking of her cubs with the forces of art or civilization as they complete the unfinished work of nature.[22] In Perriere's popular *Le Theatre des bons engines* (1539), the bear's licking represents doctrine, gained by study, which polishes the *imbecilité* of the human spirit at birth.[23] Titian, whose influence on Sidney's *Arcadia* has been demonstrated by Katherine Duncan-Jones, adopted the image of the she-bear licking her whelps into shape as his personal *imprese*, with the motto "Natura potentior ars."[24] These interpretations were almost certainly current at Wilton, since several members of the family had shown a high degree of interest in emblem and imprese literature. Fraunce himself, for example, had dedicated the manuscript and then the published version of his *Insignium, Armorum, Emblematum, Hieroglyphocorum, et Symbolorum quae ab Italis Imprese nominatur, explicatio* (1588) to Mary Sidney's brother Robert.

In addition to these associations with bear cubs, an anecdote reported of Virgil in *Lives of Illustrious Men*, a work ascribed to Suetonius, creates an explicit connection between the licking of bear whelps and the making of books. Virgil described his custom of composing a section of the *Georgics* in the morning and then condensing it in the afternoon as a way of fashioning his poem "after the manner of a she-bear," as he "gradually licked it into shape."[25] This application of the bear cub image to the writing of books was well within the interpretive repertoire of authors in the early 1590s, for this comparison of the revision of written work to a bear's licking of cubs is also made by Robert Greene in his dedication of *Philomela The Lady Fitzwaters Nightingale.* According to this dedication, Greene had written the work some time since and had just recently revised it for the Lady Fitzwater: "Asoone as I had red it ouer and reduced it into forme, lickinge it a lyttle as the beares doe their whelpes to bring them to perfection, I have resolved to make good my duty to his Lordship in doing homage with my simple labours to your Ladiship."[26] This image may well represent Greene's contemporary reading of Fraunce's striking passage through the interpretative filter of the anecdote attributed to Virgil, for in the next sentence, Green asserts the influence of Fraunce's *Countess of Pembrokes Ivychurch.* Greene has modelled his title after Fraunce's: "Imitating heerein Maister *Abraham France*, who titled the Lamentations of *Aminta* under the name of the Countesse of Pembrokes *Iuie Church.*"

While the association between bear cubs and the raw nature of recently written books seems grounded, its implications for the countess of Pembroke's role in the production of books remain problematic. As the dying bear asks Pembrokiana to make her wound wide so that her whelps may be born, Pembrokiana seems to be serving almost as a midwife; this midwife role implies the countess's role as enabler of Fraunce's works, unfinished though they may be. As the mother bear points to Pembrokiana's responsibility for their premature birth, is she commending her cubs to Pembrokiana's protection? On the mother bear's death, is Pembrokiana to shape the cubs in some way? And does this passage suggest that the countess of Pembroke is also to complete Fraunce's work, civilizing it perhaps through editing or criticizing? Or do the cubs remain, after their mother's death, forever unshaped and unrevised, signifying Fraunce's acknowledgement of the inferiority of his work? The implications of the image are at this point as uncertain as the fate of the bear whelps. But whatever the fate of this work/whelp, this passage has shifted the responsibility for its final state to the countess.

This final polishing of Fraunce's work may have been to take place in the countess's act of reading rather than in some form of editing. In a description of the whelping bear in the *Phile sapientissimi versus iambici, De Animalium proprietate,* by Gregory Bersmano and John Camerarius, two separate meanings may be gleaned from one line: "Linguaque lambens hunc glabrum sensum facit."[27] As an adjective, the Latin word *glaber* means "bald," but as a noun in means "page." Thus, this line could mean either "and with her tongue she gives sense to this bald thing," or "with her tongue she gives sense to this page." This latter translation may invest the countess with power over Fraunce's text not only as a patron able to provide money, but also as a reader able to complete a text by constructing meanings through the process of reading it aloud. The chances of familiarity of those at Wilton with Bersmano and Camerarius's text were greatly increased by the personal friendship between Philip Sidney and Camerarius, who travelled together to Hungary.[28]

While the role of enabler seems appropriate enough for a reader-patron, this supportive role is at odds with the aggression signified by Pembrokiana's shooting the bear in the first place. The prologue of the play, in which Cupid enters disguised as a shepherd, provides a context for understanding the bear whelp passage as in some sense about the countess's power as a source of literary works. According to this prologue, Cupid's dart inspires not only love but also eloquence. Cupid proclaims that even in this rural outclave, "noble thoughts wil

I send, and high conceipts wil I breath foorth / Into the lowli'est minds" (A3v). Like Cupid, Pembrokiana shoots her arrow. Like Cupid's lovers, the bear becomes eloquent. The eloquence and love inspired by Cupid's arrow provide a reason in the text for perceiving the powers of Pembrokiana's arrow as embodying the countess's power of patronage, which can make even a bear, even an Abraham Fraunce, speak.

But what does the bear say? "Death's dart, (yet sweete dart, as throwne by *Pembrokiana*)": even in the throes of mortal pain, the bear must flatter, must deny any anger directed to the person who has just killed it. In fact, for the sake of its cubs, the bear must even ask for more pain. This channeling of anger into flattery seems like an emotional experience possible, even probable, in a patronage relationship, unbalanced as it is by the power of the respective partners. When the protégé was male and the patron was female, the power relationship must have been even more skewed. Thus, the bear is female; and as Pembrokiana, like Cupid, shoots her phallic arrow, the "blunt dart" (A3v) of love, she is taking on a role that is assertive and even sexual in its masculinity. The gender reversal implicit in the countess's patronage, her power over men, apparently acts as a feminizing force to those males who experience Pembrokiana's "arrow." Pembrokiana shoots a phallic arrow, and a bear births cubs: the countess of Pembroke has engendered literary works upon a bestial, feminized author. For the woman patron, the experience is one of competence and power. For the male author, the experience is one of humiliation and pain. Fraunce does not represent the experience of whelping/childbirth as joyful creation. In Fraunce's image, the womb has replaced the penis as the organ of generativity; and in the process, what was often represented as an assertion of control, almost God-like in its power, has become instead an experience of being controlled, of mortal suffering.

Fraunce's final addition, an entire scene of over ninety lines at the end of Tasso's play, posits an alternative role for women in the production of literature, which represents Pembrokiana's aggression towards the whelping bear as freakish and perverse by comparison. By the end of the play Amintas and Phyllis, like countless numbers of other sheperds and shepherdesses, pledge their love to each other in song. According to this model, mutual love between social equals, rather than the power of a dominating lady regent, produces verse. Shepherds sing to gain romantic or sexual favors, not economic ones, from their ladies. This final, evidently happy model for the production of literature lies at the heart of the pastoral convention. But in

Fraunce's version, not even this model for a woman's power over a text is free from taint. In fact, this thoroughly disagreeable scene, in which Phyllis accepts Amintas's love but renounces any physical demonstrations whatsoever, contradicts the whole point of Tasso's play, set in the age of gold before false honor interfered in the love between men and women, when the motto was "If you will, you may" (C2).

Amintas begins his long dialogue with Phyllis with the forthright question, "Deare life, when shal I once have full possession?" (F3). She does not understand the gift he wishes, which he claims will cost her "not a dodkin," until he whispers it in her ear. She denies his suit, but agrees to let him sleep with her, dashing his enthusiasm with the requirement that he "stir not a finger." "Then let's kisse," he pleads, proffering the suggestion that she pretend his lips are roses. No. "Yf nought els, yet geue mee leave those eyes to be kissing." No. "Yet let an embracement to *Amyntas* his arms be aforded." "With good will," she replies, to his surprise and relief—but only after he fetches her some apples on a tree surrounded by bushes and briars. She then dashes his hopes by accusing him of wanting to do to her what he would do to the shaken tree: "clypt *Phyllis* must looke soe to be served" (F4). He cannot put a red rose in her bosom. He cannot even touch her hand, for "soe by the hard-gryping, hoate-kissing Lover *Amyntas, / Phillis* snowe-white hand may melt, or chaunce to be bruysed." Finally they sing a song in which they pledge their exclusive devotion to each other, followed by Phyllis's ecstatic repetition of his name before she suggests they go to see her father. As they rise, Amintas consummates their relationship in this way: "Let mee help you up: your hand is in hand of *Amyntas* / Now at last surprisde: yet I ask but a kisse for a ransome" (F4v). The play ends here, with Phyllis's kiss indefinitely deferred.

The song of Amintas and Phyllis is the only poetry directly represented in the play. Like the bear whelp scene, this final scene is filled with denied anger proceeding from a woman's power over a man. As Phyllis tantalizes Amintas by coyly agreeing to embrace him and then prudishly refusing to let him even touch her hand, her portrayal in this scene is unpleasant. Rigorous beyond the expectations of the time, Phyllis's standards of deportment between lovers are absurd within the permissive society represented in Tasso's play. Amintas, like the bear, responds to her cruelty with the utmost gentility. Like Pembrokiana's lethal arrow, Phyllis's power is also sexual, but in the traditionally passive female way of withholding sexual favors. The song that Phyllis produces in the poet is the product of repressed sexuality. While repressed sexuality also formed a necessary precondition for the expressions of desire constituting Petrarchan poets, Petrarchan ladies were traditionally portrayed as virtuously chaste rather than prudishly coy.

Her modesty contrasted to Pembrokiana's aggression, Phyllis at first appears to serve as a counter to the countess of Pembroke as a producer of literature. Yet it is possible that Phyllis represents another element of the countess's patronage, instead of or even as well as an alternative. Perhaps the countess's patronage of male authors also contained an element of repressed sexuality. Perhaps she, like Queen Elizabeth, encouraged flirtation, leading on and then frustrating the desires of her protégés. Or perhaps Fraunce himself merely adapted the conflation of the courtier and the lover current in the Elizabethan court to Wilton as a means of his own self-fashioning.

Fraunce's *Second Part of the Countess of Pembrokes Ivychurch,* his English translation of a Latin work by Thomas Watson, contains a model for the relationship between poet and reader-patron which seems much less problematic.[29] Providing an unexpected sequel to Tasso's play, this version tersely informs the reader of Phyllis's death, an event whose importance consists chiefly in a series of eleven operatic lamentations performed by Amintas over eleven days before his own suicide at her grave, at which point his dead body is transformed into the Amaranthus flower. Fraunce adds a passage to his translation in which Pembrokiana, presented with the flower that was Amintas, declares an annual commemoration of Amintas's death at a dale in Ivychurch, newly named Amintas Dale, where Ivychurch's nymphs and pastors are all to gather, wearing Amaranthus garlands. This *Ivychurch* presents a model of the relationship between poet and patron-reader shared by writers desiring immortality after death. Denied reward during his life, Amintas receives posthumous recognition. His name is eternized, and as the "nymphs" and "pastors" recite poetry at the annual commemoration of his name, he himself becomes a producer of poetry even after his death.

The Third Part of the Countess of Pembrokes Ivychurch. Entituled Amintas Dale presents a relatively subdued Pembrokiana.[30] No longer wielding a bow and arrow, she presides instead over the nymphs and pastors of her estate as they gather to recite poems from Ovid's *Metamorphoses* in remembrance of Amintas. She seldom speaks except in her role of assigning narratives—love stories for the most part—to various storytellers. The order of the tales, as well as the ones selected, are determined by a complementary discourse, controlled by the sage Elpinus, whose lengthy and learned explications threaten at times to overwhelm the Ovidian texts. Each tale concerns one specific god, discussed in order of hierarchy; and Elpinus's commentary on each legend includes a description of the pertinent god's characteristics and attributes along with an interpretation of the narrative.

The complementary discourses of the third *Ivychurch* reveal competing interpretive systems that strongly imply gender. Without Elpinus's readings, the third *Ivychurch* would be an anthology of love stories told by graceful pastoral characters under the direction of a lady regent, presented for the readers' simple enjoyment of the narratives for their own sake. In fact, the one tale that is explicated by a character other than Elpinus includes an address to "noble dames." Dieromena (probably a woman relative of Edward Dyer) explicates the tale of Iphis and Anaxarete not in terms of natural allegory, but as an exemplum for ladies to follow in choosing a suitor worthy of their love. After asserting the historical accuracy of the story, she shows its application as a lesson to ladies to regard merit more than rank in their choice of husbands:

> Then let noble dames, let Ladies learne to be lovely,
> And make more account of a gentle minde, then a gentry.
> Love makes lowest high, and highest harts to be lowly,
> And by these meanes makes both high and lowe to be lovely.
> (O4v)

Dieromena's explication, unlike those of Elpinus, represents the Ovidian tales as amorous and especially useful for gentlewomen readers.

Elpinus's explications represent the Ovidian tales in quite a different light. Elpinus's discourse creates the third *Ivychurch* as a handbook of mythology compiled from other male scholars, whose names—Cicero, Pythagoras, Plato, Solomon, Fulgentius—populate his margins, authenticating his text through an appeal to a body of masculine scholarship. Such learning is, in the nature of things, male, for males wrote it and males had primary access to it. His interpretations elevate possible intellectual uses for the narratives, their seriousness of purpose, the way they reveal "hidden mysteries" of philosophy (B2), to the discerning mind. Suppressing the sensuous pleasure and the amorous content of this Ovidian tales, Elpinus's interpretations exert strict dominance over these graceful myths. In his function as explicator, he has distinguished himself from the sexualized woman reader imagined as delighting in amorous content. Thus, the explications of Elpinus and other actual commentators, which once defended Ovidian tales from the charge of pagan sinfulness, now functioned, I suspect, to defend them from what was in the Renaissance a more serious accusation: their femininity.[31]

In the concluding interpretations by the lower-class Daphne, this gender hierarchy will be conflated with a social matrix in Elpinus's hierarchy of readers, in which the literal reader is ranked as contemptibly low. But women readers, generally excluded from the educational process that provided erudite classical readings of myths, were surely often imagined as—and perhaps often were—fairly literal readers and receptive to such aesthetic appreciations as were available to readers without university educations. Elpinus characterizes literal readers, who appreciate the sensuousness of the text, its heroic exploits and "sweete and delightsome verse," as readers of "mean conceit," of "rurall humour." Next in his hierarchy stands the moral reader, the "practicall and common wealth man," who with a higher capacity can reach beyond the "external discourse and history" to find a "morall sence." At the top of his hierarchy are those who, "better borne and of a more noble spirit, shall meete with hidden mysteries of naturall, astrologicall, or divine and metaphysicall philosophie, to entertaine their heavenly speculations" (B2). Rereading Ovidian narratives as repositories of hidden knowledge, Elpinus gives explications of this last sort. His readings privilege him as the sole decipherer of these secrets in the third *Ivychurch*, the only reader of "noble spirit" and true learning, on whom the other characters depend to understand the meanings of the narratives they recite. Rather than sharing pleasure in a community of readers, he acts as an instructor, teaching his audience the "true" meaning of the narratives.

Towards the end of the third *Ivychurch*, however, Elpinus's dominance over these Ovidian tales begins to wane. His explications become noticeably shorter and offhand. After Ergastus's tale of Hermaphroditus, the narrator points out, "Elpinus was as brief, as Ergastus had been tedious in his tale of the two wantons" (N4v); in this case Elpinus's explication consists of one paragraph of untranslated Italian. Dieromena's explication takes place in the penultimate tale; and Elpinus's interpretation, which describes the avenging goddess Rhamnusia, who does not even appear in the narrative of Iphis and Anaxarete, does not compete with Dieromena's application of her story to the situations of amorous gentlewomen readers. It is the last story, however, which presents the most serious challenge to Elpinus's discourse. The "rurall humour" of Daphne associates women readers with the lowest rank of literal-minded readers, who also had "rural humours." Daphne tells her story in prose rather than verse;

but her rambling prose, like that of the Shakespearean characters who do not speak in verse, represents her as lower class, not as learned like Elpinus. While Daphne's story deals with transformations of men into plants, her model appears to be local folk etymologies rather than Ovidian metamorphoses. Unlike the other pastoral characters, Daphne claims a female source rather than Ovid for her narrative: her story was told to her many times by her mother (O4v). Yet the scholarly allusions studding her narrative (of which she does not seem to be aware) invite recognition by learned males, and her plot bears various resemblances to classical antecedents, notably Lucan's *Icaromenippus*.[32] Thus, Daphne's tale is not the simple, uneducated narrative it presents itself as being. From two perspectives—from that of uneducated women readers as well as from that of educated males—Daphne's tale throws open the entire question of intellectual presumption and the nature of narratives.

Daphne's story relates the adventures of "certain schollers of Cambridge" who wanted to "mount up to heaven and understand those mysteries which bee above the Moone" (P1), particularly whether the predictions of astrologers about whether were correct or not. As they embarked on a sea voyage, an "Academique" offered to give them directions from the benefit of his own experience. His father had entered him in a university called a Garden, where he studied such works as "the Garden of Ladies," and "the moralization of the Georgikes," and where each student was known by the name of a plant. One day, Hemlock, Parsnip, and Thistle—the most accomplished scholars in astrology, mathematics, and philosophy—were chosen as ambassadors to heaven, which they finally entered by climbing high ladders. From this vantage they discoursed of the heavens, making fun of such errors as Lactanius's on the limits of the deluge. There, riding on some clouds they met Intellectus and Fantasie, who first warned them of the dangers of foolish curiosity before acting as their guides. Unfortunately, when they finally arrived at Jupiter's court, Parsnip and Hemlocke let Venus, Luna, Ganymede, and others choose from their gifts of fruit; and when it came time for them to present their tribute to Jupiter, their baskets were empty. In anger, Jupiter threw Hemlock and Parsnip to the ground, where they became the plants whose name they bore. At this point, Thistle threw himself upon the mercy of Intellectus, letting him peruse his long petition, which features such items as "Whosoever eateth buttered Parsnips without Pepper, may dye without Auricular confession." Intellectus had just taken Thistle to the Palace of Time, when the ship carrying the group encountered a terrible storm. At this point Pembrokiana smilingly interrupts Daphne's story, asking her to "refer the pitifull description of so wofull a shipwrack, to some other time" (O1).

Daphne's tale is confusing on various levels. Thistle meets Jupiter; folktale elements of why thistles lose their "hair" in the autumn mingle with learned allusions to Lactantius's theory of the limits of the deluge. Instead of an unlearned narrative passed from mother to daughter in an oral culture, it is really an application of folktale characteristics to scholarly concerns. Its structure is informal, moving from unlikely event to more unlikely event with no necessary conclusion. Perhaps most important, it cannot be interpreted according to any allegorical system, as Daphne herself notes: "The best is, I meane not to be so full of parables, as that *Elpinus* shall have need to make any explication" (P1).

One function of Daphne's chaotic tale is to oppose the narrative strategies of an oral culture against the learned readings of Elpinus. With its odd and uneducated narrator and Daphne's mother as its stated source, Daphne's tale poses a silent alternative to a learned and therefore primarily masculine tradition of allegorized myths. But allegorized myths were also undercut by male scholars; skepticism concerning such ways of reading was a respected intellectual position. The rebellion against Elpinus's interpretations of narrative is mounted from two perspectives: from that of unlearned women and from that of learned male skeptics alike. The learned allusions within Daphne's homely tale create a split audience which would, however, unite in agreement with her ridicule of the foolish and wrongheaded presumption of academicians and especially astrologers who attempt to understand the secrets of the universe. Since Elpinus's commentaries lay special stress on the physical or natural meanings of Ovidian myths, Daphne's tale represents a direct attack on the value of his interpretations.

As Pembrokiana laughingly defers Daphne's endless tale until another meeting, the position on the nature of narrative offered in the third *Ivychurch* remains unclear. The question posed in the third *Ivychurch* affects the other two, as well. Since the speaking bear of the first *Ivychurch* and Amintas's metamorphosis into an Amaranthus flower in the second *Ivychurch* insert both of these works within an Ovidian discourse, the perspective of Elpinus would censure both of them as frivolous, pleasurable texts without substantial didactic merit. Such a position contradicts Fraunce's apparent purpose, to amuse and probably to flatter the countess of Pembroke. The intensity of Daphne's attack on learned pretensions suggests that Fraunce himself had not achieved resolution on this matter.

The competing valuations of learned discourses may have proceeded from competing audiences Fraunce constructed for this work and from competing aims regarding these disparate audiences. His apparent attempt to charm the countess into providing patronage by depicting her as the graceful lady regent Pembrokiana presiding over her company of delightful nymphs and pastors came into direct conflict with his desire to impress members of the legal profession who might provide him employment as a solicitor. Only two years before Fraunce published the third *Ivychurch*, Mary Sidney's husband was writing a letter to Lord Burghley to recommend Fraunce for the position of solicitor at the council of the Marches of Wales. The desire to become a lawyer apparently motivated Fraunce to write *Lawyers Logike* (1588), dedicated to the earl of Pembroke, in the attempt to show how his studies in philosophy qualified him for a position in the legal profession. A reference to this work disrupts the second *Ivychurch* with the only explicit inscription of a male audience ("of some little men") in this series of works.

In the second *Ivychurch*, Fraunce defends his repetition of the word "stil" in two succeeding lines, anticipating the criticism of "some little men" who were apparently incapable of noticing that, as the narrator points out, in the first instance the word was used as an adverb and in the second as an adjective. Then the narrator proceeds with a tirade, utterly unmotivated by the text, against a critic of his *Lawyers Logike*. Apparently this critic, upon whom Fraunce heaps abuse, objected to Fraunce's inexact quotation from legal texts (H1). Fraunce's critic may well have had a point, for Fraunce's *Lawyers Logike* is rendered peculiar by his illustration of technical legal concepts by lines from Spenser's *Shepherd's Calendar*. In his illustration of Adjuncts, for example, Fraunce uses Perigot's description of Bellibone's attire:

> I saw the bouncing *Bellibone*
> hey ho *Bonnibell,*
> Tripping over the Dale alone,
> Shee can trip it very well.
> Well decked in a frock of gray,
> Hey, ho, gray is greete.[33]

This uneasy yoking of pastoral verse and legal terms points to a tension in Fraunce's perception of himself as both poet and lawyer. The pleasure offered by this pastoral verse, with its absurd refrain ("Hey ho Bonnibell"), so frivolous and nonpurposive in this context, is as out of place as Bonnibell bouncing through a serious catalogue of legal terms.

Fraunce's preface to *Lawyers Logike* attempts to explain his use of literary texts in terms that point to their femininity, countering the charge that he, author of "The Lamentations of Amyntas," is too "delicate" to serve as a solicitor. He imagines a "great Tenurist" asserting that his "easie, elegant, conceipted, nice, and delicate learning" better befits him to compose "new-found verses of Amyntas death" than qualifying him for the study of law (¶2). Fraunce's text finally exacerbates rather than resolves this polarity, and it is not surprising that he never got the position. His inappropriate mixture of discourses suggests the extent of his problem in self-definition.

Thus, Fraunce's brief inscription in the second *Ivychurch* of an audience of "litle men" who criticize his verse and his *Lawyers Logike* quite possibly reveals a second and hidden audience for the third *Ivychurch* as well, which would account for some of the tensions in this work. His role as entertainer of a female audience which enjoys versified love stories for their own sake and will allow him to amuse them at Ivychurch until something better comes along might jeopardize his reputation as a serious prospective solicitor. His representation of Elpinus might well have been initially designed to demonstrate the seriousness, the masculinity, of a privileged reader of literature, justifying its study to the earl of Pembroke or to any "Tenurists." Fraunce's most severe critic may well have been himself. Daphne's unanswered challenge to Elpinus's authority suggests the precariousness of the attempt to restore the reading of literature to the secure domination of the masculine voice of learning and purpose. But as her learned allusions suggest, her challenge itself had also been expressed as a recognized intellectual position by male scholars.

Fraunce's inscriptions of the countess of Pembroke as Pembrokiana are no more consistent than his text or his authorial persona. His inscriptions of the relationship between author and patron-reader reveal a range of possibilities. As he writes for the countess of Pembroke, is he being feminized, producing works at her desire like a whelping bear? Is he, like Amintas, achieving fame which will keep his memory alive? Can he, like Elpinus, reassert masculine control by explicating sensuous, poetic texts about love with his learning? Even these possibilities do not do justice to the crazy complexity of Fraunce's representations. What does become evident in the three *Ivychurch* works, however, is the way that attitudes towards narratives are inextricably entangled in constructions of gender. It is in the interstices of gender and attitudes towards narrative that Pembrokiana is constituted, as her power over texts is markedly diminished from her first incarnation as huntress of bears, to her second incarnation as celebrator of the dead Amintas, and finally to her third incarnation as moderator of Ovidian tales. These metamorphoses have little to do with Mary Sidney as an individual; they have everything to do with Fraunce's fashioning himself as a male author experiencing the power of a woman reader.

Fraunce includes the countess's name in the title of one additional work, *The Countess of Pembrokes Emanuel,* described on its title page as an account of the "nativity, Passion, Buriall, and Resurrection of Christ: togeather with certaine Psalmes, of David." This work, which does not inscribe the countess as a character in its text, reflected Mary Sidney's interest in her brother Philip's uncompleted translation of the Psalms, a project she had perhaps already taken up. This inclusion of the countess's name in Fraunce's title is the only hint of the existence of a religious interest which wholly constitutes Nicholas Breton's inscription of her as a character in his poem "The Countess of Penbrookes Love."[34]

Nicholas Breton: Her Love for God

While there are striking differences between Fraunce's Pembrokiana and Breton's "Countess of Penbrooke," both personae represent responses to the same gap between the countess's power over texts and the discourse of gender difference which discouraged that power. Instead of circumscribing the countess's authority, Breton rationalizes it by writing her as a religious mystic. Since Breton's "Countess"[35] is defined solely in terms of her relationship with God rather than with mortals, worldly power becomes, in theory, irrelevant. So does secular literature. Unlike Fraunce's Pembrokiana, Breton's "Countess of Penbrooke" supports only works on religious themes and explicitly abjures any writing of her own. But the real countess of Pembroke not only supported writing on secular themes; she even translated it. Some evidence points to Breton's distortions as implicit criticism of Mary Sidney's secular literary activities rather than simple ignorance. Whichever the case, patronage by Breton's "Countess" unlike that by the biographical countess posed no threat to masculine dominance; as a religious muse she served in the conventionally female role of providing inspiration to the male writer.

The name "Countess of Penbrooke" does not appear in the text of Breton's poem, which refers to its female persona only in third- or first-person pronouns. But the text implies the identity of the poem's female persona as Mary Sidney in various ways. The word "love" in the title *The Countess of Penbrookes Love* associates Mary Sidney with the poem's female wooer of God. Breton's dedication of the work to the "Gentlemen studients and Scholers of Oxford" asserts that the meditations of an honorable lady played a formative role in the writing of his poem: "The occasion, that made me first enter into this action, was to acquaint the honest mindes of virtuous dispositions, with the heavenly Meditations, of an honourable Lady." His request for leave "with this booke to honour her" echoes his dedication to the "Countess of Penbrooke," whom he also claims to honor with his book. Moreover, his dedication to the "Countess of Penbrooke" portrays her solely as a spiritual figure both in herself and in her influence on writers such as Breton himself. He uses her religious fervor, in fact, to level a criticism at the more secular courtly ideal popularized in Castiglione's *Book of the Courtier.* This criticism becomes explicit in his comparison of his "Countess of Penbrooke" to the duchess of Urbino: "If she had the beauty of Nature, you beautifie Nature, with the blessing of the spirite." Breton's dedication adapts elements of the Neoplatonic ideal—by which the lady inspires the suitor to spiritual progress—to create a model of patronage. The "favour" of his "Countess" has spiritual properties: "Let the poore pilgrime, that seeketh Paradise, finde heaven the better by your favour." Not only his "Countess's" example but also her patronage benefits her servants. Possibly under the influence of a patriotic as well as a religious impulse, Breton locates the superiority of his "Countess of Penbrooke" to the duchess of Urbino in the quality of writing she elicits from her followers: "Who hath redde of the Duchesse of Urbina, may saie, the Italians wrote well. But who knowes the Countesse of Penbrooke, I thinke hath cause to write better." Any authority exercised by Breton's "Countess" is securely contained within a religious model of patronage, through which she moves followers to conform to God's will, not her own.

In Breton's poem, a disinterest in worldly power is implicit in the refusal by his female protagonist to enjoy any pleasures the world might (and does) offer. The only audience of importance to this religious "Countess" is God himself, who gains her love and motivates her patronage. Thus, far from enjoying a recitation of Ovidian tales on her country estate Ivychurch, Breton's "Countess of Penbrooke" is left profoundly unsatisfied by the inventions of poets, whose "fancies" are, she knows, "but fained." Her dissatisfaction with secular poetry participates in a general conviction of the vanity of the world. Soldiers, peasants, merchants, lawyers, courtiers, scholars, sailors, shepherds—all come with gifts, but none of them can satisfy his protagonist's desires. Finally, realizing that "this world is but a weede" (21) his "Countess" understands that she longs only for God and wishes only to arrive at her heavenly home. Her rhapsodic and disjointed effusions, deriving from a long tradition of mysticism, sexualize her speech but render that sexualization acceptable through the divine object of her love. She has become a woman wooer, sick with love for God ("Oh love quod she, / My soule is sicke she cannot be with thee," 24). Praying that she "might leave this lothsome world" to "finde out" her "heavenly rest" (28), she falls into a trance in which she beholds God. Saints, martyrs, and angels embrace and comfort her. She awakes to wish only the love of God, which sets her "hart on fire" (28).

Resembling in her spiritual nature the "Countess of Penbrooke" depicted in Breton's dedication of *The Countess of Penbrookes Love,* the "Countess of Penbrooke" inscribed in a work entitled in manuscript *The Countesse of Penbrookes Passion* encourages poets to write on religious subjects.[36] In fact, she specifically prohibits secular themes:

Come all the worlde and call your witts together,
Borrowe some pens from out the angell's winges;
Entreat the heavenes to send ther muses hether,
To helpe your soules to write of sacred thinges;
  Prophane conceits must all be caste awaye;
  The night is past, and you must take the daye.
(10)

This "Countess" not only forbids the writing of "prophane conceits"; she also resolves not to author any writing—not even any religious writing—herself. After she prays to receive her own pen made from an angel's wing in order to write in God's honor, she decides instead to "refere unto some angel's glorie, / The hapie writtinge of his heavenlie storye" (8). While she later joins with other souls in religious song, she specifically limits her contribution to one word:

That while my soule doth thus my God adore,
I maye yett singe *Amen* althoughe no more.
(10)

Thus, unlike the real countess of Pembroke, who had already written two translations and was probably already working on her translation of the Psalms, Breton's "Countess" disclaims any possibility of authorship for herself.

Let us speculate upon the probable effect of Breton's entitling his poems after the countess of Pembroke. However much she may have engaged in religious meditation, Mary Sidney may not have welcomed Breton's female protagonist as an ideal, and especially not as an ideal associated with herself. She no doubt disagreed with his censure of secular literature, since her two translations published in 1592 were not primarily religious writings: Philippe Du Plessis Mornay's classically influenced preparation for death turns Christian only in the last quarter, and Garnier's *Marc Antoine* never turns religious at all. These translations are in no way acknowledged in Breton's poems. It is tempting to suppose that the "pen" in his adaptation of "Pembroke" to "Penbrooke" reveals a slip in his repression of her writing. Unless his spelling of her title was itself influenced by her authorship, Spenser's use of a similar form, the "Countesse of Penbroke," in one of his sonnets prefacing the *Faerie Queene* may indicate that the "Pen"form was conventional.

Breton's representation of his "Countess's" distrust of "fained" inventions in *The Countess of Penbrookes Love* and of secular writing in *The Countesse of Penbrookes Passion* might well have aroused considerable hostility towards him on the part of secular writers attempting to gain or to maintain Mary Sidney's support. His inclusion of the countess's name in his title may in fact nod to Fraunce's works as well as to Philip Sidney's *Countess of Pembrokes Arcadia.* Appearing in the same year as Fraunce's third *Ivychurch,* Breton's religious *Countesse of Penbrooks Love* may well have been experienced, and even have been intended, as a reproachful alternative to Fraunce's secular work with its secular Pembrokiana.

Whether the discrepancies between the real countess of Pembroke and Breton's "Countess of Penbrooke" signify ignorance or criticism of her writing and the secular writing of her protégés turns on the extent of Breton's knowledge of her and her work. Large gaps in Breton's biography make it impossible to ascertain absolutely the closeness of his relationship with the Sidneys and Herberts. He claims a strong friendship for Philip Sidney in his epitaph for him: "I lost a friend, such one there are no more."[37] Perhaps he knew Sidney in the wars in the Low Countries; a possibly autobiographical passage in *A Post with a Packet of Mad Letters* describes him as "wounded in the warres."[38] Four years after Sidney's death, the earl of Pembroke sent an enclosure, now lost, to the lord treasurer of England, concerning the case of one "Brittan" (possibly but not positively Nicholas Breton), a schoolmaster: "I latelie receaved lines from the Bishop of St. Davids, who complaineth of hard dealing assured to one *Brittan* a scholemaster, by Mr. Justice Walter at the last Sessions held in Brecknock."[39] The close variant of "Brittan" for "Breton" appears in Breton's work *Brit-*

tons Bowre of Delights. Two years later, Breton's first dedication to the countess, *The Pilgrimage to Paradise joyned with the Countesse of Penbrookes Love,* thanks her for rescuing him from adverse circumstances; he would have "utterly perished," he informs her, had not "the hand of your honor revived the hart of humility."

Breton was undoubtedly aware of the countess's secular activities by the time he wrote *The Countess of Penbrookes Passion,* in which the "Countess of Penbrooke" explicitly leaves even religious writing to others. *The Countess of Penbrookes Passion* was never published under that title, although a variant was published as *The Passions of the Spirit* in 1599 without Breton's name.[40] Both of Breton's editors speculate that Breton did not publish this work because of strain between him and Mary Sidney; and they believe this strain is described in a passage in Breton's *Wit's Trenchmour* (1597) that echoes the content and even the wording of his dedication to the countess in his *Countesse of Penbrooks Love.*[41]According to this passage, a generous lady, whose house was a "little Court" where God was served and religion preached, relieved the want of a poor gentleman until "by the faction of the malicious, the deceitfull working of the envious," she became disenchanted with him. Suffering from his Lady's displeasure, the gentleman begged leave to travel until on a snowy day he "fell so deepe downe into a Saw-pitte" that he "shall repent the fall while he lives" and has never since presumed to think about his Lady or her "Court-like pallace" except in prayers (2:19).

This passage from *Wit's Trenchmour* provides a strong impetus for speculation. Who were the envious, if they in fact existed? Why were they malicious? Possibly Breton's inscription of the countess as a religious character who rejected secular writing angered the secular writers such as Fraunce at the countess's estate. Michael Brennan, on the other hand, has suggested that Mary Sidney may have been offended by Breton's possible sale of *The Passions of the Spirit,* adapted from a manuscript produced for her, to the stationer Thomas Este, as well as by its subsequent dedication to a Mrs. Mary Houghton.[42] The inscription of the "Countess of Penbrooke" in *The Countesse of Penbrooks Passion,* later *The Passions of the Spirit,* suggests a third possibility: that Breton may have made a strategic error of another kind in his pursuit of patronage. The primary emotion expressed by the "Countess" of that poem is a feeling of guilt for her sins; the "plot" is fulfilled when God sends her the grace through which she can feel the true remorse of repentance, as demonstrated in her tears. In the process of moving herself (and the reader) to repentance, she perhaps grieves over sins that the countess may not have repented or, if she had, might not have wished to have laid before the public in a book. At one point, for example, the speaker in *The Countess of Penbrookes Passion* decries the sin of her "present time":

In fruiteles labours and in ruthless love:
Oh what a horror hath my harte to prove.
(3)

Breton's representation of his "countess"'s chaste repentance sexualizes her past by implying, somewhat incautiously, her previous improprieties. In this way, Breton's writing of his "Countess" is controlled by dualities present in the discourse of gender difference itself. Representations of chaste women readers condemn by contrast ordinary and supposedly lascivious women readers; these two poles oscillate unstably according to a discourse that interprets the acts of reading and writing as measurements of women's sexuality. Perhaps more straightforwardly, one wonders if Mary Sidney found Breton's description of her supposed torment of soul, so full of lamenting and repenting, entirely in good taste.

Thomas Moffett: Compassionating Silkworms

Thomas Moffett's *Silkewormes and Their Flies* (1599), a versified set of instructions on how to raise silkworms, inscribes yet another version of the countess of Pembroke. His Mira, "Lady of the plaine," is neither an Amazon like Fraunce's Pembrokiana nor a mystic like Breton's "Countess of Penbrooke." Portrayed with her female attendants in the homely domestic duties of raising silkworms, Mira is not a figure of threatening power, secular or spiritual. Perhaps because she is not represented as implementing authority over the works of male poets, Moffett can recognize her as an author, the recipient of the "Sydneian Muse" who will help Moffett write his poem. He refers specifically to her "sweete & heav'nly-tuned Psalmes" as authorizing her to enrich his own "high aspiring layes."[43] Reading his poem will provide refreshment, giving her increased energy for her own work, as he advises her in the dedication to "Let *Petrarch* sleep, give rest to *Sacred Writte,*" for "some little pawse aideth the quickest witte."

Moffett's acknowledgment of the countess of Pembroke as a writer may have had everything to do with his own independence from the power of her patronage. Moffett was not primarily a writer, nor was his career in a state of crisis. Instead, he was an established physician in his own right. According to the earl's will, written in 1596, the earl of Pembroke was his patient.[44] Moffett was also the Herberts' neighbor, in no apparent need of financial assistance; for John Aubrey records that he lived "in his later time at Bulbridge (at the mannor-house there)" near Wilton. Moffett's residence near Wilton can be established on better authority for the period in which he wrote *Silkewormes and Their Flies* (1599), for he was elected a member of Parliament for Wilton in 1597, and he buried his wife at Wilton in 1600.[45] From the vantage point of the family physician and neighbor, Mary Sidney probably did not look like a fierce huntress or spiritual phenomenon. And as an author, Moffett resembles neither a whelping bear nor a spiritual soulmate. He is instead an expert in a knowledge of use to his female audience. This version of his authorship paralleled his role as certified physician. Both activities—licensed physician and learned entomologist—are justified through expertise available primarily to males. This expertise creates for him an easy authority over his female audience, expressed within his poem as a tone of genial condescension.

While Moffett acknowledges the countess's authorship, she is addressed through most of the poem as a member of a group of women absorbed in the homely task of raising silkworms. In this way, her power as a reader and a writer is rationalized through an additional, more domestic function as a raiser of silkworms. Exerting little apparent authority even over her gentlewoman attendants, she becomes one of their number, listed with them under assumed classical names at least twice in the course of the poem. Like her attendants, she is represented as endearingly compassionate even for insects, as when, for example, the speaker consoles them for the death of the moths with the promise of the birth of new silkworms from the eggs:

> Weepe not faire (2) *Mira* for this funeral.
> Weepe not (3) *Panclea, Miraes* chiefe delight.
> Weepe not (4) *Phileta,* nor (5) *Erato* tall:
> Weepe not (5) *Euphemia,* nor (7) *Felicia* white:
> Weepe not sweete (8) *Fausta.* I assure you all,
> Your cattels parents are not dead outright:
> Keepe warme their egges, and you shall see anone,
> From eithers loynes a hundred rise for one.
>
> (F4v)

The numbers in the text refer to marginal references, which identify the personae as (2) "The Lady of the plaine," (3) "Miraes daughter," and (4–8) "Gentlewomen attending upon Mira and her daughter."

The poem's naming and characterizing of the women attending Mira creates Moffett's work as a small *roman à clef* written in part for the pleasure not only of the countess but of her gentlewomen as well. In his role as physician and neighbor, Moffett was no doubt personally acquainted with these women. Thus, it is likely that "Erato" (whatever her everyday name) was tall, and that "Felicia" was fair-skinned. In any case, Moffett's inclusion of them in his inscribed audience makes sense, for in actual practice it was no doubt these women, not primarily the countess, who would tend to the silkworms on a daily basis.

If these two versions of Mira, as a talented poet carrying on a Sidnean tradition and as a member of a group of women weeping over the fate of their silkworms, are difficult to reconcile, they point to other splits in the text. The poem itself is much more sophisticated than its title would imply. Specifically drawing on the fourth book of Virgil's *Georgics* as a model, it is, in fact, the first Virgilian georgic written in English.[46] The learned references to authors like Plutarch, Pliny, Regius, and Comes scattered over the margins also suggest an educated audience capable of recognizing these names and the way their influence enhanced Moffett's work. On the other hand, an uneducated audience is indicated by marginal explications of even simple classical allusions present in much of the poem. This identification of Titan as the sun is typical:

how they work not above nine dayes.	
1 *the sunne*	Whilst rosie (1) *Titan* nine times doeth arise
2 *Aurora, the morning*	From purple bedde of his most loving (2) friend
3 *The westerne sea*	And eke as oft in (3) *Atlas* vally dies.

(L3)

Moffett's use of classical allusions and then his careful identification of those allusions suggest that he was directing his work to at least two audiences: to the countess and her educated friends, who would acknowledge and appreciate Moffett's learning; and to uneducated women of the upper or middle classes, for whom the countess and her ladies acted as an advertisement, enticing them, too, to raise silkworms.[47] Moffett's description of his poem on his title page, in fact, as written "for the great benefit and enriching of England," shows a patriotic motive for encouraging the raising of silkworms. According to a later assertion, even the poor can enrich themselves by this activity: "No man so poore but he may Mulb'raies plant, / No plant so smal but wil a silke-worme feede" (K4). But raising silkworms is, according to the poem, no merely lower-class activity. The poem concludes with the hope that even the "Queen of Queenes . . . perhaps will hatch them twixt those hillocks rare."

This strange concluding image, of the queen hatching silkworms between her nurturing breasts, is only one way in which raising silkworms is constructed as a female activity. Silkworms are represented as appealing to women's mothering skills, their compassion. As a doctor, Moffett was no doubt aware of Galen's belief that women's particular tendency to compassion proceeded from their uterus, as expressed by one modern historian: "The effect of the uterus on the mind weakens rationality and increases the incidence and violence of passions in women: hate, vengeance, fear, anger . . . but also compassion, pity, and love."[48] The ability to feel compassion particularly characterizes Mira and her gentlewomen, who pity even the mulberry seeds that grow the trees which provide nourishment for silkworms:

> Far be it from a tender damsels hart
> On tendrest seedes to shew so hard a part.
> (G4v)

In this description of the grief of silkworm wives over their husbands' deaths, the narrator's attempt to elicit an extreme compassion from his women readers verges on parody:

> In Tuscane townes what armies did I view
> One harvest, of these faithfull husbands dead?
> Bleede, O my heart, while I record anew,
> How wives lay by them, beating, now their head,
> Sometimes their feet, and wings, & breast most true,
> Striving no lesse to be delivered,
> Then *Thisbe* did from undesired life,
> When she beheld her *Pyram* slain with knife.
> (F3v)

Cast in the roles of Ovidian heroines, silkworm wives are granted a surprising degree of subjectivity. Compassion for their grief merges with the compassion for Ovid's protagonists assumed here for women readers. Moffett's readers have already read the tale of Pyramis and Thisbe in his poem, as an explanation for why mulberries are black. Like Fraunce, Moffett here assumes women readers who interpret Ovid literally. To them, as to Dieromena, Ovid is an instructor of love rather than a stern moralist or an erudite naturalist. The Ovid claimed for Moffett's female audience is "Loves schoolmaster" (C1). Thus, Moffett's poem conflates the compassion qualifying women as caretakers of silkworms with the compassion for protagonists of love stories imagined as characterizing women's reading.

This compassion for protagonists of love stories and silkworms alike implied for Moffett's female readers takes on a specifically sexual aspect in this description of the mutal gratification silkworms enjoy in the sexual act:

> Both long, and longing skud to *Venus* forts,
> To stirre up seed that ever may remaine,
> He runs to her, and she to him resorts,
> Each mutually the other entertaine.
>
> (K1)

Anticipating Aubrey's representation of the countess's pleasure in watching horses mate, Moffett advances a voyeuristic pleasure in the sights and sounds of silkworm sex as one motive for his women readers to raise silkworms:

> Observe their gate and steerage al along,
> Their salutations, couplings, and *Adieus:*
> Heare eke their hurring and their churring song,
> When hot *Priapus* love and lust renewes.
>
> (L1)

In this passage, women's compassion has shaded into a peculiar form of lascivious interest.

Thus, like Virgil's *Georgics,* Moffett's poem is not merely about silkworms. Virgil personifies his bees to almost a humorous extent to represent a serious model for human behavior. His bees are ideal citizens of a smoothly functioning commonwealth, laboring in their distinct offices for the public good. Despite his assumption of his readers' peculiar interest in silkworm sexuality, Moffett's poem elsewhere also portrays a feminine ideal of sorts, however humorous his personification. In addition to eliciting the compassion of female readers, the grief of silkworm wives over their husbands' deaths provides a model for conjugal devotion. Silkworm wives also provide a model for dying well. The table at the beginning of Moffett's poem even singles out their "manner of dying" as a useful topic for the readers' perusal. The application to the readers' own life is made explicit in this description of the happy deaths silkworms make after laying their eggs:

> Which donne, both die, and die with cheerefull hart
> Bycause they had done al they bidden were,
> Might we from hence with conscience like depart?
> How deare were death? how sweet or voyd of feare?
> How little should we at his arrowes start?
>
> (F4v)

Their deaths prepare them for paradise of erotic bliss:

> Go worthy soules (so witty *Greeks* you name)
> Possesse for aye the faire *Elisian* greene:
> Sport there your selves ech Lordling with his Dame,
> Enjoy the blisse by sinners never seene.
>
> (F4v)

This final vision of insect bliss reconciles the silkworm wives' dual functions as romantic protagonists and as masters (or mistresses) of the art of dying well.

Despite this final reconciliation of the functions of silkworm wives, however, the female audience implied for Moffett's poem remains oddly split. Bearing resemblances to the sexualized women readers described by Vives and others, they extend their compassion for the protagonists of love stories to silkworms as well. In fact, the very raising of silkworms is represented as a kind of love story, a tale of conjugal fidelity spiced with a piquant sauce of insect sexuality. It is difficult to imagine women readers taking silkworms as a model for dying well too seriously. This interest in making a good death was no doubt directed to the countess of Pembroke, who had already translated a treatise on dying well, and perhaps to other women educating themselves in the art of dying.

Recipient of the Sidnean muse and translator of a sober treatise on dying well, the countess seems to be distinct from the uneducated female reader imagined for this poem. But as Mira, she is inscribed as weeping with her ladies over the deaths of silkworms. Does her membership in this group serve merely as an advertisement to female readers who were very unlike herself? Or is she implicated, as she weeps for her silkworms, in the foolish compassion of the sexualized woman reader? This knotty question of whether an elite female audience is defined against or in conformity with the sexualized woman reader poses itself insistently in this culture, appearing again in Sir Philip Sidney's *The Countess of Pembroke's Arcadia.* It no doubt worked itself out not only in texts, but in the subjectivities of Renaissance women as they created themselves as readers, as well.

Nathaniel Baxter: Ile be thy Patronesse

Questions of audience and purpose are much less complicated in Nathaniel Baxter's poem *Sir Philip Sidneys Ourania* (1606) because he is simply more venal. The poem itself, a catalogue of God's creation in imitation of Du Bartas's *La Semaine* (1578), is framed by a topical allegory that serves as a heavy-handed request for patronage. In this frame, Baxter reminds the countess, now the countess-dowager, of previous promises; he even fabricates a request from her dead brother to give Baxter patronage as a reward for past services as his tutor. Dedications to her daughters-in-law, her nieces, and her cousin, all of whom are inscribed in the text as members of "Cynthia's" company, widen the audience to female members of the countess's family, no doubt in the hope that if the countess did not reward him with money or with the restoration of his situation, one of them might. He may have printed the poem to flatter or to shame her into patronage, to find new patrons who might sympathize with the plight he so pathetically sets forth, or just to gain money from the public sale of a work he had originally written to appeal to a private audience.

A poem with little literary merit, *Sir Philip Sidneys Ourania* cannot be taken seriously in its claims. Baxter needed money, and his record of being twice sued in court for extracting money under false pretenses suggests that his integrity was not beyond reproach. To the little written of Baxter's life in the *Dictionary of National Biography* can be added information from legal records revealing his tendency to petty crime. In 1591 a Robert Henlack, who was robbed of his goods in London, swore that "one Nathaniel Baxter by indirect meanes hath sithence gotten £12 of the suppliantes uppon promise to help him to his goods and mony againe, pretending great skill in casting a figure."[49] Baxter's pastoral vocation did not counteract his dishonest tendencies, for two years later a widow named Jane Shelley attempted to reclaim some money and jewels which "one Nathaniel Baxter a minister did cozon her of."[50] Thus, there is perhaps an element of the con artist in Baxter's authorship of the execrable verse in *Sir Philip Sidneys Ourania,* which functioned primarily as a blatant appeal for patronage. Even Baxter's claim to have been Sidney's tutor should be regarded with suspicion, since it is not substantiated by other sources.

Baxter's dedication writes the countess of Pembroke in ways recalling Fraunce's Pembrokiana. He even uses the name Pembrokiana in his address to "Mistris Arcadian Cynthia, Maria Pembrokiana," and he describes her as holding a "dreadefull bowe, / To kill the game, if any should appeere, / Or any deadly foe approach too neere" (B3). But unlike Fraunce, Baxter does not seem immasculated, perhaps because the power of the countess seems limited simply to her wealth; Baxter describes in loving detail the diamonds and sapphires on her coronet and the gold in her buskins.[51] Within the text, the countess's power as patron and her nurturing use of that power are implicit in the model for patronage offered in the underlying narrative of the love of Cynthia the moon for the poet Endymion. By providing an antecedent for the love of a powerful woman for a worthy poet, this myth perhaps removes some of the threat from the patronage relationship by eliciting and then rationalizing the anxiety induced by the inequality of their social circumstances.[52]

Creating a religious context for this myth in adapting it to fit his personal circumstances, Baxter writes himself, as well as the countess and her female relatives, into his poem. The extent of his appeal for patronage is best conveyed by a summary of this narrative frame to his poem. He inscribes himself as the gentle shepherd Endymion, who sang "divine and sacred layes" (B2) to his flocks at Troy in Cambria. (Baxter himself was installed as a vicar of a church in Troy, Monmouthshire, in 1602.)[53] His skill as a poet or, more likely, as a preacher is indicated by Endymion's fame, which finally draws even Cynthia, identified as Astrophill's sister, and her ladies to listen to him. Stunned by her jewels, he drops his pipes. Cynthia herself stoops to rub his temples, and her ladies strive to "rouze him from his Trance" (A4); but he cannot rise until Cynthia lays aside "her Majestie, that daunteth rurall pride" and urges him to "Cast feare away, Ile be thy Patronnesse: / While *Cynthia* lives *Endymion* is sure" (B4v). Modestly, he asks only to remain on his hill. Cynthia agrees, although she feels that he should ask for more, repeating her request that he sing his "Melodious Notes of sweetest Harmonie, / For such does please the highest Deitie," and (in a somewhat disjunctive tone) "comfort us after our weary Howers, / Which we have spent in gathering Gilliflowers" (B4v).

Besides her admiring response to Endymion's skill, Cynthia's promised patronage is represented as a sign of her love for her brother Astrophill, a name Sidney had chosen to represent the poet-lover in his sonnet sequence *Astrophel and Stella.* After Endymion's 3,000-line list of the elements, the plants and animals of the earth and sea, and the metals within the earth, he sees a "gentle Knight come pricking on" (M3v). Lifting his beaver, the knight reveals himself as Astrophill, or more specifically, when Cynthia's three attempts to embrace him fail, as the ghost of Astrophill. Reviving from her faint, Cynthia begs him to speak to her. He replies to her with the revelation that Endymion (nicknamed "Tergaster," a Greek version of "Backster" or "Baxter") had been his tutor, and he directs her to patronize him: "My dearest Sister keepe my Tutor well." After Astrophill mounts back up into the clouds on Pegasus, Cynthia turns to Endymion with the following promise:

> This Mount (quoth she) take for thy mansion:
> Here shalt thou dwell, and feede thy little flocke,
> I with my Ladies, will encrease thy Stocke.
> (N3)

For a while he lived "in reputation / Expounding Oracles of Theologie" (N3). Then, somewhat like Breton's poet, whose patronage was also terminated by envious ill-wishers, Endymion met his downfall through the agency of "envies sophistication," no doubt of the "false Lividus" who "brought it about, / That *Cynthia* had him in suspicion." He was "cast downe / By Envies practise and great *Cynthias* frown" (B1). But the entire truth will never be known, for, as Endymion concludes, "Sith Tragaedies have a bloody end, / During his life, he will not have it pend" (N3).

In addition to setting a new limit to how blatant a request for patronage could be, Baxter's inscription of the countess of Pembroke as Cynthia is noteworthy for a detail that became central to versions of her authorship by Spenser and by herself. Baxter's Cynthia expresses a desire to die in order to join her brother. When Astrophill's ghost returns to heaven, Cynthia desires to follow him:

> *Cynthia* would needes ascend *Olympus hill,*
> To live or dye, with blessed *Astrophill.*
> Nature perswaded her to stay a while.
> Her time prefixed was not yet assign'd.
>
> And yet to spend in contemplation,
> The better part of her remaining dayes:

Which vow she keepes in veneration,
Witnesse her learned Poems, and her Layes,
So often crowned, with Arcadian Bayes.
(N2v)

Baxter's representation of the countess's wish for death, inspired by a devotion to her brother, as motivating her literary activities presents a model which removes many of the anxieties associated with women's writing in the English Renaissance. According to this model, writing is not associated with a desire to impress an audience or to seduce a lover, but becomes instead an unworldly activity, a rejection of the things of this world as mere vanity. However much the work of the countess (inscribed as Cynthia) may be "crowned, with Arcadian Bayes," public recognition is not acknowledged as her goal. Her primary audience, according to this representation, is private, not public—apparently her contemplative self or perhaps her brother in heaven. Her primary motivation, according to this model, is that of passing the tedious time before her desired death. A number of elegies and epitaphs by women in the period suggests that this model in fact worked, allowing them to write and even sometimes to publish poems of grief over dead sons and fathers.[54] One of the most famous, "The Lay of Clorinda," may well have been written by the countess of Pembroke.

Edmund Spenser: Clorinda's Elegy

The inscriptions of the countess of Pembroke by five writers suggest a factor influencing the thoroughness of the effect of gender ideology: generally, the greater an author's need for Pembroke support, the more threatening the power he attributed to the countess and the less likely he was to recognize her as an author. Fraunce included no references to Mary Sidney's authorship, while Breton's "Countess" explicitly leaves writing to others. An exception to this tendency is Baxter, who refers fleetingly to the "learned Poems, and her Layes, / So often crowned, with Arcadian Bayes" of his inscribed countess figure. The more secure Moffett acknowledged her work, although in an admonishment to interrupt it: "Let *Petrarch* sleep, give rest to *Sacred Writte.*" Spenser, however, represents the sister of Astrophel as mourning her brother in a poem, "The Lay of Clorinda," which was included in his *Astrophel* (1595), a collection of elegies for Sir Philip Sidney written by various authors. According to the speaker of *Astrophel*, Clorinda was the actual author of "The Lay of Clorinda": "In sort as she it sung I will rehearse."[55] Whether Mary Sidney or Edmund

Spenser wrote "The Lay of Clorinda" is still in dispute; critical opinion appears to be veering towards the countess.[56] Whichever the case, Spenser's inscription of the countess as an author reveals the conditions which permitted a woman to be represented as speaking in print. It apparently took an author as established as Spenser to inscribe her explicitly as a poet, and even to publish literary texts represented as her work.

In addition to his reputation as poet, Spenser's relative independence from the power of her patronage may have freed him to cross this cultural boundary. There is no evidence that he depended upon her patronage or that she strongly influenced his literary or political career. A stanza from the *Faerie Queene* quoted in Fraunce's *Arcadian Rhetorike* (1588) two years before the *Faerie Queene's* publication may suggest that Spenser's manuscript was circulating at Wilton.[57] Spenser's dedicatory sonnet to Mary Sidney prefacing this work describes her primarily as the sister of Sir Philip Sidney, whom she resembles: "His goodly image living evermore, / In the divine resemblaunce of your face."[58] Perhaps some reward for this dedication prompted his reference to her "manie singular favors and great graces" in his dedication to her of *The Ruines of Time* (1591), but his primary reasons for dedicating this poem to her is because of her membership in the Dudley family, for whose renown this work is "speciallie intended"; the bulk of the dedication concerns Spenser's attachment to her brother.[59] Perhaps the strongest statement of her patronage of Spenser is Colin's reply to the question, "But say, who else vouchsafed thee of grace," in *Colin Clouts Come Home Again* (1595):

> They all (quoth he) me graced goodly well,
> That all I praise, but in the highest place,
> *Urania,* sister unto *Astrophell.*[60]

Nevertheless, while Spenser apparently profited in some way from the countess's support, there is no evidence that he spent time at Wilton or that she exerted a major influence upon his literary projects.

Even Spenser's inscription of the countess, however, reveals the shaping pressures of the discourse of gender difference. Unlike the elegies spoken by male figures in Spenser's *Astrophel,* "The Lay of Clorinda" begins by posing a pressing issue for a woman writer, the problem of audience:

> Ay me! to whom shall I my case complaine,
> That may compassion my impatient griefe?
> (217–18)

She cannot address the heavens, for they caused the catastrophe of Astrophel's death. She cannot address men, for they are equally and wretchedly subject to "heaven's ordinance." She can express her sorrow only to herself:

> Then to my selfe will I my sorrow mourne,
> Sith none alive like sorrowfull remaines:
> And to my selfe my plaints shall back retourne,
> To pay their usury with doubled paines.
>
> (19–22)

Clorinda's representation of herself as her sole audience contradicts the elegy's frame, which creates an audience for her. Spenser's first speaker addresses *Astrophel* to "shepherds" (1), although he is well aware that they of "nycer wit" might "hap to heare" (13–14) or read the elegy. More specifically, the first speaker presents Clorinda as one of several shepherds gathered together to mourn Astrophel's death; the other shepherds are, presumably, within listening range. This contradiction can be explained by the process of *Astrophel's* composition. Probably various authors wrote their elegies individually before Spenser gathered them together in *Astrophel*.[61] Still, it is striking that, while other authors may not mention a specific audience, Clorinda is the only author who denies the presence or possibility of an audience. In this evocation of the solitary mourner, the author of the Clorinda poem is working well within a pastoral tradition; but it is a pastoral tradition none of the other poets in the collection takes up. Clorinda's isolation as a poet does not last long, however. A few stanzas later, she imagines a female audience of "shepheards lasses," whom she urges to break their garlands (37), and by line 54, she tells "shepheards" that they will never see the like of Astrophel again. By addressing a male audience, Clorinda is crossing a boundary line drawn around female public speech. The factors enabling her to cross that line become clearer on analysis of the other female listeners and speakers in *Astrophel*.

The presence of a female audience, often shepherdesses or nymphs (water or wood), is not uncommon in the pastoral tradition. Their function, sometimes shared with male figures, is to feel compassion, to weep or even to die in sympathy for the deceased. Sometimes, however, they join in the mourning with plaints of their own. Thus, the distance from these female mourning figures to Clorinda is not great; and their lamentations, individually or in concert with a poet, help to explain why Clorinda is allowed to speak her "lay." The two separate treatments of Stella in *Astrophel* provide a range of possibilities imagined for a female mourner. In the first poem of *Astrophel,* Stella (here Sidney's wife, not Penelope Rich) does not merely mourn. She dies in her grief (in actuality she remarried); and the gods, taking pity on her devotion, turn both Astrophel and Stella into a single flower. Her function as mourner remains in the flower's ability to hold dew:

> And all the day it standeth full of deow,
> Which is the teares that from her eyes did flow.
> (191–92)

Thestylis's poem, spoken after Clorinda's, reveals intricate strategies enabling a woman's poem to be presented while evading the problem of addressing an audience. Thestylis's poem includes a reported elegy for Astrophel's death by Stella, who is overheard apparently only by the speaker, of whose presence she seems unaware. Any suspicions of a desire to influence an audience are also allayed by Stella's expressed wish to die. Accusing Astrophel of leaving her alone, "plung'd in a world of woe" (122), Stella can find no contentment on earth since Astrophel, her only treasure, lies in a grave. She wishes, of course, to join him in heaven: "As here with thee on earth I liv'd, even so equall / Methinkes it were with thee in heav'n I did abide" (116–17). Finally, her grief participates in the pathetic fallacy on a grand scale, to associate her with natural forces rather than with civilized arts. Her expression of grief is followed by a "lake" (125) of tears, which create a number of interesting effects. Her tears make her even more beautiful than the weeping Aurora, and Cupid bathes in them before he dries her eyes. All nature weeps with her, and the rainstorm which follows for "many a day" threatens the destruction of the earth by flood. Ships are swallowed up. The caves along "Medway's silver streames" cry "Phillip!" Nymphs and shepherds join in the general moan, along with the speaker, who refers to the "teares we weep" in his address to Astrophel's spirit in heaven.

These two versions of Stella suggest two ways that women figures contribute to the genre of elegy. First of all, while Spenser's shepherds and sylvan gods are known to weep, tears are especially associated with women, whose compassion supposedly characterizes their gender. Secondly, women serve as mediators, figures of transition, between the world of civilization and the world of nature. Recent work in anthropology reveals the ways that women are associated cross-culturally with untamed nature and defined that way in opposition to men, the purveyors of civilization.[62] In the pastoral tradition shepherds, too, operate in somewhat this way, partaking of a natural scene, freed at least nominally from the constraints of court society. But both in her metamorphosis into a flower and in nature's imitation of her weeping, Stella is associated as part of nature in a way more pronounced than is true for shepherds, except for Astrophel himself, whose actual death has already made him nonhuman.

The audience imagined in the first lines of Thestylis's poem combines both these female attributes in the persons of weeping nymphs:

Come forth, ye Nymphes, come forth, forsake your watry bowres,
Forsake your mossy caves, and help me to lament:
Help me to tune my dolefull notes to gurgling sound
Of Liffies tumbling streames: come, let salt teares of ours
Mix with his waters fresh. O come, let one consent
Joyne us to mourne with wailfull plaints the deadly wound.
(1–6)

The compassion of Thestylis's nymphs, a characteristic expected of female audiences in general, makes them dependable weepers, a particularly appropriate audience for expressions of sorrow. As denizens of caves and streams, their grief is only one step away from the pathetic fallacy; they imply the effect of Astrophel's death on nature itself. Such figures are not exclusively female. Sylvan gods and male rivers also grieve. But females, especially nymphs and muses, by far outnumber males in this function.

Unlike Clorinda and Thestylis's Stella, nymphs and other female figures do not often speak independently to an audience. In their grief, Thestylis's nymphs are allowed to speak only in concert with the speaker of the poem. In the next poem, "A Pastoral Aeglogue," female figures from nature speak independently but not to an audience: the shepherd Colin describes Pales, surrounded by nymphs and oreads, weeping "A floud of teares to bathe the earth" (58). Leaving their springs and bowers, Pales and her female followers mourn in "wailful tunes" in "hollow caves," accompanied by the howls of wolves (71–77). The next elegy, set within the frame of a dream vision, includes the songs of male and female birds responding to a mourner's grief for Astrophel: Philomell, a female nightingale "that knowes full well / What force and wit in love doth dwell" (29–30); a female turtle dove who sings her praises of Astrophel's loyalty to his mate; and a male swan who dies after singing a funeral dirge. One final female figure haunts the genre of elegy. Her presence is implied in Clorinda's lay, when Clorinda believes that "the woods, the hills, the rivers shall resound / The mournfull accent of my sorrowes ground" (23–24). This figure is Echo, the actual voice of a natural force, repeating the words she hears. In "A Pastorall Aeglogue," Colin asserts that "Eccho will our words report" (34).

Even if female figures do not often speak independently in pastoral elegy, their sheer numbers may well have had the effect of legitimating the genre as appropriate for a woman's voice. In addition to their numbers, their plaints present elegy as an "uncivilized" form, a spontaneous outpouring of emotion, to be judged on the basis of its sincerity, not its art. This perception of elegy is voiced in "A Pastoral Aeglogue" as the shepherd Colin urges the unlearned Lycon to express his grief for Astrophel:

> Ah, Lycon, Lycon! what need skill, to teach
> A grieved mynd powre forth his plaints?
> Hath the pore turtle gon to school (weenst thou)
> To learne to mourne her lost mate? No, no, each
> Creature by nature can tell how to waile.
>
> (15–19)

The opening of *Astrophel* expresses something of this sentiment, as the speaker addresses his rhymes "rudely dight" solely to lowly shepherds. If any of "nycer wit" should hear or read them, they must remember that the purpose of this elegy, which was "made not to please the living but the dead," is not to impress but only to move to pity (12–18). This description of this elegant and learned poem is, of course, inaccurate; but as a fiction, it may have played a role in enabling Clorinda's verse by representing it as a spontaneous outpouring of feelings, to be judged by the intensity of its grief rather than as a crafted poem demanding recognition for its learning.

Thus, while the pastoral elegy remained an appropriate genre for male writers, various characteristics made it especially hospitable to a woman writer faced with a gender ideology hostile to her writing. There was within pastoral itself a sense of apology, a posture of humility. Sung in a natural setting by lowly shepherds, who were portrayed as learned only in the ways of nature and their own hearts, pastoral was itself perceived as "simple" or "natural," at the opposite pole of more complicated and "civilized" genres like epic poetry. For this reason, youthful writers, some of whom may, like Virgil and Spenser, have had epic yearnings, adopted pastoral as appropriate for their inexperience. The pastoral defended a woman author from the accusation of flaunting her learning, of asserting herself as a "real" poet. A woman who wrote a pastoral elegy, in particular, was authorized not by her reason but by her emotions; Clorinda's elegy is merely a verbal expression of what, according to gender ideology, women were able to do: to weep.

Finally, the elegy solves the audience problem faced by women writers. Even if an audience is present, it only enables grief. The speaker of an elegy is not searching for worldly fame or attempting to impress potential lovers. The death of the loved one is often depicted as actually or potentially emptying out any meaning from the speaker's life. Since the beloved is dead, what does worldly acclamation signify? These conventions were, of course, poses, and probably meant to be recognized as such. The most uneducated of shepherds frequently reflected an uncanny knowledge of works by Theocritus and Virgil as well as a remarkable sense of the intricacies of prosody.[63] No matter how truly distressed by the death of a loved one, authors of elegies found meaning in the act of writing poetry and no doubt, like other poets, were pleased by acknowledgments of their skill. But these poses, no matter how transparent, enabled the countess of Pembroke (if she was in fact the author of Clorinda's lay) to write a public elegy, or (if she was not) at least to be inscribed as a poet.

The constructions of gender that enabled Clorinda to sing her lay may have enabled Mary Sidney to carry on a significant part of her literary career. Her literary activities began as a devotional act to her brother, as she edited and published authorized versions of his work. The letter prefacing her 1593 version of *The Countess of Pembrokes Arcadia* represents her efforts as a homely and maternal act of love rather than as a scholarly activity. She is washing its face, which had been dirtied by Greville's 1590 edition: "The disfigured face, gentle reader, wherewith this work not long since appeared to the common view, moved that noble lady, to whose honour consecrated, to whose protection it was committed, to take in hand the wiping away of those spots wherewith the beauties thereof were unworthily blemished."[64] But beyond love for brother, her version of authorship drew upon a larger cultural preoccupation which functioned in a similar way: the art of dying. As a bereaved sister, she could write elegies on her brother's death. As we shall see in Chapter 3, her representation of herself as yearning for death was not, however, absolutely centered on her brother. Also influenced by her mother and her husband, she turned her attention to the heroines who died so gracefully, their beauty never diminished, in the works she translated by Garnier and Petrarch.

Modern Constructions of the Countess of Pembroke

The rationalization of Mary Sidney's power over texts was not limited to the Renaissance. Until recently, much of what was believed about the countess of Pembroke proceeded from a later discourse of gender difference. Let us look first at the "facts" about Mary Sidney, as they have been passed down in standard literary histories. Before the recent attention attracted by her verse in the last decade, she was known as a patron (or patroness) of writers who supported the projects of her revered brother Philip.[65] Thus, at her wealthy husband's estate at Wilton, she offered hospitality to writers who continued her brother's experiments in quantitative verse and who wrote closet dramas to reform the English stage according to the precepts of Sidney's *Apology for Poetry.* These works, inspired by the "neoclassical spirit" of this group, were doomed to fall outside the mainstream of enduring literary monuments.[66]

This literary history written about the countess of Pembroke is permeated by, indeed has been largely created by, a modern discourse of gender difference. Until recently, her own writing, considered separately from her brother's, has been largely relegated to the silence surrounding the writing of other Renaissance women, while her role as a patron has been stressed and even exaggerated. Decades of literary historians have gathered writers into her group on the slimmest of pretexts: a dedication to her of one work also dedicated to thirty-four other people; a writer's friendship with another writer she may have patronized; patronage of a writer by her son William after the period of her own residence at Wilton.[67] Clearly, as a patron, but not as a writer, the countess fit an expectation of what women were supposed to do. She served as a model to hold up to other women, to encourage them also to be helpmates, not achievers; to nurture, not to create. This use of the countess is particularly explicit, for example, in an essay published in 1927 by Felix Schelling entitled "Sidney's Sister, Pembroke's Mother": "Moreover, need we all, save for the personal pleasure that is in it, need we all be creative? Is there not a function as necessary in its way to the healthy flourishing of literature, music, and art, all but as important as creation itself? . . . And woman, in the degree of her more exalted ideals, may remain, let us hope, after all, for the future as she has been heretofore, the truest patron of poetry and the arts."[68] Schelling's essay represents Mary Sidney as an example of a woman qualified by her gender to respond to art. In arguing for the importance of this skill, Schelling creates a dichotomy between responding and creating which almost by definition excludes patrons as writers. While he celebrates the presence of women writers in his own society, implicit in his use of the countess as the model for a nurturing woman patron of male writers is the assumption that, with some eccentric exceptions, women are not creative.

When elsewhere in his essay Schelling represents women patrons as writers, he praises them for not taking their accomplishments seriously. He uses their aristocratic femininity to discount later women writers as unattractively masculine:

> The cultivated Elizabethan women who encouraged letters, graciously received the praises of poets, and dabbled in writing, as did their lords and husbands, and with about equal success, could little have dreamed of such a person, for example, as scandalous Mistress Aphra Behn of Restoration times, the first English professional literary woman, who wrote plays, poetry, and fiction with the swagger and abandon of a man . . . Even Mrs. Katherine Philips, the Matchless Orinda, as she was dubbed . . . would sorely have puzzled my Lady Pembroke.[69]

While some of Schelling's claims may well have been accurate (if difficult to prove), his essay lacks any awareness that the association of writing, and especially of public writing, with masculinity was socially constituted rather than a natural occurrence. He appears to be reinterpreting the countess in terms of his contemporary discourse of gender difference.

Sexual stereotyping has not stopped at the exaggeration of the countess of Pembroke's patronage. Her very support of male writers was motivated, it is still almost universally claimed, by the attempt to further her brother's projects; she apparently had none of her own that did not overlap with his. A recent biographer who has made valuable contributions to the understanding of the countess as a poet in her own right is only following along in the tradition of literary scholarship when he deduces from "letters, dedications, diaries, public and private records" that "the dominant passion of her life seems to have been her devotion to her brother's literary and cultural ideals." From the dedication of her translation of the *Psalms* to her brother's "angell spirit," for example, he has analyzed a line of "intense intimacy" to see a "veil" lifted "very briefly, unwillingly, even unconsciously" on the true nature of her passion for her brother. Recalling Aubrey's gossip that Mary and her brother lay together, this critic suggests "a degree of intensity of feeling between Philip and Mary, especially on the side of the Countess" so that "there is no doubt that the deepest emotional commitment of her life was to her brother, both before and after his death."[70]

While I do not wish to deny Mary Sidney's sisterly love for her brother or his influence upon her even after his death, this emphasis upon her relationship to Philip Sidney has led to an unfortunate distortion of the perception of her own literary activities. While she did complete her brother's translation of the *Psalms*, her two major "programmes" of sponsoring quantitative verse and reforming the English stage appear to be largely the fictions of literary historians. Her supposed support of quantitative verse is based on ignoring numerous works dedicated to her, and even written by her, in other poetic meters. While Fraunce wrote his wretched hexameters, Breton, for example, wrote his *Countess of Pembrokes Love* in regular iambic pentameter. Moreover, the actual extent of her influence on Spenser, the major force behind these supposed experiments in quantitative verse, is questionable.[71] More blatantly, the countess's supposed attempt to reform the English stage is based upon attributing to her influence plays by Thomas Kyd and William Alexander, neither of whom ever dedicated any works to her or showed any acquaintanceship with her during her lifetime, while eliminating from consideration such works as Abraham Fraunce's translation of Tasso's *Aminta*.[72] Fraunce's inclusion of her name in his title *The Countess of Pembroke's Ivychurch* renders the absence of his work from discussions of her dramatic program more than an oversight.

The power of a modern discourse of gender difference is demonstrated in the way that these discussions include works by writers she did not know and exclude works which are even titled after her. By perceiving her solely as the intellectual functionary of her brother, completing those projects and only those projects that he would have completed if he had lived longer, literary historians have again created a model of what a woman was supposed to be: a passive vehicle responding to an active male agent. The effect of these modern representations is to erase her as as subject in her own right. While the countess of Pembroke composed some quantitative verse and translated a closet drama, a closer examination of work by her and by those whose work she certainly supported reveals that her programs were more varied and complex than literary history has allowed.

There is one final way in which this modern discourse of gender difference has played a part in the representation of the countess of Pembroke and her circle. In the emphasis on quantitative meters and closet drama, this group is portrayed as excessively rule-oriented, out of touch with the "real" creativity of the late sixteenth century. As a standard literary history has put it, "For Mary, we may infer, rules were the essence of literature."[73] It was this representation that apparently moved T. S. Eliot to champion her cause in his essay "An Apology for the Countess of Pembroke," in which he attempted to depolarize the creative and critical faculties. According to Eliot, her influence upon Spenser, who influenced Marlow, who influenced Milton, was sufficient to "rescue the Countess of Pembroke's friends and relatives from obscurity, enough to dignify their critical efforts, to raise them from the ignominy of well-born amateurs of the arts, or obscurantist supporters of a fastidious and sterile classicism."[74] Even if the extent of Mary Sidney's influence over Spenser were not open to doubt, the truth value of Eliot's statement is questionable. Do we believe, as we read it, that the successful influence of one man can redeem a whole group from such a heavy charge?

With Eliot's defense of the countess of Pembroke and her circle against the charge of being "obscurantist supporters of a fastidious and sterile classicism," the modern discourse of gender difference has moved full circle. "Fastidious," "sterile": these adjectives convey the image of the old-maid schoolteacher, obsessed with rules of grammar and behavior and having little contact with life as lived by her students. This image of the spinsterish, rule-bound schoolteacher strongly resembles the modern representation of Mary Sidney as she censures popular drama, attempts to uplift popular taste, and sponsors plays of refined speeches rather than violent action. These activities imply a sterility of imagination, a denial of the messy, human impulses that compose "real life." This stereotype lies at the opposite end of the spectrum from Aubrey's malicious sexual gossip, which also occasionally informs modern critical views. Rather than being a revaluation of the countess, this reversal responds to a modern revaluation of sexuality.

Whereas the Renaissance discourse of gender difference delegitimated women's writing and reading by sexualizing it, this modern discourse of gender difference seems to be delegitimating the countess' patronage by desexualizing it. The chaste, virginal reader-heroine of the Renaissance is reread as the frigid schoolmarm, terrified of being touched. While the content of these representations of the countess has changed in compliance with a changing discourse of gender difference, the function of these representations has remained the same. The activity of criticism has increasingly made it necessary to reread not only former times, but also our own.

Chapter 2

The Countess of Pembroke's Arcadia and Its (Com)Passionate Women Readers

The title of Sir Philip Sidney's *Countess of Pembroke's Arcadia* grants a privileged position to the countess of Pembroke as a reader. Since it identifies the work as in some sense *hers*, it asserts the importance of her reading in the book's very production. Sidney's dedication confirms the primacy of his sister's role as reader: the work was written at her desire, mostly on loose sheets of paper in her presence; it was written only for her, and it was to be kept to herself "or to such friends who will weigh errors in the balance of good will."[1] As his sister rather than his patron, Mary Sidney gained her power as reader through her love rather than through her wealth or her husband's connections. Thus Sidney, unlike various other authors dedicating their works to the countess, reveals no ambivalence towards his sister's influence or condescension towards her reading. If he fits her to the role of compassionate woman reader who will "blame not, but laugh at" the follies of his work, the fault is not in her passionate nature but in the represented worthlessness of the work itself, which calls out for pity.

The compassion of "fair ladies" is another matter. The first of the two versions of *The Countess of Pembroke's Arcadia (The Old Arcadia)*, never published until the twentieth century, inscribes a female audience explicitly addressed by its narrator fifteen times, usually as "fair ladies."[2] Signifying their own passionate natures, the compassion of fair ladies for the increasingly dubious exploits of lovers exemplifies the sexualization of women's reading through the discourse of gender difference. Sidney would have encountered this discourse directly in inscriptions of female readers in works such as Ariosto's *Orlando Furioso* or George Pettie's *A petite Pallace of Pettie his pleasure* (1576). Oscillating wildly between representing their "cortesi donne" or "gentlewomen" as courtly noblewomen and contemptible whores, these inscriptions by Ariosto and Pettie reveal ambivalence not only towards women readers but also towards texts imagined as appropriate for them.[3] In Sidney's work, however, the value of "reading like a woman" finally remains unsettled rather than negated. At stake in the *Old Arcadia* is not only the value of compassionate readings by "fair ladies" of either gender, but also, according to the discourse of gender difference, the masculinity of authors who write romances which elicit their compassion.

The revised *Countess of Pembroke's Arcadia (The New Arcadia)* rewrites the feminine as an aspect of its revaluation of passion in general. As onlookers gaze at the dying heroine Parthenia through "spectacles of pity," compassion becomes, for both genders, a positive trait deriving from a sense of common humanity rather than from guilty sexuality. Pyrocles' assumption of the name "Zelmane" rather than "Cleophila" also signals a major change from the *Old Arcadia*. Disguising herself as a boy and finally dying in Pyrocles' service, the original Zelmane's sacrifice counteracts some of the potential degradation of Pyrocles' cross-dressing as an Amazon. Finally, the princesses Philoclea and Pamela attain the status of heroines through their loyalty to their princes, expressed in their preference for death rather than marriage to anyone else. In the *New Arcadia*, Parthenia, Zelmane, and the princesses all become the heroines, rather than the victims, of their passion; for largely through their willingness to die, passion itself has assumed new value as a motive for heroic constancy.

The revaluation of the feminine and of passion in general contains immense significance for the reading and writing of romances by male authors. But the constraints imposed by the discourse of gender difference upon women's authorship remain unchanged within the two versions of *The Countess of Pembroke's Arcadia*. While male protagonists freely narrate their experiences to female auditors, women are generally permitted to narrate their experiences only to other women. Even then, their stories, especially stories by lower-class women, are notably brief and subject to sudden interruption. Poems by female protagonists, to a greater extent than those by male protagonists, are permeated by guilty sexuality. The constraints surrounding women's authorship are represented as internalized; for Gynecia and Philoclea, poetry itself becomes a form of silence or, more radically, of self-erasure. But if aristocratic women authors negate their own authorship, readers are not directed by the text to share this negation. While the text faithfully records the gender ideology restricting female authorship, upper-class women characters reveal themselves as able authors of verse of high quality.

In its focus on women readers and women writers, this chapter departs from much of the recent critical work on *The Countess of Pembroke's Arcadia.* My focus on women readers and writers seems appropriate, however, for a text named after a woman, dedicated to a woman, and inscribing women readers in its original version. The perception of *The Countess of Pembroke's Arcadia* as a text read by women was, in fact, repeatedly echoed in successive centuries. Yet modern critics have convincingly read Sidney's text as immersed in the religious and political concerns of his day, concerns for which ordinary women have appeared to play only a peripheral role.[4] My examination of *The Countess of Pembroke's Arcadia* does not deny the significance of these readings. Not only was Sidney capable of addressing a split audience, but this divergence of subject matter is also not as great as it might at first appear. *The Countess of Pembroke's Arcadia* is structured on a series of hierarchical relationships—between reason and passion, monarch and subject, father and child—which it posits and then renders problematic. The relationship between the sexes—man and woman, husband and wife, male writer and woman reader—occupies a well-defined space within this pattern. For this reason, gender concerns lie at the very center, not the periphery, of political and religious thought. Much work remains to be done in exposing the presence of gender ideology in these areas.[5] My goals are, for the moment, more modest. Rather than devaluing readings which privilege state politics and contemporary religious thought, I intend to show that in its exploration of the power of women readers over male writers, and in its changing constructions of gender itself, *The Countess of Pembroke's Arcadia* was only following out the logic of a controlling set of analogies.

Giving Birth to the Text

Sidney's creation of a role as a sympathetic reader for his sister in his dedication is predicated upon an oddly feminized role as author for himself. He is the mother of *The Countess of Pembroke's Arcadia;* he has given birth to the work. While the metaphor of birth for the production of a work of literature was not uncommon, Sidney carries the metaphor through with an unusual degree of specificity. He has experienced the anxiety, common among pregnant women, that he will give birth to a monster. His book does not, like most works imagined as "brain-children," remain an infant. Sidney worries about his child's safety as he learns to walk "abroad," and like a good Renaissance parent, he places his child in the service of a competent and loving adult, as he requests that the countess protect it by giving it her livery. While this anxiety about a growing child's welfare was no doubt experienced by loving fathers as well as mothers, Sidney's construction of fatherhood precludes such concern. Sidney is not only a worried mother craving indulgence for his child: he is also an unloving father, wishing, according to the Greek custom, to murder his baby by exposure, casting it "out in some desert of forgetfulness."

Sidney's assumption of both parental roles, represented as such polar opposites, suggests the internalization of both voices, one lavishing nurturing sympathy upon its child and the other threatening lethal severity. Both internal voices are projected upon external audiences. Mary's role of compassionate reader implies its opposite, the hostile reader. Lying outside the safe circle of his sister's protection await the "severer eyes" which endanger the safety of the manuscript if it walks abroad. Was this audience solely a projection of Sidney's psyche, or did it have any external reality? This hostile audience may well have embodied the sentiments of a misogynistic humanistic tradition, represented by Burghley and others in the Elizabethan court, according to which the reading and writing of poetry were activities unsuitable for grown men.[6] The possibility that the circulation of a literary manuscript, probably his *Astrophil and Stella,* to the court could have done Sidney harm was, in fact, expressed by a character in Ben Jonson's *Epicoene,* who asserted that a writer friend would not repeat Sidney's mistake, endangering his "rising i' the state" by becoming known for his poems.[7]

The "Fair Ladies" and the Judges

The two audiences described or implied in Sidney's dedication of the work to his sister present some striking similarities to the two audiences structuring the *Old Arcadia.* Several critics have ably discussed the way that the *Old Arcadia* entraps the reader by presenting Euarchus's severe rereading of the protagonists' exploits delineated so sympathetically in the first three books.[8] This entrapment is facilitated by a supposedly inconsistent narrator, who oscillates between encouraging a "moral holiday"[9] and advocating strict morality. The narrator's alleged inconsistencies become explicable, however, when considered in the light of his two inscribed audiences. The first three books are repeatedly addressed to fair ladies, dependably compassionate towards the lovers' exploits and tolerant of their foibles. Their compassion, unlike the countess's, is represented as proceeding from their own passionate natures, subject to envy and voyeurism. Practicing the sexualized reading imagined for women by gender ideology,

Sidney's inscribed female audience functions as a rhetorical ploy, to guide readers of both gender to "read like women" in the first three books. In the last two books, all references to fair ladies drop out of the texts. In a deft act of reader entrapment, readers are led to judge not only the lovers, but their own readings, with the sudden intrusion of the rational (if sometimes inaccurate) perspective of a court of law rather than a court of love. The judge of this court is the just Euarchus, who, like the internalized Greek father of Sidney's dedication, sentences his own son to death.

To seduce readers into sharing the sexualized readings of the inscribed female audience, the narrator's addresses cast Sidney's *Old Arcadia* into the aristocratic interaction between courtier and lady popularized by such works as Castiglione's *Courtier.* When Sidney's narrator addresses his ladies as "fair," we cannot be sure of their physical beauty, but we can be sure that the narrator is courteous. Ann Rosalind Jones has shown that the value of this courtly model was increasingly interrogated by a more pious model of desire circulating among the bourgeoisie.[10] Perhaps this sober model encouraged the undermining of the courtly interaction between Sidney's narrator and women readers. In any case, Sidney's inscribed women readers mark the dubious morality not only of the narratives addressed to them, but also of courtliness in general. Yet the rejection of fair ladies does not stand as the final word. Their perspective, however flawed, on the events of the *Old Arcadia* finally poses a genuine alternative to Euarchus's severe reading.

The fifteen apostrophes to "fair ladies" or "worthy ladies" in the first three books of the *Old Arcadia* create the narrator as a courtier, fashioning his own gentility through his elegant speech directed to ladies. Ever solicitous of his ladies' pleasure, he introduces the eclogues after the first book, for example, to ease his "fair ladies of the tediousness of this long discourse" (55). He wishes their admiration, as he candidly remarks in his account of Dorus's killing of a bear: "Doubt you not, fair ladies, there wanted no questioning how things had passed; but because I will have the thanks myself, it shall be I you shall hear it of" (51). Several addresses, such as the chatty reminder that Musidorus was last seen in a "grove by the two lodges," considerately restore past narrative events to the audience's possibly hazy recollection. Other addresses refine the text from the crudities of the real-life experiences it supposedly depicts, such as the sighs which interrupt a love song, or the panting of fleeting shepherds. These addresses imply the gentility not only of the narrator, but also of the inscribed female audience, able to recognize and respond to the narrator's self-fashioning.

But the very gentility of the fair ladies implicates them, rather than absolving them, in a series of moral flaws, as the narrator calls upon them several times to empathize with even the undesirable traits of the characters, which they supposedly share. The narrator suggests, for example, that some of his women readers may understand the envy of the women in Basilius's court when the prince Pyrocles praises Philoclea's beauty because they themselves may also have felt such envy at another woman's beauty: "You ladies know best whether sometimes you feel impression of that passion" (39). In this passage, the narrator directs towards his ladies the same tolerance that he asks of them for his characters. His teasing tone suggests the intimacy born of prolonged association, through which he has learned their foibles but does not judge them.

In another aside, the narrator demonstrates his own compassion towards his characters, assuming that his fair ladies will share his sympathy for Pyrocles when, stricken by love, he disguises himself as an Amazon to be near Philoclea: "And thus did Pyrocles become Cleophila—which name for a time hereafter I will use, for I myself feel such compassion of his passion that I find even part of his fear lest his name should be uttered before fit time were for it; which you, fair ladies, that vouchsafe to read this, I doubt not will account excusable[11] (27). Love apparently excuses even sex without marriage, for when Pyrocles achieves sexual consummation with his beloved Philoclea, the narrator discreetly closes the door on the lovers with a congratulatory aside: "He gives me occasion to leave him in so happy a plight, lest my pen might seem to grudge at the due bliss of these poor lovers whose loyalty had but small respite of their fiery agonies. And now Lalus's pipe doth come to my hearing, which I hope your ears, fair ladies, be not so full of great matters that you will disdain to hear" (243). Some complexity of tone in this aside turns on the interpretation of "great matters," which can be read either to signal the lovers' aristocratic, as opposed to shepherdly, status or else to refer to the lovers' sexual activities. In the former sense, the narrator is pointing to his female readers' membership in the upper class, requesting their tolerance for the songs of the lower-class Lalus. In the latter sense, the narrator is slyly teasing his readers, saying in effect, "I know that you would rather hear more about what the lovers did in bed, but I am now going to move the scene to the shepherds' eclogues, instead." No doubt both meanings were operative.

The following passage suggests that his readers' interest and even experience in sexual matters is, in fact, an integral part of their aristocratic natures. Fair ladies will not condemn lovers for their passions: some of them may also have felt the instantaneous passion of love, just like the Duke Basilius (who did not see through Pyrocles' disguise) and his wife Gynecia (who did):

> But so wonderful and in effect so incredible was the passion which reigned as well in Gynecia as Basilius . . . that it seems to myself I use not words enough to make you see how they could in one moment be so overtaken. But you, worthy ladies, that have at any time feelingly known what it means, will easily believe the possibility of it. Let the ignorant sort of people give credit to them that have passed this doleful passage, and daily find that quickly is the infection gotten which in long time is hardly cured. (49)

In his appeal to the ladies' own experience of love, the narrator takes care not to insult them. Those who have not caught this "infection" are the "ignorant sort of people." On the surface level, "ignorant" simply means lacking knowledge; on another, "ignorant" implies membership in the lower class. The narrator's aside directs us to read adulterous passion according to the text of courtly love, not of religious doctrine. While love is "doleful," it is not sinful, and it even signifies an aristocratic heart.

The narrator also counts on an audience experienced in matters of the heart to sympathize with the pain of Pyrocles/Cleophila as he/she inflicts psychological pain on Philoclea in order to enable their union: "But, O you that have ever known how tender to every motion love makes the lover's heart . . . judge, I pray you, now of Cleophila's troubled thoughts" (211).

Increasingly, the narrator stretches the sympathies of fair ladies to cover progressively more dubious situations. When Pyrocles/Cleophila manipulates the affections of Basilius and Gynecia so that, in their attempt to commit adultery with him, they actually sleep with each other, the narrator's description of "poor" Gynecia's reaction when her husband lays his "lovingest hold" upon her in bed and addresses her as Cleophila, implies the readers' pity rather than their condemnation: "In what case poor Gynecia was when she knew the voice and felt the body of her husband, fair ladies, it is better to know by imagination than experience; for straight was her mind assaulted partly with being deprived of her unquenchable desires, but principally with the doubt that Cleophila had betrayed her to her husband—besides the renewed sting of jealousy what in the mean time might befall her daughter" (227). Clearly, this text in no way advocates adultery; its depiction of Gynecia's tortured soul feelingly represents the agony of her situation. Yet the text makes clear that the source of her anguish is more the fear of betrayal and the loss of her object of desire than remorse over her sexual act. The narrator does not demonstrate any discomfort over the omission of any larger moral context. His admonition to ladies to know her plight by "imagination" rather than "experience" is strikingly mild and suggests, in fact, that such experience was open to them.

By the end of book 3 of the *Old Arcadia*, a variety of destructive acts have taken place in the name of love. Pyrocles has slept with Philoclea, Musidorus decides to rape the sleeping Pamela (he is prevented only by a band of attacking brigands), Basilius has sent his own daughter to woo Cleophila into an adulterous relationship, and Gynecia and Basilius have committed adultery (albeit with each other). Yet, largely because of the narrator's asides, these characters are presented sympathetically, as unfortunate victims of an irresistible love, and therefore not responsible for their actions. The narrator and his inscribed audience have read the protagonists' exploits through the eye of compassion, born of their own passionate natures inclined to love.

In book 5, Euarchus vehemently censures this perception of love as an irresistible force, a perception guiding the readings by fair ladies in the first three books. When Pyrocles claims that "love offered more force" (394) to him than he had to Philoclea, and when Musidorus similarly appeals to "love's force" (402), Euarchus renames the princes' love as "ill-governed passion," redefining real love as composed of reason, not passion, which can "never slide into any action that is not virtuous" (407). Trying the protagonists for their crimes, real and supposed, Euarchus reads their actions through the eye of reason, following the laws of Arcadia to condemn Philoclea and Pamela to perpetual celibacy and Pyrocles, Musidorus, and Gynecia to immediate and violent death.[11] Euarchus's reading is to some extent a misreading. Gynecia's confession to the murder of Basilius is false, for he himself had insisted on drinking the potion. Pyrocles chivalrously denies Philoclea's complicity in their act of love, insisting that he forced her. Yet, even if all the facts were known, the sentences would still stand; for, as Euarchus points out, "the wickedness of lust is by [Arcadian] decrees punished by death, though both consent" (406).

More than lovers are on trial at the end of the *Old Arcadia*. Euarchus's judgement condemns, by implication, the genre of romantic fiction and its readers.[12] The compassion the narrator and his fair ladies share for the lover, born of their own amorous experiences, now signifies sexual guilt; and readers who have empathized with the lovers are now also implicated in their deeds. This guilt is perhaps implied as early as the description of "everlasting justice" that opens book 4. The repeated use of "our" draws readers, especially any readers who have just been titillated by the bedroom scene at the end of book 3, onto the dock of "everlasting justice," which uses "ourselves to be the punishers of our faults . . . making our actions the beginning of our chastisement, that our shame may be the more manifest, and our repentance follow the sooner" (265). Such titillation was, in fact, assumed by the narrator, who teased his female audience for preferring to hear more about the "great matters" transacted between Pyrocles and Philoclea than the eclogues. Thus, Sidney's fair ladies have provided first a pretext for the narration of pleasurable texts about love and then, in the supposed unworthiness of their readings, a reason to condemn them.

But the value of romantic fiction and its (allegedly) female readers is not so easily dismissed. As numerous critics have mentioned, the ending of the *Old Arcadia* is inconclusive if not contradictory.[13] Basilius rises from the dead; and Euarchus's judgments, reasonable as they may be, are not enacted. Constance Jordan has eloquently argued that Basilius's restoration embodies a providential imposition of equity, a "divine and universal feminine principle operating beyond literal applications of law."[14] This harmoniously androgynous view provides satisfying closure to the conflict between gendered readings of the *Old Arcadia:* finally the readers of the *Old Arcadia* are offered an opportunity to be both compassionate and judgmental, to read simultaneously as women and as men. Others, however, have rejected the reading of Basilius's restoration as an act of divine providence, to perceive, with Richard McCoy, the conclusion of the *Old Arcadia* as constructed upon glaring "contradictions between moral values and fictive rewards."[15] For these, the dismissal of all charges, just as well as unjust, against the protagonists represents the victory of the pleasures of romantic fiction over the correctness of moral principles. Demonstrating loyalty to lovers, to compassionate readings, to romantic fiction itself, this victory is based not in reason but in love. The narrative, like its protagonists, remains appealing even in its guilt.

Reason : Passion : : Male : Female

These two ways of reading the events of books 1 through 3—first, according to the passion of fair ladies, and then, according to the reason of Euarchus—conform to a binary pattern of thinking which provides a necessary link between gender and reading in the Renaissance.[16] The respective genders of the fair ladies and Euarchus reflects a general association of women with passion and men with reason. Dating back as far as Aristotle's *Politics,* this perception of gender difference was widely institutionalized through the legal, educational, and medical systems.[17] The following homily on marriage, for example, was required by law to be read in English churches from 1562 onward: "The woman is a weak creature not endued with like strength and constancy of mind; therefore, they be the sooner disquieted, and they be the more prone to all weak affections and dispositions of mind, more than men be."[18] The dichotomy between the perspectives of the fair ladies and Euarchus was only strengthened by the disqualification of women as witnesses in a court of law, owing to their *"levitas, fragilitas, imbecillitas, infirmitas."*[19] This widespread perception of gender was not, of course, absolutely rigid. Women such as Queen Elizabeth and Margaret Roper were admired for their intellectual abilities; and men were not necessarily condemned for expressing feelings of passion and grief. Yet these gender categories persisted even in their exceptions. Women who displayed intelligence tended to be represented as possessing a masculine understanding, and a weeping man could be described as playing the "woman with his eyes."[20]

As the marriage homily indicates, this representation of gender difference justified the containment of women within a domestic hierarchy. Just as reason is to govern passion, so the husband is to govern the wife; for ideally, if not always in fact, husbands, supposedly less subject than women to the persuasions of passion, possessed the superior reason requisite to command their charges. This hierarchy was further reinforced through its analogic relationship with the state.[21] Within the realm of politics, the king represented the head of the body of state, exerting his reason over his subjects, who performed the functions of the stomach and other organs to insure political order.[22] Thus, the hierarchical relationship between reason and passion underlay an entire series of other hierarchical relationships, between mind and body, king and subject, man and woman.

The way in which the *Old Arcadia* renders these conventional hierarchies problematic perhaps finds its source in the Calvinist pessimism about the incorruptibility of reason.[23] Once reason is recognized as capable of depravity, its right to absolute authority over passion is no longer unarguable. The *Old Arcadia* never seems to suggest that passion should rule reason; the best that passion can achieve is equality, as shepherds representing "Passion" argue with shepherds representing "Reason" in an eclogue that "fellowlike" they were "together born" (136). This crucial debate between Reason and Passion ends in a standoff, as both parties agree to "give place" to "heav'nly rules."

While Calvinism's radical ideology was played out in political and ecclesiastical issues, some of which are explored in both the *Old* and the *New Arcadia,* the subjection of wives to husbands was, if anything, strengthened within the English Renaissance.[24] Perhaps under the influence of the logic of its own analogical method, perhaps under the influence of the doctrine of courtly love, both versions of the *Arcadia* are remarkable for the way they render problematic the relationship between male and female, like that between Reason and Passion. As in the argument between Reason and Passion, both sides are voiced: on the one hand, the dominance of male over female and on the other, the innate equality of the sexes. Like most issues in the *Arcadia*s, this one is never resolved.

This analogy that reason is to passion as male is to female is present, for example, in the shepherd Dicus's criticism of the lovelorn Dorus for the power he, as a male, has given to mere women: "A man to fear a woman's moody eye, / Or reason lie a slave to servile sense" (139). Dicus presents a positive example of this analogy in his song honoring the marriage of Thyrsis and Kala in which he asks Virtue to knot their vow, so "that still he be her head, she be his heart." The lines of authority are softened but still present, so that ideally Thyrsis will "lean to her, she unto him do bow" (247). The aged Geron uses his own marital situation to describe a similar domestic ideal. Geron's wife is able to command his household and also to obey him; and he praises women's "sweet supple minds which soon to wisdom bow, / Where they by wisdom's rules directed are, / And are not forced fond thraldom to allow" (263). It is, ironically enough, the evil Cecropia in the New Arcadia who expresses this code most forcefully in her attempt to convince her son Amphialus to rape Philoclea: "For indeed, son, I confess unto you, in our very creation we are servants; and who prayeth his servants shall never be well obeyed . . . show thyself a man; and, believe me upon my word, a woman is a woman" (534).

This conventional doctrine does not remain unchallenged. Cecropia's argument is based on specious logic, and Amphialus remains unconvinced. More generally, Sidney's treatment of several major male characters casts doubts upon their abilities to direct by "wisdom's rules." Rendered ridiculous by senile lust, Duke Basilius, for example, is not likely to rule a wife as strong-willed as the tragic Gynecia. While Gynecia's sexual desire for Pyrocles strengthens the model associating women with passion, she is, unlike her husband, treated with considerable respect by the text, which affords her an unusual degree of interiority by granting her at least three substantial soliloquies and even a dream.[25] In her ability to understand the reasonable code of behavior but not to act upon it, she is likened to rather than contrasted with the princes, depicted in the same psychological situation. Of all the lovers, it is Pamela, not the male lovers, who successfully exerts her reason to control her increasing passion for Musidorus, if only temporarily: "Pamela was the only lady that would needs make open war upon herself, and obtain the victory; for, indeed, even now find she did a certain working of a new-come inclination to Dorus. But when she found perfectly in herself whither it must draw her, she did overmaster it with the consideration of his meanness" (55).

Both versions of Sidney's *Arcadia* may well have been intended and sometimes perceived in part as an apology for women. On the first page of the *Old Arcadia*, for example, the princesses are introduced with the following description, which affirms the equality of their "gifts" and those of women in general with other "reasonable creatures": "Both so excellent in all those gifts which are allotted to reasonable creatures as they seemed to be born for a sufficient proof that nature is no stepmother to that sex, how much soever the rugged disposition of some men, sharp-witted only in evil speaking, hath sought to disgrace them" (4–5). Pyrocles echoes this defense of women in his assertion to Musidorus that since women "(if we argue by reason) are framed of nature with the same parts of the mind for the exercise of virtue as we are," then they are undeserving of the cruelty of men who "like childish masters, think their masterhood nothing without doing injury" to women (21). While this specific passage is somewhat less prominent in the *New Arcadia*, its general respect for women remained prominent at least to one near contemporary, for the *New Arcadia* was the only literary work cited as evidence in women's defense in William Healy's *Apology for Women* (1608).[26]

Thus, the way in which the versions of the *Arcadia* depict males as subject to passionate excess at least as much as females challenges the symmetry of the analogy that reason is to passion as male is to female. This unsettling of a powerful binary pattern of thought may underlie the character distinctions drawn among the two youthful royal couples. While all four eventually succumb to passion, the elder Pamela and Musidorus tend more to reason, while the younger Philoclea and Pyrocles tend more to passion. Philoclea succumbs to her sexual desire, engaging in premarital sex with Pyrocles, while Pamela extracts from Musidorus a vow (almost broken in the *Old Arcadia*) that he will not attempt her chastity. Pyrocles falls in love before Musidorus, who marshals all his reasonable arguments against that "effeminate love of a woman" that "doth so womanize a man." Pyrocles' adoption of feminine apparel creates him as the more feminine, and therefore the more passionate, of the two princes.

The confrontation between Pyrocles, dressed in Amazonian garb, and Musidorus, shocked by his friend's excess, demonstrates the way that the *Old Arcadia* deconstructs but does not demolish the analogy of reason : passion :: male : female. While males are as prone to passion as females in the *Old Arcadia,* nevertheless, passion remains associated with women. When Pyrocles falls in love, his cross-dressing points to the way in which the very act of falling in love with a woman is effeminizing, the mark of the failure of the masculine reason to conquer feminine passion.[27] Before he himself succumbs to love, Musidorus argues along these lines to the love-stricken Pyrocles: "Remember . . . that, if we be men, the reasonable part of our soul is to have absolute commandment, against which if any sensual weakness arise, we are to yield all our sound forces to the overthrowing of so unnatural a rebellion. For to say I cannot is childish, and I will not womanish" (19).

While Pyrocles argues for women's virtue, he himself finally submits to the same metaphor. When he hilariously embodies Musidorus's theory, literally becoming "womanish" by dressing as an Amazon, his song confirms that his exterior change accurately expresses his inward state, his "poor reason's overthrow," the way his "reason to his servants gives his right." He is transformed to a "woman's hue" (29) not only because he is obsessed by a woman, but also because that very obsession reverses the desired hierarchy of reason and passion in his soul. Disturbing overtones confirm that this transformation proceeds beyond a change of clothes. The loving detail lavished by the text upon his Amazonian costume, which exposes the small of his leg "to show the fairness of the skin" (27) invests his newfound femininity with a strong homoerotic appeal. Even more unsettling is the subsequent use of pronoun "she" to refer to Pyrocles in his female attire. It appears that the text, in its portrayal of Pyrocles in his Amazonian attire, invites the reader to enjoy the erotics of sexual mix-up.

Reading Like a Woman

The way that passion's overthrow of reason makes a character "womanish" contains extraordinary significance for the formative role of gender in the act of reading. Certainly in the first three books of the *Old Arcadia,* Pyrocles' transvestitism strongly suggests the circumstance of the male reader encountering words addressed to "fair ladies." Like Pyrocles, that reader must adopt a female disguise to be privy to this discourse. While this crossing of gender roles was not uncommon for women readers of texts addressed to males, the phenomenon was perhaps less usual for males, whose access to texts addressed to women was limited by their less frequent availability. The discomfort possible to this experience is perhaps suggested in an exaggerated form by Pyrocles' reaction when he recognizes that the voice which had made "so lively a portraiture" (181) of his own miseries belongs to Gynecia. His initial sense of identification yields to horror, and he breaks out in a "cold sweat" as if he had "been ready to treat upon a deadly stinging adder" (183).[28] Just as Pyrocles "reads" his own passions only to discover how much he shares with a woman, the male readers of the *Arcadias* are called upon to "read like a woman" and in the process perhaps discover layers of their own defective masculinity.

The dialogue between Boulon and Plangus, related by Histor in the *Old Arcadia*, makes explicit the way that men's reading is to differ from women's reading. A male reader, unlike a woman reader, is expected to respond according to reason, not passion. The "wise Boulon" is reported by Histor to have struggled with his own response to Plangus's tale of woe, in which Plangus expresses his fears that his beloved Erona, imprisoned by the evil Queen Artaxia, may lose her life. Boulon does not sympathize with Plangus because compassion, according to Boulon, is effeminizing, a signal of reason's loss of control:

Thy wailing words do much my spirits move,
  They uttered are in such a feeling fashion
  That sorrow's work against my will I prove.
Methinks I am partaker of thy passion,
  And in thy case to glass mine own debility—
  Self-guilty folk most prone to feel compassion.
Yet reason saith, reason should have ability
  To hold these worldly things in such proportion
  As let them come or go with e'en facility.

. . . .

For what can breed more peevish incongruities
Than man to yield to female lamentations?

(150–51)

Boulon conquers his womanish sympathy for Plangus to refuse him pity; but the court party apparently did not, for "so well did Histor's voice express the passion of Plangus that all the princely beholders were stricken into a silent consideration of it; indeed everyone making that he heard of another the balance of his own troubles" (152). Predicated upon its own sexual guilt, the sympathetic reception of the court party, male as well as female, suggests the femininity of males and females alike in their responses.

Histor's account of the interchange between Plangus and Boulon implicates Sidney's own narrative, itself reporting the adventures of lovers to a courtly audience. If we are meant to hold with the "wise Boulon" that a real man does not "yield to female lamentations" in sympathy for such tales, then what are we to make of the male reader or, even more, of the male writer of the *Arcadias?* If we believe that the sentiments of "wise Boulon" were entertained even partly in the Renaissance and by Sidney, then responding to the *Arcadias* themselves may have posed a challenge to the masculinity of male readers. Its challenge to the masculinity of a male writer becomes clearer in the reworking of Histor's account in the *New Arcadia,* where Plangus's tale remains unchanged, but the narrative situation is altered in various ways that mark the importance of gender. In the *New Arcadia,* Plangus tells his tale to Basilius, not to Boulon; the interchange was first written down by Basilius and then copied by Philoclea, rather than remembered by Boulon and transmitted orally by Histor. Finally, the audience for the "Complaint of Plangus" is a group of women (and one male in female disguise), not a mixed group. All of these changes feminize the narrative situation of the "Complaint of Plangus."

Basilius's act of writing down the interchange between himself and Plangus has made it, in some sense, his literary creation. The text directs less positive feelings towards him than it had to the "wise Boulon." Not only has the representation of Basilius's desire for Pyrocles/Zelmane cost him some dignity; but the response registered for this audience is critical, as Pyrocles/Zelmane remarks: "One may be little the wiser for reading this dialogue, since it neither sets forth what this Plangus is, nor what Erona is." More importantly, as Basilius later reveals, Plangus had told him his plight in order to receive military assistance, which Basilius had denied him, claiming "the course of my life being otherwise bent." Instead of assisting him (other than lending him a guide to Euarchus), Basilius sets down his dialogue "at an idle time."

Literary authorship has, in Basilius's instance, become an alternative for heroic action, a signal of Basilius's self-indulgent escapism in his pastoral retreat. If yielding to "female lamentations" is feminizing, then Basilius's act of writing casts his masculinity in doubt, for, as he later confesses, his "vehement compassion" for a prince so "pulled down" by love motivates his poem. In this "vehement compassion" he resembles the emotional "fair ladies" inscribed in the *Old Arcadia*. Writing has become the natural result of passionate reading. Writing, like passionate reading, implies passionate excess, as Basilius's description of his authorship makes explicit: "I could not temper my long idle pen in that subject" (398).[29]

Considering these circumstances, Basilius's evident pride in authorship, as he relates his writing to Pyrocles/Zelmane and lets Philoclea copy it, is rendered inappropriate, especially in contrast to the purely oral interrogation of the "wise" Boulon. Histor is acting appropriately for his name in relating this dialogue to the Arcadian audience, and his performance indicates a prodigious memory. Philoclea, on the other hand, has merely copied the dialogue, not remembered it; and her act perhaps suggests a filial admiration for her father that is more loyal than discerning. Finally, in the *New Arcadia*, the "Complaint of Plangus" is told to a group of women, whose stories tend to reveal an interest in love. The gender of this group contributes to a sense of the "femaleness" of Plangus's "lamentations."

The way that Basilius's writing calls his masculinity into question may reflect upon the writing of the *Old* and the *New Arcadia*. Portions of the *Old Arcadia* were written when Sidney was in retreat from the court because of his misplaced advice to the queen about her marriage. In a 1580 letter to Sir Edward Denny, he described his enforced leisure as "unnoble," preventing him from engaging in the "fitte imployments" of the active life.[30] When he was writing the *New Arcadia*, he was still separated from significant opportunities for heroic action. Is there a sense in which he, like Basilius, set down the plaints of lovers for the delight of ladies? Is it possible that his narrator's addresses to "fair ladies" in the *Old Arcadia* represented not only a strategy of entrapment, but also Sidney's judgement of his own narrative as effeminizing? This question must be taken all the more seriously when it becomes clear that the feminizing of Basilius as as writer represents part of a consistent pattern of gender construction, especially within the rich array of narrative situations in the *New Arcadia*.

In the *New Arcadia*, men generally tell stories to men for the purpose of heroic action; if they do not, then the text erects flags of distress around the narrative situation. For example, twice near the beginning of the *New Arcadia*, male characters withhold their stories despite direct queries from other male characters. When the shepherds who rescue Musidorus from drowning ask him, "What cause then, made you venture to leave this sweet realm?" they are greeted with his non-answer, "Guarded with poverty and guided with love."

When they repeat their request so that his host Kalander will know "how to proportion his entertainment," Musidorus replies only that his entertainment should be low.[31] Kalander's long description of the country of Arcadia to Musidorus is completely appropriate to his role as host, yet his repeated apologies reflect his discomfort at speaking for a length of time that is, in fact, not unusual in the *New Arcadia.* The narrative told by Kalander's steward to Musidorus about the events leading up to the capture of Kalander's son needs no apology. Musidorus requests the story for the purpose of heroic action and then responds appropriately by arming himself, gathering an army, and rescuing the lad.

Most of the stories told by a man to a man are relatively short; only Kalander's initial narrative extends over ten pages. Several of the stories told by a man to a woman, in contrast, are considerably longer. One of Musidorus's two tales lasts for thirty pages, while Pyrocles' covers thirty-five pages. The length of these tales told to Philoclea and Pamela, respectively, suggest the appropriateness of a female audience for narratives eliciting amatory rather than heroic action as a response. Musidorus tells Pamela of his own heroic exploits to reveal or to compose a self in contrast to his shepherd's disguise. Pyrocles' tales provide various inducements to Philoclea to love him. The tale of the promiscuous Pamphilius underscores Pyrocles' loyalty; the adventures of the lustful Andromana act as a "foil" revealing "the warrantableness" of Philoclea's favor to him. The love of Helen, queen of Corinth, for the noble Amphialus supplies a noble precedent for Philoclea's love for a suitable object (him). Finally, the moving tale of Zelmane demonstrates that a woman can love a man, and even dress as a man, without becoming unchaste. In telling Zelmane's story, Pyrocles fulfills Zelmane's request, to speak of her "folly" not with "scorn, but with pity" (366). All of these stories represent attempts to elicit admiration or pity from their female audience. Philoclea and Pamela act out the role of fair ladies by responding to their storytellers with sexual desire.

This use of a female audience, whether fair ladies or princesses, reflects ambivalence towards what is now called fiction as an activity appropriate for active males. While the princes fashion themselves as lovers by telling lengthy narratives to their ladies in this pastoral idyll, they are escaping from their duties as soldier-heroes.[32] Just as Basilius's relation of the tale of Plangus and Erona represented an inappropriate alternative to providing military aid, the princes' narratives also represent an alternative to a pressing heroic task: the rescuing of Erona. In order to avenge herself upon Pyrocles and Musidorus for their role in her brother's death, the evil Artaxia has confined this lovely and worthy princess in a castle, where she will be held for two years, after which time she will be executed unless Pyrocles and Musidorus do not "in person combat and overcome two knights" (404). The clock is ticking away.

Speculations: Reading the Author

Although any hypotheses about an author's biographical relationship to his work must of necessity remain speculative, it seems possible that the division in the *New Arcadia* between heroic action and pastoral storytelling mirrors the circumstances under which *The Countess of Pembroke's Arcadia* was written. Like the princes, Sidney himself was in pastoral retreat, whether because of the queen's disapproval or because of social pressure, at his sister's estate.[33] The title of Sidney's work not only pays tribute to his sister; it also advertises itself as reading appropriate to a woman. Like the princes, Sidney is addressing amorous tales to a female audience to while away their time. Like Basilius and the princes, Sidney no doubt spent much of this time with women; and the criticism levelled by the text against Basilius and the princes for their neglect of their proper duties—governing Arcadia and rescuing Erona, respectively—perhaps creates Sidney's own pastoral idyll, even if involuntary, as culpable. According to this gendering of the narrative act in the *New Arcadia,* Sidney's description of his work in his dedication as a "trifle," providing no "better stuff' than "glasses or feathers," may not have been entirely motivated by modesty.[34]

This personal reading of Sidney's own situation into the gendered circumstances of the *Old* and *New Arcadia* gains credibility from a letter Sidney wrote to his friend the humanist Hubert Languet in 1578, which reveals Sidney's dissatisfaction with his inactivity in the political realm: "For to what purpose should our thoughts be directed to various kinds of knowledge, unless room be afforded for putting it into practice, so that public advantage may be the result, which in a corrupt age we cannot hope for?"[35] Attempting to find some benefit in his retreat, he represents his withdrawal from court as an opportunity for self-examination. But he finally exposes this optimism as a role: "Do you not see I am cleverly playing the stoic? yea and I shall be a cynic, too, unless you reclaim me." Like any Sidnean self-representation, this reading is rife with ironies. Even as he praises self-examination, his letter clearly expresses a preference for action. He has not become a stoic; he is, instead, "cleverly playing" the stoic to make the best of a bad situation. The potential for cynicism was present in 1578, when he was probably beginning the *Old Arcadia*. By 1580, Languet warned him that his friends were fearing that "the sweet pleasures of lengthy retirement may to some degree relax the vigour with which you formerly rose to noble enterprises."[36]

Ladies Do Not Tell Stories to Men

The sense that the narration of lengthy texts to women may not have been entirely appropriate for a heroic male did not, however, render long narrations appropriate for a female. Despite its sympathy for women, the *New Arcadia* conveys a strong sense of the danger of women's speech through positive and negative *exampla*. Parthenia, held up with her husband Argalus as the ideal couple in the *Arcadia*, is praised for the infrequency of her speech: "Her speech being as rare as precious; her silence without sullenness; her modesty without affectation; her shamefastness without ignorance; in sum, one that to praise well, one must first set down with himself what is to be excellent, for so she is" (88). Even silence could not repress the sexuality of women's "speech," for Parthenia's lips, though closed, still express a mute invitation on her wedding day: "Her lips though they were kept close with modest silence, yet with a pretty kind of natural swelling they seemed to invite the guests that looked on them" (109). This description of Parthenia's lips suggests one pressure exerted on women to conform to a cultural norm. Paradoxically, silence, which prevents the supposedly overwhelming sexuality of women's speech from endangering their reputations, is presented as itself a means for attracting sexual attention. The extent to which silence itself is eroticized is demonstrated in Pyrocles' blazon of the mistress's tongue, which portrays the mistress's rarity of speech as itself an erotic object of desire:

> Of precious pearl the double row,
> The second sweetly-fenced ward,
> Her heavenly-dewed tongue to guard,
> Whence never word in vain did flow.
> (288)

The sensuousness of this description conflates women's very ability to speak, whether realized or not, and women's sexuality.[37] The eroticism located in this organ of women's speech is as complex as it is potent. The moisture of the dew appeals to the sense of taste; in this context "heavenly" perhaps connotes its lusciousness. Its sensuousness is so overwhelming that it requires guarding, for the power of its verbal/sexual expression is implied by its very containment. On the other hand, its dew comes from heaven, and it is safely guarded. Teeth prevent speech from coming out and alien tongues from coming in. Speech and silence, sensual and chaste: the boundaries between these opposites have become so tenuous that they come to imply each other. Silence, and the modesty it connotes, have become means of sexual arousal, as even the outrageous Andromana knew when, in the very prison cell where she was attempting to force the princes into compliance with her sexual demands, she tried to attract them by modesty, as well: "Earnestness dyed her cheeks with the colour of shamefastness, and wanton languishing borrowed of her eyes the down-cast look of modesty" (349).

For Parthenia, the ideal of modesty pervades even the act of reading. In perhaps an indirect rebuke to the fair ladies of the *Old Arcadia*, Parthenia's reading is totally governed by her husband in a way that precludes any real pleasure in a text for its own sake: "The messenger . . . found Argalus at a castle of his own, sitting in a parlour with the fair Parthenia, he reading in a book the stories of Hercules, she by him, as to hear him read; but while his eyes looked on the book, she looked on his eyes, and sometimes staying him with some pretty question, not so much to be resolved of the doubt as to give him occasion to look upon her. A happy couple" (501). Parthenia derives pleasure from her husband's reading, not from the text itself. She questions him to gain his attention, not to resolve her own curiosity. The strenuous containment of Parthenia's reading in this scene, presented as the epitome of domestic bliss, implies the way in which even reading, not to mention writing, can potentially threaten the master-servant relationship between husband and wife. The dynamics of Parthenia's reading reflect her loving subservience to her husband; and the narrator proceeds to comment upon the scene in paradoxical terms which soften, but do not deny, the direction of power: "He ruling, because she would obey, or rather because she would obey, she therein ruling" (501).

Constraints against women's public speech are evident in the striking absence of poetry by women shepherds in the eclogues. That Pyrocles, disguised as an Amazon under the name Zelmane, can recite his poetry out loud without negative comment or surprise represents these strictures as internalized rather than externally imposed. His skill implies that women shepherds were prevented from similar displays of their own virtuosity by lack of skill rather than by cultural constraints. Constraints against "purposeful" speech are apparently stronger, however, for even Pyrocles must justify his oration to rebels threatening the safety of the royal party. His speech represents his speech as an inversion of natural order that the rebels themselves have precipitated; for a woman speaking to men is, according to Pyrocles, an "unused thing," occurring only because they have "forgotten all man-like government" (384).

The one time that women disguised as shepherdesses offer to perform eclogues, disaster results. Secluded in their rustic retreat, Pamela, Philoclea, and the disguised Pyrocles are approached by six maids. Explaining that they were "stirred with emulation" (442) of their male shepherd friends as well as with affection for the royal party, the group offers to perform for the princesses and the Amazon. Danger flags signalling female sexuality appear throughout the passage. These maids had been even willing to perform for a mixed group, for they claim that they had stopped at the lodge to invite Basilius and his attendants there first. They are dressed in scarlet petticoats pulled up to leave their legs naked; their breasts are "liberal to the eye." Taking the willing princesses and Pyrocles/Zelmane to a clearing in a forest, they offer them repast that is fraught with female sexuality: "The maids besought the ladies to sit down and taste of the swelling grapes, which seemed great with child of Bacchus, and of divers coloured plums, which gave the eye a pleasant taste before they came to the mouth . . . their cool wine . . . seemed to laugh for joy to come to such lips" (443).

It is, of course, a cruel hoax. The picnic is followed by capture, not eclogues. Twenty armed men rush out of the woods to convey Pamela, Philoclea, and Pyrocles/Zelmane to the castle of the evil Cecropia, where they endure torture and threatened death, never to emerge in the work Sidney left unfinished. The maids were not really shepherdesses. They were Cecropia's gentlewomen, led by Artesia, known for the "sharpness of her wit" (517), who was persuaded to the deed by the promise of marriage to Cecropia's son Amphialus. Although Artesia and her woman never recite their promised eclogues, the association in this episode of female authorship with aggressive female sexuality shapes several of the narratives and poems by women in the *New Arcadia*.

The danger posed by narratives told by women is contained in various ways, one of which is the restriction of audience to members of their own gender. Only two women tell narratives to men. Queen Helen tells her story to Musidorus at his command; since he has just been attacked by her attendants, she can hardly withhold an explanation. She concludes her account by submitting herself to male judgement: "Now weigh my case, if at least you know what love is" (127). She probably escapes the criticism potentially leveled against female narrators in part because of her role as queen, which authorizes some public speech,[38] and in part because of her role as unrequited lover, which tempers possible aggression by placing her in a submissive position to a man.

Dido is not so fortunate, and the text censures her aggressive tendencies in various ways. Her story, reported by Pyrocles/Zelmane, also provides a needed explanation, for Pyrocles has just prevented her from putting out the eyes of the fickle Pamphilius. She presents her narrative as a monitory tale to prevent Pyrocles from behaving like Pamphilius towards women.[39] Dido's explanation for her behavior—that Pamphilius had judged "another fairer" (338)—does little to mediate her unwomanly aggression. The text remains critical of her unwomanliness, even faulting her actions in defense of Pyrocles, for whom she died, "over-boldly for her sex" (346). Dido's unwomanly aggressiveness is, I believe, not unconnected with the fact of her narration of her story to Pyrocles. She is the kind of "unwomanly" woman, the text implies, who would relate her story.

Women Who Tell Stories to Women

All the other narratives by women in the *New Arcadia* are told to other women. The discovery of Philoclea's copy of her father's poem "The Complaint of Plangus" initiates Pyrocles' request for more information about the plight of Plangus and Erona. Philoclea and Pamela oblige him, and Miso and Mopsa insert their stories, as well. The motive of narration is strikingly void of seduction or heroics. Philoclea and Pamela are satisfying Pyrocles' curiosity; Mopsa seems to be telling her down-to-earth form of chivalric narrative more or less for her own amusement; the criticism of love stories motivating Miso's poem is severely undercut by indications of her own sexual interests. This absence of ostensible motive is unusual, perhaps even gender-specific; for in the *New Arcadia,* men's narratives tend to be organized by a heroic or sexual purpose unless, like Basilius, their full masculinity is in doubt.

The circumstance of narration among these women appears, in some respects, surprisingly egalitarian. Miso suggests that (after her story) they draw straws to determine the order of story-telling so that her daughter's speech is as privileged as that of princesses. Radical in the highly aristocratic *New Arcadia,* this social levelling exists only among the women, however; the text reasserts class differences by heaping abuse upon Miso and her daughter Mopsa. Miso's many vaunts of her beauty include the "certain wrying" (309) of her neck which she thought becoming; Mopsa must wipe her mouth before her narration, "as there was good cause" (311). The potential threat posed by women who tell stories to marital as well as class hierarchy is also implicit in Miso's assertion that the shortest cut should speak first, for "when you are married, you will have first and last word of your husbands" (307). As with class hierarchy, however, this threat is neatly contained by expressing it through an unattractive, cloddish character.

The constraints against female speech are not entirely lifted even when the auditors are also women. Women in the *New Arcadia* are not allowed to talk for very long; and this central core of female narration is notable for its overall brevity and for the number of interruptions. Not including a reading of Basilius's "Complaint of Plangus," the stories of Philoclea, Miso, Mopsa, and Pamela together take up only eighteen pages, about half the number of pages of Pyrocles' single narration to Philoclea. The narratives are interrupted three times. Miso's interruption shows the aggression possible to female authorship as she bursts in with her demand that "I will first have my tale" just as Philoclea is about to hand the narrative thread to Pamela. Philoclea stops Mopsa's one-page chivalric narrative because of its ostensible lack of form, bribing her with a public audience on her wedding day and her best gown. Mopsa's pleasure with the offer of the larger audience, "that it should grow a festival tale" (312), is represented, like everything else said or done by this lower-class family, as unseemly. The most abrupt of the interruptions, Basilius's arrival, stops Pamela's narration immediately. Its suddenness shows the strength of Basilius's prerogative, as well as his lack of interest in female discourse. "Not able longer to abide their absence," Basilius comes "suddenly" among them to convey them to their lodgings, not even letting Pamela finish her sentence.

Originally recited by the grave Dicus in the *Old Arcadia*, Miso's description and poem of Cupid provide an especially valuable opportunity to examine how narrative circumstances were shaped by gender in the Renaissance. Discus's hostility to love is an opinion offered with some seriousness in the *Old Arcadia*.[40] While the narrator admits the possibility that Dicus's low estimation of love may proceed from "mischances of his own," he surmises that it may also proceed from "a better judgment, which sees the bottom of things" (64). Certainly Dicus's estimation of love as a "toy," an estimation which the aged Geron shares, reflects a viewpoint widely expressed in the humanist tradition. Placed after the love plaints of Lalus and Dorus, Dicus's grim condemnation of romantic love extends, by implication, to the ethos governing the first three books themselves; and his portrayal of Cupid as a hangman anticipates the judgement of Euarchus against the lovers. Within the context of the eclogues themselves, Dicus's poem elicits a serious reply in the relation of the story of Erona, condemned to unhappiness in love because of her blasphemies against Cupid.[41]

Unlike Dicus, Miso is not the author of her poem; she has heard it from a "good old woman," who heard it from "an old wise man" who heard it from "a great learned clerk" who "gave it him in writing" (307). Unlike Dicus's poem, Miso's poem with its surrounding narrative is not allowed the dignity of a valid protest. The ladies "make support" (310) of it, while Pyrocles/Zelmane, who "could scarce suffer those blasphemies (as she took them) to be read," asks Pamela to continue the very story of Plangus and Erona which Miso had interrupted with her complaint. Because of the omissions of Erona's blasphemies against Cupid in the *New Arcadia* version, the narration of this story at this point represents a negative response to Miso's censure of the "tittle-tattlings of Cupid" (307) rather than a serious reply.

The text sets up Miso's poem to encourage readers to react like Pyrocles/Zelmane and the princesses. Miso's authority as a poet is drastically undermined by her sexuality and that of the "good old woman" who was her source. This "good old woman" distorts this versified warning against love as an endorsement of promiscuity, as she charges Miso to "do what thou list with all those fellows one after the other, and it recks not much what they do to thee, so it be secret; but upon my charge, never love none of them" (309). Because Miso endorses the old woman's reading of the poem, she and her source are both disqualified even as readers, their sexuality rendering them incapable of interpreting even this simple Cupid poem. Miso's own account that only a few days before hearing the poem, her priest had informed her privately of the origin of Cupid in the "belly of fair Venus" suggests that she already shared the old woman's perspective.

Rather than condemning, by inference, the opening books of the *New Arcadia*, Miso's accusation of Philoclea's narratives as the "tittle-tattlings of Cupid" gives point to the common cultural representation of women as obsessed by love and of female speech as frivolous. Unlike Dicus, Miso is implicated in her own accusation. The text's unpleasant rendering of her sexuality and the sexuality of her female source provides the by now familiar link between female sexuality and authorship; and even the authorship freely allowed to Dicus is, for Miso, demoted to textual transmission. While the contempt for the sexuality of Miso and her "good old woman" expressed in the text is certainly exacerbated by their membership in the lower class, the poems of aristocratic women in the *New Arcadia* are also (dis)organized by their sexuality in a manner not apparent in poems by aristocratic men.

Philoclea's Stain: Sexual Guilt and Female Authorship

While this central core of female narration contains most of the stories told by women, all three major women protagonists—Philoclea, Pamela, and Gynecia—do recite and even write poetry, usually of their own creation. While the *New Arcadia* does not in any simple sense portray actual practices, the circumstances of their recitations reveal the nature of the constraints against poetry performed or written by women. For the most part, women sing their songs to themselves, overheard by eavesdropping males without their knowledge. Philoclea sings two poems in her own room, where she "like a solitary nightingale bewailing her guiltless punishment and helpless misfortune" had performed to herself "meaning none should be judge of her passion but her own conscience" (681). Gynecia confines her recitation of poetry to a dark cave, supposedly far from listening ears, unless it be those of the "plaintful ghosts" and "infernal furies" whom she addresses as her audience.

Religious poetry performed within the family, however, did not pose a problem; and all three protagonists join Basilius to sing a hymn to Apollo (396). Poetry requested for entertainment by a dominant male was also permissible; for, just as many women no doubt soothed the anxieties of fathers and husbands with their songs, Philoclea sings some verses at her father's request to "divert" his "thoughts from the continual task of their ruinous harbour" (659).

Pamela exchanges amorous verses with Musidorus, but the circumstances of this exchange suggest that she is trespassing against sexual constraints, drawing grave consequences upon herself and her companion. Eloping from Basilius's pastoral retreat, Pamela and Musidorus have already crossed the boundaries of behavior acceptable in Arcadia, not only placing Pamela's reputation at severe risk but also endangering the heir of the Arcadian crown, a treasonable offense.

This sense of trespass of sexual as well as geographical boundaries becomes more apparent when an exchange of songs between Musidorus and Pamela culminates in Musidorus's lullaby, which puts Pamela to sleep. This slumber allows Musidorus the opportunity to lean over her prone body, putting his face down to hers, "sucking the breath with such joy" (653) that he wishes no other food. In the *Old Arcadia,* he decides to rape her. In both *Arcadias,* the scene is redolent with such dangerous sexuality that, when the brigands emerge from the forest to kidnap them, there is a sense in which, according to the mores of the time, they are partly responsible for their own capture.

Sexual guilt permeates the verse of all three women. Deep in a cave, Gynecia writes a poem comparing the darkness of the cave and her own moral blindness: "This cave is dark, but it had never light/ . . . I darkened am, who once had clearest sight" (635). A poem Pyrocles writes in the same cave confirms these associations, extending them to cover his own situation. For Pyrocles, "passions dark" have "clos'd in dungeon dark / My mind, ere now led forth by reason's light" (632). Pyrocles, like Gynecia, has been driven to the cave by bondage to sexual passions, and his recognition of his own plight in Gynecia's song can be seen to confirm the feminization of his mind through his abandonment of reason.[42]

Gynecia's poems, however, contain two elements not present in the verse of Pyrocles or any other male. The first is the association of passion with death. Her cave signifies not only her moral blindness, but her grave, a dark engulfing maternal "bosom": "Come cave, become my grave: come death, and lend / Receipt to me within thy bosom dark." This grave is only the extension of her wretched condition of death-in-life: "Thus then my form, and thus my state I find, / Death wrapped in flesh, to living grave assign'd" (633). But if her guilty passion for Pyrocles has brought her to this plight, an earlier drama suggests that in her loyalty to Basilius she would fare no better. In this dream, she finds the noisome dead body of her husband who embraced her, saying "Gynecia, leave all, for here is thy only rest" (376). Both of these conditions are reified in Euarchus's verdict that she be executed by live burial in her husband's grave. Paradoxically signifying both her engulfment by her passion for Pyrocles and the psychological consequences of her enforced marriage to Basilius, this punishment is the logical physical representation of her inner psychological state. Even though she was in fact innocent of Basilius's supposed death, it is no wonder that she does not protest her innocence.

The other element represented in Gynecia's verse not present in that of male poets is the way her written poem represents the inadequacy of writing. She concludes her first of two poems, a description of her "dark ugly night," with the couplet: "An end, an end: my dull'd pen cannot write, / Nor mazed head think, nor falt'ring tongue recite"

(634). Her second poem concludes in a similar vein: "No Cave, no wasting wax, no words of grief, / Can hold, show, tell, my pains without relief" (635). Unable to represent the extent of her wretchedness and moral confusion, writing is represented as futile.

In a poem Gynecia writes on the belly of a lute, writing is not only futile; it is a form of silence. Reversing the usual significance of writing as an act of public speech, Gynecia contrasts singing and writing to find the latter more appropriate to her state, not because of its ability to communicate her mind, but because of its silence. Because her song is now only an inarticulate cry, because her hand is "benumb'd with fortune's daily blows," because her mind is "amaz'd," she can no longer sing. Asking her lute to be silent, to "within thyself thy tunes enclose" (662), she writes upon it instead. She asks that the melodies the lute plays hereafter be silent ones: "And though my moans be not in music bound, / Of written griefs yet be the silent ground."

The silenced lute itself becomes an evocative representation of a silenced woman. Within the imagery of Gynecia's poem, the lute becomes personified, a friend or gentlewoman servant to its "mistress." This personification perhaps proceeds in part from the lute's curves, especially the prominent "belly" (662) upon which Gynecia writes. The function of this lute is to grieve for its mistress; the black ink of Gynecia's words becomes the lute's "mourning weeds" for her mistress's death. This depiction of words as a mourning garment is evocative in two ways: on the one hand, the image presents words as mute signifiers. What matters is not what they say, but the meaning of their color. On the other, it appears that the lute's grief, like the grief of Spenser's Clorinda, enables writing. In this lute poem, like her cave poem, Gynecia closely associates the act of writing and the death of a woman tormented by sexual guilt, as she cries, "Black ink becomes the state wherein I die" (663).

Philoclea also writes a poem against writing, associating it not with silence but, more radically, with erasure. Her poem associates death with chastity rather than with moral blindness, and portrays death as an ideal state, not merely a relief from present wretchedness. Before the events of the *New Arcadia* began, Philoclea had written on a marble stone within a forest a poem affirming her chastity. The words of this poem literally become "blots," stains demonstrating her fall from spiritual virginity. When, after falling in love with Pyrocles, she revisits the site of her poem only to find the words blotted, she makes the connection between textual and sexual spot explicit: " 'Alas,' said she, 'fair marble, which never received'st spot but by my writing, well do these blots become a blotted writer' " (242). Philoclea's parallel between her writing (spots on the otherwise fair marble) and her newly sexual self (now a blotted writer) eloquently attests to the dangerous sexuality implicated in female authorship by contemporary gender ideology. Her words have been smudged, erased by natural process, probably by moisture, just as her identity has become stained, erased, "blotted" by sexual guilt.

Philoclea's second poem conveys not only a changed sense of her sexual nature, but an altered valuation of her earlier writing:

> My words, in hope to blaze my steadfast mind,
> This marble chose, as of like temper known:
> But lo, my words defac'd, my fancies blind,
> Blots to the stone, shames to myself I find.
> (242)

According to this poem, her writing even of a chastity poem was itself already a "spot" on its pure white marble blankness. The pure white marble, like a pure white bedsheet, signifies chastity, the basis for a woman's identity, for her moral and social value in this patriarchal culture. Writing on the marble, like bleeding on the sheet, signifies loss of that identity. Implicated in sexuality to this extent, to write is, paradoxically enough, to deface the purity of the white stone, to erase.

The way that Philoclea's second stanza itemizes further reasons for the inferiority of her words to a blank marble stone attests to the power of contemporary cultural constraints against women's writing:

> My words full weak, the marble full of might;
> My words in store, the marble all alone;
> My words black ink, the marble kindly white;
> My words unseen, the marble still in sight,
> May witness bear how ill agree in one
> A woman's hand with constant marble stone.

Philoclea's poetry is not only guilty; it also partakes of the other attributes commonly ascribed to female language: weakness, excessive volubility, insubstantiality, transience. The invisibility of her "unseen" words appears to be a characteristic of the words themselves, not a constraint imposed upon them. Her gender has disqualified her as an author, and it is no accident that she did not have "present commodity" (242) or means of writing it down. From this perception of the nature of her words, what would be the point?

But if the sexual guilt of female authorship is represented as an agonizing experience, Philoclea's representation of virginal chastity also resonates with disturbing undertones. The constancy of marble stone is the constancy of self-negation, of a detachment from other humans and from human needs that denies the possibility of a full emotional life. While the marble is "full of might," it is also "all alone." While it is "in sight," it is "white," blank, conveying nothing. The implied ideal that a woman's hand should be like "constant marble stone" suggests a flight from humanity, perhaps even a desire for death. Writing outside on marble stone has, in itself, an association with death, with marble tombstones engraved with names of the deceased.

These associations are even more explicit in Philoclea's chastity poem, in which she rejoices that the stone's "pureness doth present / My purest mind," that its "temper hard doth show / My temper'd heart." Because of her purity and her hardness, she will, like the stone, be "in sight," for "after-livers" will know her virtue. The choice of "after-livers" as her validating audience suggests a fantasy of her death. This fantasy becomes explicit in the final lines of the poem, when she describes how her "constant" course will lead her to "Chastity," into whose maternal bosom her soul will fly at her death. The alternative to sexual guilt is not, according to this representation, a sexually loyal marriage to a loved and respected husband, but a chilly withdrawal from human need that foreshadows and is best fulfilled in death itself; for in death a woman's hand does best "agree" with "constant marble stone." The extent to which this imagery functions as actual metaphorical equipment through which to perceive her sexual desire is chillingly demonstrated by its presence in her confession of her love to Pyrocles: "Shall I labour to lay marble colours over my ruinous thoughts? Or rather, through the pureness of my virgin-mind be stained, let me keep the true simplicity of my word" (330).

The values controlling this imagery of "marble colours" and "stain" run counter to the values of romantic prose narratives: as the heroine of a romance, Philoclea is supposed to return Pyrocles' love. This conflict in values, between the high estimation placed upon "truth" to one's own chastity and the high estimation placed upon passionate love of another, disappears in the captivity episode of the *New Arcadia,* which offers a powerful opportunity of heroism to women. Imprisoned deep within the castle of their evil aunt Cecropia, Philoclea and Pamela maintain their selfhood through their determination to die rather than to submit to marriage with their cousin Amphialus.

That's Why the Lady Is a Stoic

The contradiction between the demands of romantic love and those of chastity, especially female chastity, is concealed rather than resolved in the captivity episode of book 3 of the *New Arcadia*. With Musidorus outside the castle walls and Pyrocles/Zelmane in another cell, the chastity of Philoclea and Pamela is endangered not by romantic love, but by the specious logic and even physical torture through which Cecropia attempts to force one of them (either one of them will do) to marry her son. Their "truth," their self-contained, inner identity, is now defined by their loyalty to their princes, demonstrated through their willingness to die rather than through the presence or absence of their sexual desire. Through conquering the fear of death, the princesses transcend not only sexual guilt, but all other desires of the flesh. Their willingness to die alters the perception of love from a guilty sexual passion to a motive for heroic constancy. In their new roles as constant lovers who bravely face imprisonment and even death, the princesses have been moved from object status, the means through which the princes demonstrated their merit, to subject status, heroines (or female heroes) in their own right.[43]

The heroism of the constant woman lover draws from various sources: from romantic heroines who die for love, from martyrs who die for their religious beliefs, and from Stoic heroes who demonstrate their equanimity by dying well. Romantic heroines were represented in numerous collections of English prose romances; Bandello's well-known tale of Romeo and Juliet, for example, appeared in William Painter's *Palace of Pleasure* (1566). The choice by Juliet and other heroines to die rather than to live in a world without their beloveds created a role for women which heroized rather than denigrated their love for men. The self-sacrificing love of Philoclea and Pamela for their princes casts a romantic glow over the otherwise severe demeanor of the religious martyr, whose influence is apparent in Pamela's long reply to Cecropia defending the existence of God. While a long medieval tradition offered ample precedent for women martyrs, an even more influential model in sixteenth-century England was John Foxe's *Actes and Monuments*, a widely read compilation of the trials and deaths of Protestant men and women martyred during the Catholic reign of

Mary Tudor.[44] The specific contribution of the Protestant martyr was the authorization of a model of female heroism enabling speech and even rigorous intellectual debate on religious topics. Pamela's impassioned yet immensely informed and logical arguments against atheism owe a debt to this model.

Finally, the emphasis of the captivity episode on the princesses' resignation to death, even to each other's death, also points to the influence of Stoicism.[45] While religious martyrs are often represented as dying gladly, Stoics tend to display an equanimity which reflects an independence of the inner self from the whims of fortune rather than a belief in rewards in heaven. Resignation to death is the final test of the true Stoic's ability to endure whatever fortune sends without resistance or complaint. In their common contempt for the rewards of this world, Christian martyrs and Stoics overlapped in their form of heroism; in fact, these two perspectives merged in a Christianized form of Stoicism especially popular near the end of the sixteenth century.[46] Philip Sidney would have read at least one tract of Christianized Stoicism, written by his friend Philippe du Plessis Mornay and later translated by his sister Mary as *The Discourse of Life and Death.*[47] While classical Stoicism did not advocate dying for love or for any other passion, the fortitude with which Sidney's princesses face death may embody an application of Stoic philosophy to the circumstances faced by women.

Understanding that the function of book 3 is to create the constant heroine from these various sources makes sense of what might otherwise seem gratuitously morbid. The heroic strength of the princesses's constancy can be elicited only through a variety of increasingly severe tests, which at times verge on the sadistic. The princesses respond to these tests in pointedly different styles, delineating the parameters of heroism which women can display without trespassing gender lines.[48] Both styles reveal the continued pressure of gender ideology in the text's evident concern that the heroism of the princesses, like that of romantic heroines, never seem masculine or strident. Thus, Pamela's majesty shows the extent of feisty assertiveness allowable in an attractive woman; Philoclea's sweetness shows that impressive courage need not jeopardize appealing femininity.

The first and probably the mildest test is Amphialus's wooing of Philoclea. Philoclea's victory over the temptation offered by the wealthy and attractive Amphialus himself, richly apparelled in black velvet embroidered with pearls and jewels (448), kneeling at her feet to offer his absolute devotion (449), shows that her resolve cannot be shaken merely by a handsome face and large financial resources. Recognizing the danger posed to her constancy by Amphialus, Philoclea prettily combines female frailty and strong resolve as, nearly fainting, "slowly lifting up her eyes upon him, with a countenance ever courteous but then languishing" (451), she expresses her determination to die rather than to endure dishonor. She receives Amphialus's 164-line poem (475–80), "after her wonted sorrowful (but otherwise unmoved) manner" (480). She is equally unmoved by Cecropia's "reason." As Cecropia depicts the fulfillment as wife and mother following on her marriage with Amphialus, she is to Philoclea only a "tedious prattler" (461), unsuccessfully distracting her thoughts from Pyrocles.

Pamela's confrontation with Cecropia brings out a more vigorous form of heroism. While Philoclea uses "sweet and humble dealing" to avoid the assaults of her aunt, Pamela "with the majesty of virtue did beat them off" (465). While the lovelorn Philoclea finds sanctuary from her aunt's speeches in thoughts of Pyrocles, Pamela mounts a vehement defense not only of her own actions but of the order of the universe itself. What has become one of the most celebrated passages of the *New Arcadia* begins when Cecropia points to the folly of Pamela's reliance on virtue by alleging the nonexistence of God. Her "cheeks dyed in the beautifullest grain of virtuous anger," her eyes glistering "forth beams of disdain," Pamela interrupts her aunt with the injunction, "Peace, wicked woman, peace, unworthy to breathe that dost not acknowledge the breath-giver" (488) before launching into her eloquent and impressively learned sermon. Through Pamela's eloquent speech, the text creates an intellectual heroine empowered to display her learning. Critical debate concerning the sources of Pamela's attack against Cecropia's atheism suggests the depth of the learning allowed her by the text.[49] But whether her learning is derived from Christian or classical sources, the formative model for this highly verbal heroine is the Protestant woman reader/martyr whose exhibition of learning is enabled by disputations with the "damned"—the devil, Catholics, or atheists like Cecropia.

The princesses' temptations proceed from inducements and verbal arguments to threats of physical death and to actual torture. The severity of their plight, made explicit when they are actually placed upon a scaffold "to be kept as ready for the slaughter" (546), elicits two contrasting demeanors, both expressive of a willingness to die, both attractive to onlookers.

> One might see in Pamela a willingness to die rather than to have life at other's discretion; though sometimes a princely disdain would

> sparkle out of her princely eyes, that it should be in other's power to force her to die. In Philoclea a pretty fear came up to endamask her rosy cheeks; but it was such a fear as rather seemed a kindly child to her innate humbleness than any other dismayedness: or if she were dismayed, it was more for Zelmane than for herself. (546)

Next, in a passage that surely contained considerable erotic appeal for at least some readers, the two women are actually tortured, repeatedly whipped with rods by spiteful old women. After her first beating, Philoclea kneels, "with tearful eyes and sobbing breast" (552), begging that Cecropia would pity her and take her life rather than torment "a poor gentlewoman." Pamela shows no signs of pain, defying Cecropia with a little smile, "but such a smiling as showed no love and yet could not but be lovely" (553). Resolving to die, both women take comfort in thoughts of their loved ones, Philoclea resting her mind in the thought that "she should die beloved of Zelmane" (553) and Pamela commanding Musidorus in her mind to "live long, that thou mayest long love the chaste love of thy dead Pamela" (554).

Finally, Cecropia threatens the princesses with the most severe test of all—not their own deaths, but each other's. Cecropia first threatens Philoclea with Pamela's death. Sure in her own resolve for death, Philoclea is equally sure of her sister's: "Since in herself she preferred death before such a base servitude, love did teach her to wish the same to her sister" (556). Putting her resolve to the test by beheading the "sharp-witted" Artesia in Pamela's clothes, Cecropia gains from the meek yet defiant Philoclea only the plea to "let me follow my Pamela whom ever I sought to follow" (559). Philoclea's eloquent pleading for death is further elicited by Pyrocles, whom Cecropia sends to persuade Philoclea to marry Amphialus and live. Cecropia next stages a mock execution of Philoclea, thrusting her head up through a hole in a scaffold into a bloody basin so that it appears that she was beheaded. Philoclea's mock beheading only brings from Pamela the vow to starve herself, never more receiving "sustenance of them that had been the causers" of her sister's murder (569). All of the efforts of Cecropia and of her successors only call forth increasingly vehement expressions of a desire for death from the princesses. United in this common wish to die, they continue to delineate two versions of the constant heroine in their individual styles of fortitude. Pamela scorns death as only a "bugbear," while Philoclea takes on a humbler role, wishing only that Pamela, her "school-mistress" in this subject, might live, "to see me say my lesson truly" (580). Facing death "nobly" (580), the stately Pamela remains appealing to men; facing death "sweetly" (580), Philoclea remains a stalwart heroine despite her femininity.

Unlike Pamela and Philoclea, Pyrocles faces death "sadly and desperately" (580); this contrast portrays the princesses as the more adept in resigning themselves to death. Pyrocles' most spectacular failure at resignation occurs after the mock execution of Philoclea. Crying out in "a wild fury of desperate agony" (563), he farcically bungles suicide by braining himself against a wall. After coming to, he spends all day and night bewailing Philoclea's death only to be rebuked, near dawn, by a mysterious gentlewoman who had been listening to him all the while and who criticizes him for bemoaning her "who hath in one act both preserved her honour and left the miseries of this world" (567). Pyrocles' retort, "O woman's philosophy, childish folly," constructs resignation to a beloved's death as a female characteristic. The term "philosophy" also associates women's resignation with a Christianized form of classical thinking by foregrounding a resemblance between the veiled Philoclea and Boethius's character "Philosophy." Coming to a prisoner's cell to instruct him in resignation to the world's injustice, Philosophy declaims a compendium of classical thought composing *The Consolation of Philosophy,* whose author was later proclaimed a Christian martyr.[50] Pyrocles shows himself comically inept at receiving consolation as, in response to the woman's suggestion that he might someday find a better love, he rushes forward to strike her. He is prevented from such an ungallant deed only by the discovery that he has been speaking with his beloved Philoclea all along.

Another instance of the princesses' superiority to Pyrocles as disciples of this "woman's philosophy" is even more clearly related to gender. The sisters' code of resigned fortitude shows itself in opposition to the more active heroic virtue exercised by Pyrocles, who directs his attentions towards escape rather than towards endurance.[51] Allying himself with Artesia and Clinias, Pyrocles initiates a plot to free the sisters which involves the poisoning of Amphialus. Preferring "perpetual imprisonment than consent to destroying her cousin" (519), the compassionate Philoclea will have no part in the scheme, while the principled Pamela refuses to stoop to such "falsehood" (520). Heroic resignation has interfered with active heroism, and the plot fails. Towards the end of the captivity episode, it is only with great effort that Pyrocles convinces the sisters to pretend to wait upon their father's consent to marriage to gain time for possible rescue, a ploy that causes no one any harm.

The construction of contrasting female and male versions of heroism may well explain other aspects of the captivity episode as well. As the princesses endure increasingly violent inducements to marry, the knights engage in gruesome battles and hopeless tournaments. By juxtaposing the vulnerable humanity of the soldiers to the grisly details of the battle against Amphialus to free the princesses, the text elicits pathos for the defeated rather than admiration for the victors. Who could rejoice over the death of the "beautiful" Agenor (467) or over the "old knight Aeschylus" (469) in the arms of his son, or of Amphialus's tender young squire Ismenus? Far from glorious, the battle is continually described in the most gruesome terms, the battlefield littered with dismembered parts, arms "whose fingers yet moved," hearts "now with deadly violence opened," and "fouler deaths" which "had uglily displayed their trailing guts" (469). The morbidity of the text suggests the emptiness of military heroism, which causes such futile suffering.[52] The heroic constancy practiced by the princesses appears increasingly attractive in contrast with the empty heroism of the battlefield.

Despite the gorgeous costuming, courtly *impreses,* and the impeccable manners of their participants, the engagements of single combat finally fare no better than the gruesome battle as glorious examples of heroic prowess. In these descriptions, too, the pathos over the death of the defeated finally outweighs the admiration for the victor. The courteous encounter between Amphialus and Phalanthus, in which no one dies (496), quickly gives way to Amphialus's killing of the hero Argalus (506). The values of romantic love and of heroic valor have come into conflict. Even Amphialus weeps at the death of the loving husband of the worthy Parthenia (509); even Amphialus finds little satisfaction in a martial fame that does not gain him the love of Philoclea (509).

The battle between Amphialus and Parthenia, disguised as the Knight of the Tomb, marks the victory of the values of romantic love over heroic valor. "Astonished with grief, compassion, and shame" (528) over its unintentional killing of Parthenia, Amphialus breaks his sword and takes to his bed. His skill as a warrior creates him not as a military hero, but as the unwitting villain of a love story whose popularity will be soon demonstrated by its many copies and imitations in the seventeenth century.[53] This defeat has already been thoroughly prepared for by earlier descriptions. Parthenia's death represents, in fact, the end point of a pattern evolving throughout the martial encounters in the third book, which even in the initial battle scene had shifted attention from the victors to the defeated. The pathos of her death is different in degree but not in kind from the pathos over the earlier deaths of the "beautiful" Agenor, the aged Aeschylus, the young Ismenus. Taken together, these episodes suggest the shallowness and the cruelty of an egotistical military code. With this demise of the values of heroic valor, Sidney's much-cited aim for the *New Arcadia,* the presentation of the princes as epic heroes, is emptied of meaning.

The pathos of Parthenia's death performs another function, also prepared for by other characters in book 3. Like the princesses, Parthenia shows her courage in the face of death, for her goal is not to win, but to lose. She eloquently expresses her intent to die in the morbid appointments of her armor: "In an armourall painted over with such a cunning of sorrow that it represented a gaping sepulchre . . . his bases, which he wore so long as they came almost to his ankle, were embroidered only with black worms, which seemed to crawl up and down, as ready to devour him" (526). Like the princesses, Parthenia remains feminine in her heroism; she dies beautifully as well as bravely. Even wounded in her armor, her beauty "was nothing short of perfection." Her "dainty blood" ran like a river on the alabaster of her neck creating an "island of perfectest white." Her wounds "all-looked-upon through the spectacles of pity, did even increase the lines of her natural fairness" (528). Parthenia's death not only represents the victory of the values of romantic love; it also confirms one of the few forms of heroism available to women in the Renaissance: the ability to die well.

The Spectacles of Pity

The heroism created by the ability to die well depends upon an audience response different from that elicited by an epic hero. The "spectacles of pity" focussing the onlookers' gaze on the wounded Parthenia must also be worn by the audience of the text if this form of heroism is to work. Through these spectacles the defeated, not the victorious, emerge as heroes. While in the *Old Arcadia* pity is construed as an irrational feeling to which women were unfortunately prone, in book 3 of the *New Arcadia* pity is not represented as suspect. Book 3 does not spring any trap on the compassionate reader; it does not offer any "spectacles of judgment" through which to qualify a reader's sympathetic response. The endorsement of pity as an appropriate reader's response represents a radical change from the relationship between reader and text in the *Old Arcadia.* Does this change suggest that the text has granted male readers permission to "read like a woman," to come into contact with that "female" aspect of themselves capable of compassionate responses to a text? Or that Sidney is writing primarily to a female audience whose compassion is anticipated?

Both possibilities seem to apply. The text seems to sanction "female," compassionate readings from its male as well as its female readers, for "reading like a woman" is no longer shameful when the qualities associated with women are represented as noble rather than degrading. This shift has already been anticipated in Pyrocles' sympathetic response to the original Zelmane. This rereading of "female" passion was already implicit in the *New Arcadia* with the revealing substitution of "Zelmane" for "Cleophila" as Pyrocles' assumed name.[54] As a rearrangement of "Philoclea," "Cleophila" suggests that way that Pyrocles' love for Philoclea confirms the reversal of the hierarchies of male/female and reason/passion described in his poem "Transform'd in show." In the *Old Arcadia,* Pyrocles' transvestitism rendered him absurd; his female clothing signified the humiliating defeat of his reason by his passion. Pyrocles' assumption of the name "Zelmane" in the *New Arcadia,* on the other hand, moves towards the rereading of the value of passion realized in book 3. The dignified death of the original Zelmane in Pyrocles' service elevated love from passion to vocation. No longer a dangerous passion to be conquered, love becomes a motive for heroism, a means of conquering the fear of death. By revealing his compassion for a woman who loved him, Pyrocles' adoption of Zelmane's name signals his empathy and even his attempted participation in this now-noble female passion.

Pyrocles has "become" Zelmane in a very different sense than he had "become" Cleophila. By book 3 of the *New Arcadia,* his self-denying ability to love signifies noble heroism, not passionate excess. If the text levels a criticism at Pyrocles, it is not that he has become effeminate, but that he has perhaps not become effeminate enough. While his imprisonment offers him the same opportunities for the passive heroism offered to women—endurance, loyalty, fortitude—he never entirely conforms to this model of heroism that is portrayed as female in the *New Arcadia.* As, near the end of the fragment, he steps forward to attack the brutish Anaxius, he is named "Pyrocles" rather than "Zelmane" for the first time since donning his female attire. In this act, Pyrocles shows that the active heroism appropriate to his masculinity still predominates even over the ennobled form of female heroism explored in book 3. But rather than denigrating the form of heroism practiced by women in this book, his reassertion of traditional masculine heroism in his battle with the surprised Anaxius renders the virtues of fortitude and patience all the more gender-specific. Taken together, Pyrocles and Musidorus represent an eloquent statement of divided values, with Pyrocles offering a resigned form of heroism to which he is not, by gender, suited, while outside the castle walls Musidorus continues to participate in a masculine form of heroism increasingly exposed as futile.

There is another less optimistic way in which the captivity episode may have performed its operations upon some readers proceeding from another, less wholesome gaze made possible by the "spectacles of pity." As onlookers gather around the body of Parthenia to admire her "dainty blood" running like a river on the alabaster of her neck to create an "island of perfectest white," the beauty of her dying body may have elicited a sexual as well as, or even instead of, a compassionate response. This reading can be performed upon the sufferings, and especially the whippings, of the princesses, as well. From this perspective, the desiring female body banished from the captivity episode has become instead a suffering female body that invites male desire. The valorization of the female body as the site of heroic virtue becomes, then, a mask covering sadistic voyeurism based on pleasure in women's pain. Rather than being promoted to subjects through their heroic constancy, the princesses and Parthenia can be reduced again to sexual objects of a perverted impulse allied to necrophilia.[55]

Speculations: Equipment for Living

The captivity episode in the *New Arcadia* can also be read as an attempt to construct a form of heroism appropriate for young women who are under pressure to marry husbands chosen by their parents, and for young brides who are living in the households of their mothers-in-law.[56] The problem faced by women forced to marry against their will no doubt impressed itself upon Sidney with special urgency in the summer of 1581, when his beloved Penelope Devereux married Richard Rich. Cecropia's attempts to flatter, argue, and torture Pamela and Philoclea into marrying Amphialus represent a nightmare version of a relatively ordinary situation, apparently faced by Penelope Devereux as well as by numerous other aristocratic women in the Renaissance.

This reading of the captivity episode is legitimated by contemporary responses which assume the influence of Penelope Devereux upon the *New Arcadia*. One seventeenth-century reader states that the *New Arcadia* was Sidney's expression of devotion to Penelope Rich as if it were a matter of known fact: "No man is so ignorant as hath not at least heard of the excellent worke of Sir Philip Sidney called Arcadia which was cheefly intended to the honourable memory of this Lady Penelope." Another seventeenth-century reader interpreted Philoclea to refer to Penelope Rich.[57]

An identification between Philoclea and Penelope Rich is also assumed in a manuscript set of imaginary epistles exchanged between characters named Sir Philip Sidney and Penelope Devereux. Like other near-contemporaries, the author of these epistles perceives the *New Arcadia* as a literary monument to Penelope Devereux. For this author, however, the captivity episode recorded not her "honourable memory" but her "unconstant change" as she, unlike the princesses, acceded to pressure to marry. This author shows no embarrassment in reading the *New Arcadia* within a biographical framework:

> So longe as doth Arcadias name survive
> so longe thy graces in that name shall live
> by which all readers shall deride as strange
> My constant love, and thy unconstant change.

The character "Sidney" censures "Penelope"'s accession to parental demands to marry Richard Rich:

> Princes may force the body, not the mind
> The mind's a temple, free and hallowed Cell
> Which Tirantes cannot raze, nor strength compell.

Admitting her fault, this imagined "Penelope" regrets her weakness:

> The fault was mine I should have been tormented
> Even unto death and yet not have consented.[58]

That is, "Penelope" asserts that she should have acted as the princesses did in fact act in the captivity episode, defying death rather than agreeing to marry a man she did not love.

While Sidney may have written the *New Arcadia* in part as a response to one woman's acquiescence to parental demands, his creation of constant young heroines who defy formidable authorities would no doubt have appealed to large numbers of actual women facing a similar situation.[59] The fairy-tale distortions of the captivity episode—the evil, scheming aunt; the ever-good princesses; the valiant knights—make it easy to overlook the relevance of this model for the behavior of real women. But, as with fairy tales, these distortions simplify the complexities of real life to create fantasies of considerable power. For example, few if any young women were actually threatened with death. But the language of the anonymous epistles, particularly "Penelope's" reply that she "should have been tormented / Even unto the death and yet not have consented," suggests that this exaggeration possessed an imaginative truth.

While the grotesque dynamics controlling the captivity episode markedly exaggerated actual parental pressure, aspects of this exaggeration may have contained more than merely imaginative truth. There is at least one documented case of the practice of one of Cecropia's more sordid strategies in an early-seventeenth-century household. Fourteen-year-old Frances Coke, a wealthy heiress who resisted her father's demand to marry Sir John Villiers instead of her beloved Henry, earl of Oxford, was "tied to the Bedposts and whipped till she consented to the Match."[60] Possibly this violence was practiced, or at least used as a threat, in other households as well. Whether such practices were primarily threatened or real, the effect of reading the courageous response of Pamela and Philoclea even to whipping must have been powerful for young women also facing the prospect of an undesired marriage. The captivity episode no doubt provided them a means by which they could perceive their resistance as heroic.

Another group of women may also have derived consolation from the *New Arcadia.* The captivity episode reflects in exaggerated form the situation of young brides living in their husbands' houses under the supervision of their mothers-in-law. For these women, the events of the captivity episode must have been immensely gratifying. When Amphialus learns of his evil mother's cruel treatment of the virtuous and uncomplaining princesses, he goes berserk with guilt and anger. He rushes towards Cecropia with his sword outdrawn. Thinking that her son intends to kill her, she falls from a high tower. Cecropia does not die, however, until she sees her son stab himself, writhing under the burden of his unbearable remorse for the way he has unknowingly allowed his mother to treat the princesses. This episode no doubt provided pleasant vindication for any young woman living with a difficult mother-in-law: the wicked mother-figure is blamed by the remorseful son for the grief she has caused the innocent young woman, the silently suffering victim of her tremendous cruelty.[61] The exaggerations of an ordinary situation within the *New Arcadia* would only have increased its reading pleasure.

The creation of the constant heroines in book 3, which almost certainly provided "equipment for living" for numbers of young women, no doubt accounts in part for the large female audience for the *New Arcadia* described in numerous references in the seventeenth century.

At a time when opportunities for heroism for women were limited, the *New Arcadia* offered its female audience a means through which they could perceive themselves as heroic in their everyday lives. The translations of the countess of Pembroke provide some evidence for reading book 3 as a source of consolation for women, for they, too, delineate a romanticized form of the constant heroine in ways that suggest the applicability of fortitude and self-sacrifice to women's lives. In which direction did influence travel? Was Sidney's text formed by his sister's philosophy, or was her philosophy formed by his text? Perhaps it was a shared discourse between the two. But it did not remain private. At least one woman reader interpreted the *New Arcadia* as an injunction to women to endure any hardship for love. The eloquent presence of the pronoun "us" in the concluding sentence Mrs. Stanley added to her 1725 "modernization" of the *New Arcadia* implies a personal application of this model: "Time and Assiduity (at least in love) will conquer every difficulty, and pay us double Interest for every Disappointment which we have or can endure."[62]

The constant heroine, who endured misfortune and even faced death without complaint, who would sacrifice even her own life for her beloved, provided a model of passive endurance rather than of healthy self-assertion. The cost of such heroism was high. Richard McCoy's criticism of the princesses for their "dangerous quietism" is equally applicable to women who practiced this form of heroism in everyday life.[63] As the next chapter will suggest, the heroics of constancy often served to deny or to mask other powerful emotions, and especially rage.

The Reception of the *New Arcadia*

The role of constant heroine offered women readers of the *New Arcadia* appears to have been lost upon seventeenth-century male readers, who continued to represent women readers of the *New Arcadia* as culpably frivolous and dangerously sexual. The reception of the *New Arcadia* reveals the essential conservatism of the imagined effect of gender on reading. Generally, men read the *New Arcadia* as a serious work, revealing either political insights about the "growth, state, and declination of Princes, change of Government, and laws" or moral guidance, "Examples, (as directing threads) to guide every man through the confused Labyrinth of his own desires, and life."[64] The *New Arcadia* as read by women would hardly seem to be the same book. For example, a mid-seventeenth-century parody, which adopts the plot of the *New Arcadia* to reflect the political circumstances leading up to the Civil War, describes the work as presenting political meanings for male readers and sartorial meanings for women readers. For men, "Court follies hee discovers, and / What makes comotions in a land," while women may benefit from it "even to the dresse / That shadowes ore their nakedness."[65]

As represented by seventeenth-century male writers, the primary response of women readers to Sidney's *New Arcadia* was sexual arousal. In a poem by Charles Cotton, for example, the narrator comes upon his "nymph" by a river as she is reading the *New Arcadia*. In a scene oddly reminiscent of Pyrocles' observation of Philoclea's naked body as she bathed, Cotton's poem makes it clear that his woman reader's pleasure is sensual rather than intellectual:

The happy object of her eye
Was Sidney's living *Arcadie*
Whose amorous tale had so betray'd
Desire in this all-lovely maid,
That whilst her cheek a blush did warm,
I read Love's story in her form
  And of the sisters the united grace,
  Pamela's vigour in Philoclea's face.[66]

Cotton's narrator is, like Pyrocles, a voyeur. As he watches the sexual arousal of his woman reader, he attests to the erotic pleasure possible to males imagining female responses to this work. A seventeenth-century translator finds a different use for female arousal. He builds on the response of "fair ones" to the *New Arcadia* as a way to sell his translation of Achilles Tatius's steamy romance, *Loves of Clitophon and Leucippe:*

A while lay by
blessed Sidney's Arcady:
Here's a Story that will make
You not repent Him to forsake.[67]

Although his reaction is monitory rather than admiring, Wye Saltonstall constructs a similarly sexual female audience, warning that a woman should not be allowed to read "loves historyes," such as *Amadis de Gaule* and the *Arcadia*, for in them she "courts the shaddow of love till she know the substance."[68] By 1599, cheap editions of the *New Arcadia* demonstrated its popularity among the middle classes;[69] and Thomas Powell's advice to parents to supervise their daughters' reading reveals negative attitudes towards class as well as towards gender. Powell's rejection of the *New Arcadia* as inappropriate reading for middle-class women shows his fear that the sexual immorality of upper-class women will contaminate their morality and, perhaps even more damaging, their utility:

> Let them learne Cookery and Laundrye. And instead of reading Sir Philip Sidney's *Arcadia*, let them learn the grounds of good huswifery. I like not a female Poetess at any hand. Let greater personages glory their skill in musicke, the posture of their bodies, their knowledge in languages, the greatnesse and freedome of their spirits, and their arts in arreigning of mens affections at their flattering faces: This is not the way to breed a private Gentlemans Daughter.[70]

What was the effect of these representations of women readers of the *New Arcadia* upon women at the time? Did reading the *New Arcadia* constitute an act of defiance?[71] Did some women readers conform to these representations by obligingly providing the predicted sexual responses? Did others find the constant heroine created in book 3 all the more impelling as a model for behavior because of her difference from the frivolous gentlewoman reader? And what was the effect of these representations upon women who wished to write? Powell's inclusion of the statement "I like not a female Poetess at any hand" in his admonition to parents shows his association of women readers and writers alike with sexuality and frivolity. For a woman who defied these representations of women readers and writers to compose her own work, the heroics of constancy offered a possible discourse, despite its cost. She could, like Pamela and Philoclea, eloquently attest to her willingness to die.[72]

Chapter 3
The Countess of Pembroke and the Art of Dying

Taken as a group, Mary Sidney's translations from Mornay, Garnier, and Petrarch suggest an interest in the art of dying which apparently gained strength not only from her grief over the death of her brother Philip, but also from her mother's impressive death, from her husband's expressed desire to die, and from the preoccupation with the topic evidenced by her culture in general.[1] In the common representation of the countess's literary activities as motivated entirely by her love for her brother, critics are drawing upon a perception that she herself was partly responsible for conveying. Like Spenser's elegiac version of Clorinda, Mary Sidney's own version of her authorship functions to deny the existence of dangerous sexuality or of a desire for worldly power. Her representation of her various literary activities as an extended elegy for her famous brother enabled her writing at a time when the boundaries were tightly drawn around women's public speech or published words. While her participation in the *ars moriendi* tradition was no doubt sincere, the desire for death permeating her authorship also accomplished two related functions: first, it provided a means of heroism accessible to Renaissance women through their constancy to their husbands, and second, this heroics of constancy was also able to serve as a mask for anger simultaneously elicited and denied.

Since no reasons were usually required for a woman's translating religious works for her own perusal,[2] the countess's construction of a version of authorship was perhaps necessitated by her preparation of a copy of the Psalms translated by her brother and herself for presentation to the queen in 1599. Accompanying (and accounting for) this presentation copy were two dedicatory poems, both composed by the countess, one to Queen Elizabeth and the other to the spirit of her deceased brother, Philip.[3] Margaret Hannay has written ably on the political messages embedded in both poems, which exhort the queen to support the Protestant cause on the mainland espoused by Sir Philip Sidney.[4] Despite, or more likely because of, this political agenda, these presentation poems portray a modestly unpolitical version of the countess's authorship. In the requisite dedicatory poem to Queen Elizabeth, Mary Sidney presents her translation as rent owed to the queen; and, as befits a woman author, this rent takes the form of cloth. Together she and her brother have woven a livery robe which they now present to Her Majesty as her due in exchange for those "nighe feelds where sow'n [her] favors bee" (line 39).

The dedicatory poem "To the Angell spirit of the most excellent Sir Philip Sidney" sets up a split audience for the translation, written not only for Queen Elizabeth but for the late Philip Sidney. In fact, in oblivious contradiction to the previous poem addressing her work to the queen, the first line of "To the Angell spirit" claims her deceased brother as the countess's only audience, to whom the work is "alones addres't." Since this second poem was not required, as was the first, for this presentation copy, its inclusion represents a strong statement. Its primary function seems to be the invention of an acceptable version of the countess as an author-translator; her version of authorship in this poem is notable for its use of several of the authorial strategies created for Clorinda in Spenser's *Astrophel.* After deflecting any anxieties about her attempt to influence a royal audience through her writing, the countess (like Clorinda) also disclaims any "Art or skill" on her part, attesting to the source of her poetry as "simple love" for her brother.

Like Spenser's Clorinda, the countess creates her authorship as a form of mourning. Not only is Philip the countess's only meaningful audience, but he is also her poetry's real author, inspiring her after his death:

> To thee pure sprite, to thee alones addres't
>   this coupled worke, by double int'rest thine:
>   First rais'de by thy blest hand, and what is mine
> inspir'd by thee, thy secrett power imprest.
>
> (1–4)

Merely completing what her brother would have finished had "heav'n spared" (74) his life, she is not a "real" poet asserting the independent subjectivity of an author. Far from serving as a means of self-display, her writing serves only to express her love for her dead brother, according to this striking image:

To which theise dearest offrings of my hart
dissolv'd to Inke, while penns impressions move
the bleeding veines of never dying love:
I render here.

(78–81)

In using her blood for ink, she represents her writing as almost a physical rather than an intellectual act, literally writing from the heart's feelings rather than from the head's thoughts. The next lines make clear that her work proceeds from love, not from learning:

These wounding lynes of smart
sadd Characters indeed of simple love
not Art nor skill which abler wits doe prove,
Of my full soule receive the meanest part.

(81–84)

Far from desiring worldly recognition, Mary Sidney's representation of herself as wishing only to join her brother in death forms a poignant conclusion to this poem:

I can no more: Deare Soule I take my leave;
Sorrowe still strives, would mount thy highest sphere
presuming so just cause might meet thee there,
Oh happie chaunge! could I so take my leave.

(88–92)

The countess's concluding desire for death implies her absolute detachment from any desire to influence the affairs of this world through her writing. This yearning for death is the fitting conclusion for her dedicatory poem, which constructs her translation of the Psalms, produced through Philip's inspiration and addressed solely to his eyes, as a conversation with her deceased brother, as an intermediate stage of communion with the dead for which her own death represents the only wholly satisfactory fulfillment. This desire for death will be shown to permeate her version of authorship, exerting powerful control over the other works which she not only translated, but allowed to be published.

With what seriousness can we take Mary Sidney's version of her authorship? The dedicatory poem to her brother's spirit suggests that her self-representations can neither be taken at face value nor wholly discounted. While her devotion to her brother and even her desire to join him in death cannot be denied, the contradictions which fissure her representation of her authorship make visible the pressure exerted against women's writing at that time. Poetry proceeding from "simple love" does not require meticulous consultation with numerous versions of the Psalms and their commentaries; an artless expression of love does not "extend the technical range of English versification," as a modern editor claims for her translations.[5] Poetry intended solely for the reading of an "Angell spirit" is not presented formally to the queen, nor does it advocate even subtly the political policy of supporting Protestants on the Continent. If her translations were informed primarily by her goal to die well, why, then, did she allow their publication? It is not clear whether these unresolved contradictions proceed from a gap between the countess and the mask of authorship she assumes or more deeply within her character, from a conflict posed by her dual identity as woman and as writer. What is clear, however, is that in the Psalms as in her other translations, her representation of herself as wishing to die formed an integral and necessary condition for her presentation of her work to the public eye, for her presentation of herself as an author.

Mary's own expressions of devotion for her brother Philip were no doubt partially responsible for the conventional understanding of her other literary projects as motivated by sisterly dedication. But this attribution of motive does not go very far in explaining her actual choice of works to translate. Critics who generally agree that she translated Philippe du Plessis Mornay's *Discours de la vie et de la mort* because her brother had begun a translation of another work by that author do not speculate upon why the countess chose to translate that particular work instead of another. Scholars' claims that her translation of Robert Garnier's *Marc Antoine* supposedly forwarded Sir Philip Sidney's attempt to reform the English stage along the principles laid out in his *Apology for Poetry* never seem to wonder why, if she wished to reform the English stage, she chose a notable example of closet drama, never intended for the stage at all? If her translation of Petrarch's *Trionfo della Morte* was truly an embodiment of her "idealized love" for her brother, why did she choose a poem which depicts the excellent death of a woman, rather than of a man?[6]

Mary Sidney's representation of her desire to die expressed at the end of her poem "To the Angell spirit of the most excellent Sir Philip Sidney" suggests an additional discourse underlying her version of authorship, which she shared not only with her brother Philip but also with her mother, her husband, and many other late-sixteenth-century Elizabethans. Taken together, these three translations by the countess of Pembroke—her *Discourse of Life and Death* (1590) from Philippe du Plessis Mornay's *Discours de la vie et de la mort*, her *Antonie* (c. 1590) from Robert Garnier's *Marc Antoine*, and her *Triumph of Death* from Petrarch's *Trionfo della Morte*—reveal an interest in the art of dying, particularly by beautiful heroines who die for love. Mornay's essay is an explicit *ars moriendi* tract that develops its argument against the fear of death along a peculiarly stoicized version of Christianity, while Garnier's play and Petrarch's poem feature appealing female protagonists who demonstrate their heroism by dying well.

The countess's translations of the works by Garnier and Petrarch reveal her struggle to apply Mornay's insights to the specific situation of women. These three translations demonstrate her response to the *ars moriendi* literature and to the heroics of constancy as these concerned women at the end of the sixteenth century. By exalting the ability to suffer without complaint, to endure any affliction with fortitude, Stoicism was consonant with other models in the Renaissance that recommended silence and obedience in the face of adversity as praiseworthy female behavior. Similarly, the scene of the noble death repeatedly portrayed in the *ars moriendi* tracts offered a model of heroism that women might emulate without violating the dominant sexual ideology. The countess's translations embody a female literary strategy through which women could be represented as heroic without challenging the patriarchal culture of Elizabethan England.

Not only did translating works about women who die well provide the countess with viable women heroines, but her subject also worked to absolve her as author from the charge of attempting to seduce or to gain power through her writing. Presenting women who die well as models to emulate strongly implied her own involvement in making a good death. After all, a woman who studies methods of dying has, it would seem, declared her distance from such transient concerns as illicit sexuality or other forms of control over men.

This creation of heroines who demonstrate their purity by their willingness to die well draws power from the captivity episode in Philip Sidney's revised *Arcadia,* which presented a revaluation of women and of passionate love. Rather than sharing in the guilty sexuality of the "fair ladies" addressed in the *Old Arcadia,* the princesses become constant heroines in the *New Arcadia*. Through their passionate love for their princes, they show control over, rather than capitulation to, their emotions; for through their love they conquer their fear of death. From this model Mary Sidney may well have constructed a form of authorship, also heroized by the willingness to die, exonerating her from the sense of sexual contamination surfacing with special strength in episodes of female authorship in Sidney's work.

Heroizing women for their willingness to die was hardly limited to the Sidneys. This form of heroism was a cultural cliche, set forth in a multitude of works read in the Renaissance, from Boccaccio's *De Claris Mulieribus* to Chaucer's *Legend of Good Women* to Castiglione's *Book of the Courtier.* In all of these works, the willingness to die was represented primarily as a means of exonerating women from the charge of sexual guilt. In Castiglione's work, for example, Cesare Gonzaga mounts an impassioned defense of women by demonstrating their continence through an array of grisly examples of women who "have chose rather to dye then to lose their honesty" not only in the "olde time" but even in his day.[7]

These gory accounts of glorious female deaths, usually suicides, were explicitly offered for imitation in the lives of young women in tracts on women's education in the Renaissance. Vives's influential *Instruction of a Christian Woman* (1592) recommends that girls be informed about the examples of virtuous women.[8] The kind of virtue he intends becomes apparent in the no fewer than twelve stories he recounts of women who preferred death, usually by suicide, to submitting to sexual dishonor. These women represent only a small portion of those "infinite in number, that had leaver be killed, headed, strangled, drowned, or have their throtes cut, then loose their chastitie" (H5v–H7v). Vives was not unique in his approach to female education. In recommending appropriate readings for young girls in his *Mirrhor of Modestie,* Thomas Salter elevates "Lucres, Portia, Camma," and Christian martyrs, all of whom preferred ghastly deaths to dishonorable lives, as examples of "vertuous Virgines and worthie Women" through which an Elizabethan girl "maie increase and augmente her vertue by immytatyng their lives."[9] How did these examples affect young Elizabethan girls? The lesson was clear, even if few women were actually offered the necessary conditions for an exemplary suicide in their personal lives. By preferring death to dishonor (should it be offered), they could attain the stature of heroines, cleansed from the possibility of contamination from unauthorized sexuality. This lesson may well have influenced Mary Sidney's version of authorship, as well. Through translating works about women who died well, she cleansed her writing from the contamination of the illicit sexuality inherent in female authorship.

The countess's decision to translate Mornay's *Discours de la vie et de la mort* sets her writing within an additional discourse which presented an opportunity for heroism more capable of enactment within the actual lives of its adherents. From the late Middle Ages, the *ars moriendi* tradition provided a means of attaining or proving spiritual worth. Numbers of Elizabethans attempted to implement its lessons in their lives by making a good death, although what was considered to be a good death depended upon which version a dying person chose to follow. Nancy Lee Beaty traces how, by the late sixteenth century, authors of *ars moriendi* tracts had rung at least three separate changes upon the original fifteenth-century source, which offered practical advice to arm dying persons against the devil's final temptations, especially the temptation to despair.[10] First, several Protestant tracts adapted a Catholic technique of meditation to inspire the dying person with the religious devotion fitting for an exemplary death. Second, and less satisfactorily, Calvinist tracts included expositions of dogma not always directly helpful to the act of dying itself; this strategy reflected the strain the *ars moriendi* tradition created within the Calvinist theology, according to which a person was already elect or damned, despite deathbed behavior.

When the countess chose to translate Mornay's *Discours de la vie et de la mort,* she was turning to a somewhat Christianized version of the third form of *ars moriendi* tract, which ignored the deathbed to focus instead on philosophical arguments persuading the reader not to fear death. Even in its most classical form, this third, humanistic version developed a Stoic view that need not have conflicted with church doctrine; for its pervasive sense of the illusory nature of worldly fortune was thoroughly present in church teachings as well. But in practice this classical perspective drastically deemphasized the personal relationship between man and God, the sense of sin, and the recognition of Christ as Redeemer that composed the cornerstones of both Catholic-influenced and Calvinist tracts on dying. Despite the introduction of a Christian emphasis in its final quarter and despite its occasional scriptural allusions scattered throughout, Mornay's tract is characterized by all of these aspects of the humanistic form of *ars moriendi.* An avid Calvinist, Mornay seems an unlikely author of a primarily humanist, as opposed to a Calvinist, tract. His *Vindiciae contra tyrannos* posits reason as a servant of faith, not as a source of belief in itself. Yet, as Diane Bornstein shows in the introduction to her edition of Mornay's discourse on death, the major portion of Mornay's work is so permeated by Stoic philosophy that when Mornay refers to

Christian immortality at the end of the work, "it almost strikes a jarring note."[11] This perception of Mornay's work as primarily Stoic in emphasis is confirmed by Mornay's addition of selections from Seneca's letters in its 1576 edition.

Increasingly, the *ars moriendi* tradition in all its rich and various forms offered itself as a source of consolation and as a means of heroism to women and men, and from the countess's time and into the seventeenth century, women as well as men were praised for dying well in tracts of widely differing theoretical bases. Twelve years before the countess's translation of Mornay, a Catholic-influenced tract included spiritual counsel addressed to "my Daughter."[12] The next year in a vehemently anti-Catholic Protestant tract, a speech to be read to the dying person by a minister or friend is suffused with references to "B.S.N.," that is, Brother, Sister, or Name."[13] Seven years after the countess's translation of Mornay, an immensely popular tract recommends itself on its title page to persons subject to unexpected deaths: mariners, soldiers, and women in childbirth.[14]

Dying well presented women with one of the few forms of heroism available to them. In fact, the countess's own mother, Mary Sidney, was publicly praised for her excellent death. No less eminent a work than Holinshed's *Chronicles*, published in 1587, recorded the noble death of the elder Mary Sidney in great detail:

> During the whole course of her sicknesse, and speciallie a little before it pleased almightie God to call her hense to his mercie, she used such godlie speeches, earnest and effectual persuasions to all those about hir, and unto such others as came of freendlie courtesie to visit hir, to exhort them to repentance and amendement of life, and dehort them from all sin and lewdness, as wounded the consciences, and inwardlie pearsed the hearts of manie that heard hir. And though before they knew hir to exceed most of hir sex in singularitie of vertue and qualitie; as good speech, apt and readie conceipt, excellence of wit, and notable eloquent deliverie (for none could match hir, and few or none come neere hir, either in the good conceipt and frame of orderlie writing, indicting, and speedie dispatching, or facilitie of gallent, sweet, delectable, and courtlie speaking; at least that in this time I my selfe have known, heard, or read of) yet in this hir last action and ending of hir life (as it were one speciallie at that instant called of God) she so farre surpassed hir selfe, in discreet, wise, effectual, sound, and grounded reasons, all tending to zeale and pietie, as the same almost amazed and as-

> tonished the hearers to heare and conceive such plentie of goodlie and pithie matters to come from such a creature. Who although for a time she seemed to the world to live obscurlie, yet she ended this life, and left the world most confidentlie, and to God (no doubt) most gloriouslie, to the exceeding comfort of all them (which are not few) that loved or honored hir, or the great and renowned house whereof she was descended.[15]

This public praise of the death of the countess's mother demonstrates the possibilities for heroism offered to women by the *ars moriendi* tradition. A woman "who seemed to the world to live obscurlie" could yet leave the world "most confidentlie, and to God (no doubt) most gloriouslie." This emphasis upon the elder Mary Sidney's "discreet, wise, effectual, sound, and grounded reasons" suggests that she may have been following the Calvinist version of *ars moriendi,* although her exhortations to onlookers to "repentance and amendement of life" may have been less dogmatic than a purely Calvinist form would admit. Whichever the exact version of *ars moriendi* the countess's mother followed, the emphasis upon her eloquence of writing and of speech, unmatched by any that the compiler had known or read of, demonstrates the way in which dying enabled the elder Mary Sidney's display of her skill with language or, even more, public recognition of a skill she had demonstrated during her lifetime. On her deathbed, her eloquence could not entice lovers or gain worldly power for her. Although her exact words were never set down, this praise creates the countess's mother as a kind of author and even a kind of preacher, whose devout sentiments pierced the hearts of all who heard her. Her mother's death, and perhaps equally important, this public recognition of her mother's eloquence in death, may well have exerted yet another formative influence upon the countess's version of authorship.

The countess's choice to translate an *ars moriendi* tract may also have been influenced by, or may have influenced, her husband, the earl of Pembroke, who was also apparently a practitioner of the art of dying well. Five years after her translation of Mornay's tract, her husband's letter of condolence to Sir Francis Hastings for the death of his brother Henry, third earl of Huntingdon, locates an actual desire for death within the countess's immediate family. The earl's letter reads like more than a usual letter of condolence; it is a small *ars moriendi* tract in its own right. His self-description is striking enough to warrant quoting the passage at length:

> In the mean time I request you to take neither that nor your brother's death more to heart than Christianity and wisdom should: for as in showing some passions we seem men and no stones, so in being too sorrowful we may show ourselves turtles and no men. You are not ignorant that three hundred days lamenting the death of Moses could not recall that mild, wise and godly duke from death: and verily were ours as long, as great and as true a sorrow (wherein I with yourself will ever bear a part) yet we cannot, or (if we love him) we should not bring him again to life, or rather to another death. Might it have pleased the giver and taker of souls to have ransomed one life with a thousand, no doubt there are no fewer in England that would have stood betwixt him and the arrow: since whose death I may truly write thus much of myself, I dream of nothing but death, I hear of nothing but death, and (were it not for others' farther good) I desire nothing but death. The departure of Sir Roger Williams did much trouble me, more the irrecoverable sickness of Sir Thomas Morgan: but never any more, or so much, as the wanting of him for this little time of my pilgrimage, with whom I hope to live ever. I mean your most honourable deceased brother, whom now we want, but hereafter shall want indeed. Thus desiring God to comfort you and us all with His holy spirit, I rest your assured loving friend.[16]

The earl's letter is structured upon an emotional contradiction. In his letter urging Hastings (and himself) not to mourn more than "Christianity and wisdom" would allow, he creates himself as a mourner *in extremis,* affected by no one's death—not Sir Robert Williams', not Sir Thomas Morgan's—as much as Huntingdon's. Since Huntingdon's death, in fact, the earl writes, "I dream of nothing but death, I hear of little but death, and (were it not for others' farther good) I desire nothing but death." And, rather than diminishing with time, their sense of loss will only increase for this friend and brother "whom now we want, but hereafter shall want indeed." These sentiments contradict Pembroke's stated purpose of urging Hastings to moderate his grief.

This contradiction may derive from several sources. The earl's "desire for nothing but death" was no doubt also affected by the severity of his own recent illness. His wish had apparently nearly been granted; for about three weeks before 24 December 1595, when this letter was written, the retainer of his brother-in-law Robert Sidney had written of the earl: "Truly I hard, that if my Lord of *Pembroke* shuld die, who is very pursife and maladife, the Tribe of *Hunsdon* doe laye Waite for the Wardship of the brave yong Lord."[17] Thus, the earl of Huntingdon's death no doubt provided a catalyst for the earl of Pembroke's reflections on his own death. In his creation of himself as mourner, the earl of Pembroke may have been, perhaps unconsciously, providing a contradictory model for how he himself would like to be mourned: intensely, as an expression of how much he was loved, yet moderately, so as not to cause grief to those he loved.

A close analogy, if not a source, for this contradiction also presents itself in the writing of Seneca. While the earl mentions Christianity, alludes to Moses, and asks for God's comfort, the consolations he offers are, for the most part, based on reason, not on Christian faith, as he explains that mourning would not bring Hastings back and that if it did, Hastings would only have to die again. Excessive mourning does not show lack of faith in God's divine plan; it shows the bereaved to be "turtles" (i.e., turtle doves) "and no men." The gender anxiety suggested by that comparison is consonant with the Senecan tradition, for in this sentiment, Pembroke is echoing the beginning of Seneca's letter of consolation to Marullus: "You are like a woman in the way you take your son's death."[18]

In his rational explanations dissuading Hastings from excessive mourning, the earl, like Seneca, displays his control over his emotions. But for this control to be impressive, the emotions themselves must be shown to be intense. Thus, the earl must also create himself as mourner, perhaps even competing with Hastings for the honor of most bereaved mourner. His letter of consolation provides a model for Hastings to follow, heroizing its author as a mourner *par excellence* who is nevertheless able, through the skillful exercise of his considerable rational faculties, to master his grief. This contradictory claim of rational detachment and intense grief becomes understandable within Stoic philosophy. A strong emotion, whether grief or rage, is a necessary precondition for the heroism of the detached Stoic, whose peaceful resignation is rendered admirable only in proportion to the emotional turmoil it negates. This contradictory aspect of Stoicism will be seen to operate within Senecan plays addressed to women, as well.

While the earl of Pembroke's letter to Henry Hastings cannot be surely classified within the Stoic branch of the *ars moriendi* tradition, its Senecan resonances suggest a shared concern with the countess of Pembroke, translator of Mornay's *Discours de la vie et de la mort*. The countess and her husband were not alone in their interest in Seneca, for in the late sixteenth century, Seneca was rapidly replacing Cicero as a primary classical influence.[19] By 1581, all of Seneca's plays had been translated into English, and his influence upon the English stage in the plays of Chapman, Marston, Shakespeare, and numerous others is indisputable.[20] Several of Seneca's nondramatic works were available in translation—*De Remediis Fortuitorum*, translated by Robert Whyttinton in 1547, and *De Beneficiis*, translated by Arthur Golding in 1578—but translations of Seneca's works were hardly necessary to aristocratic readers fluent in Latin. Perhaps more influential on the popularity of Seneca's philosophy were Continental works of Neostoicism like Lipsius's 1584 *De Constantia*, Montaigne's 1580 *Essais*, and du Vair's 1585 *La Philosophie Morale des Stoiques*.[21]

While an interest in Seneca was by no means confined to any one gender, there are indications of the felt applicability of the Stoic ideal to the situation of women in the Renaissance. By the seventeenth century, moralists had made the usefulness of Stoic philosophy to women's domestic situation explicit, but the particular appropriateness of Seneca's letters to women was apparently sensed earlier.[22] For example, a 1589 portrait of the countess of Cumberland holding the works of Seneca along with a Bible and a book of alchemy represents the centrality of the Stoic ideal to the presentation of a well-known Elizabethan woman.[23] Even the restrictive Luis Vives encouraged women to read Seneca.[24] Writings of Seneca were translated by various women, including, apparently, Queen Elizabeth.[25]

The reason for the attractiveness of Seneca to Renaissance women is not difficult to comprehend. Perhaps more than any other contemporary philosophy, Stoicism was consonant with the sexual ideology of the time. The Stoic ideal as expressed in Mornay's *Discours de la vie et de la mort* is as follows: the apparent "goods" of this life—love, wealth, fame—are illusory, for they cannot bring true satisfaction. Instead, they subject one to the destabilizing emotions of hope and fear, joy and sorrow, which attend the revolutions of the wheel of Fortune. Only by disengaging from earthly desires can one gain a sense of what is real and enduring; from this detachment one achieves the equanimity of soul to bear any misfortune, even death, without complaint. Death, in fact, provides a welcome release from the miseries of life; and the calmness with which one greets one's own death measures the extent to which one has achieved a superior understanding of the illusory nature of the pleasures of this life.

This Senecan ideal ennobled the behavior that was hoped for from women. It heroized the enforced nonparticipation of ordinary women (as opposed to queens) in the public arena; for one who understands the transitory nature of worldly events, detachment from the hustle and bustle of public affairs was to represent true wisdom. Stoicism's emphasis upon passive endurance over heroic action and its privileging of inner composure as a positive virtue provided a powerful model for heroism that was accessible to women. If they could not fight on the battlefields, if they could not administer justice in the law courts, if they could not gain properties by charming an aging queen, yet they could prove their worth, if only in their own eyes, by enduring whatever fortune sent without resistance or discontent.

This ability to endure misfortune without complaint was consonant with the passivity that had been associated with women from the time of Aristotle, who allowed women excellence in the "imperfect" or passive virtues of *continentia, verecundia,* and *tolerantia,* or chastity, modesty, and long-suffering. While the story of Eve rendered women's chastity suspect by the time of the Renaissance, women's superiority in endurance, or long-suffering, was reinforced by biblical precedent, especially in Proverbs.[26] Perhaps the most important factor contributing to Stoicism's appeal to women proceeded from its unusual structure as a discourse, in the way in which its creation of a view of the ideal man was not predicated upon his superiority to women. Unlike other Renaissance discourses, which defined the ideal man in opposition to irrational and/or sinful women, the Stoic discourse defined its hero, the sage, in opposition to the powerful, those whom Fortune raised up and cast down. Its villain was not Eve, but Alexander.[27] Predictably, Stoicism, the one text which did not strongly construct a view of women as a weak or sinful Other, became in fact the discourse which enabled the countess's writing.

Mary Sidney's *Discourse of Life and Death* was a close translation of Mornay's tract, which until its final quarter based its argument more on reason than on faith or Scripture, to move inexorably towards the conclusion that death is to be welcomed, not feared. After an introductory collection of soothing metaphors for death—the haven for the toiling mariner, the end of a weary journey, "our true home and resting place" (27)—Mornay embarks on a thorough disquisition of the ills endemic to each stage of life. A baby or small child is miserable, "neither receiving in his first yeeres any pleasure nor giving to others but annoy and displeasure" (28); as he grows, he "falleth into the subjection of some Schoolemaister" to study only with "repining" (29). As a youth, he becomes subject to the bondage of passion, which aims only to "cast him into all viciousness" (31).

While the miseries of the first stages of life were endured by aristocratic little girls as well as boys, the illusory ambitions of middle age for which Mornay saves his special fervor refer almost exclusively to male experience. Money, that "vile excrement" (34), can never content the covetous. Worldly honor repays us only with "smoke and winde," as those "great about Princes" or "commanders of Armies" (36, 37) can witness. Soldiers hazard their lives, often losing an arm or leg, for princes who do not love them. Courtiers lose their ability to command themselves through their constant flattery of the prince. If a courtier is raised to a "great height," the prince "makes it his pastime . . . to cast him downe at an instant" (38). Especially subject to the wheel of fortune, courtiers endure the envy of their inferiors at their height and then, "disroabed of their triumphall garment" (39), are known by no one. Even at their height, their pleasure is spoiled by their fear of loss and their ambition to climb yet higher. Even princes are the most miserable of men, and numerous monarchs have attested to the anxiety which attends the crown. Escape from the world provides no respite. The world follows us even into the desert, and if it does not, "we finde greater civill warre within our selves" (50). Even learning is an empty vexation of the spirit leading to no self-knowledge, for it brings "on the minde an endlesse labour, but no contentment" (54), failing to pacify "the debates a man feeles in himselfe" (54). The only stage easily applicable to ordinary women is old age, which gathers in only the "plentifull harvest of all such vices as in the whole course of their life, hath held and possessed them" (55). Death provides a welcome release.

Despite occasional references to Lot and Solomon, this first three-quarters of Mornay's tract is essentially secular. His Senecan approach is so strong that the Christian hope for heaven is temporarily forgotten: "Tell mee, what is it else to bee dead, but to bee no more living in the worlde? Absolutelie and simplie not to bee in the worlde, is it anie paine?" (60–61). The classical orientation of most of his argument becomes explicit in Mornay's introduction to the final, Christian fourth of his tract: "But unto us brought up in a more holy schoole, death is a farre other thing: neither neede we as the Pagans of consolations against death" (62). Christians who have faith in God need not fear death. We should neither seek death (for that is cowardice) nor flee it (for that is childish). Through death, God will provide us "true quietnesse" and "pleasures whiche shall never more perish" (72). We must "die to live" and "live to die." This Christian ending did not substantially alter Mornay's perception of this work as imbued with Stoic philosophy, for he issued the work in 1576 with selections from Seneca's letters, which were later appended to an edition of Mary Sidney's translation in 1606. In his preface to Seneca's selected letters, Mornay explains his use of Seneca's views: Seneca arrived at a perception of "le vanite de l'homme . . . seulement avec son jugement natural et quelque connoissance et experience."[28] Christians, then, should be all the more able to attain the same knowledge and resignation to God's will.

Mornay's treatise applied the Stoic ideal primarily to the life course led by men, not by women. Sheltered at home, aristocratic young Englishwomen seldom had the opportunity to be cast into any dramatic, immediately recognizable forms of viciousness by their passion. More strikingly, few women had the chance to experience the emptiness of being "great about Princes" or commanding armies. While they could enjoy the fruits of the wealth of their fathers and husbands, women did not, as a whole, have the opportunity personally to strive in the world, attempting to climb higher, becoming ever more thirsty for worldly honors. Instead, their rise or fall depended for the most part upon the rise or fall of their close male relatives. While dying to live and living to die would seem to represent a goal women could attempt to reach, the specific application of Mornay's Senecan philosophy to the lives of women was yet to be made.

Strong evidence suggests the the countess's translation of Garnier's *Marc Antoine,* with its heroic portrait of a female protagonist, Cleopatra, is an attempt to apply Mornay's philosophy to the situation of Renaissance women. First, the translations of Mornay's treatise and Garnier's play were probably intended as a pair, for they were published in the same volume. Secondly, the content of the two works is strikingly similar. The chorus of act 1 of *Antonie,* for example, reads like a versified *Discourse of Life and Death.*

Nature made us not free
When first she made us live:
When we began to be,
To be began our woe:
Which growing evermore
As dying life dooth growe,
Do more and more us greeve,
And trie us more and more.[29]

The chorus to act 3 recites a virtual paean to death:

Death rather healthfull succor gives,
Death rather all mishapps relieves,

> That life upon us throweth:
> And ever to us doth unclose
> The doore whereby from curelesse woes
> Our wearie soule out goeth.
> What Goddesse else more milde then she
> To burie all our paine can be,
> What remedie more pleasing?
>
> (L3v)

But it is the central figure of Cleopatra herself who most prominently employs Stoicism in her heroics of constancy. From Antony's opening speech, the suspense of the play revolves around whether or not Cleopatra will betray him to Caesar to save her own kingdom and her life. Much of the middle of the play consists of debates between Cleopatra's followers, who attempt to dissuade her from her decision to die, and Cleopatra, whose contempt for life and desire for death would impress any Stoic philosopher. The play ends with Cleopatra's ringing resolution to die as soon as she has performed the proper obsequies for Antony's corpse. In her absolute rejection of the possibility of saving her life and perhaps her crown by living subject to Caesar, Cleopatra attains the stature of a constant heroine in her insistence on death.

Cleopatra's desire to die for love would not have been endorsed by Seneca or Mornay. Neither writer makes any distinction between mature love and the "tyrannical passion" felt at the height of youth. An Elizabethan explication of Seneca asserts that love is madness, although not as severe a madness as the lust for riches.[30] Love, according to Seneca, is one of those passions that bind a human to Fortune's wheel; emotional dependence on another person's affections prevents the attainment of complete calm. For Cleopatra, however, love is the agency through which she rises above the caprices of Fortune, as she declaims to the absent Antony:

> And didst thou then suppose my royall hart
> Had hatcht, thee to ensnare, a faithles love?
> And changing minde, as Fortune change cheare?
>
> (G4v)

For Cleopatra, the prospect of loyalty to a defeated Antony, even a dead Antony, outweighs her realm, her children, her own life. And it is her love for Antony, not just her ability to face death, that motivates her bravery. Far from a beastly passion, this love is an integral part of her humanity, as she exclaims to one of her women: "Without this love I should be inhumaine" (H5).

Cleopatra's renunciation of her ability to protect the interests of her children and her realm as well as her own life understandably displeases her fellow Egyptians; and much of the central portion of *Antonie* is composed of their attempts to dissuade her. Her exchange with Charmion is typical:

> CHARMION: Live for your sonnes.
> CLEOPATRA: Nay for their father die.
> CHARMION: Hardhearted mother!
> CLEOPATRA: Wife kindhearted I.
> (H5)

Diomede soliloquizes his wish that the queen would cease mourning and charm Caesar to gain back her crown, saving them all from disaster. But despite the wishes of her followers and despite Antony's suspicions that she will betray him, Cleopatra never wavers in her resolve. As the curtain falls, she bends weeping over Antony's corpse, her own suicide delayed only until she can give Antony his "due rites."

Cleopatra's determination to die provides two means through which ordinary women could demonstrate their heroism. Cleopatra's loyalty to the defeated Antony heroizes the domestic virtue of a wife's loyalty to her husband despite the vicissitudes of fortune. Representing this usually passive attribute as heroic ennobles a wifely response perhaps often taken for granted. Second, just as the countess's mother compensated, according to Holinshed, for the obscurity of her life with a noteworthy death, any woman could die well. But there is a difference between Cleopatra's orientation towards death and that of the elder Mary Sidney. Holinshed represented the elder Mary Sidney's speeches as demonstrating Christian virtues, as she exhorted those standing around her deathbed to "repentance and amendement of life," persuading them "from all sin and lewdness" and proving herself a virtuous Christian in much the same manner as a man would do. In contrast, Cleopatra combines the attributes of Stoic and wife. By defining herself in terms of her relationship with a man, Cleopatra represents a specifically female deviation from the Stoic ideal as it applied to men, who died declaiming philosophical, political, or moral sentiments, not their love for their wives.

Repeatedly calling Antony "husband," Cleopatra is portrayed as a faithful wife instead of the adulteress of legend. The absence of any hint of illicit sexuality or even of Egyptian sensuality suggests the way in which Cleopatra's willingness to die cleanses her from sexual taint. Her overtly sexual lines are delivered only over Antony's dead body. These lines, which conclude the play, represent her wished-for death as an erotic act:

> A thousand kisses, thousand thousand more
> Let you my mouth for honors farewell give;
> That in this office weake my limmes may growe,
> Fainting on you, and fourth my soule may flowe.
> (O2v)

This eroticization of death was hardly novel in a period when "to die" signified the act of intercourse. Yet the confinement of Cleopatra's sexual impulses to an expression of desire for death represents a striking deviation from the conventional representation of this exotic queen of the fertile Nile.

This unusual suppression of Cleopatra's sexual nature suggests insights into the way in which the resolve to die cleanses a heroine of sexual taint. The intent to die well apparently cannot coexist with a desire for sexual love in one woman character. These two kinds of woman protagonists—the ascetic, loyal heroine who proves her heroism through her resolution to die and the alluring, seductive heroine who demonstrates her sexual power through attracting men with her abundant charms—are not combined until the stunning death scene of Shakespeare's Cleopatra. Quite possibly these diers and seducers are polarized because of their represented differences in their control over their emotions. It would seem that, in theory, a dying woman who can control her fear of death can also be expected to control her sexual appetites; a woman who cannot control her sexual appetites cannot be expected to control her fear of death. Yet whether they make love to them or die for them, both kinds of female protagonists define themselves in terms of their love for their men.

A sequel to Mary Sidney's *Antonie,* Samuel Daniel's *Tragedie of Cleopatra* (1594), confirms the refashioning of Cleopatra as a constant heroine. According to its dedication to the countess of Pembroke, Daniel's play was written to complete the plot line begun in the countess's translation. In an amusing personification of the plays, Daniel represents his play's wifely submission to the countess's *Antonie,* claiming that he would have continued to write sonnets had not the "well grac'd *Anthony,* / Requir'd his *Cleopatra's* company." In fact, Daniel's play was explicitly written at the countess's request; it was "the worke the which she did impose . . . who onely doth predominate my Muse."[31] For this reason, his portrayal of Cleopatra as the incarnation of the most elevated form of Stoicism[32] seems to develop Mary Sidney's perception of Cleopatra in her own translation, and Daniel's play in some sense completes her attempt to create the constant heroine from the materials of Stoic philosophy and romantic love literature.

Daniel's contribution to the countess's project to fashion a constant heroine becomes most visible in his addition of an interchange between two philosophers. This passage, which has no parallel in other treatments of the subject, connects Cleopatra's heroic resolve to die to abstract philosophies which are supposed to reconcile adherents to their deaths. Almost certainly pointing to Mary Sidney's translation of Mornay's tract, Daniel portrays two philosophers who, unlike Cleopatra, bewail their cowardly inability to conquer their fear of death despite their learning:

> And yet what blasts of words hath Learning found
> To blow against the feare of death and dying?
> What comforts unsicke eloquence can sound,
> And yet all failes us in the point of trying.
>
> . . . .
>
> For when this life, pale Feare and Terrour boords,
> Where are our precepts then, where is our arte?[33]

In this passage Cleopatra is represented as capable of embodying what even learned philosophers could not: the highest Stoic principles as adumbrated in learned tracts reasoning against the fear of death. The probable reference to the countess's translation of just such a tract by Daniel's addition provides further reason to perceive Cleopatra's form of heroism as an application of the perspective on death expressed in Mornay's treatise to the situation of women.

While Cleopatra only resolves to die in the *Antonie,* she actually accomplishes her death in Daniel's *Tragedie of Cleopatra.* With Antony already dead, Daniel's foregrounds an issue implicit in the countess's version. In Cleopatra's heroic resolution to die, she not only proves her love for Antony; she also thwarts Caesar. In contrast to Garnier's *Marc Antoine,* Daniel's play stresses Cleopatra's triumph over Caesar even more than her loyal love. As Cleopatra applies the asps to her body, for example, her long speech barely mentions Antony until the last lines; even then he is almost subordinate to Caesar in her thoughts:

> Witnesse my soule partes free to *Antony,*
> And now prowde Tyrant *Caesar* do thy worst.
> (5.1608–9)

At the moment of her death, serene and heroic, her focus is on her resistance to Caesar's will:

> And in that cheere th' impression of a smile,
> Did seeme to shew she scorned Death and *Caesar,*
> As glorying that she could them both beguile,
> And telling Death how much her death did please her.
> (1626–29)

In Daniel's version of the story, then, Cleopatra not only proves her Stoic disregard for death and establishes her identity as true wife; she also demonstrates her freedom from male tyranny as represented by Caesar. This pointed refusal to subject herself to Caesar, implicit in the countess's translation and explicit in Daniel's play, suggests that underlying Cleopatra's heroism is a resentment of male domination.

Cleopatra's defiance of Caesar reveals an expression of anger behind the mask of resigned endurance and perhaps suggests a function of this mask for women in the Renaissance.[34] Pertinent to Cleopatra's heroics of constancy is Gordon Braden's recent analysis of the way in which Stoicism from its inception depended upon an intense emotion over which the sage could exert rational control. The earl of Pembroke's letter of condolence to Henry Hastings heroized his control over his emotions by, paradoxically, demonstrating the intensity of his grief. For Braden, the emotion most frequently radiating from the hot core of Stoic detachment was not grief, but "the most paralytic kind of anger." Convincingly bridging the chasm between Seneca's quietistic philosophy and the grotesque violence of his plays, Braden shows how the "inner passion which bursts upon and desolates an unexpecting and largely uncomprehending world" in Seneca's plays formed the precondition for the achieved calm of the Stoic sage.[35] Rather than directing his urge for power outward like the Senecan avenger, the Stoic sage directs his competitiveness inward, achieving his victory over himself, rather than over the external world. Not a philosophy of political resistance, Stoicism directed the sage's will against his own urges, not against authority. The ultimate assertion of control over the self was expressed in his suicide.

If Braden's model is applicable to Mary Sidney's translations, what were the violent emotions underlying her interest in the daunting self-control of her constant heroine? Was she attempting to deal with an intense grief over the deaths of her brother Philip and other family members? What are the implications of Daniel's emphasis upon Cleopatra's defiance of Caesar in his continuation of the countess's translation? Was this focus solely Daniel's contribution, or was he influenced by an understanding of the countess's psychological needs? Was the countess also angry at a form of temporal authority—her husband, perhaps, or, more generally, cultural restrictions of some sort? Mary Sidney's biography provides few clues. Although she married a man considerably older than herself, there are no significant rumors of unhappiness in the match. Her project to create a constant heroine may have derived some of its impulse from a general situation common to Renaissance women, rather than a personal need of her own.

Daniel's dedication of "A Letter from Octavia to Marcus Antonius" to the countess of Cumberland in 1599 suggests the applicability of the angry model of Stoicism to at least one Renaissance woman. Rewriting the Antony and Cleopatra story from the viewpoint of the jilted Octavia, this passionate letter minces no words about the sexual nature of Cleopatra, that "incestuous Queene, / the staine of Aegypte, and the shame of Rome" (stanza 2, lines 2–3), that "delitious Dame . . . royall Concubine and Queene of lust," as Octavia pleads with Antony to leave off his unseemly dalliance and to return to the arms of his "wronged wife *Octavia*" (stanza 1, line 3).[36] While the wording of Daniel's dedication remained discreet, the parallel between Octavia's situation and that of the countess of Cumberland's must have been patently apparent to anyone who knew her. Like Octavia, the countess remained at home while her dashing husband engaged in numerous sexual liaisons at court and elsewhere, eventually causing their separation.[37] Daniel's dedicated letter may well have traced a self the countess of Cumberland had already articulated, for it was she who had had her portrait painted holding a copy of the works of Seneca in 1589.[38]

Daniel's epistle to Margaret, countess of Cumberland, published in 1603, is more detailed in its delineation of the countess of Cumberland as a constant heroine. Daniel portrays his "Countess" as under seige, enclosed within the "region" of her self, where she requires the protection of the "brasen walles" of her "cleere conscience" from the workings of malice:

> That whatsoever here befalles
> You in the region of your selfe remaine;
> Where no vaine breath of th'impudent molests,
> That hath secur'd within the brasen walles
> Of a cleere conscience, that without all staine
> Rises in peace, in innocencie rests;
> Whilst all what malice from without procures,
> Shewes her owne ougly heart, but hurts not yours.[39]

Daniel's model of the heroism of the "countess of Cumberland"[40] depends upon the strength of her anger. Without strong beseiging forces, her victorious defense of her "region" of her self would not be remarkable. Without the threat of "staine," her preservation of her "cleere conscience" would not be admirable. Her forceful exclusion of any normal angry response to malice from the walls of her city in order to enjoy the peace of innocence suggests the powerful centrality of her anger, the impossibility of psychological peace, except by a mapping of the self that divides rather than integrates its territories, pitting them in conflict against each other. His character's imagined enclosure of herself has, in Braden's terms, created a "zone" in which she knows "no contradiction," an area in which she can exert absolute power and control.[41] But the very need to create this zone reflects Daniel's sense of her powerlessness over the forces of a hostile world as well as over the chaos he imagines raging within her.

Daniel's epistle and his dedication of "A Letter from Octavia to Marcus Antonius" to the countess of Cumberland were perhaps influenced by Samuel Brandon's version of the Cleopatra story, *The vertuous Octavia* (1598), itself no doubt influenced by Daniel's *Tragedie of Cleopatra* (1594).[42] Brandon's play confirms the applicability of the heroics of constancy to Renaissance women angered by the indignities they received from their philandering husbands. Its final lines, in fact, present Octavia as a model for its readers, presumably especially its female readers, to follow:

> But those that know not, let them learn in me:
> That vertuous minds can never wretched be.
> (5.1846–47)

This creation of a heroics of constancy capable of being played out in actual women's lives may well have been influenced not only by Daniel's play but also by Mary Sidney's translations, for Brandon's play was dedicated to Lucia Audelay, the mother of one of the countess's closest aristocratic neighborhors, Mary Thinne, mistress of the estate of Longleat, only a few miles from Wilton House in Wiltshire.[43]

Like Daniel's "countess of Cumberland," Brandon's Octavia has moved the site of conflict from the outside world into her own psyche. Unlike Daniel's "countess," Octavia engages in active warfare rather than passive retreat as, fearing psychic extinction, she enlists the aid of virtue to arm her soul before her upcoming battle against her emotions:

> O vertue, thou that didst my good assure,
> Arme now my soule against proude fortunes might:
> Without thy succor I may not endure,
> But this strong tempest will destroy me quite.
> (2.1.682–85)

She finally wins. Despite the sad state of Octavia's marriage at the end of the play, its triumphant presentation of her successful struggle to keep a "vertuous minde" types the play as more comic than tragic. Shunned by her husband, enduring every affront he can offer, Octavia appears to glory in the strength of mind with which she greets her husband's final cruel demand, that she leave his house:

> True fortitude doth in my soul abound,
> My honor scornes the height of fortunes pride.
> The worst that can befall me is but death:
> And O how sweete is his lives sacrifize,
> On vertues altar that expires his breath.
> (5.1836–40)

Despite Octavia's claim throughout the play that her love for Antony remains undiminished, a bitter subtext of anger is not difficult to discern in her scornful honor, in her fantasy of death. Her annihilation of her anger results in her imagined annihilation of her self as, like a true Stoic, Octavia asserts her absolute control over her soul in her yearning for death. The aptly titled "vertuous Octavia" now fantasizes her sacrifice for the cause of the very virtue for which she is named. Once arming her against her interior armies, her "vertue" now provides the location of her glorious capitulation, the altar upon which she yearns to be sacrificed. Despite the symptomatic shifts to the masculine pronoun, revealing the culture's construction of all heroism as being in some sense masculine, the passivity of Octavia's imagined sacrifice upon an altar fulfills a compliant female role, the appropriate culmination of her denial of anger. She effaces her current emotional needs to displace them into a desire for death, for in death her heroism can be safely and fully acknowledged. Brandon's *The vertuous Octavia* presents, as perhaps a better play would not dare, the pathology from which the heroics of constancy drew its strength.

Mary Sidney's translation of Petrarch's *Triumph of Death,* which she was working on in 1599 but never published, provides another powerful model for female self-effacement. Petrarch's prominent placement of Laura among a troop of women whose chastity has just won a victory over love inserts Laura securely in the tradition of women like Lucrece who were willing to sacrifice their lives for their chastity. While Laura does not actively choose death, her brave anticipation of the news of its arrival demonstrates her sexual purity in much the same way as this often-cited female suicide. Her resignation probably provided a more usable model for Renaissance women readers than the willed deaths of other heroines held up to young Elizabethan girls for imitation.

Like Cleopatra and the other constant heroines, Laura defines herself even in death in terms of her relationship with a man, as she tempers her welcome of death with regret for the sorrow it will bring the poet:

> This charge of woe on others will recoyle,
> I know, whose safetie on my life depends:
> For me, I thank who shall me hense assoile.[44]

The passivity of Laura's death, surpassing even the sacrifice fantasy of Brandon's Octavia, represents a striking departure from the *ars moriendi* tradition. While after her death Laura admits that "the crosse / Preceeding death, extreemlie martireth" (2.46, 47), her death scene, "deservedly famous for its serene beauty,"[45] conveys no sense of her physicality or of her pain. She fades like a flame; her whiteness resembles snow. Taking no active role, neither exhorting her friends to repentance as did the countess's mother, nor engaging in Cleopatra's lengthy internal debates, Laura gains admiration through her beauty:

> Right lyke unto som lamp of cleerest light,
>   Little and little wanting nutriture,

Houlding to end a never-changing plight.
Pale? no, but whitelie; and more whitelie pure,
Then snow on wyndless hill, that flaking falles:
As one, whom labor did to rest allure.
And when that heavenlie guest those mortall walles
Had leaft: it nought but sweetlie sleeping was
In hir faire eyes: what follie dying calles
Death faire did seeme to be in hir faire face.
(1.163–72)

In the *Triumph of Death,* "making a good death" has been radically revised. The scene of Laura's death demonstrates not her religious fervor, not her detachment from the illusory pleasures of the world, but her beauty. Laura's beauty is in fact best displayed in death, in its affirmation of her recumbant passivity, of her ethereal insubstantiality, of the absolute erasure of her person. All of these had already occurred in the *Canzonière,* in which she had always represented an externality, a projected fiction by which the male poet measured his fame, his work, his ontology.[46] While the depiction of Laura in *Triumph of Death* was perfectly understandable according to the artistic goals of Petrarch, who was not writing an *ars moriendi* poem or even a biographical statement about Laura, the countess's apparent acceptance of Petrarch's perspective implied in her choice to translate this *Triumph* is disturbing.

Perhaps the representation of Laura functions less as a model for dying well than, like the versions of Octavia, a model for living heroically. Her example shows how any woman can fulfill the function of spiritual guide, molding her words and actions to benefit her man on his pilgrimage to heaven. Returning to the poet as a spirit after her death, Laura exposes the elaborate fiction she had created to mold his behavior, encouraging him when he despaired, appearing angry with him when his suit became too hot, all out of her loving concern for his spiritual health:

A thousand times wrath in my face did flame,
My heart meane-time with love did inlie burne,
But never will, my reason overcame.
(2.100–102)

Laura's modulation of her display of emotion to respond to the poet's needs rather than to her own feelings demonstrates a control of her passions far exceeding the poet's. Ironically, she reverses the pattern presented by Octavia. Laura controls her love to make it appear as anger, rather than controlling her anger to emerge victoriously loving. But the principle remains the same. Laura, like the Stoic heroines, creates her heroism through the absolute mastery of her feelings. Yet this mastery represents a form of self-erasure, for her inner drama is determined solely by the needs of the poet. While the idealized and insubstantial character of Laura herself does not admit ambiguity, her model for heroism represents the same mixture of anger and love, the same self-effacement disguised as self-mastery, as that offered by the constant heroines.

The art of dying emerging from the countess of Pembroke's translations bears varied fruits; its roots reach deeply into several substrata of soil. Most immediately, her intellectual and accomplished family provided fertile topsoil for her creation of the Stoic heroine. Written up by an eminent historian, her mother achieved an excellent death; writing a somewhat Senecan letter of condolence, her husband revealed a more Stoic preoccupation with death; her brother influenced her or, perhaps even more generously, let himself be subject to her influence when he created the princesses as constant heroines in the captivity episode of the *New Arcadia.* In addition to her family, Mary Sidney was no doubt also influenced by wider cultural trends, by the popularity of the *ars moriendi* tradition, by the Senecan revival, and by the numerous Christian Stoic sages making good and even learned deaths at the end of the sixteenth century. Beneath these lay the barren clay of the sexual ideology of the Renaissance, according to which she twisted both *ars moriendi* and Stoicism to create heroines who not only perceived themselves in terms of their men, but who also demonstrated their willingness to annihilate their inner selves by effacing their anger.

Perhaps the deepest influence on Mary Sidney's translations was a fundamental need to find a form of heroism applicable for her time and gender. Her translations held up mirrors in which Renaissance women could be perceived as heroic. Cleopatra's constancy to Antony exalts the domestic virtue of a wife's loyalty to her husband despite the turnings of the wheel of Fortune. Through this representation of Cleopatra, women could view themselves, in their simultaneous love for and anger at their husbands, as worthy protagonists in the drama of their own lives. Through Laura, women could perceive themselves as spiritual authorities, bearing upon their virtuous shoulders the responsibility for their husbands' immortal souls. If women could not win public admiration for remarkable deeds in the outside world, they could at least attain dignity in their own eyes as constant heroines, giving of themselves, submerging their rage and sorrow beneath the smooth surface of equanimity. And when the time came, they all had the opportunity to die gracefully.

Both Cleopatra and Laura are, finally, models of negation. Each model defines women as important solely in terms of their relationships with men, even in the most private and solitary act of death. Militant images of self-aggression and self-enclosure characterizing the adaptations of the constant heroine by authors connected with the countess of Pembroke reveal the destructive potential of this means of channeling rage. These negative aspects of the constant heroine remind us that the Countess was a translator, not an author in her own right. In both the literal and the broad sense, she translated a male perspective on women. The Cleopatra of the *Antonie* is the creation of Robert Garnier; Laura is the creation of Petrarch. Both of these female heroines bear striking resemblances to Lucrece, Portia, Iphigenia, and the other women who "died well" to prove their sexual purity to a patriarchal culture.[47]

We should not be too quick to criticize Mary Sidney for the disturbing implications of her constant heroines. There were few alternatives. The Renaissance offered women few healthy models for encouraging the expression of justified rage or for acknowledging the heroism of their ordinary lives as they bore with husbands whose marital infidelities were so generally condoned within the culture that these infidelities could not even be effectively protested. The countess made good use of her limited material to enable not only her writing, but even more astonishingly, her publication of her translations. A woman's publication of her work without apology or subterfuge was extremely rare in the Renaissance. Unlike the learned Anne Bacon, the countess did not first submit her translation to the discerning eye of male authority.[48] No sympathetic friend obliged her by "betraying" her work to the press. She presented her work to the world in her own person, even marking the date and place of completion at the end. The countess of Pembroke's publication of her translations presents a model if not of heroism, then at least of courageous intellectual assertion that was made possible by her creation of these Stoic heroines, from whose very self-effacement and beautiful deaths she created a viable version of authorship.

Chapter 4

The Heroics of Constancy in Mary Wroth's *Countess of Montgomery's Urania*

Especially when contrasted with the countess of Pembroke's association of authorship with the art of dying, Mary Wroth's composition of the first romance written in English by a woman appears remarkably unresponsive to the pressures exerted against women's writing in the Renaissance. An original work rather than a translation, *The Countess of Montgomery's Urania* runs to almost 590,000 words in its two sections: a folio printed, with or without Wroth's consent, in 1621 and suppressed shortly thereafter, and a shorter manuscript in Wroth's holograph existing in a single copy now in the collections of the Newberry Library.[1] The sheer volume of this published and unpublished writing demonstrates that Wroth's work represented a determined effort carried out over a period of time. Moreover, rather than denying the sexuality possible to women's authorship, Wroth, through various allusions in this romance, capitalizes upon scandalous events of her own life, especially in the plot centered on the work's primary heroine, the "all loving" Pamphilia, readily recognized by contemporaries as referring in some sense to Wroth herself.[2] Wroth's creation of herself as author was inextricably bound up with her creation of herself as lover. Far from deflecting accusations of sexuality, Wroth's romance heroizes women who love; and expressions of permissible female sexuality are not always confined to the marriage bed.

Wroth's version of authorship was not only explicitly sexual; it was also implicitly angry. Far from soothing anxieties about the power of female speech over an audience, Wroth's overt allusions to contemporary scandals at court incurred the antagonism of powerful figures, including King James himself.[3] The possibility that a very real anger motivated various episodes of topicality, however she may have denied her intent to others or even to herself, cannot be easily dismissed. Moreover, the angry model of female Stoicism which Samuel Daniel offered the countess of Cumberland receives full expansion in Wroth's characterization of Pamphilia. Pamphilia's constancy to Amphilanthus makes of Wroth's romance an angry text; for to induce the rage Pamphilia successfully conquers, the narrative must detail Amphilanthus's infidelities. These descriptions of Amphilanthus's wavering loyalties create an accusatory topicality at least potentially embarrassing to Amphilanthus's real-life referent (probably William Herbert).[4] This model of female heroism is refracted numerous times through the narratives of other heroines. Demonstrating their worth through their psychological victories over their own rage, these women define a heroics of constancy predicated upon the intensity of their anger, without which such victories would scarcely be impressive. Yet their constancy cannot remain absolute, or they would remain silent. The narratives through which Pamphilia and others finally, after repeated provocations, relate their wrongs creates anger as a central motive of authorship.

Surveying Wroth's Vast Romance

This chapter will inevitably stress (pseudo-)autobiographical connections within *Urania,* especially those which shed light upon conditions of authorship and the related heroics of constancy. By focussing on episodes involving women authors, I will foreground circumstances granting women license to speak or write. By focussing on episodes involving constant lovers, I will foreground the anger implicit in the heroics of constancy. But to select these issues is to ignore others, and the very attempt to articulate a stable viewpoint runs counter to the shifting movement of Wroth's vast romance, which denies any hegemony of position. For example, while I stress the heroism of constancy practiced by her women characters, this form of heroism is eloquently criticized by Urania herself. While I note that Urania argues "against her minde" to save Pamphilia's life, nevertheless these criticisms are still voiced within the text. And the pessimistic perspective of Pamphilia and even of the narrator concerning male constancy is itself belied by many contentedly constant husbands in this romance. A brief survey of *The Countess of Montgomery's Urania,* with special attention to its complex and open-ended structure, is necessary to offset these inevitable distortions.[5]

The rejection of singleness of perspective or unity of form is essential to the aesthetics organizing, or refusing to organize, *Urania.* Rejecting stability of viewpoint, Wroth has written a romance which, like its characters, is buffeted about by a sea as wavering and unpredictable as human desire. Like the destination of the despairing Amphilanthus, who throws himself on a boat bound for anywhere (MS I, 34Ar), the placement of its events often seems arbitrary. With its often abrupt transitions ("But now it is time to leave these affaires to *Mars*, and let his Mistris have her part," LL4v), it frequently arrives, like its characters, by shipwreck. Thus, readers of this chapter may find themselves at times startled by unexpected events or puzzled by suddenly introduced characters; this experience reproduces the sensation of reading Wroth's romance itself, enriched by scores of plots and hundreds of characters, some of whom reappear numerous times and some of whom do not.

While there is no clear pattern to the romance's wealth of untidy details, *Urania* is loosely structured upon at least three open-ended devices: a series of enchantments, the relationship between Pamphilia and Amphilanthus, and the multiple refractions of events and issues encountered by Pamphilia through dozens of other plots and characters. Prominent among the enchantments are these: the magical imprisonment of various female protagonists within the Towers of Desire, Love, and Constancy, to be resolved upon the entrance of the "valientest Knight and loyallest Lady" (F4v) into the tower of constancy; the enchantment of the Rocky Island, during which Pamphilia and others are imprisoned in a theater where they imagine they see their loves until they are freed by the entrance of "the man most loving and most beloved" and "the sweetest and loveliest creature, that poore habits had disguised greatnesse in" (RR4v); the apparent disappearance of Amphilanthus into the "hell of deceit," where Pamphilia sees jilted mistresses poised to raze her name from his exposed heart (QQQ2v); and the search for the lost children of Urania and others, who embark upon a ship for Naples only to be conveyed to the Inaccessible Rock (MS I, 22Br). All of these require the efforts of communities of characters, many of whom encounter their own adventures in the process. Unlike the oracle structuring Sidney's *Countess of Pembroke's Arcadia (The Old Arcadia)*, these enchantments impose no necessary conclusion to Wroth's romance, for another rescue, another spell, always lies just beyond the narrative's horizon.

Moving in and out of these enchantments, the relationship between the constant Pamphilia and the fickle Amphilanthus constitutes a second element overarching much of Wroth's romance. A fuller detailing of the oscillations of their prolonged association appears in the Appendix. In brief, however, their relationship may be summarized in this way: Amphilanthus leaves his previously beloved

Antissia for Pamphilia, only to become distracted by Musalina while Pamphilia is enclosed in the theater of the Rocky Island. Feeling remorse, he pledges his love to Pamphilia again until they are separated during a hunt; here Pamphilia sees a vision of Amphilanthus in the "hell of deceit." Reunited again, Amphilanthus and Pamphilia are married in a contract which is not yet legally binding. Later, falsely informed that Pamphilia has married while he was off on an adventure, Amphilanthus marries the princess of Slavonia but does not consummate the union. He discovers his mistake in time to attend the marriage of the king of Tartaria and the sad Pamphilia. While the king is off on a trip, Pamphilia and Amphilanthus acknowledge their love for each other with a passionate kiss. They travel together to the court of the king of Tartaria, where they reside happily and relatively chastely with the king as well as Pamphilia's friend Urania and her husband.

In the last pages, the romance suddenly inserts the events of Wroth's own marriage, ended by the death of her husband followed soon after by the death of her only son, with the apparent death of the king of Tartaria, which leaves Pamphilia as the mother of a boy who also soon dies. Here the text becomes inconsistent. When Pamphilia returns to her native country with Amphilanthus, the king of Tartaria is inexplicably present on shipboard. As with the enchantments, there is no necessary conclusion to this plot. Marriages to other partners do not seem to have any effect on the love between Pamphilia and Amphilanthus, and the possibility that the narrative may be continued by Amphilanthus's being tempted by yet another pretty face can never be safely discounted.

To foreground the relationship between Pamphilia and Amphilanthus is, of course, to neglect others. The friendship between Pamphilia and the title character Urania, whose somewhat less complicated story is also included in the Appendix below, remains constant through much of the romance. Some major events of Pamphilia's life also occur to Bellamira and Lindamira, two other women characters who also appear to represent versions of Wroth. The difficulties confronting Pamphilia are by no means limited to self-reflexive characters: they are refracted through sometimes dozens of plots and scores of characters. These refractions form another open-ended structuring device, for one set of circumstances gradually gives way to another set of circumstances. Various narratives about women married against their will gradually yield to narratives about the happiness of second loves, which gradually yield to narratives about sad constant heroines whose beloveds leave them for yet a second time.

The strewing of the issues and even the facts of Wroth's life over a vast panorama creates not only a loose structure for the romance, but also a socioliterary context transcending any personal biography. Near the beginning of the folio, the several accounts of a woman with a beloved who is married to a man against her will provide a good example of the way Wroth's romance includes but moves beyond her biography to reflect upon the place of a lover, sometimes chaste and sometimes not, within an arranged marriage from a variety of viewpoints. By heroizing the loyalty of the character Limena to her lover Perissus after her marriage to the jealous Philargus, the first story presents a poignant critique of arranged marriage. A monitory message to aristocratic parents can be read in the self-recriminations of Limena's mother, who dies of grief for her participation in the marriage negotiations when it appears that the cruel Philargus has murdered her daughter. Limena's final union with Perissus, blessed by the dying Philargus himself, validates her constancy to her beloved. After many variations of this situation, this issue more or less expends itself in the history of a fishing maid, who reconciles herself to an undesired marriage by ruling her affections so strictly that even her husband cannot object to her chaste enjoyment of her beloved. Through this range and sheer number of narratives, Wroth's romance not only resists closure; it also constructs this problem attending arranged marriages as societal, not merely individual. This issue, arising in part from the life of Wroth and of unknown others whose marital secrets she betrayed to paper, no doubt reflects the multiplicity of ways aristocratic couples coped with arranged marriages in Jacobean England.

If there is a viewpoint emerging as central to the folio, it is a preoccupation with love, be it for spouse or for beloved, as a means of defining the self. The desire of male and female characters alike to find, keep, or lament a love partner controls many of the plots. The manuscript continuation, while detailing the marriage of Pamphilia to the king of Tartaria and their subsequent friendship with Amphilanthus, increasingly moves away from affairs of the heart to brave deeds by noble knights: battles with giants and griffins, mysterious gifts of magic swords, and other stuff of chivalric romance. Emerging as a special preoccupation, however, is the recovery and identification of lost children. One major episode on this theme is the rescue of the royal offspring of the folio's protagonists from the Inaccessible Rock, involving several heroes over hundreds of pages. In addition, the first episode in the manuscript includes a mysterious account of a ten-year-old or five-year-old boy (five on MS I, Br; changed to ten on MS I, Bv) and his infant sister, raised far from their parents in secrecy under the protection of the wise sage Melissea. The description of them as "the bestborne princes of the Easte, butt nott as yett to bee knowne" (MS I, 2Ar) implies that their obscurity is temporary. Years later, their parentage becomes apparent in the revered Parselius's immediate love for them and in his recognition of his face in the girl's and of his wife's face in the boy's (MS II, 5Ar). An astonishing number of the offspring of the folio's protagonists are transported from their parents by mysterious or nefarious means, only to turn up later as attractive and competent youths. The most prominent of these is called "Faire Designe" after the cipher on his garments; the intensity of Amphilanthus's instinctive love strongly implies his paternity.

While the manuscript continuation contains few explicit examples of self-referentiality, Wroth's experience of motherhood may be reflected in the combination of physical distance and continued concern which characterizes parental relationships in the manuscript portion. She herself experienced absence from her own illegitimate son and probably from an illegitimate daughter as well. In an apparent reference to living arrangements for her son in 1615, her father Robert Sidney approved his wife's "putting Wil away, for it had bin to greate a shame he should have stayde in the hous."[6] Yet this shame by no means curtailed her family's commitment to her son, for in 1640, through "my Lord of Pembroke's good mediation," the king granted Wroth's son "a brave living in Ireland."[7] Perhaps as an expression of its author's wish, the manuscript continuation erases the stigma of illegitimacy in accounts of at least two natural offspring. Perissus, for example, is overjoyed to discover his natural brother, identified by the coat-of-arms on his wine bowl at his forest nuptials (MS II, 2Bv–3Ar). Andromarcke, natural son of Polarchus, engages in various adventures and is gladly included by the royal company gathered at the end of the manuscript.

By the end of the manuscript continuation, most of the histories begun in the folio have reached some closure. The heroes of the folio have aged. Some of them, recognizing the futility of earthly life, have become pilgrims; others have died; one of them (male) has even got fat. After extensive wanderings, exhausting both physically and emotionally, most of the primary protagonists have found contentment and permanent addresses. But the accounts of their children have just begun. How will the beautiful Sophie, whisked away by a lady in a chariot drawn by dragons, be recovered to rule her kingdom? Under what circumstances will Faire Designe discover his identity? The manuscript continuation ends in mid-sentence with Andromarcke's relation of the most recent news of Faire Designe to Amphilanthus (his probable father) in the hearing of Pamphilia (his probable mother) and the court party:

> And Sir your faire designe hath now left all things (beeing certainly informed by severall wisards, especially the sage Melissea that the great Inchantment will nott bee concluded thes many yeeres, nay never if you live nott to assiste in the concluding, soe his search is for you, resolving nott to leave you if once found, till that hapy hower come, and in this Island hee is seeking adventur; the best, and hapiest I assure my self wilbee in finding you; Amphilanthus was extreamly (MS II, 31Br)

The folio had also ended in mid-sentence; and the repetition of this device, together with the general resistance of Wroth's romance to closure, strongly suggests its deliberateness. Wroth's handwriting confirms her disinclination to leave a narrative section mid-sentence; for changes in ink and in thickness of nib habitually occur at the beginning, not the middle of sentences.[8] Undoubtedly a tribute to her uncle's revised *Countess of Pembroke's Arcadia,* which also ended in mid-sentence, Wroth's fragment asserts her literary as well as biological relationship with Sir Philip Sidney. But Wroth's ending differs significantly from Sidney's in one important aspect. Some critics who believe Sidney's mid-sentence ending to be deliberate perceive it as revealing an authorial paralysis caused by the growth of his narrative beyond its structuring oracle.[9] Wroth's mid-sentence ending, on the other hand, is thoroughly consonant with the general looseness of her form, which embodies a refusal to structure, to organize, and even perhaps to mean. Any structuring principle in *The Countess of Montgomery's Urania* derives from the concerns and events of Wroth's own life, which had not yet ended. More than authorial paralysis or an artful defiance of literary convention, Wroth's mid-sentence ending signifies a shift of focus from the events of her own life and the society of her peers to a life-affirming absorption in the never-ending events of the lives of the next generation.

Safety in Disgrace

In its survey of various alternatives for married women and their beloveds, in its preoccupation for lost (and not necessarily legitimate) children, Wroth's romance owed much to the unusual circumstances of her own life. Her ability to write this relatively scandalous romance was enabled by a change of fortune that had thrust her from the center to the margins of her society by the late 1610s and early 1620s, when she was writing *The Countess of Montgomery's Urania.* At the age of eighteen, she had been married to a man whose love of dogs and hunting had gained him the notice of King James. At nineteen, she became one of Queen Anne's much esteemed "dancing ladies," cast in choice roles in masques such as Jonson's *Masque of Blackness* (1605) and, later, his *Masque of Beauty* (1608). But then, her husband's death in 1614 left her with tremendous debts; and the death of her son in 1616 prevented her from the use of estates that he would have inherited. Her fortunes blighted by financial exigencies, her reputation at court apparently went into total eclipse when she bore the first of two illegitimate children, the fruits of an adulterous liaison with her cousin William Herbert, third earl of Pembroke.[10]

Thus, by her early thirties, Mary Wroth had perhaps less to lose from the hostility elicited by her writing than other women might. She did not have to worry about falling from a position of security and public esteem; she had already fallen. Widowed, she did not continue to benefit from her husband's association with King James; but her husband's death also enabled her to use her time and talents as she wished, participating in literary activities and literary friendships at her own discretion. Beset by debts, she frequently encountered the antagonism of unpaid merchants and survived; perhaps this experience made her less vulnerable to the prospect of antagonistic readers. The mother of two illegitimate children, she did not have to protect her reputation from any aspersions of sexuality elicited by her writing. She was already proven guilty as charged.[11] Wroth's creation of herself as a writer only added one more item in her catalogue of transgressions against the behavior expected of an aristocratic woman in the Renaissance.

Safe Houses

If Wroth's location on the edge or even outside of the sanctions of her culture enabled her writing, her location within a powerful family milieu was also essential. She was not only a woman; she was a Sidney. Until her marriage, she was even, like the celebrated aunt for whom she was apparently named, a Mary Sidney; and this shared name may well have rendered Mary Wroth's identification of her authorship with that of the countess of Pembroke all the more likely.[12] She had powerful male predecessors, as well. The possessive form of the title of *The Countess of Montgomery's Urania* reflects her use of her famous uncle Philip, author of *The Countess of Pembroke's Arcadia*, as one model in her creation of herself as a writer. Her long sonnet sequence, "Pamphilia to Amphilanthus," presented at the end of the published section of her romance includes specific imitations of poems written by her father, Robert Sidney.[13] While she was probably not responsible for the presence of the names of her uncle and her father validating her as a writer on the title page of the published portion of *Urania*, her identification with her prestigious literary relatives may have provided some private self-authorization, as well.[14]

Safety in Poetic Numbers

The Sidney family provided more than illustrious predecessors. In addition to the works written by Mary Wroth's father, uncle, and aunt, there is evidence of a flourishing literary culture within the immediate circle of her cousins, at least two of whom wrote numerous poems in manuscript. Her cousin Elizabeth Sidney, daughter of Philip Sidney and wife to Roger Manners, fifth earl of Rutland, was praised by Ben Jonson as a better poet than Philip Sidney; unfortunately, none of her poetry has survived to test his judgement.[15] The L'Isle papers record numerous visits between the cousins before Elizabeth's death in 1612.[16] Wroth's cousin and lover William Herbert, son of the countess of Pembroke, also wrote poetry, published after his lifetime by John Donne the younger. One poem, "Had I loved butt att that rate," not reproduced in the published collection but attributed to Herbert by three manuscript sources, is even included in Wroth's *Urania*.[17] While manuscript transmission is difficult to ascertain, especially since most of the original manuscripts have been lost, we know at least that Wroth read some of Herbert's manuscript verse; and it would seem probable that all three cousins shared their work.

The title of *The Countess of Montgomery's Urania* assigns a determining influence to the reading of Susan Vere Herbert, the countess of Montgomery, wife to Mary Wroth's cousin Philip Herbert, younger brother of William Herbert. While she may not have written poetry herself, both of her parents did; her mother Anne Cecil, author of four epitaphs for Susan Vere's brother, provided an early model for female authorship.[18] Thus, Vere's family provided another "safe house" in which women could write, and perhaps increased her receptivity to the presence of women poets among her cousins by marriage. Furthermore, the countess of Montgomery was Wroth's neighbor at Enfield, and the physical proximity of their estates allowed Wroth easy access to the countess of Montgomery as a reader.[19] According to Wroth's title, her romance belonged to the countess of Montgomery in some sense. Perhaps the countess's responses, actual or imagined, played a significant role in Wroth's composition.

The formative influence of an immediate audience within Wroth's own family is appropriate to the apparent origin of Wroth's work as a manuscript to be circulated among a limited number of readers. Significantly predating the composition of the romance, Wroth's sonnet sequence, passed in manuscript among her friends, probably provided the impetus for *Urania,* which expands upon Pamphilia's constancy to the unreliable Amphilanthus.[20] The social nature of manuscript poetry creates an especially important role for actual readers known by the author, as opposed to the anonymous readers of the printed book. Sprinkled with poems addressed by characters to each other, mentioned offhandedly by their authors and eagerly read by kindly insistent friends, Wroth's romance probably reflects actual literary practices within her circle. This possibility is rendered all the more likely by the topical nature of *Urania,* in which "Pamphilia," transparently signifying Wroth herself, addresses her poems to "Amphilanthus," whose romantic betrayals suggest the appropriateness of that name. "lover of two," for William Herbert.[21] Whether or not Wroth decided at a later point to allow publication of her work, its origin in this close circle ameliorated the pressures against women writers in her larger culture. The earl of Rutland's censure of his wife for keeping "table to poets" suggests that the boundaries around these safe spaces permitting literary activities for artistocratic women in the Sidney family were, however, permeable.[22]

Masquing Authorship

It is possible that Mary Wroth's performances in masques at court also worked to enable her authorship. Just as her cousins provided an environment receptive to her composition of poems, so the court and various upper-class families provided a space in which she was permitted to act in plays, a practice widely condemned by the broader culture. As Prynne's *Histriomastix* (1633) was later to show, the public at large did not approve of the acting of masques at court; and women of aristocratic rank who condescended to tread the boards even of courtly stages were vulnerable to identification as "notorious whores."[23] The presence of paid female actors on the public stage was unthinkable. Yet at court, Mary Wroth was able safely to flout cultural prohibitions against women's acting to experience herself as a performer before an audience. This experience may have prepared her for an identity as author, also a form of public performance, even if the audience was limited to friends.

Wroth's acting experience apparently extended beyond her period at court and into the time of her composition of her romance. Josephine Roberts's meticulous tracing of provenance identifies Wroth's unpublished play *Loves Victory* as a manuscript once possessed by Sir Edward Dering, a friend who invited various members of Wroth's family to his house. Dering organized private theatricals acted by friends and neighbors at his estate, probably in the early 1620s; and it seems likely that Wroth may have participated, even writing her play for such a group. Expanding upon an episode in *The Countess of Montgomery's Urania,* Wroth's play suggests an audience receptive to her authorship.[24]

Wroth's creation of herself as a writer and dramatist may have also been influenced by her friendship with Ben Jonson, who addressed various poems to her as well as dedicating his play *The Alchemist* to her. Since Jonson was also entertained by Wroth's cousin Elizabeth, countess of Rutland, he may also have formed part of Wroth's manuscript readership; in fact, a poem Jonson wrote to Wroth explicitly refers to his "exscribing," or copying out, her sonnets.[25] The effect of these theatrical activities can be traced in *Urania* itself, for, as will be discussed below, various characters in her romance act out masques, and various key enchantments take place in theaters. A major character, Melissea, whose prophecies perform the authorlike role of structuring the actions of the characters, herself puts on masques of her own composition. At one point Wroth's narrator describes the romance itself as a play, in which a "new seane must be found, and fram'd" for an immodest woman lover to act (MS I, 3aAv).[26] This perception of her romance as playlike conformed to a powerful precedent, for her uncle had divided his *Old Arcadia* into five acts.

Determining Guilt of Intent

While Elizabeth Sidney Manners and William Herbert both wrote poetry in manuscript, neither of them published any of their work; and Wroth's play as well as a large section of her romance have yet to appear in print. Did her aunt's example encourage Mary Wroth to publish a portion of her romance in 1621? Or did she intend for her work, like her cousins,' to remain in manuscript? Modern scholars have puzzled over the evidence concerning Wroth's relationship to the published portion of *The Countess of Montgomery's Urania,* noting the irregularities of the career of Wroth's printer, the unconventional omission of all prefatory material in the published work, and the conclusion of its narrative with the word "and."[27] In her letter to the duke of Buckingham requesting a warrant to prohibit the further sale of her book and to enable her to call back copies already sold, Wroth herself claimed that copies of her romance "were solde against my minde, I never purposing to have had them published."[28]

While solid reasons exist for perceiving the publication of Wroth's romance as unintentional on her part, probably no discussions of Wroth's relationship to the published volume can be conclusive. It is clear that the published text of Wroth's romance presents itself as unauthorized by the author. But because of the cultural pressures against openly intentional publication of original secular works by women, these apparently solid reasons may represent a deceptive façade plastered over a thin wall of subterfuge. Wroth's relationship to the published work was probably unclear even to her contemporaries. In her letter to the duke of Buckingham, for example, how is her tone of grieved innocence over the "strang constructions which are made of my booke contrary to my imagination" to be read? Undoubtedly some readers made bad guesses as to the real-life identities of some of the characters. But there can be no doubt that *Urania* contains various episodes of fairly transparent topicality, most clearly those centering around Pamphilia and Amphilanthus. As will be discussed below, characters within the romance itself perform topical readings, as they guess that the complaint of Lindamira, for example, alludes to the "real" situation of the character narrating her story. These internal spates of transparent topicality make it difficult to dismiss the probable topicality of the work itself.

Thus, to what extent can Wroth's apparently earnest protestations inspire belief? Considering the pressure exerted against women's authorship, it would be easy to understand why a woman writer of an original romance might protect herself by making publication appear involuntary. Or perhaps her role was truly ambiguous: a copy of her romance may have found its way to the publisher, and she may have simply refused, or neglected, to take action to stop it. Perhaps she truly did not know that publication was in process. Like many determinations of intent, the extent of Wroth's participation in the publication of her work can never be finally decided. Discussions of the issue might well, however, include mention of its topicality, which introduced more than an element of scandal into a few of the many episodes of Wroth's romance. Descriptions of violent family quarrels, of bedroom exploits, and of other highly personal material even in a closely circulating manuscript were already acts of verbal aggression. But by transforming morsels of salacious gossip into incidents of public exposure, the intentional publication of such material would have been, at least to the eyes of its victims, vicious.

Arousing Ben Jonson

Whatever her intentions, Mary Wroth became a published woman author in 1621. Her period of fame and/or notoriety was brief. The scandal aroused by the topical allusions in her romance caused its withdrawal from sale by December 1621, and from the time following its initial appearance until recently, few authors or critics have evidenced knowledge of its existence. The few early reactions to Wroth's writing, however, provide valuable evidence of the reception of her work.[29] Of special interest are the contrasting responses of her friend Ben Jonson and the hostile Edward Denny, both of whom construct their versions of Wroth's authorship in blatantly sexual terms. Their poems deserve to be quoted in full, beginning with Jonson's praise of her sonnets in his "Sonnet to the noble Lady, the Lady Mary Wroth":

I that have beene a lover, and could shew it,
    Though not in these, in rithmes not wholly dumbe,
    Since I exscribe your Sonnets, am become
A better lover, and much better Poet.
Nor is my Muse, nor I asham'd to owe it
    To those true numerous Graces; whereof some,
    But charme the Senses, others over-come
Both braines and hearts; and mine now best doe know it:
For in your verse all *Cupids* Amorie,
    His flames, his shafts, his Quiver, and his Bow,
    His very eyes are yours to overthrow.
But then his Mothers sweets you so apply,
Her joyes, her smiles, her loves, as readers take
For *Venus Ceston*, every line you make.[30]

Since line 3 refers to his "exscribing," or copying out, her verse, Jonson's sonnet probably describes his response to Wroth's poetry before publication. Jonson's accomplished but by no means transparent poem seems to represent this act of transcribing as itself a sexual response to a seductive text. Since he has copied her verse, he claims to have become not only a better poet (possibly by learning from her literary techniques), but also a better lover. How can poems make him a better lover? In the first two lines, Jonson's narrator claims that his identity as a lover has been shown, not in the rhythms of "these" (his poems), but nonetheless in "rithmes not wholly dumbe." The most obvious referent for these rhythms, it seems to me, are the rhythms of the vocalized sexual act. Thus, Jonson's narrator seems to be equating the rhythms of the sexual and the textual act. His narrator has become a better lover through reading Wroth's poem, not just because lovers write poetry, but because the writing of poetry *is* a form of making love. The "rithmes" of verse have become one with the "rithmes" of sexual intercourse.

The amorous imagery of the next quatrain provides further evidence for the presence of this textual and sexual equation by describing the double effect of Wroth's work on his "Muse" (narrator as poet) and on himself (narrator as lover). Both are overcome by the graces of her verse, which charm the senses with "*Cupids* Armorie," whose shafts, quivers, and bows, together with erotic flames, point to obvious anatomical referents. Wroth's verse also overcomes "braines and hearts" with the "sweets" of Venus, softening erotic aggression with maternal tenderness. The content of Wroth's sonnet sequence, which consists largely of sad poems by an abandoned woman narrator written in conventions that were by then old-fashioned, does not in itself account for the intensity of this erotic reaction.[31] The narrator's arousal (poetic and sexual) seems instead to form a response to the sexuality inherent in Wroth's act of authorship (her own "rithmes"). This implicit sexuality was no doubt exacerbated by the sequence's reversal of traditional Petrarchan roles through its presentation of a female wooer as narrator, however conventional her sentiments. The traditional identification of the narrator of a sonnet sequence with an aspect of the poet (probably accurate in Wroth's case) further collapses the distinction between a response to a work and to its author, between textual and sexual arousal.

Jonson's last lines generalize this sexual response to Wroth's work to other readers who, like him, perceive every line as a "*Venus Ceston*," a girdle described in the fourteenth book of Homer's *Iliad* as having the power to arouse the beholder with passion. Just as the girdle of Aphrodite (the Greek Venus) had the capacity of arousing Jove, or any beholder, to passion, so Wroth's poem is said to have the capacity to arouse its readers. What is the source of this aphrodisiac-like power? Is it the property of amatory verse in general, or of verse written by women, or just of sonnets written by Wroth? Representing her authorship as the conventionally female task of sewing, the description of Wroth's poetry as an item of female apparel suggests that the power of her verse to arouse relates either to her gender in general or to her person in particular. This image also plays with earlier representations by Hyrde and others of women's reading as sewing. By providing a Venereal source, Jonson's representation of Wroth's garment/poem empties out the traditional associations of sewing with modesty and chastity.

Jonson's comparison of Wroth's lines to Venus's ceston is a fitting conclusion to his sexual compliment, for his classical source also uses it to associate sexual desire with feminine eloquence:

> In whose sphere
> Were all enticements to delight, all Loves, all Longings were,
> Kind conference, Faire speech, whose powre the wisest doth enflame.[32]

Thus, Wroth's verse, containing "all enticements to delight" as well as "faire speech," supposedly strikes the reader, helpless to resist, with sexual passion. According to Homer, the effect of Venus's ceston on Jove had been at least equally impressive, arousing the king of the gods to lust even after his wife.

The multivalence of possible meanings for Venus's ceston makes of Jonson's allusion a dubious compliment. In Homer, Aphrodite's ceston had enabled Hera to perpetrate fraud, helping the Greeks to a bloody victory over the Trojans. In his marginal notes explaining Venus's ceston in his *Hymenaei,* Jonson alludes to Homer: "*Venus* girdle, mentioned by *Homer, Ili.* which was fain'ed to be variously wrought with the needle, and in it woven *Love, Desire, Sweetnesse, soft Parlee, Gracefulnesse, Perswasion,* and all the *Powers of Venus.*"[33] In the *Hymenaei* itself, Jonson subjugates the erotic power of the ceston to Reason, which is the center of a circle of dancers who represent Venus's girdle. In *Volpone,* however, the fraudulent aspect of the ceston again becomes visible, as Mosca likens "the strange poeticall girdle" to gold, able to transform "the most deformed" to loveliness (4.2.100–102).[34] This instability of meaning for Venus's ceston makes of it an apt signifier for the pleasure and simultaneous suspicion of that pleasure elicited by sensuousness in poetry in the Renaissance. Thus, for Jonson as for Philip Sidney, female authorship foregrounds an anxiety already present about the nature of the appeal of poetic texts.

And Oysters Do Not Make Pearls

A poem written by Edward Denny in response to *Urania* provides an unambiguously negative reading of the female sexuality permeating

Wroth's authorship. Angered by Wroth's apparently accurate allusions to a violent family scene, in which Denny's attempt to murder his daughter as punishment for her adultery was prevented only by his son-in-law, Denny assembles several provocative representations of female authorship in a poem he authored, entitled "To Pamphilia from the father-in-law of Seralius" in a contemporary manuscript:

Hermaphrodite in show, in deed a monster
  As by thy words and works all men may conster
Thy wrathfull spite conceived in Idell book
  Brought forth a foole which like the damme doth look
Wherein thou strikes at some mans noble blood
  Of kinne to thine if thine be counted good
Whose vaine comparison for want of witt
  Takes up the oystershell to play with it
Yet common oysters such as thine gape wide
  And take in pearles or worse at every tide
Both frind and foe to thee are even alike
  Thy witte runns madd not caring who it strike
These slanderous flying f[l]ames rise from the pott
  For potted witts inflamed are raging hott
How easy wer't to pay thee with thine owne
  Returning that which thou thy self hast throwne
And write a thousand lies of thee at least
  And by thy lines describe a drunken beast
This were no more to thee than thou hast donne
  A Thrid but of thine owne which thou hast spunn
By which thou plainly seest in thine own glass
  How easy tis to bring a ly to pass
Thus hast thou made thy self a lying wonder
  Fooles and their Bables seldome part asunder
Work o th'Workes leave idle bookes alone
  For wise and worthyer women have writte none.[35]

Most of Denny's representations of Wroth's authorship are highly gendered. The first line—"Hermaphrodite in show, in deed a monster"—portrays her writing as a transgression of the boundaries of gender that renders her half-male, a monster of nature. Next, the bestial connotation of "damme" (line 4) creates her subhuman but still female; constituted entirely of anger, she gives birth, her foolish offspring revealing the folly of her "spite." Denny's oyster image alludes to Wroth's offending passage, where a pearl signified the obscurity of the blame, "sought for" but "rarely found," laid upon the "noble blood" of Seralius (i.e., Denny) by his daughter's scandal.[36] Unmistakably gendered in Denny's description, the oyster image seems to locate the possibility for female authorship squarely in the genitalia which are "thine," or Wroth's. The association of oysters and genitalia derives in part from a visual similarity between the two halves of the opened shellfish and the symmetrical labia of women's private parts; this similarity was no doubt responsible for the later attribution of aphrodisiac properties to oysters. Further evidence for the presence of this sexual association in Denny's poem is presented by his use of the image to accuse Wroth of promiscuity. Oysters like Wroth's are "common" and they "gape wide" to take in pearls or "worse," not discriminating between "frind and foe." The association of pearls with words in the biblical injunction not to throw "pearls before swine" further contributes to the viability of the oyster as an apt image for author.

Denny's development of his oyster analogy presents a striking dislocution: oysters *make* pearls rather than "gaping wide" for them. Oysterial creativity was well known in the Renaissance and easily associated with the physical creativity of women. The 1601 edition of Pliny's *Historie of the World*, the *locus classicus* commonly consulted for information on such matters, was unmistakably clear on this point. Echoing Pliny in his phrase "gape wide," Denny's erasure of the oyster's ability to manufacture pearls reveals a telling distortion of standard information. Denny's gendering of the oyster itself derives from Pliny's, which is striking enough to warrant quoting:

> When the season of the yeere requireth that they should engender, they seeme to yawne and *gape*, and so doe open *wide*; and then (by report) they conceive a certaine moist dew as seed, wherewith they swell and grow bigge; and when time commeth, labour to be delivered hereof: and the fruit of these shellfishes are the pearles, better or worse, great or small, according to the qualitie and quantitie of the dew which they received.[37]

Denny's suppression of the fact that oysters produce pearls suggests the intensity of his anxiety about the possibility that women can author words of real value. He distorts received knowledge about pearls to fit his image to a male-oriented discourse, so that the valuable "pearls" for which the oysters "gape wide" take on a distinctly phallic association. Instead of being the words produced by the oyster/author, pearls have become the phalluses that oysters/genitalia gape for and, presumably, engulf. The sexual anxiety permeating his image suggests an important motive for the suppression of women's authorship in the Renaissance.

Denny's next image, of the flames rising from a pot, presents an unusual image for female authorship; for it seems to accuse Wroth of drunkenness, a meaning that is confirmed by his claim that her lines describing a "drunken beast" aptly refer to their author. The allegations of irrationality and irresponsibility inherent in the image are not unfamiliar, however, to representations of women's speech. Wroth's work as a "Thrid," or thread, recalls the way in which Jonson's image of Venus's ceston constructs female authorship as sewing. "Fooles and their Bables" is a gender-mixed representation. Indicating a fool's office, a bauble was a baton attached to a carved head; Shakespeare uses the phallic implications of the image.[38] Is Denny suggesting that Wroth is inappropriately masculine, as well as foolish? Or perhaps an operative association of "bable" is "babble," meaningless language produced by babies and women.

Denny's final and presumably strongest argument against Wroth's authorship is its inappropriateness to her gender, for "wise and worthyer women have writte none." While undoubtedly many wise women were not authors, Denny knew of at least one who was; and this line suppresses knowledge that he himself reveals in a letter to Wroth also dated soon after the publication of Wroth's romance. His advice to Wroth to write religious works rather than "lascivious tales and amorous toys" contains a reference to Wroth's aunt, the countess of Pembroke, who "translated so many godly books, and especially the holy Psalms of David."[39] Denny's representation of this devout form of authorship also depends upon a suppression of the secular content of the countess's published translations from Garnier and Petrarch. As perhaps more competent poets would not, Denny has revealed in his anger the mechanisms operating within the larger Renaissance culture through which women's authorship was contained.

Aunt Antissia's Legs

Far from idiosyncratic, Jonson's and Denny's representations of women authors encode cultural attitudes similar to those structuring versions of authorship present in *Urania* itself. Lord Denny himself could hardly have been more cruel than Wroth's own romance in its representation of a woman writer named Antissia.[40] The text guides readers to concur in the criticisms leveled at Antissia's authorship, for most of the major characters of the work subscribe to them. The initial description of her literary activities is related by the reliable character

Rosindy to Pamphilia and Amphilanthus, Urania and Steriamus, Dalinea and Parselius, Antissius and Selarina, and Selarinus and Meriana, who provide a powerful communal context for her censure. While the dependably compassionate Pamphilia grieves for her follies, even she judges Antissia's apparent madness as just punishment for her follies (MS I, 7Ar); and even this amount of compassion receives the objection of Antissius, one of Antissia's nephews. Far from taking affront at Rosindy's character assassination of Antissia, Antissius contributes the gratuitous criticism, which locates the basis of his aunt's low value in her body, as he informs the others that the "smalls" of her legs are "nott very small," for "my Aunte is well underlayd, nott shaped for dauncing" (MS I, 6Ar).

While Antissia is not, like Denny's representation of Wroth, a hermaphrodite, Rosindy's comparison of her to an effeminate male accuses her of an unseemly transgression of gender boundaries: "If you did Madame butt see her speake, you would say you never saw soe direct a mad woeman such Jestures, and such brutish demeaner fittinger for a man in woemans clothes acting a Akilles, then a woeman, and more a princess" (MS I, 7Ar). Even after Antissia's repentance and cure, the narrator still cannot forgive her masculine aggressiveness of speech. The last mention of Antissia in the text, when, after her rescue from an amorous giant, she is conducted to the borders of a country by its king and his troops, describes her as "filling them with as much noisfull discourse as the trumpets, and drumms" (MS II, 9Av).

While Antissia is not a drunk like Denny's author, her "witte runns madd"; her poetry is a form of madness requiring cure. In her retirement at her husband's estate, she hires a tutor to aid her in study to keep her mind busy. Unfortunately, the tutor had become mad "in studying how to make a peece of poetrie to excell Ovid"; he had come to her attention as he walked on the sand, "roaring out high strained lines" (MS I, 7Ar). Antissia's language also takes on a bizarrely Ovidian coloration, as, for example, she describes herself at one point as a "secound Niobe in tears of Joye to melt for this unlooked for hapiness" (MS I, 6Av). On the pretext of searching for some ancient relics of the gods, her loving husband Dolorindus lures her to St. Maura, the island home of the wise Melissea, who puts her to sleep in a bed which sinks into a lake of warm water, where she remains immersed for twenty-four hours. As she wakes, she is served a drink of forgetfulness so that she will not be shamed by the memory of her past behavior (MS I, 8Br–v). Despite Melissea's drink, she does remember her authorship, perceiving it as madness:

> Idleness, with an unsteddy braine . . . led mee to a studdy able to unsettle a more serious braine then ever mine was and soe I learnt Poetrie . . . which in the parfection is butt a delightfull frenzie, and in that kind I was of most excelling, for perfectly I was possest with poetticall raptures, and fixions able to turne a world of such woemens heads into the mist of noe sence, and such learned furies, as have that title of poetticall furie, which in true sence is distraction, and in to that I fell. (MS II, 8Br)

According to Antissia's description, poetry itself is madness, whether indulged in by men or women, although it is apparently implied that women are more apt to have their heads turned because their brains, like Antissia's, are perhaps less "serious." Rosindy's interpretation makes explicit the connection between Antissia's madness and the diminished ability to study that is innate in women: "Beeing a dangerous thing att any time for a weake woeman to studdy higher matters then their cappasitie can reach to, and indeed she was butt weake in true sence, but colorick ever, and rash" (MS I, 7Ar).

Finally, the cultural pressures against women's authorship revealed in Denny's allegations of Wroth's inappropriate sexuality also structure Antissia's authorship. Among the self-authored songs with which she and her tutor vex her husband aboard ship is Antissia's expression of sexual arousal, in which she proclaims: "Venus, my deere sea borne Queene, / Gives mee pleasures still unseene" (MS I, 8Bv; in *PMW*, pp. 198–99). Her explanation to her husband that her poem expresses only her love for him does little to mitigate the censure of even this tolerant man: "Did ever a chaste lady make such a songe, ore chaste eares endure the hearing itt, fy fy Antissia if you will write, write sence, and modestie, nott this stuff, that maides will blush to heere . . . your poeticall furies . . . thus in raving rime bury truth of modestie" (MS I, 8Br).

It is apparently not only Antissia's poetry itself, but also her creation of herself as an author that incurs Rosindy's scorn. Among the products of her "babling" and her "frivelous discourse" (MS I, 6Ar) is a masque she has her household act out before Rosindy. While Rosindy admits that "some things were tollerable," he has no patience with her own pride of authorship: "To illustrate her owne glory," Antissia "did soe commend, and overvallue . . . as verily itt made mee not esteeme it att all" (MS I, 6Av). Rosindy takes pains to distinguish the writings of "meere poets" from the permissible verse of the lovers who compose his audience: "Such a heigth of poetry which att the best is butt a frency, and yett in Lovers itt is a most commendable, and fine qualitie beeing a way most excellent to express their pretious thoughts, in a rare, and covert way, butt they are meere poetts thus I spake of when I condemned poetry, this way I adore itt, butt my Aunts raging, raving, extravagent discoursive language is most aparently, and understandingly discerned flatt madnes" (MS I, 7Ar).

Rosindy's distinction between the authorship by lovers and by his aunt breaks down. Poetry is a frenzy commendable to lovers but despicable in Antissia. Yet Antissia's poems create her as a lover of her own husband. Renaissance lovers, including the lovers in Wroth's romance, also sometimes employ "extravagent" language and classical allusions. Rosindy's claim that he "adores" poetry by lovers but condemns poetry by "meere poetts" locates the value of poems in their origin rather than in their artistic merit. Or is perhaps the real difference, unstated in the text, in the degree of public exposure of poems? Lovers in Wroth's romance, and perhaps within the Sidney households, circulate their poetry closely to a few friends who request it. Antissia's proud performances of her verse and of her allusion-laden language lack reticience.

The blurred distinction between the poetry of lovers and of "meere poetts" informs *Urania*, for the communal hostility levelled against Antissia implicates Wroth's own narrative. While Wroth's language is not as ornate as Antissia's, or even as Philip Sidney's, it is hardly plain. Wroth's romance also owes a debt to Ovid in, for example, an episode of familial violence ending in the metamorphosis of a fleeing girl into a fountain's nymph through the agency of Diana (MS II, 16Bv).[41] Like Antissia, Wroth wrote at least one dramatic piece, expanded in fact from an episode in the romance, apparently for performance in a private household. And so did the sage Melissea, consulted reverently by many of the protagonists, whose presentation of a masque of her own composition presents a positive model of authorship by a woman. Why is Melissea's masque admired and Antissia's reviled? The text's disjunctions reveal unresolved contradictions in attitudes towards women's authorship. Wroth's extended representation of a woman writer clearly reflects in some way upon her own authorship. Is Antissia an alter ego or a debased self-image? Does Antissia function as a kind of lightning rod to ground otherwise destructive cultural prohibitions against women's writing?[42] Or does her mad form of authorship, present only in the manuscript continuation, reflect the increasing anxieties of the author of *The Countess of Montgomery's Urania* prompted by the outcry greeting Wroth's published folio?

The Heroics of Constancy

Antissia's function in the folio portion of *Urania* provides some insight into the implications of her authorship for Wroth's. Even the "anti" in her name foregrounds how, in both the published and unpublished portions of Wroth's romance, she functions as a negative example. In the continuation, she embodies a negative form of authorship; by mid-folio, she embodies a negative form of woman lover. Her dual function is apparently not random. Rosindy's depiction of her mad authorship was initiated by his memory of her jealousy, and according to him, her poetic frenzy is a manifestation of the same irrationality motivating her "jealous fitts" (MS I, 6Ar). The disjointed behavior Rosindy observes of her as author resembles that of a jealous woman of Pantaleria, as Antissia falls from one passion into another, mixing singing, speaking, crying, and laughing. Rosindy's image of a valentine to express the fragmentation of her identity perhaps suggests some connection between erotic and poetic furies. She was, according to Rosindy, "soe discomposed as if pieces of all [her emotions were] throwne in a hatt . . . like Valentines to bee worne by severall persones, noe one to have them all" (MS I, 6Ar).

Issues of authorship are integrally related to issues of love in *Urania*. The implications of Antissia's dual role are better understood within the matrix of female heroism set forth in the folio. One primary accomplishment of the folio portion of Wroth's romance is to redeem the cultural stereotype informing, for example, Philip Sidney's "fair ladies," obsessed by love and compassionate to a fault, from aspersions of sexual frivolity. Like the *New Arcadia*, Wroth's romance creates heroines who demonstrate their self-control through their constancy.[43] Unlike Sidney's Stoic princesses, Wroth's heroines do not generally reveal their inner determination through a desire for death. They mourn and they pine, but, except for a few minor characters, they seldom die.[44] In fact, for the major protagonist, Pamphilia, constancy to the man she loves does not prevent her marriage to someone else.

Among its various narrative strands, *The Countess of Montgomery's Urania* develops a heroics of constancy by presenting a number of women who are cruelly deserted, at least for a time, by the men they love: Dalinea (R2), Allarina (AA3v), Alena (BB3–BB4), Liana (EE2), Bellamira (SS3), Lady Pastora (YY1), Dorolina (FFF4), Musalina (GGG2v), Lindamira (GGG4), Pelarina (LLL1v), a woman of Pantaleria (MMM4), Mirasilva (PPP2), Antissia (MM4), and most notably,

Pamphilia herself (AAA4). These women react to their rejections in various ways, usually through strategies which suppress anger, sometimes in the form of jealousy. These constant heroines are sisters to the female Stoics of Brandon and Daniel, for the heroism of both groups is predicated upon an internal battle through which the protagonists emerge triumphant over their own emotions. Pelarina's account of her inner struggle task explicitly sets forth the task faced by the forsaken women in Wroth's romance: "I discover'd how neere I was to bee an ordinary lover after losse, which is to grow neighbour if not inhabiter with hate" (LLL2v). "Ordinary" lovers do not overcome their anger; heroic ones do. Anger represents the silent precondition for the heroism of the constant woman lover. Pelarina overcomes hers by going on a pilgrimage to Jerusalem, returning to live "the rest as she had begun her dayes in fervent zeale and affection" (LLL2v) to the man she continues to love.

Wroth's narrator extends little sympathy to women who do not achieve this constancy. Beginning "Christian-like," the woman of Pantaleria, engaged in Urania's service, loses control over her rage, compared to a shameful pregnancy: "I carryed [my lover's scorn] with infinite paine secret from knowledge, suffering what Beasts never doe, yet Christian like, I ever strove to turne my selfe from violent hurt, but being so great with rage as no longer able to conceale it, I returned to some land of an Uncle of his" (MMM4). When she falls distracted from one passion into another, from crying to singing and twenty other such passions, the narrator criticizes her for "having profited but little in her Mistrisses service for loving exactly well" (MMM4v).

Perhaps the most satisfactory reaction to betrayal belongs to Allarina, who, donning Diana's garments, declares "I love my selfe, my selfe now loveth me" (BB2).[45] But such independence does not represent a true alternative in an age when women were economically dependent, and Allarina eventually marries the lover who had previously scorned her (EEE4v). Bellamira and a widowed sister to the ambassador to Brittany excuse their lovers by blaming themselves; but the triviality of their supposed offenses—a slight or even imagined imperfection in beauty (SS3), a belief in warnings (later proven accurate) of a lover's infidelity (MM3)—reveals that their deflection of blame points to their own virtuous loyalty, not to any role they played in their own forsaking. Sometimes rejected women deflect their anger into irony, as for example in Bellamira's conjecture that her lover had forsaken yet another woman, "not meaning to bee a Phaenix among men-lovers, for feare of envy" (SS3). In the manuscript continuation, Veralinda exclaims that she "would nott my selfe have my Lord Constant, for feare of a miracle" (MS I, 21Br). These ironic statements provide bitter comment upon the essentialist excuse made for men, that their inconstancy is a condition of their gender, a "naturall infirmitie" belonging even to "the kindest, lovingst, passionatest, worthiest, loveliest, valiantest, sweetest, and best man" (AAA3; see also BB4).

Most of the women, including Pamphilia herself, suffer in a "silence" which paradoxically, provides the impulse for the generation of many narratives, told as confidences to a few sympathetic friends, and of many sad poems, kindly demanded or accidently overheard by passers-by. Pamphilia relieves her grief, which is said almost to cause her death, in a long defense of constancy elicited by the objections of her friend Urania offered "against her owne minde" (CCC3) to save Pamphilia's life.[46] As the primary heroine of the romance, Pamphilia provides a model of heroism for women in her unswerving loyalty to the lover who has forsaken her, pointing out, "To leave him for being false, would shew my love was not for his sake" (DDD3v). In the first episode of enchantment in the folio, Pamphilia's heroic constancy makes of her the "loyallest Lady," who, with the "valientest Knight" (F4v), can free women lovers imprisoned in the towers of Desire, Love, and Constancy. As Beilin points out, Pamphilia "becomes" Constancy as she takes keys from the figure of Constancy, "at which instant *Constancy* vanished, as metamorphosing herself into her breast" (T3).[47]

The inner conflict underlying Pamphilia's achieved constancy is explored to some extent in her poetry. In fact, she claims that "rage" motivates some of the sonnets she has written under the name "Lindamira," whose signification of Pamphilia herself is revealed by the slip, conventional in this topical mode, into the first person. When, after fourteen years of grief, "Lindamira" finally complains, Pamphilia apparently revises her words into poetry: "[Her] complaint, because I lik'd it, or rather found her estate so neere agree with mine, I put into Sonnets . . . I will with the story conclude *my* rage against him; for thus the Booke leaves her" (GGG4; my italics). But Lindamira's complaint is curiously devoid of the rage which her author claims to motivate it. Any jealousy is deflected into doubts of her own worthiness or of the depth of their love:

I am not Jealous, they so well do fare.
But doubt my selfe lest I lesse worthy am,

Or that it was but flashes, no true flame,
Dazl'd my eyes, and so my humour fed.
(*PMW*, p. 178)

The sonnets Pamphilia writes under her own name are more explicit about the workings of jealousy. In the final sonnet of her crown of fourteen sonnets,—each of which takes the last line of the preceding sonnet as its own first line—she, like the constant heroines of Daniel and Brandon, employs a military metaphor to describe her internal conflict:

Curst jealousie doth all her forces bend
To my undoing; thus my harmes I see.
Soe though in Love I fervently doe burne,
In this strange labourinth how shall I turne?
(*PMW*, p. 134)

The question itself reveals her doubts about her victory over the forces of "curst jealousy" at this point in her sequence. In addition, by repeating the first line of the crown, this final line creates an enclosing labyrinth of passion from which art provides no exit.[48] This deferral or denial of solution is necessary for the generation of the poetry in the sequence, for her last poem links her conquest over her inner turmoil with the cessation of writing. The achievement of the "quiett of a faithfull love" precludes "the discource of Venus, and her sunn." "Storyes of great love" are appropriate to "young beeginers," not to her. By its very nature, absolute constancy produces only silence; and so Pamphilia ends her sequence with these lines promising an end to writing:

And thus leave off, what's past showes you can love,
Now let your constancy your honor prove.
(*PMW*, p. 142)

Thus, authorship in *Urania* is inextricably entangled in the heroics of constancy. Language—expressions of anger and of pain, and even of loyalty and of forgiveness—is generated by a speaker's distance from the final achievement of true resignation, for resignation itself is productive only of silence.

Incipient in the Stoic heroines of Brandon and of Daniel, Wroth's heroics of constancy probably represents a response to a real situation faced by a number of contemporary aristocratic women such as Daniel's countess of Cumberland, often isolated (or stranded) on country estates while their husbands freely roamed the courts and countryside. The way that Wroth's romance expands upon the basic plot of her sonnet sequence points, however, to a literary as well as a social genesis. The gender reversal necessitated by Wroth's adoption of the role of Petrarchan lover transforms the conventional dynamic between poet and beloved. Chastity creates the distance from the beloved that produces the poetry of male Petrarchan poets. A male beloved so preoccupied would be, to some eyes, comic, or at least vulnerable to accusations of effeminacy. For Wroth's sequence, then, the necessary distance between poet and beloved is created by the male's infidelity. The dynamic created by the beloved's infidelity would predictably contain anger, along with grief and longing, as one manifestation of desire.

Anti(ssia)'s Rage

Understanding female authorship in *Urania* as indicative of inner turmoil (without which constancy would not be heroic) provides some insight into the choice of Antissia as an author. The authorship of an explicitly angry poem is realized, not by Lindafilla or Pamphilia, but by Antissia, who, after her rejection by Amphilanthus in favor of Pamphilia, portrays herself as constituted through anger:

> And since I can nott please your first desire
> I'le blow, and nourish scorners fire,
> As Salimanders in the fire doe live
> Soe shall those flames my being give.
> (*PMW*, p. 164)

Her anger does not predominate at this time, however, and she immediately burns her verse, begging pardon of love and expressing melancholy, rather than rage, by mourning her loss in a seat she has made at the top of a willow tree. Her resolution does not last for long. Instead of conquering her anger, she takes out a contract on Amphilanthus's life, sending both her nephew Antissius and her lover Dolorindus out to kill him (QQ1, VV1). Even though she later repents her resolve as she weeps over a dead body she supposes to be Amphilanthus's, in the context of the heroic constancy practiced at such cost by so many forsaken women, her attempt to have Amphilanthus killed is remarkable—humorous, refreshing, or shocking, depending upon the orientation of the reader.

Antissia defines by contrast the heroics of constancy practiced by the other women. The differences between her reactions and Pamphilia's are rendered all the more dramatic by the identical object of their love, for it was Antissia whom Pamphilia replaced as Amphilanthus's beloved. Antissia's own poem portrays her as constituted by the anger that must be suppressed, with a greater or lesser degree of success, by the other women characters. Antissia seems to function in much the same way in her role as author, embodying the negative cultural attitudes towards women's writing that must be suppressed, with a greater or lesser degree of success, in order for any woman, including Wroth, to write in the Renaissance. Thus, Antissia serves as a container, a disposal site, into which rage over inconstant lovers and anxiety over authorship can be placed to prevent contamination from spreading further into the romance. But like any object of marginalization, the character of Antissia reveals what is in fact central enough to the discourses of love and of authorship to warrant suppression.

The representation of Antissia as mad author exists in contradiction to, not in resolution with, the portrayals of sane authors in the text. Wroth's romance provides no justification or explanation for the communal approval of Melissea's authorship of her masque. This contradiction reflects a wider disjunction within the Renaissance culture. Within the circle of Wroth's cousins, female authorship was permissible; within the wider culture it was not. Thus, the cultural anxieties constituting Antissia's authorship are not answered, and perhaps are not answerable; they simply coexist with images of successful authorship by women.

Antissia's anger as a lover reflects a contradiction of a different kind, from which even the Sidney family was not exempt. As Carolyn Swift has noted, despite the text's occasional recognition of marriage as a trap, there were few realistic alternatives offered aristocratic women who did not wish to become financial encumbrances upon their possibly unwilling families.[49] Wroth's romance seems to offer another similarly culturally induced contradiction in one Renaissance discourse of love, inside or outside of marriage. While a woman's love for a man, whose "naturall infirmitie" necessarily causes him to leave her, is doomed to cause her pain, this very love remains the primary means through which she can prove her value to herself and possibly to others. Since, in marriage or in love affairs, there was little women could do to translate their anger outward to alleviate its social cause, these cultural contradictions were internalized, to be reproduced within their own psyches. Thus, the validity of Antissia's anger, fully experienced by other forsaken women inside and no doubt outside Wroth's romance, is not denied. Instead, existing in silent contradiction to other culturally generated financial and emotional desires, its containment organizes the creation of the constant heroine, one of the few heroic forms of self available to Renaissance women.

Towering Desires

The enchantment in the Towers of Desire, Love, and Constancy reveals, to a limited degree, a consciousness of the heroics of constancy as a mechanism of emotional confinement, enclosing its women subjects through its operations upon their own desires. When a group of male and female characters are shipwrecked on Cyprus, they all drink a magic water that inflames them with passions. The men's passions range from a desire to perform heroic deeds to a desire for a beloved: Parselius desires to settle the sons of the king of Albania on their rightful throne; Steriamus and Selarinus wish to devote themselves to Mars and knighthood; Leandrus desires to find and win Antissia. The women's passions, on the other hand, are all confined to forms of desire for a beloved. While the men's desires, including Leandrus's love for a woman, propel them away from the towers to wander a vast expanse of exterior space in search of the objects of their passions, the women's passions drive them to imprisonment within an interior space: Selarina is locked in the Tower of Desire because of her "uncessant desire" for her prince; Urania and her maid are locked in the Tower of Love.[50]

The arrangement of the three towers creates a hierarchy of desire, according to which constancy represents the highest level. Women who enter the Tower of Constancy prove their superior accomplishment as lovers. But all three towers confine the women against their will, and the phallic shape of the towers perhaps suggests an awareness of the role played by a masculine system of sexuality in this enclosure of women. Most startling is the narrator's sudden internalization of this enchantment, which renders heroic constancy irrelevant. Representing the victims of all three towers as prisoners in the "throne of love," this internalization levels the hierarchy of the towers. Whether women feel sexual desire, true affection, or heroic constancy, they are all merely prisoners to love; and their imprisonment lies within their own psyches: "Thus were the women for their punishment, left prisoners in the throne of *Love:* which Throne and punishments are daily built in all humane hearts" (G1).

Yet within this very description of the destructive effect of love, the text rebels, negating its protest against the enclosure of women through their own desires. The *e* on "humane" betrays an instability of meaning proceeding from the unstandardized spelling of the Renaissance, when *humane* could mean at the same time "human" or "humane" (*OED*). "Human" undercuts the gender distinction implicit in the enchantment of the women in the towers. "Humane" elevates prisoners of love as superior in feeling. This devious praise echoes a doctrine of love voiced by the sage Melissea to Pamphilia in a description that reverses the meaning of the "throne" of love: "Love indeed hath a more steddy place, and throne of abiding when in such Royall harts" (MS I, 22Av).

From prisoners within the enclosures of love, women can become the houses within which love is enclosed. A self-description by the sympathetic Philastella expands upon the spiritual nobility conferred by the entertainment of love in a lover's heart through a silent allusion to Ovid's story of the visitation of Jupiter and Mercury upon the humble Philemon and Baucis: "Love who is Lord of all brave royall minds, hath like the heavens beheld my lowly breast, and in it taken lodging, gracing it with humbling his great Godhead, to embrace a true, and yeelding heart . . . love dwels in me, hee hath made me his hoste" (NN3) Philistella's claim that she is "made, maintained by love, and in love shaped, & squared only to his rule" (NN3) is approved by her friend Urania, whose sympathetic response provides a convenient guide for the response of receptive readers.

This view of women as ennobled by the love that constitutes their entire identity emerges as one main perspective of the romance. Some of Philastella's phrases echo in the narrator's praise of Pamphilia and her friend Orilena, for example, for being "made" by love: "Surpassing passion, excellent, still governe, how delicate is thy force? How happie thy rule, that makes such excellent women thy subjects? made so by thy government, instructed by thy skill, taught by thy learning, and indeed made by thee" (RR1).

The Constant Narrator

Thus, despite the awareness of the pain and disappointment that love causes various sympathetic characters, most notably Pamphilia, the narrator continues, for the most part, to value love, expostulating in love's praise even near the end of the manuscript continuation: "What is riches, what is fortunes of estate, what indeed is any thing, noe nott honor itt self though the rarest of earthly treasures, without that inestimable Juell, Love" (MS II, 17Br). The emotional contradiction elicited by this optimism in the face of the disappointing events of the Pamphilia-Amphilanthus plot reproduces a cultural contradiction, in which women are expected, even by themselves, to remain loving to their men despite infidelities or other inducements to rage. This contradiction is most apparent in the narrator's attitude towards Amphilanthus. Forsaking Lucenia, Antissia, Pamphilia, Musalina, and then Pamphilia again, Amphilanthus's incorrigible infidelity, encoded in his very name, provides the major structuring device of Wroth's romance. Yet the narrator's early infatuation with him as "the worthiest man the earth carried" (QQ4) is unchanged well into the manuscript continuation, when, moving to an episode in which he forsakes Pamphilia for the queen of Candia, the narrator inscribes an audience equally devoted to him: "Amphilanthus whos name butt named is sufficient to call all eares, and harts to attend him" (MS I, 25Bv). Like Pamphilia, the narrator seems ever ready to forgive him again. The narrator's feelings for Amphilanthus are in no way qualified by his numerous infidelities, for she singles him out from a shipwrecked party that includes Urania and others for special attention: "Butt divers great ones are in distress especially Amphilanthus, who must nott bee forsaken, though hee hath proved a forsaking lover" (MS I, 32Av).

One mechanism controlling the narrator's undiminished enthusiasm for Amphilanthus becomes apparent in a commentary on his final approaching infidelity to Pamphilia. When, like forsaken heroines, she blames his inconstancy on his gender, it appears that the narrator herself is a practitioner of the heroics of constancy:

> You or hee will say Fate did itt, indeed itt is most true, poore Fate is made the couler when such Fatall stormes fall, butt itt is a strange, and rare thing in reason thus all men should bee borne under that fatall rule of unconstancy, for when did any one see a man Constant from his birthe to his end, therfor woemen must thinke itt a desperate destinie for them to bee constant to innconstancy, butt alas this is woemens fortunes, and by that unfixed sex to bee blamed as if stained with ther guiltines. (MS I, 4Bv)

After expressing anger in her refusal to blame fate, the narrator concludes by sadly assenting to an ill that has no remedy, exclaiming "alas this is woemens fortunes." This movement from justified outrage to weary resignation demonstrates that the narrator, too, is a proficient practitioner of the heroics of constancy.

The narrator's projection of a "you" willing to excuse Amphilanthus's actions through the workings of fate inscribes readers even more sympathetic to Amphilanthus than she. In their unwavering affection for Amphilanthus, these inscribed readers are altogether consistent with those inscribed earlier, whose "eares, and harts" were ever ready to attend that apparently irresistible hero. Their affection for Amphilanthus is undeterred by their own sad experiences of love, for the narrator discloses that some of them have, in fact, even experienced Antissia's jealousy. When Antissia discovers Pamphilia embracing Rosindy, whom she mistakes for Amphilanthus, the narrator inscribes an audience who has similarly suffered Antissia's emotional anguish: "But those who know that languishing paine, also know, that no perfect satisfaction can be, unlesse the humour it selfe with satisfaction doe quite leave the possessed" (N2v). Since these inscriptions surface just at the time of Amphilanthus's real or imagined infidelities, any actual readers who accept the role offered by these inscribed readers must suppress the negative feelings for Amphilanthus elicited by empathy for Pamphilia's grief. Thus, Wroth's romance performs the same operations upon its readers as those undergone by constant heroines in the text.

The (Com)Passionate Narrator

The narrator's constancy exists in harmony rather than in disjunction with her passionate compassion to the erring Amphilanthus. In fact, her constancy represents an especially difficult extension of the compassion, often punctuated with the word "alas," which she offers almost all of the characters. In one instance the narrator's concern takes on a distinctly maternal cast as she urges the readers to rush to relieve the distress of a group of shipwrecked characters: "Butt wee must not dally with the story, they are wett" (MS I, 32Br). The narrator's compassion is usually elicited, however, by characters who feel the joy and especially the anguish of love. For example, when Amphilanthus, searching for Pamphilia, unknowingly passes near her, the narrator commiserates over present and future events alike: "Alas Pamphilia his helpe was neare thee, but thou must not have it lent thee, but loose more . . . Alas unfortunate Lady, what will become of you? this is the last time for some moneths, hee shall come so neare, but yeares before his affection bee so much" (SS1). When the valiant king of Tartaria falls in love with Pamphilia, the narrator accuses love of a false dealing that is eventually belied by the apparent happiness of the king's marriage with Pamphilia despite her continuing love for

Amphilanthus: "Alas brave Rodomandro thus thou shouldst fall from one shipwrack into an other, and one soe much more dangerous . . . Love, O love thus you play, thus you blinde, thus you flatter, thus indeed you Jugle, and play faulse with all men" (MS I, 7Br).

This compassion proceeds from the narrator's own experiences with love, for she, too, has felt its sometimes deceptively dangerous power: "Brave Amphilanthus was never without that pretty thing to play withall, ore what most plays with us, dallying hope, a vapor rising from the spleene of wayward love" (MS I, 33Bv). The "us" of this complaint links the narrator's experience with that of the inscribed readers, who have also, it must be remembered, felt the "languishing paine" of jealousy like Antissia's. Thus, Wroth's narrator and the inscribed readers share a common background of amorous experiences. *The Countess of Montgomery's Urania* is told by a lover to lovers. Its narrative situation depends upon a writer and an audience who share a mutual obsession with love, according to the narrator: "Love is a subject so delightfull, and alluring, as it not onely winns, but commands the very soule to the hearing, or writing of it, so wholly possessing, as it caused this amorous accident, and yet will not permit a resting here, but proceedes to *Amphilanthus*" (AAA1v).

The Constancy of Compassionate Fair Ladies

This narrative situation is reminiscent of that determining the first three books of Sir Philip Sidney's *Old Arcadia*. Wroth's narrator and inscribed readers seem to be produced by the same values creating Sidney's narrator and his sympathetic "fair ladies," whose compassion for the morally dubious exploits of lovers, proceeding from their own complicity in amorous activities, lures unwary readers into a textual trap. Wroth's narrator and audience show just as much compassion for their lovers, whose frequently extramarital activities would seem to be just as morally dubious. The confession by Wroth's narrator that she values "that inestimable Juell, Love" over "riches," over "fortunes of estate," and even over "honor itt self" (MS II, 17Br) does little to assuage suspicion over the nature of her compassion.

Unlike Sidney's *Old Arcadia*, however, Wroth's romance springs no trap. No stern judge intervenes to interrogate the reasonableness of compassion for lovers. No alternative viewpoint challenges the judgement of Wroth's narrator and inscribed audience, who together shepherd readers to an unquestioned compassion for an array of suffering lovers. And, unlike the *New Arcadia*, *Urania* does not reserve this compassion for deserving Stoic heroines like Sidney's Parthenia or the Arcadian princesses whose resignation to death proves the stern metal of their souls. Compassion is repeatedly extended to lovers indulging in premarital and extramarital affairs, including those which involve a lover's "boldly possessing" what a mistress "freely gave" (Z2v).

Wroth's text flashes no danger signals even when Pamphilia utterly abjures the role of wisdom in love: "Truth of love, which is a supreme power, commanding the eyes, and the heart: what glory were it to him to have a cold part of wisdome to rule with him? No, his honor is to be alone . . . his knowledge wanting no advice . . . who is in truth all wisdome" (AA2). This startling perspective upon the amorality of love in *Urania*, marking it off especially from Sidney's *Old Arcadia*, may have been enabled, according to Wroth's aesthetic, by the gender difference of their authors.

An episode of verse reception appears to construe a preference for reason in love as originating from gender rather than from virtue. When a group listens to the songs of shepherds and shepherdesses, the women especially enjoy the songs of shepherdesses, two of which—a constancy poem and a farewell to love—Pamphilia causes to be written down. When Amphilanthus blames the "mayde for accusing him so unjustly" (T4), a shepherd obliges him by singing a song in praise of love approved by reason, which pleases him better. As Amphilanthus's utter irrationality in his conduct of his own love affairs suggests, his desire for a song of reasonable love bears no connection to his own amorous behavior. But his preference may well reflect a cultural expectation sometimes at odds with actual taste. This gesture towards a gendered aesthetics partially accounts for the distance of Wroth's romance from the moral concerns organizing her uncle's.

Ungendering Aesthetics

This brief episode in which a man and woman respond differently to the same poems exists at odds with the usual narrative situation within *The Countess of Montgomery's Urania*, which is remarkably ungendered. Men and women alike exchange their stories on less than the slightest pretext, and often without any specific motive beyond the relief of their feelings or the pleasure they might provide. In sharp contrast to Sidney's *Old* and *New Arcadia*, women tell their stories freely to each other and to men without interruption; men tell stories to women without any apparent intent to seduce them (although love may sometimes result); and, perhaps most incredibly, men repeatedly pour their hearts out to other men.

Thus, the narrative situation inscribed in *Urania,* with its compassionate narrator and its readers similarly obsessed by love, is refracted dozens of times within the work itself without regard to gender. A mutual preoccupation with love, not the gender of the audience, creates the conditions for a narrative. When Leonius requests the grieving Cilandrus to tell his story, Cilandrus asks him first if he is a lover, for if he is not, Cilandrus's story will be wasted and Leonius will "no more esteeme of it, then of an old tale" (EEE2). Steriamus invites Dolorindus to relate his love plight, for he himself is afflicted by love: "Tell mee then all your woe, and know you speake to woe itselfe in speaking unto me" (X1). Perissus permits himself to tell his grief to Urania "because you are, or seeme to be afflicted" (B2v). Bellamira confides the events of her sad life to Amphilanthus because he, too, looks sad (SS3).

These representations of compassionate males, who sometimes weep and even embrace each other, cross gender boundaries to deny the construction of compassion as a primarily female trait. An episode at Mira's pyramid suggests that Wroth's romance presented this compassion as a deliberate substitute for the more traditionally sanctioned competitive aggression. When Alarinus, grieving over his deceased Mira, challenges Peryneus, lamenting the death of Elyna, to fight to determine whose was the worthiest lady, nymphs force the two to settle their dispute by telling their histories instead. At the end of their narratives, the two men embrace in sympathy, their agonistic impulse quelled (SSS2). Another episode challenging conventional gender boundaries occurs when an old man in a small boat (actually the king of Romania) offers to tell his "wofull'st and most disastrous history that ever Princely eares gave attention to," which will "encrease compassion, and passion" in an audience of royal males. As he cries during his own narrative, all of the princes join in, their compassion amplified by their own problems; and together they interrupt his account "with sobs, and groanes, every one having equall feeling of sorrow, though for several things" (G1v).

The compassion women extend to each other exists at variance with the core episode of female storytelling in the *New Arcadia,* in which women interrupt each other's narratives. Limena's invitation to Dorolina is not unusual for other women in Wroth's romance: "I have beene as you are afflicted, and never felt more felicitie then in discoursing my woes, besides, I see you are apt to discover your passions to these places, why not then as well to us, who are, and ever will be sensible of passion?" (FFF4). In *Urania,* women speak freely not only to each other, but also to mixed groups and even to solitary men. According to Amphilanthus, in fact, women are the best narrators of stories of love. To Amphilanthus it is especially lovely "to heare love described, and related by a woman, out of whose lipps those sweet passions more sweetely proceeded" (II1v). Yet, unlike the women in Sidney's romance, Wroth's female characters can tell their stories to men without impugning their reputations. A richly dressed maiden whom Amphilanthus discovers fishing, for example, even walks alone with him along a beautiful riverside as she tells him the history of her amorous past. She is, like most women, attracted by his charms, for "she could not but extreamely admire the loveliness of Amphilanthus" (II1v). Yet her husband is not jealous, and neither is her beloved. She has succeeded in ruling her "affection by virtue" (II3v) to such an extent that, after two years of marital unhappiness, her husband now trusts her entirely, even with her beloved. And so, it seems, does the text.

Whose Ceston?

Amphilanthus's response to the fishing maid's narrative resembles Ben Jonson's to Wroth's romance. Like Jonson, Amphilanthus becomes a lover: "Then made he some excellent verses, the subject being desire, and absence, and so much was he transported, as he stood not like a beholder, but as an Actor of loves parts" (II3r). Amphilanthus does not implicate the female narrator in his transformation from passive audience to an "Actor of loves parts." He does not displace any sexual guilt upon her or even accuse her of seductive intent. Seemingly impervious to his response, the fishing maid remains happily content with her husband and chastely affectionate to her beloved. This episode provides an example of how women's speech to men in Wroth's romance does not imply sexual guilt or gender-inappropriate aggression. While this interchange between Amphilanthus and the maid confirms the capacity of women's language to elicit a sexual response, the placement of responsibility for that response rests upon the audience rather than upon the storyteller.

The mechanism through which guilt is displaced upon the reader rather than upon the narrative suggests a strategy germane to Wroth's own authorship. The fishing maid's free speech about her own history to a man she does not know well transgresses cultural prohibitions limiting women's speech that organize such encounters in Sidney's *New Arcadia*. The implications of her freedom of speech for Wroth's freedom of authorship are rendered evocative by various blurrings of the boundary between spoken stories and written texts in the Renaissance. Perhaps the most important such blurring justifies the powerful prohibition against women's publishing as a form of speaking in public, supposedly censured by Saint Paul when he forbade women to speak in church. In addition, written texts were often experienced as spoken when they were read aloud, as they often were among aristocratic Renaissance women, who read to their servants, or who were read to as they sewed. This overlapping of spoken narrative and written text enters Wroth's romance in such confusing statements as Amicles' claim that he has experienced "soe many adventures as wowld fill a whole Vollume to recite them" (MS II, 4Ar; see also MS II, 4Br).[51] Finally, as will be discussed below, the distinctions are blurred by central spates of self-referential topicality through which Wroth, like the fishing maid, purports to tell her "own" story; in these episodes Wroth displaces other forms of textual guilt, in addition to sexual guilt, upon a voyeuristic reader.

As in the narrative of Amphilanthus's fishing maid, the cues implicating *The Countess of Montgomery's Urania* in a discourse of sexual guilt are notably absent. This absence is all the more remarkable because its inscription of a compassionate narrator and an audience of lovers, refracted many times in the narrative circumstances among characters within the romance, repeatedly points to its own seductiveness. The compassion which permeates its narrative situations, including the frame of narrator and inscribed audience, makes *Urania* a seductive text by evoking a discourse of courtly love, according to which pity can lead to sexual desire. This power of compassion to inspire sexual love becomes most explicit in an episode near the beginning of the romance. In eliciting Urania's compassion with his story of his lost Limena, Perissus almost moves her to love him: "She did pitie him so much, as this had almost brought the end of some kind of pitie, or pitie in some kind love: but she was ordain'd for another, so as this prov'd onely a fine beginning to make her heart tender against the others comming" (C4).

Perissus, like Amphilanthus's fishing maid, seems unaware of and certainly unresponsible for Urania's nearly loving response; his heart remains pledged to Limena. Yet in its capacity to arouse pity, his story remains seductive despite any intent of his. The way in which "pitie" produces free-floating love prepares Urania for her fated lover suggests seductive possibilities for Wroth's collection of lovers' stories. The narrator's enormous compassion for her characters guides her readers to pity them as well, perhaps in the process becoming, like Urania, themselves more vulnerable to love. This ability of books to prepare women's hearts for lovers accounts for the following representation of Dalinea's reading, interrupted by the arrival of a stranger named Parselius, her brother's friend and soon to be her husband: "Her Ladies who attended her, were a little distant from her in a faire compasse Window, where also stood a Chaire, wherein it seemed she had been sitting, till the newes came of his arrivall. In that Chaire lay a Booke, the Ladies were all at worke; so as it shewed, she read while they wrought" (O3v). Bringing him under the "State, where two Chaires being set," Dalinea listens to Parselius "discoursing of adventures," at first centering upon her brother's brave exploits. From narratives follows conversation, from conversation proceeds a desire for more conversation, which leads her to love Parselius. Parselius's conquest of Dalinea began with his skill at narration, for his "discourse had made his way, by taking first her eares prisoners" (O3v). Since Dalinea is already a lover of reading, her fall for a well-presented text seems inevitable.

Women Who Write Poetry

Since poetry is even more thoroughly entangled in amorous discourse than narratives, it would seem even more likely to endanger the reputations of women authors. Poets woo, but virtuous women do not; so a virtuous woman poet, especially a writer of love poems, would seem to be an anomaly in the Renaissance. But not in *The Countess of Montgomery's Urania*. Rather than constructing a gender-specific circumstance enabling women's authorship of poetry, Wroth's romance simply denies any difference between the conditions controlling the production of poetry by men or by women. Like the telling of stories, the writing of poetry is unusually gender-neutral in Wroth's romance; and unlike Sidney's Philoclea, her woman poets seldom accuse themselves of guilty sexuality. Moved by the heights and, more usually, by the depths of love, men and women alike confess their feelings in meter throughout Wroth's romance. Even for the unprepossessing Musalina, becoming a poet was a "necessary thing" upon her abandonment, "and as unseparable from a witty lover as love from youth" (GGG2v). The queen of Naples's ability as a poet is described as a "Princely" virtue: that "rare lady" was as "perfect in Poetry, and all other Princely vertues as any woman that ever liv'd" (RR3v). The number of good women poets makes Amphilanthus's comment to Bellamira on her ability as a poet as "rare" for women a more accurate description of Renaissance England than of Wroth's romance: "You did . . . touch upon a quality rare in women, and yet I have seene some excellent things of their writings" (TT3). The writing of verse does not apparently compromise masculinity either; for Amphilanthus, like other princes of that fictional place and time, was "brought up in that, next to the use of Armes" (P4v).

Amphilanthus's respectful appreciation for the aesthetic qualities of Bellamira's verse exists in tension with another kind of response exerting strong influence upon women's verse, which makes the absence of sexual guilt in women's poems all the more startling. The women poets in Wroth's romance write poems in the thrill of the chase as well as in abandonment. In using their poetry as a means of seduction, women poets are following a path well worn by the metrical feet of male poets. Wroth's male character Lamprino, for example, reveals his love to his beautiful kinswoman in poems written in the third person, "leaving itt to her favour to accept the understanding, or her cruelty" (MS II, 3Ar). She rejects him tactfully by praising his poetry without acknowledging his flirtatious message. Various women poets—Allarina, Pelarina, and even Pamphilia—also pretend to desire an aesthetic response to their poetry while their real hope is for an amorous one. "Knowing that they might speake in kind for me, and yet my selfe not beg againe" (BB1v), Allarina sets down her feelings in verse to inform her beloved of her passion. Her despair over his continued scorn leads only to more poetry, so that "some said, my prose was gone, and that I onely could expresse my selfe in verse." Pelarina's cold beloved is even worse. Instead of responding unambiguously to her love poems, he merely turns down the leaves of her book at poems "he thought touched or came too neere, or I imagine so" (LLL2v), leaving her to her own miserably confused conjecture. The technique works for Pamphilia, however. Showing her poetry to Amphilanthus, she betrays herself with a blush. Ascertaining that she did not merely "counterfeit" love in her verse, Amphilanthus first guesses himself as her beloved and then tests the accuracy of his conjecture by catching her in his arms, to find that "she chid him not" (MM1v).

The shy/bold offerings of these lovers construct a devious form of topicality, which in turn creates a double-layered text appealing to a double audience. An amorous audience will recognize themselves as signified in the texts and may, like Amphilanthus, reward the exhibition of lovers' desires with caresses. A tactful but unreceptive audience will suppress, or pretend to suppress, obvious topical readings. Refusing their own signification, they may respond, or pretend to respond, by constructing the poem as pleasurable artifact whose beauty can be experienced and praised in a distanced manner. Thus, lovers' poems simultaneously partake of the contradictory elements of tortured confession and charming ornament, reflecting the contradictory desires to exhibit amorous feelings and to deny them by calling them art.

This form of topicality contains important implications for *Urania,* with its main plot proceeding from just such a sequence of poems offered by Pamphilia, whose topical allusion to Wroth can be admitted or denied, to the object of her love. Like lovers' poems, Wroth's romance presents itself as a pleasantly refined work of art written to amuse courtly readers; like lovers' poems, this representation exists in striking contradiction to disturbing episodes of transparently personal content. Thus, the author of *The Countess of Montgomery's Urania* deviously shifts responsibility for the work's occasionally scandalous material to the reader by offering it under the thinnest of topical veils.

This double audience of knowledgeably voyeuristic/discreetly unaware readers finds its ultimate progression in the present/absent audience also frequently created for lovers' poems in *The Countess of Montgomery's Urania.* Not all lovers address their poetry to their beloveds; many of them confess to the air, to an absence that almost always conceals a presence. Believing themselves alone, lovers in Wroth's romance often find relief for intense emotional pain by setting feelings to meter, only to be overheard or read by compassionate audiences, whose fortuitous appearances far exceed the laws of chance. Near the beginning of Wroth's romance, for example, Urania enters a cave only to find a poem whose very first line, "Here all alone in silence might I mourne," declares the absence of an audience as necessary to the composition of its text. But, like other such texts, it is inevitably found, and its author Perissus, unlike Sidney's Gynecia, is consoled.

The repetition of this unlikely narrative circumstance is based upon an authorial fantasy. Just as rape fantasies enable a woman to imagine sexual pleasure without acknowledging voluntary participation in a forbidden act, this fantasy of the present/absent audience permits the exposure of personal feelings without admitting responsibility for such exhibitionism. Like the voyeuristic/discreet audience, the present/absent audience shifts the guilt for its disclosures upon the voyeuristic reader, who could, after all, have moved on. Thus, both versions of the double audience are created by the head-on collision of two conflicting desires: the compulsion to relieve intense feelings by expressing them to a receptive audience and a requirement for reticence deriving from social prohibitions and from an impulse of self-protection. This contradiction, which lies at the source of many works of art, is rendered particularly acute in the work of a

Renaissance woman, whose public speech and writing faced special obstacles imposed by her culture. Wroth's impassioned denial in a letter of any intent to "give cause of offence," her innocent grief to be "thus much mistaken"[52] despite the volatile material inscribed in her romance, suggests that, in contradiction to the mechanisms of her own text, her writer's-audience-that-is-always-a-fiction was discreetly unaware or even absent.

Devious Topicality

By representing itself as light fare for discriminating palates, *Urania* provides readers a viable excuse for ignoring its topicality. Filled with leisurely spates of storytelling among aristocratic characters for little apparent motive, *Urania* offers itself, like the supposedly charming poems of lovers, as an ornamental source of pleasurable amusement. The following exchange, with its stories mixed of fact and fiction, seems particularly self-referential: "The Queenes of *Naples* and *Cicely* kept alwaies together, and never failed walking in the sweet woods . . . there they passed the time together, telling stories of themselves and others, mixed many times with pretty fine fictions, both being excellently witty, and the Queene of *Naples* rare in Poetry" (FFF3).

In one of the few gendered markers of a narrative situation, the title's naming of a woman as the formative audience for *The Countess of Montgomery's Urania* represents Wroth's work as an act of friendship between women. Like the stories exchanged between the queens of Naples and Cicely, the romance requires for its completion no verifiable result: no heroic endeavor, no seduction, no revelation of a hidden identity. Like the stories exchanged between these queens, *The Countess of Montgomery's Urania* also conveys a discursive sense of pleasure with its stories, first of lovers and then of their grown-up children, which meander over several hundred pages without any clear destination or obvious point.

In the "title" in its title, *The Countess of Montgomery's Urania* represents itself as reading appropriate to upper-class readers; lower-class readers would presumably be called away from such lengthy entertainments by other duties. The artist who drew the title page of the folio catches this quality of well-heeled recreation with a drawing of an excessively well-dressed man and woman about to set off arm-in-arm over a well-manicured estate, complete with formal gardens, which features the towers and the theater-on-a-hill that serve as the locations of two episodes of enchantment in the folio. This work, the title page implies, aims only to please.

But, as in the frequently agonized content of lovers' poems, the events detailed in many of Wroth's histories disturb the smooth surface of this representation. Many of them participate in a form of topicality as devious as that determining the love poems. Pretending to offer mildly amusing narratives for the enjoyment of a courtly audience, narrators repeatedly reveal their own tortured histories complete with cues alerting their auditors to the presence of personal content, such as, most obviously, the conventional slip into the first person. When Antissia concludes her sad story of a deserted widow with the plaint, "Unfortunate I . . . but little happier then you see me now" (MM3), Pamphilia smiles at her apparently unintentional disclosure, and Amphilanthus, politely disguising his understanding, bids her to proceed. In response to Dorolina's urgings to disclose her sorrow, Pamphilia tells the story of Lindamira, also slipping into the first person at the end. Dorolina masks her recognition of the personal application of Lindamira's tale with a polite façade of ignorance, thinking it "some thing more exactly related then a fixion, yet her discretion taught her to be no Inquisitor" (HHH2).

In her tactful response, Dorolina, with the other courtiers, offers a role to the discriminating reader. Readers who choose to acknowledge the presence of personal material by cooperating in the creation of topical meanings are themselves made responsible for the scandal exposed by their own voyeuristic gaze. They have alternatives. Readers can choose, like the compassionate Dorolina, to pretend that these narratives which more than point to—which, indeed, headline—their self-referentiality are merely stories. Such considerate averting of the eyes, which attests to the aristocratic breeding of an audience, does not proceed from blindness. It represents instead, to turn a phrase, a willing suspension of belief.

Offering this role as courteous reader was not an altogether benign act on the part of the text or its author. Probably most readers who recognized themselves or their family and friends in this text were coerced to gloss over the insult to prevent self-disclosure of their private scandals. Lord Denny's protest was, in its way, remarkable. His anger at Wroth's representation of his near-murder of his own daughter for adultery not only reveals him as rude or even lower-class according to the narrative conditions inscribed within *Urania*; it also implies the accuracy of her allusions. No doubt most of those who read or heard about Denny's verses were as interested in his implicit confession to his attempted murder of his daughter as outraged on his behalf.

How many other readers remained privately offended, without

daring to call attention to their own scandals by any public protest? Wroth's romance probably contains more topicality than a modern audience can know. A contemporary comment by John Chamberlain claims that Wroth had offended "many others" besides Lord Denny: "Many others she makes bold with, and they say she takes great libertie or rather licence to traduce whom she please, and thinckes she daunces in a net."[53] And Wroth's letter to the duke of Buckingham requesting a warrant to stop the sale of her romance complained of "strang constructions" made of her book two months before she received Denny's verses; perhaps others besides Denny had been offended. Edward Le Comte has noted Wroth's encoding of the events leading up to the murder of Sir Thomas Overbury in 1613 in the story of a gentlewoman who, in loyalty to her lover, refused her husband his sexual rights for three years.[54] While there is no means of proving the accuracy of tantalizing disclosures of bedroom activities (or their absence), they must have intrigued readers not personally involved. What were the reactions of the Lady Essex?

It is tempting to perceive scandalous episodes like these in *Urania* as acts of literary revenge upon the society that had cast its author out of its circle for transgressions that seem almost mundane among the array of possibly topical accounts of adultery, incest, and murder in her work. While many of the allusions can no longer be ascertained by modern audiences, the text erects a prominent scaffolding of hermeneutic potentiality by offering prominent cues to the presence of topical allusions to private scandals, some of which were probably decipherable by contemporaries. For example, gratuitously extraneous details point, accurately or not, to real identities beneath pastoral names. One pronounced example occurs near the end, when in the midst of a story about her scorn of love, a sad lady divulges that she had been bred with a widow's son, three years older than herself, and her four daughters; furthermore, this widow had been the fourth wife of her husband, who had had one son and one daughter by his first wife, one son and two daughters by his second wife, and six daughters by his third wife (MS II, 30Av). Since none of this impressive array of progeny enters the narrative, the reader is sent scurrying elsewhere—to records of family trees, perhaps—to make sense of these disclosures. Whether any sad lady actually possessed this configuration of relatives, the text has performed its operations upon its readers merely by making them wonder about a real-life referent.

Thus, whether they allude to topical circumstances or not, statements like Belizia's claim to be the daughter of an earl marshall (ZZZ3) or a forester's claim to be the third son of the earl to whom the prince gave charge to his best forest (OO4) tantalize any curious reader, Renaissance or modern, with the prospect of forthcoming exposures of private information about public personages. Prominently placed statements of "faigning" stories also alert readers to their truth (BB4; GGG3). Not all of these topical allusions are accusatory. Many are confessional, concerning Mary Wroth and her own family. These confessions are often signaled by near-anagrams which Wroth adopts from Sidney's romance. Just as Sidney's "Philisides" unmistakably pointed to "Philip Sidney," so "Bersindor" points to "Robert Sidney" (Rober Sidn), "Treborius" to some "Robert" (Robert ius), "Bellamira" to some beautiful "Mary" (Bella/Mari).

Mistaking discretion for blindness, a New Critical position leery of mistaking literature for life would deny that the text triggers these topical mechanisms. Such caution ignores not only the obvious operations within the text, but also attitudes towards the genre at the time, inconsistent with a perception of romance as a self-sufficient artifact. The genre was strongly influenced by Tasso's recommendation that romance mix fact with fiction to ensure a serious reception of its literary novelties.[55] According to a character in John Barclay's *Argenis,* whose Latin version was published in the same year as Wroth's folio, intermingling fiction and fact provides the interpretive uncertainty necessary to win assent to its ethical system without alienating the audience. Its concluding recovery of a cabinet with a little key points to the importance of a topical level of interpretation; and in his translation, Robert Le Grys even appended a key to the text to identify the main characters in response, he claimed, to the request of King Charles himself. This topical aspect may have been responsible in part for the work's popularity, indicated by the three different translations of *Argenis* produced in less than a decade.[56]

While the topicality of Barclay's work was purportedly political rather than personal, this distinction fades in such newsworthy items as that the son of Queen Hyanisbe (Queen Elizabeth) is, as it turns out, the heir of Meleander (Henry III of France).[57] Similarly, the romance written by Wroth's own uncle contained topical allusions, including the unmistakable "Philisides" to signify himself. The political allegory of Philisides' beast fable mixes with more personal topical references, such as the apparent allusion of Philoclea to Penelope Rich. Thus, it was not Wroth's topicality itself that was unusual. Why did it provoke sufficient outrage to shut down the publication of *Urania?* Perhaps her refusal even to pretend that her topicality was political, rather than personal, removed one justification for her allusions. Perhaps her gender made her more vulnerable to such silencing. Or perhaps the content of her topical allusions to violent private occurrences in households such as Lord Denny's was simply too shocking for influential members of the reading public to tolerate. Wroth's disclaimers of malicious intent no doubt proceeded in part from critical perceptions of the genre of the romance, but she used these precepts to enable the divulgence of libellous disclosures without accepting responsibility for their consequences. In the Renaissance, her romance was withdrawn from sale. Earlier in this century, she would perhaps have been liable for suit in a court of law.

Exhibiting Her Self

While the motive of revenge cannot be entirely dismissed, Wroth's inscribed acts of narration suggest another reason for the topicality of her romance. An internal compulsion to speak rather than to endure psychic destruction motivates the narrators of various self-referential histories within the romance. The relevance of this motive to Wroth's own authorship is strongly implied by the representation, accurate or not, of these histories as her own.

The person most subject to topical allusion in *The Countess of Montgomery's Urania* is Mary Wroth herself, who portrays the events of her own life under at least three romantic identities: Pamphilia, Bellamira, and Lindamira.[58] Despite the differences in their stories, all three protagonists share various characteristics. They are all the victims of love for an inconstant lover during their marriages; yet their extramarital affections do not incur the disapproval of the ever-compassionate narrator. All three write poetry, and the authorship of these self-referential figures provides insight into the version of authorship Wroth used to enable her own writing. While all three characters maintain fronts of loving forgiveness, the unflattering details they reveal reflect badly upon figures transparently representing Wroth's husband (in Bellamira's narrative), Queen Anne (in Lindamira's narrative), and William Herbert (in Pamphilia's narrative). For all of them, these revelations, and their license to tell them, are sanctioned by an appeal to emotional compulsion, the relief of their feelings necessitated by an impending threat of damage to their inner selves.

An undeniably sympathetic character, the constant Bellamira tells her sad story to the disguised Amphilanthus. When an evil servant falsely tells her beloved she is betrothed and then tells her that her beloved is betrothed, she accepts the earnest Treborious, her father's choice, from lack of hope. After his visit to her husband's estate, the king commands her presence at court, where she sees her beloved tilt. Her husband, who delights in hunting, dies; and her son's death follows soon thereafter. When her beloved remains false to her, she retreats to the cave containing the tomb of her son. Even more than the deaths of her son and her husband, she mourns her lover's betrayal, which she describes as her "last, and greatest loss" (TT3). Her poetry, an exercise taught her by her "undoer," is much admired by Amphilanthus; and his approval prompts her to compose more verses.

Pointers to Wroth's self-referentiality in Bellamira's story include Bellamira's name (beautiful Mari) and her husband's, Treborius (Robert + ius); the king's visit to the Wroth estate, mentioned both in a letter from Wroth to Queen Anne and in a poem from Jonson to Robert Wroth; and the sequence first of her husband's death and then of her son's.[59] Robert Wroth's love of hunting is witnessed by Ben Jonson's poem to him beginning "How blest art thou, canst love the countrey, Wroth."[60] A contratopical element includes her son's love of hunting, for Wroth's son died as a small child. Bellamira's history includes the mildest revelations of the three. Its primary aggression is reserved for the villanous servant who falsely informed first her beloved and then her of the other's betrothals. Her virtuous attempts to deflect her anger towards her lover, who left her when he was assured of her faith, also suggest the "naturall inconstancy" of Wroth's lover, implied elsewhere to be William Herbert. Bellamira's portrait of her cloddish husband is most unflattering. In the hopes of hearing news of her beloved, she commended his "ordinary talke when hee praised rude sports, or told the plaine Jests of his Hunts-men" (TT2v). This petty criticism hardly seems appropriate for a loyal widow, whether she be Bellamira or Wroth herself. In addition, any grief Bellamira felt over her husband's death is eclipsed by her grief over her son's death and, especially, over her lover's falseness, which represented her "last, and greatest" loss (TT3). The slightness of her husband's role in Bellamira's history and in her emotional life suggests that Wroth used Bellamira's story to express some degree of passive anger at her husband, as well as at her lover and his false informant, even after his death.

By far the most extensive and absorbing use of self-referential topicality, arching over the entire romance in both its published and unpublished parts, is the narrative of Pamphilia, whose relationship with Amphilanthus structures *Urania*. To Denny's identification of Wroth as Pamphilia can be added cues from the text. Like Sidney's "Astrophil and Stella," the sonnet sequence "Pamphilia to Amphilanthus" included in the folio triggers topical identifications. These are amplified by the name Rosindy (Ro Sidny) for one of Pamphilia's brothers, for one of Mary Wroth's brothers was also named Robert Sidney after her father. Pamphilia's sister Philistella, a name with a distinctly Sidnean ring, may allude to Mary's sister Philippa, who, like Philistella, died in childbirth.[61] Apparently in a final attempt to provide more congruence between Pamphilia's life and Wroth's, the last pages of the manuscript relate, with remarkably little fuss, that Pamphilia becomes a widow, "yett the mother of a brave boy, who soone . . . died" (MS II, 29Br).

Textual cues also point to Amphilanthus's identity as William Herbert, the father of Wroth's two illegitimate children. Her inclusion of a poem ascribed to Herbert, "Had I loved butt at that rate," as written by Amphilanthus probably extends beyond literary tribute to identification.[62] Like Amphilanthus, brother to Pamphilia's best friend, Urania, Herbert was brother-in-law to Wroth's friend the countess of Montgomery. The accuracy of the detail repeated from the Bellamira story that he married when an evil servant falsely informed him that his true beloved was betrothed cannot be verified; but his reputation as a philanderer gained him notice in Clarendon's *History of the Rebellion* as "immoderately given up to women," especially those of "wit and spirit and knowledge," to whom he "sacrificed himself, his precious time, and much of his fortune."[63]

Within this reading of Pamphilia as a version of Wroth, the narrator's practice of the heroics of constancy towards Amphilanthus becomes absolutely understandable; for, decoded in this way, *Urania* can be read as a record of Mary Wroth's forgiving constancy to her fickle lover. For Pamphilia's constancy to be heroic, Amphilanthus's infidelities must be cruel and blatant. They are. By recording them in its text, *The Countess of Montgomery's Urania* exposes material which, according to the etiquette of lovers, should remain unspoken. By exalting its heroine's constancy, *Urania* becomes, like other narratives told by constant female characters who mask their rage, an angry text. Yet her devious topicality permits Wroth, like other constant heroines, to point to her own very noisy silence as a mark of her constancy.

The evidently self-referential story of Lindamira, which Pamphilia tells only under the urging of Dorolina, records anger towards the court more than to her lover. Lindamira, eldest daughter of "Bersindos" (Rober ssidn), was so favored by the queen of France (England) that she seldom left court. Her unspoken love for a man who did not know of her love was hardly scandalous. But what is the reader supposed to make of the delicious detail that the queen mother loved him, too? At the time, there was no queen mother; for Mary Stuart, James's mother, had been executed by Queen Elizabeth in 1587. Apparently the reference to the queen mother was a red herring, for the word "Mother" soon disappears from the account: it was the jealousy of the queen (Queen Anne) which, prompted by malicious gossip, precipitated Lindamira's otherwise inexplicable loss of favor and subsequent exile from court. It was the queen, not the queen mother, who "borne a Princesse, and match'd to a King, yet could not resist" the power of love. "Deceived in her greatnesse," Her Majesty forgot that "in Loves Court all are fellow-subjects" (GGG3v). Does the confusion of the persons caused by the brief substitution of "Queen Mother" for "Queen" provide the interpretive uncertainty necessary for Wroth's disavowal of responsibility for her allegations? Those involved would have had no doubts.

Wroth's own experience of masques is embedded in this moving detail of the suddenness of her disgrace: "*Lindamira* remaining like one in a gay Masque, the night pass'd, they are in their old clothes againe" (GGG3v). Lindamira's impeccable loyalty to the queen, claiming to "love her displeasure, since shee hath honour'd me," heroizes its author but further damns the queen as arbitrary and unfeeling. Wroth's presentation of Lindamira as the innocent victim of amorous intrigues at court involving even the queen must have been offensive to powerful figures, including no doubt the queen's royal husband.

Liana's Cabinet

Pamphilia's slip into the first person reveals Lindamira's story as her own; and Lindamira's motive for telling a self-referential story may inscribe, or, more likely, be represented as inscribing, Wroth's possible motive as well. Lindamira herself silently endures the queen's disfavor and her husband's jealousy for fourteen years before her misery drives her to compose a poem of complaint. Her license for authorship is, paradoxically, her fourteen years of silence, a mark of her constancy that, oddly enough, does not seem to be compromised by her complaint. Internal compulsion motivates the episodes of authorship in all three narratives. Driven by the intensity more than by the length of her sorrow, Bellamira's grief over her beloved's betrayal causes her to put "her thoughts in some kind of measure, which else were measureless; this was Poetry" (SS4). She shows her loyalty in her complaint by patterning her activity after her lover's; she is, even in describing the pain he has caused her, loyally imitating him. Like a courtly reader, Amphilanthus obligingly praises her skill rather than acknowledging her content; but the choice of Amphilanthus at all adds a poignant present/absent sense of him as audience in the text. Present for Bellamira, he is absent from Pamphilia. A false lover himself, he approves Bellamira's poems describing the pain caused by her false lover, who is, since both Pamphilia and Bellamira signify aspects of Wroth, a version of himself.

Like Lindamira and Bellamira, Pamphilia tells her story under emotional compulsion, to provide relief necessary to her troubled mind. Her confession is elicited, and justified, by the sympathetic urgings of Dorolina and the court party to reveal the source of her sorrow. Pressing Pamphilia to tell her story, Dorolina likens the emotional condition of a silent women to threads in embroidered cloths which become worn unless paper is laid between them. The papers on which an author writes resonate with the papers which prevent the destruction of the sewn outlines of the self, represented as an embroidered work of art vulnerable to the workings of time and bad handling. According to this image, refusing to tell one's troubles is bad housewifery. This justification of woman's speech by inner necessity declares the right of the self-referential heroines, and by implication that of Wroth herself, to speech and to authorship.

The inner necessity licensing women's speech in this image of the fretted threads organizes the image of Liana's cabinet as well. Liana's cabinet provides another evocative metaphor claiming emotional necessity as license for women to speak. Liana, believing herself betrayed by a lover for whose love she had resisted her father's "unfatherly tortures," describes her compulsion to speak through an image of an over-filled cabinet: "When I had endured a little space (like a Cabinet so fild with treasure, as though not it selfe, yet the lock or hinges cannot containe it, but breake open): so did the lock of my speech flie abroad, to discover the treasure of my truth, and the infinitenesse of his falshood, not to bee comprehended" (EE2). The lock which must break under pressure from what it contains calls up associations with prohibitions against women's speech, which must "flie abroad" under the pressure of its "truth." Locks work only on containers that are not overfilled; their inhibiting function depends to some extent upon the volition, or the condition, of the contained.

While Liana is not herself a poet, the practice by Pamphilia and other women characters of keeping their poetry in their cabinets also makes this image resonate powerfully with women's authorship. Written "truth," too, cannot be forever contained; but must burst forth, like a cabinet filled with verses, into public view, whether that public is the audience of a manuscript or of a published work. While men no doubt also put their poetry into cabinets, the cabinet image seems evocatively female, as a representation of a dark, secret, interior space where "meaning" grows until it forces itself out into the world. Finally, it is not only Liana's "truth" which flies abroad, but also the "infinitenesse" of her beloved's "falshood." In this image, Liana's cabinet links the silence required of the constant heroine to the words required of an author. The constant lover's heroism is predicated upon her beloved's infidelities, which produce a desire to speak, to grieve, to blame. The silence in which she endures her pain measures her constancy. But the image of Liana's cabinet implies that a constant heroine can break her silence under compulsion without impugning her virtue or loyalty. If the lock does not break, the cabinet will.

Pamphilia's self represents one final location of the necessary compulsion of speech. Soon after her wedding, when Pamphilia finds herself alone, she is finally able to express her grief over her loss of Amphilanthus. The text uses an image of burning in a closed place to permit her passionate complaint to the vacant air: "Passion beeing so fierce, soe strange if truly felt, and on noble cause as itt is like a secrett fire pent close in, butt noe longer having inward meanes . . . it breaks out in flames, ore wurse, consumes the place itt is penned in to ashes, soe had her hart dunn, such true fire of passion possessing itt, had nott itt gained this delivering her paines in her secrett waulke" (MS II, 12Av). Unlike most such confessions, hers is not actually overheard; but her reddened eyes betray her to Amphilanthus and, when he rids himself of other company, lead to their mutual recognition of their love, satisfactorily revealed by his placement of groaning kisses upon her willing mouth. His kisses are apparently justified within this text so sympathetic to lovers by the tears which remain as traces of her lament, spoken, like Liana's truth, to prevent the destruction of her inner self. No cues within the text blame this noisily silent practitioner of the heroics of constancy for the expression of the passion that leads eventually to her union with Amphilanthus. She was, evidently, silent as long as possible.

The confinement of the fire to an enclosed place that represents Pamphilia's self resonates with Liana's cabinet. In a trace of a pregnancy metaphor, Pamphilia's "delivering" of her pains provides reason to perceive her enclosed space as specifically female. An implicit link to women's authorship may also exist in a rare destruction of a woman's poem in this romance. Sitting on her bed with her cabinet and candle, Pamphilia takes the "new-writ" lines and "gave them buriall" (H2v). How did she give them burial? Did she tear them up?

Did she burn them? How did women authors commonly destroy their work? Sometimes, surely, sitting alone late at night in a candlelit chamber, they must have burned their poems. This possible practice among women poets provides an authorial association that is strengthened by the word "penned." As the fire threatens to consume the "place itt is penned in to ashes," the "place" readily becomes paper. The word "penned" creates a surplus of meaning linking the destruction of poems by fire to destruction of the self. Like the containment and flying forth of Liana's truth, "penned in" and "penned" moves beyond punning to suggest the paradox of women's speech and writing in the Renaissance.

Illusions of Love

The topicality of *The Countess of Montgomery's Urania* is highly sophisticated: it constructs ambiguous and even contradictory roles for its readers (who are to pretend ignorance of the real-life referents for the allusions sketched out elaborately before them) and for authors (whose angry narratives are justified only by long-continued silences). While these roles are not to be dismissed offhand (undoubtedly *some* readers and writers conformed to them), neither are they to be taken at face value. Inscriptions of three works of art demonstrate a similarly high level of self-consciousness within the text concerning its own processes; these inscriptions reveal three complex models for the possible place of a text within the lives of its readers. The first of these is demonstrated by a book read by Pamphilia that had more significance for her life than she knew. In striking similarity to Wroth's own romance, this book details a woman's affections for an inconstant lover: "The subject was Love, and the story she then was reading, the affection of a Lady to a brave Gentleman, who equally loved, but being a man, it was necessary for him to exceede a woman in all things, so much as inconstancie was found fit for him to excell her in, hee left her for a new" (LL4v).[64] Exclaiming upon the author's disloyalty to love, Pamphilia throws the book from her and, happily confident of her own beloved, she places her hand upon her breast to feel the presence of Amphilanthus's true heart within her. Pamphilia's book turns out to be more accurate than her own predictions. The same cultural texts that determine the contents of a book determine as well the behavior of its readers. As a member of the same culture that formed her book, Pamphilia is forced to experience within her own life the plot of the very text she had rejected.

Melissea's masque—which in form and content is not unlike entertainments, such as Wroth's own *Love's Victorie,* that were performed on country estates—suggests the opposite possibility. A young seafaring lad woos a dainty sea nymph, only to be counselled against love's vanity by an unusually convincing old man. The three conclude the masque by singing their refusal to love. When Pamphilia sighs over the lad's fickleness, Melissea labels her work a "phansie," not applicable to Pamphilia's life: "You are non of this madame, nor is this butt a phansie, for love indeed hath a more steddy place, and throne of abiding when in such Royall harts" (MS I, 22Av). Melissea's masque, as opposed to Pamphilia's book, pretends no large truth. Written to please the taste of the queen of Frigia, it does not reflect the realities of its wider culture beyond the court. Its real "meaning" is, in fact, in its function as ruse, to allow Melissea to speak to Pamphilia alone.

To what extent does the reduction of Melissea's masque to a "phansie" reflect a corresponding sense of country entertainments and, by implication, the unreality of the masques of the Jacobean court? If it does reflect a sense of the true character of these entertainments, then this episode provides an unparalleled example of a contemporary reaction to court masques by one who had actually acted in them and reveals that all members of the Jacobean court were not seduced by masques' "illusions of power."[65] How does this disillusionment reflect upon Wroth's own romance? As discussed above, Wroth's romance was implicated in masques and even formed the basis for one; and so it would not be difficult to perceive Melissea's work as a reflection of Wroth's own. Was there a sense in which this episode points to Wroth's own writing as a "phansie," possibly also limited by the aristocratic tastes of the readers, like the countess of Montgomery, for whom she wrote it?

The unreality of the Jacobean masque, as well as its implications for Wroth's romance, appears in the third prototype for the relationship of fictional works to the lives of their readers. Pamphilia and Urania, shipwrecked upon an island in the Adriatic, come upon a beautiful round building. When they open the door, they find "as magnificant a Theater as Art could frame" (RR4v) with a throne and four rich chairs of marble. The text flags warnings in its description of their curiosity for such vanities: "Needs this richnes must be neerer beheld and (like women) must see novelties; nay even *Pamphilia* was inticed to vanity in this kind" (RR4v). As mysterious music plays, Urania and Pamphilia sit in the chairs as the gate locks behind them, to remain enchanted until the arrival of a man "most loving and most beloved" and of a lady in poor habits that disguised "greatnesse." Far from being unhappy, Urania and Pamphilia are immobilized by the satisfaction of their desires; for they believe that they see their loves "joying in them" (RRv). The danger posed by their enchantment with theater is clear. While Pamphilia basks in the illusion of Amphilanthus's love, he has found himself another beloved. Pamphilia realizes her mistake when the doors of the theater open to reveal the real Amphilanthus. As Pamphilia rises in her chair, she sees his new love, Musalina, and knows herself betrayed.

The reference to Jacobean masques is implied by the throne in this theater, which seats the royal presence that formed such a determining role for masques performed for James. The masquelike coloration of the episode is intensified by the several disguises, from shepherdesses to Egyptians, of those who attempt to release Pamphilia and Urania. In its representation of the enjoyment of theater as a pleasant enchantment from which its audience needs rescue, this episode reveals how the pleasures of theatrical illusion dangerously blind its audience to unpleasant realities. Does this insight reflect an awareness of the illusory nature of the representations of royal power played out in masques performed for James, later proving so lethal for Charles?

This episode implicates *The Countess of Montgomery's Urania* and perhaps the genre of romance in general within its criticism of fictive illusions. Like the theater which enchanted Pamphilia and Urania, romances were said to possess special appeal for women, attracted by such "novelties."[66] While the story of Pamphilia and Amphilanthus sounds a minor chord, many of the narratives in Wroth's romance end happily for lovers. Like Pamphilia and Urania, its readers, by identifying with its characters, no doubt also experienced the illusion of being loved. In this episode, *Urania* reveals a consciousness of the dangers of fiction. This prototype implies that romances, like Jacobean masques, provided a refuge from disagreeable aspects of life; and by providing readers an illusory sense of the fulfillment of readers' desires through fiction, such works may have prevented the actual fulfillment of desires in life.

Scenes of Reading

A discussion of *The Countess of Montgomery's Urania* cannot end here; for no treatment of Wroth's romance would be complete without an analysis of the many and various scenes of reading in this work, which are extremely . . .[67]

Chapter 5
Singing with the (Tongue) of a Nightingale

Besides the countess of Pembroke and Lady Mary Wroth, there appears to have been another woman writer in the Sidney circle, the anonymous author of three copiously revised holograph poems included in the Bright manuscript (British Library, Additional MS 15,232). The watermark of the manuscript's paper, Briquet, 9665, indicates that these three holograph poems were composed no earlier than 1580–84; copied into blank pages or spaces left between other poems in the manuscript, they appear to date somewhat later than the other contents of the volume.[1] A late-sixteenth- or early-seventeenth-century date is consonant with the author's hand, which appears, for reasons stated below, to be that of a woman. Her membership in the Sidney family or circle is indicated by the nature of the Bright manuscript itself, whose several associations with the Sidney circle include the presence of the most accurate extant texts of twenty-six poems from Sir Philip Sidney's *Astrophel and Stella*.[2] The actual author of these poems may never be ascertained: the manuscript itself includes no attribution, and handwriting samples are no longer extant for prominent candidates such as the countess of Pembroke's only daughter Anne and Mary Wroth's younger sister Catherine.

These three holograph poems, which differ radically in content and in persona, provide an uncommon opportunity to study three possibilities for authorial self-creation attempted by one poet, apparently over a relatively brief span of time. Together, they reveal a poet of unusual adaptability. The first and third holograph poems, especially, demonstrate her ability to imitate, even to mimic, remarkably different authorial voices from poems current in her day. As imitations, these poems attempt accommodations to discourses circulated among male poets; for this reason, the first and third poems reveal perhaps even more about the barriers to women's writing in the Renaissance than the ingenious versions of authorship offered by the writings of the countess of Pembroke and Lady Mary Wroth.

In the first holograph, the author assumes with considerable accuracy the earnest, sober voice characteristic of the turgid mid-sixteenth-century aesthetic; like the poets of *Tottels Miscellany,* she inculcates readers in morality, in this case by avowing the superiority of virtue to beauty. The conformity of her first version of authorship to a patriarchal model of women espouses cultural precepts advocating the absence of women's desire. As was perhaps not unusual for other didactic poems of this time, her voice remains indistinguishable from the voices of handbooks, sermons, and other works instilling virtue in young ladies.

Echoing the syntax of Sir Philip Sidney as well as the wording and content of sonnets by Sidney and other courtier poets, the first six lines of the third poem show that the author is equally capable of mimicking the voice of the courtly sonneteer. Material excised from the poem suggests, however, that the role of courtier-poet was not comfortable for this author; and in the second six lines of the poem, the voice of the sober moralist interrupts the voice of the urbane courtier. The centrifugal force of these competing discourses fragments the poem, spinning the final lines off into a chaotic poetics. Reflecting male attitudes and male experiences, the aesthetics of courtly poetry which empowered numerous male authors did not empower her; and the way in which the discourse and the poetic of the first poem rupture the third one provides insight into the exclusion of women poets from the ranks of courtly sonneteers of the English Renaissance.

Only the second poem offers an authorial role that serves as a successful vehicle for women's speech: the nightingale whose song becomes increasingly optimistic about love as winter yields to spring and then to summer. Less easily traced to other poetic voices, the voice of this poem remains consistent, uninterrupted, seemingly reflective of an unconflicted authorial role. But this relatively successful song of the nightingale exists only through the suppression of another voice. Optimistic even by Renaissance standards, this poet's version of the nightingale, explicitly named Philomela, both elicits an awareness of its Ovidian myth of the violated virgin whose tongue was cut out and requires an absolute suppression of awareness of that myth. With her anger as present/absent as her tongue, the nightingale Philomela presents a powerful analogy for women writers in the Renaissance. Her tongue mutilated so that she cannot speak, Philomela becomes a figure for silenced anger. When her tongue is restored to her in her shape as a nightingale, her silence remains just as profound. Instead of lamenting her rape or accusing her rapist, she is required by the constraints of the culture which has created her to sing sweet songs of love.

The cultural conditions which formed this anonymous poet's version of authorship are best understood against an array of Renaissance Philomelas, all of whom represent a version of the poet created by writers within the Sidney family, including Philip Sidney and Mary Wroth, as well as by much-read writers like Spenser and Shakespeare. The gaps between these Renaissance versions of Philomela and her Ovidian source make visible the otherwise hidden swervings and omissions caused by anxieties about women's anger that formed such a formidable precondition for women's authorship in the Renaissance.

Her Sweet Roman Hand

The identification of the handwriting of these holograph poems as belonging to a woman was first made by the late Peter J. Croft and corroborated by R. E. Alton, both prominent paleographers expert in Renaissance writing.[3] The difference between the writing of men and women of that time proceeded from the difference in their education, not from handwriting characteristics innate to either gender. While most aristocratic men and women could write both italic and secretary hand, aristocratic women favored the italic; indeed, in his text on handwriting, *The Pens Excellencie* (1617?), Martin Billingsley specifically recommends teaching women to write italic because of its greater ease.[4] This tendency perhaps informs "the sweet roman hand" of Maria which Malvolio attributed to Olivia in Shakespeare's *Twelfth Night* (3.4.28). Of eighteen anonymous poems copied into the Bright manuscript, these holograph poems represent the only examples of italic.

More significant, however, is the difference in the relative amount of writing that aristocratic young men and women actually engaged in over the course of their education. Rather than reading and writing being taught simultaneously, reading was commonly taught first and then, after students achieved a sufficient level of literacy, writing was taught. Cressy has noted that women of this time consistently lagged behind men in their ability to sign their name on official documents, but his conclusion that they were illiterate is undermined by his own observation that writing one's own name was not commonly taught early in the writing curriculum.[5] Since writing was taught later than reading, it was quite possible for a student to be able to read but not to write, and it was certainly possible for a student to be much more fluent in reading than in writing.

This combination of fluent reading and awkward writing would seem to be especially likely for aristocratic young women in the Renaissance. Aristocratic young men, usually sent away to school, commonly wrote more often and, therefore, with more facility. Young women, staying at home where they spent much of their time sewing, attending to household tasks, or reading, had less occasion to write. Thus, the very clumsiness of the hand, with its lack of an assured rhythm, its large number of pen lifts, and the uncertainty of direction of its ascending and descending strokes, so at odds with the relative sophistication of some of the poetry, strongly indicates a young woman as the probable author of these holograph poems.[6]

Sidney Provenance

Several indications point to the provenance of the Bright manuscript within the Sidney circle. Its inclusion of the most accurate extant texts of twenty-six poems from Philip Sidney's *Astrophel and Stella* show its close descent from a copy owned by the countess of Pembroke by 1588.[7] The first lines of two of the eighteen anonymous manuscript poems explicitly echo first lines from Sidney's poetry.[8] Also significant is the presence of one line from the third holograph poem in the manuscript continuation of Mary Wroth's *Urania*. Since "sprites" and "spirits" were essentially the same word (*OED*), the holograph poem's line "Pulle up your spryttes" represents a close variant of the line "Pull up your spiritts" (MS II, 25Bv), spoken by the character Leutissia in the unpublished portion of Wroth's romance. If Wroth or the author of the holograph was not quoting from a third source or composing the same line independently, this holograph line may represent a quotation either from or by Wroth's manuscript. Sidney provenance is all the more probable because of the close circulation of both the Wroth manuscript and the Bright manuscript. There are no other known quotations from Wroth's manuscript continuation, which apparently existed only in a unique holograph copy; few persons outside the immediate family even seemed to be aware of its existence. The close circulation of the Bright manuscript is suggested by the absence of any of the eighteen anonymous poems in other manuscripts or published volumes.

That the manuscript originated specifically within the Robert Sidney family may be indicated by the name "Hen fell" scribbled lightly in a Renaissance hand at the bottom of the inside front cover, for a "Mr. fell" was with Robert Sidney at Hampton Court in 1612 and promised "to be shortly at Penshurst" with Robert's wife.[9] An origin within the Sidney circle, and especially within the Robert Sidney family, is also consonant with the subsequent ownership of the manuscript by Charles Montague, first Baron Halifax, whose arms were stamped on the cover between 1700, when he first became a baron, and 1714, when he was created earl of Halifax; for the Montagues were related by marriage to the Robert Sidneys.[10] Robert Sidney's second daughter, Catherine, niece to the countess of Pembroke and sister to Mary Wroth, was the first wife of Lewis Mansell; Mansell's third wife was Lady Elizabeth Montague, aunt to Charles, first Baron Halifax. Elizabeth Mansell could have come across a volume belonging to her husband's first wife and have passed it along to her nephew, well known in his own time for his literary interests. Another possible mode of transference lay in the close friendship between Robert Sidney's eldest son Robert and Walter Montague, uncle to Charles Montague, first Baron Halifax.[11]

While the handwriting of the three holograph poems strongly suggests a young woman whose labored italic has not yet achieved easy fluency, writing sometime near the end of the sixteenth century or the beginning of the seventeenth, the actual identity of this author will probably never be determined. The handwriting of comparatively few women of this period has survived, and most extant holographs date from late in their lives when they had attained enough power to negotiate business of some sort. Many of the few surviving letters are not holographs, but scribal copies signed at the end. Finally, many of the holographs are in secretary rather than italic hand. Thus, if the holograph hand in the Bright manuscript does belong to a woman, especially to a woman who died young, it is unlikely that she will be identified. Comparisons of handwriting samples that do exist indicate that the poems were not written by the countess of Pembroke, by Lady Mary Wroth, or by Sir Philip Sidney's daughter Elizabeth, the countess of Rutland, whose poetry, no longer extant, was so highly praised by Ben Jonson.[12]

Among the many women who left no handwriting samples, at least two young women of the Sidney family would seem to be promising candidates: Anne Herbert, daughter of the countess of Pembroke, who died in 1604 at about the age of twenty-one, and Catherine Sidney, Mary Wroth's younger sister closest to her in age, who died in 1616 at about the age of twenty-seven.[13] The manuscript's associations with the Robert Sidney family make of Catherine Sidney a particularly likely candidate. Catherine's marriage to Lewis Mansell, whose subsequent marriage made him an uncle to the first Baron Halifax, places her centrally within one possible area of provenance of the Bright manuscript. Even during her evidently unhappy marriage to Lewis Mansell, she frequently returned to Penshurst to visit her father's estate, where Mary Wroth also spent considerable time.[14]

"A most Careles Content of favore or disgrace"

The first of the three holograph poems in the Bright manuscript exists in three versions of six lines, all written on the same page. Perhaps originally intended as a final copy, the first version of the first holograph is painstakingly copied out with only one revision, possibly a copying error. But the author was apparently dissatisfied enough with this version to write two more, each containing additional revisions, in a looser, less self-conscious manner. In contrast to usual manuscript practice, the handwriting of the interlinear changes is less careful than the writing of the normally placed lines, indicating that the author, unconcerned that such changes be easily read, perceived the second and third versions as rough copy not finished enough for readers. An ending mark at the end of the third version perhaps indicates that the author perceived it as ready to be copied in final form. These three versions of this first holograph poem offer an unusual opportunity to analyze revisions of a poem written according to the mid-sixteenth-century aesthetic still in use, for example, at the countess of Pembroke's estate near the end of the sixteenth century.[15]

These are the three versions of the first holograph, with angle brackets to indicate material too blurred by water damage to read.

Version 1

A most Careles Content of fauore or disgrace
I fare esteem the Inwarde guyftes above <those of the face>
The fairest flowers fade when they forgoe the so<nne>
And beauty yealdes unto oulde agge the glory she had woune
But virteu will abyed allthough the flowers faulle
glory
Succeedyng agge will still renew the ~~good~~ good and all

Version 2

A most Careles Content of fauor or disgrace
thoes
I passe not for ~~noe~~ owtward partes wher virteu hath no place
coullers stayne by drappes or wth
The fayrest ~~flowers fade when they forgoe~~ the sunne
And Beauty doeth no longuer byed then youthfull bludde will runne
laste ~~byed~~ sweet wch tyem canne not make sower
But all good guyftes ~~Continew and faulle not wth the flowere~~
The glory of a virtuus lyeff Increaseth every hower

Version 3

A most Careles Content of fauor or disgrace
suche owtward shape I sett at naught wher virteu hath noe place
~~for fayrenes as the flowers fades~~
Good partes cann not Corrupt nor wth the Carcas dye
fades ~~and~~ coulleres change
good
when fayrnes ~~as the flower fades~~ and beauty faulles awrye
Hye glory to your selfe report shall euer rayse
If cheaffe Content on virteu leanes, and not by beauty stayes—

My edited third version of the first holograph is as follows:

A most careless content of favor or disgrace,
Such outward shape I set at naught where virtue hath no place.
Good parts cannot corrupt nor with the carcass die;
When fairness fades, good colors change, and beauty falls awry.
High glory to yourself, report shall ever raise
If chief content on virtue leans and not by beauty stays.

The first line, "A most Careles Content of fauore or disgrace," appears to represent a quotation of the words of another voice, a *donnée* derived from some source outside the poem; for despite the line's irregular metrics, which exist in striking divergence with the unfaltering iambs of the exceedingly regular poulter's measure of the other lines, this is the only one to remain unchanged through all three versions. Perhaps this first line identifies the poem as a reply to another poem with a similar first line, much like the iteration of the line, "Come live with me and be my love," from Christopher Marlowe's "The Passionate Shepherd" in "The Nymphs Reply to the Shepherd," attributed to Sir Walter Raleigh. The large number of "Aunsweres" written to or by friends in *Howell His Devises* (1581), a volume of poems written by a family retainer at the countess of Pembroke's estate, shows the prevalence of writing verses as replies at Wilton. Perhaps the practice was common among the Sidneys in general.

The apparent youth of the writer, together with the heavy-handed morality of the poem, also suggests the possibility that this first line formed some sort of schoolroom exercise in a type of poetry writing particularly appropriate for young women. In her diary, written in the late sixteenth and early seventeenth century, Grace Sherrington, Lady Mildmay, describes a collaborative writing effort initiated by her adored governess. According to this diary, which is one of the most specific available representations of the actual teaching offered to a young woman in the Renaissance, Grace Sherrington was encouraged to compose original poetry for the same reason she was taught to sing Psalms and to sew: to inculcate in her a moral discourse to control her own sexuality. Observing "the monstrous spectacle" of a man and woman "of impudent behaviour one towards another," her governess asked her to make one stave and she another until they wrote four or five verses "very wittily and sharp against such licentious behaviour." This was done, according to Sherrington, for her instruction, "to take heed of the lyke and to abhor and despise the same."[16]

Whether originating from another poem or from a governess or other role model, as a *donnée* the line "A most Careles Content of fauore or disgrace" situates this first holograph poem within a discourse lying outside the poem itself; its content strongly suggests that this discourse shared prominent features with Stoicism. This poem attempts, in fact, much the same task as that of the countess of Pembroke's translations, which adapted the tenets of the primarily male-oriented discourse of Christianized Stoicism to create a form of heroism appropriate for women. This poem also applies Stoic-like precepts to a predominantly women's issue. "A most Careles Content of fauore or disgrace" expresses one of the most powerful impulses behind Stoicism, to become "careles," or without care, not basing one's "content" or happiness upon "fauore or disgrace," to rise above the mutations of Fortune by finding an inner center which does not fluctuate according to worldly status. This poet applies this spiritual goal to the specific situation of women by connecting the experience of "fauore or disgrace" with the possession of beauty. Associating favor with youthful beauty and disgrace with the physical ugliness inevitable in the aging process, the author exhorts the reader to rely instead on virtue, which does not alter with age.

Because the irregularity of the metrics of the first line makes it possible for the stress to fall on either syllable, the word "content" can possess another meaning besides "satisfaction." Stressed on the first syllable, "content" can also mean what is contained within the self, one's own substance (*OED*). Especially with this second meaning, the versions of the first holograph poem juxtapose two strategies for composing a self, the first relying upon the ephemeral beauty of youth, claimed as inferior to the second, relying upon unchanging virtue to construct a more lasting self. The speaker presents herself as an example for the reader to follow in creating a self which is not subject to the ravages of time. In the first version, she esteems the "Inwarde guyftes;" in the second and third, she does not care, or "passe," for those outward "partes" or "shape" "wher virteu hath noe place." By the end of the last version, she turns directly to the reader, to promise that "Hye glory to your selfe report shall euer rayse" if the reader depends upon virtue rather than upon beauty.

The poetics of the poem make it clear that the speaker represents a version of author, for these admonitions to rely upon virtue rather than upon beauty reach out to control its aesthetics, accurately reproducing the sound and sentiments of the "drab" poetry popularized in mid-century collections such as *Tottel's Miscellany* but still practiced in the late sixteenth century.[17] The unflaggingly regular metrics of its poulter's measure, its general lack of sensuous detail, its mild alliteration, its undeveloped personifications, its neat two-line units of thought, and, above all, the dependable morality of its sentiments, accurately create the author of this poem as a "drab" poet. Designed to instruct more than to delight the reader, the very aesthetics of drab verse were based upon the preference of virtue to beauty, which was, according to the countess's drab poet Thomas Howell, "the bayte of Vanitie," a manifestation of the insubstantiality of the physical world.[18] Like other drab poets, the author of this holograph poem primarily offers good advice to appeal to the reason of readers, not sensuous imagery to appeal to their senses. Like other drab poems, the value of this holograph poem appears to lie in its usefulness as a moral guide to the path of virtue, not in the amount of pleasure the readers derive from its beauty.

The value that the poem places on inner virtue, which need not change over time, rather than upon physical beauty, which decreases with age, is consonant both with Stoicism and with drab aesthetics. While not written according to a primarily Stoic discourse, drab poems share with Stoicism an attempt to find a stable center of identity within a world made undependable by the arbitrary affections of princes and mistresses. This desire for permanence is well expressed not only in the typical content of drab verse but also in the unchanging regularity of its poulter's measure. Possibly it was this conjunction of Stoic doctrine and drab aesthetics that enabled the author of the poem to take a step not attempted in Sir Philip Sidney's captivity episode or in the countess of Pembroke's translations. Unlike Pamela and Philoclea, or Cleopatra and Laura, the speaker of this poem does not require beauty as one condition for her heroism. Nor does she require the love or admiration of men. She has composed a self in this poem which is not contingent upon any outside reality or vulnerable to the biased opinion of contemporaries. She has composed a self which is complete, immutable, immortal in the seemingly reliable and enduring "report" of the ages.

Yet despite this independence from the affirmation of males, the heroism constructed in this holograph is formed as much on its own negation as that of the protagonists of the countess of Pembroke's translations, and it is perhaps as implicated in a desire for death. In the rejection of physical beauty as a reliable source for composing the self, the poet has repudiated sexuality and life itself. The opposition created in the poem between beauty and virtue also creates an opposition between body and soul; and this alienation from the body becomes increasingly marked in the three revisions of the poem. All three versions at some point in their composition associate the body with flowers that fade and thus reject the body for the transience of its beauty. The second also rejects the body for its sexuality, associating beauty with the passions of "youthfull bludde." The third rejects the body for its mortality, associating it with the "Carcas" which will corrupt and die. This repudiation of the body finally implies a longing for death itself, as the time when the separation of body and soul is most complete, as the time when "report" shall raise its voice to proclaim the glory of the virtuous self to succeeding generations. In this expressed longing for death, this poet was perhaps influenced by the version of authorship used by the countess of Pembroke.

It is difficult for a modern reader to judge the success of this or any didactic poem. This poet's painstaking revisions, which tend to move the poem from sensuous image to direct statement, show an organizing aesthetic at odds with modern sensibilities. The underlying view of a reality so simple and so unambiguous, where virtue did not need to be defined, where posterity could be depended upon to report whether one had it or not, was no doubt as reassuringly true to the poem's original readers as it may seem irritatingly pat to some modern ones. It does seem clear, however, that this poet has succeeded in creating herself as a didactic author. Her success in constructing this version of authorship for herself probably derives from several sources: from the authority of the person or poem contributing the *donnée* of the first line; from the happy coincidence of impulse underlying the Stoic sentiment and the drab aesthetic through which it was expressed; and especially from the way in which the poem's virtuous teachings forward the patriarchal project of containing the sexuality of women. A young woman who relies on virtue rather than on beauty for her value is not in danger of losing her chastity. Neither is she in danger of attempting to seduce an audience, for the audience she wishes to influence will report her virtue only after she is safely dead.

"Hardon that harte" against Courtly Sonneteering

Unlike the heavily revised first holograph, the third holograph was apparently complete until line 10, where "spryttes" replaces "wyttes" on the base line, with the revision of line 6 added above its line at a later time. The poem is copied with some care, although the thick descenders near the end of the poem suggest that the author was not too concerned with the neatness of its appearance on the page. The poem is as follows:

Loue by the beames of beauty settes on fyer,
breakes fourth in sparkes by coullers, and by voyce,
sumtyes fayre wourdes, sumtyemes denyes desyer,
feades upon feare, and in hoope doeth reiouce.
syttes in the harte, and shyneth in the eyes
                                        suche deuotyon lyes.
Rulles as a Queene where ~~weaknes she espyes~~
If to your lyeffe a stronguer staye you seake
Reason requyer (the ennemy to loue)
Hardon that harte whiche was but ouer meeke
Pulle vp
~~Awake~~ your ~~wyttes~~ spryttes the other waye doe proue
vannety will vanyshe and quyght decaye
wher as discretion beareth the swaye

My edited version of the third holograph:

Love by the beams of beauty sets on fire,
Breaks forth in sparks by colors, and by voice,
Sometimes fair words, sometimes denies desire,
Feeds upon fear, and in hope doth rejoice,
Sits in the heart, and shineth in the eyes,
Rules as a Queen where such devotion lies.
If to your life a stronger stay you seek,
Reason require (the enemy to love).
Harden that heart which was but over meek,
Pull up your spirits. The other way do prove.
Vanity will vanish and quite decay
Whereas discretion beareth the sway.

It is difficult at first to believe that the author of the first holograph also composed the first six lines of the third one. Gone are the unrelenting poulter's measure, the two-line units of meaning, the lack of sensuous detail, the heavy didacticism, the earnest moral tone. A single unit of meaning with nine verbs, these six lines are the most syntactically complex of any in the holographs. From the initial trochee of the first line, this poet has mastered the metrics, language, and imagery of the courtly sonneteers of the late sixteenth century, and particularly of Sir Philip Sidney. The poet employs three of the four most frequently used words in Sidney's verse—"love," "eyes," and "heart"—in these six lines.[19] More tellingly Sidnean is the complicated syntax of the first six lines, with their one subject predicated by eight verbs. The capacity of love to cause the lover to "burn" in fire, the presence of love in the heart and eyes, the unpredictability of the beloved's response: all of these are conventional for the Petrarchan sonnets written in England.[20] Despite the small awkwardness of the lack of parallelism in line 3, this poet has successfully created herself as a courtly sonneteer.

Unlike Lady Mary Wroth's sonnets, which transpose the expected gender of lover and beloved to represent the poet figure as a woman wooer and the beloved as a fickle male, this poem leaves the conventional Petrarchan dyad of male lover and female beloved unchanged. The beautiful "colors" and voice as well as the shining eyes strongly imply a woman beloved. Like other women beloveds, she remains an object, a lovely but essentially passive vehicle through which Love works upon the lover. Only the lover is granted subjectivity, in suffering the day-to-day vagaries of hearing "fair words" and then experiencing denied desire. The poet has adapted the Petrarchan convention to accommodate her gender in one respect, however. She has loosened the traditional connection between lover and poet figure. By describing the force of love rather than by addressing herself to a beloved, the author does not necessarily conflate the poet figure with the lover. Instead, the poet figure seems to assume the stance of a third party, not explicitly identified with either member of the Petrarchan couple.

The revision at the end of the sixth line, where "weaknes she espyes" is changed to "suche devotion lyes," anticipates the criticism developed in the final six lines of the poem. The reinterpretation of the lover's passion as "devotion" suggests that, in this poem, the represented weakness of the courtly lover violates the bounds for self-criticism even in this highly self-critical genre. The phrase "weaknes she espyes" points to a conservative definition of gender as the source of evident discomfort with the Petrarchan convention. A reading of a courtly lover's devotion to his beloved as "weaknes" impugns his masculinity, enabling Love to rule as a "Queen." The choice of the word "espyes" to describe Love's alertness to a lover's weakness suggests an unpleasant element of opportunism, rather than regality, in Love's domination. Since Love works through the beloved rather than being entirely identified with her, the poem does not accuse the beloved of exercising an unseemly power over the lover. But this unrevised version of line 6 suggests that this subjugation of a male lover to Love, portrayed as a queen working her effects through a female beloved, influenced the rejection of the Petrarchan convention in the final six lines of the poem.

This anxiety about appropriate gender roles is more fully developed in the final six lines of the poem, which represent the courtly lover as feminized by passion, his heart "meek" and soft, in need of hardening by Reason, the "enemy to love." This anxiety was in no way peculiar to this holograph poem. The gendered Renaissance opposition of manly reason to feminizing passion shaped, for example, the unrevised *Countess of Pembroke's Arcadia*, especially its depiction of Pyrocles, whose poem "Transform'd in show, but more transform'd in mind" represents his transvestite appearance as revealing his inner condition. Possibly the lover's supposed weakness of reason influenced the poem's initial representation of his "wyttes" as asleep, later revised to an instruction, evidently quoted from Wroth's manuscript, to "pull up" his "spirits."

The two halves of the third holograph thus split neatly into two representations of the Petrarchan lover, valued differently according to the perspectives of two competing discourses. Much like Euarchus's stern rereading of the young princes' love as passion, these last six lines use reason, not courtliness, as their measure of manhood. Just as Euarchus's judgement glances not only at the lovers but also at romantic fiction, such as *The Countess of Pembroke's Arcadia* itself, the criticism of the Petrarchan lover in these last six lines also necessitates the rejection of the courtly poetic. Abjuring the sensuous beauty of the first six lines, the final six lines are generally written according to the mid-century drab aesthetic. The metrical complexity of the first six lines gives way to a simpler iambic pentameter with an initial trochee in lines 7 through 10. Syntactical complexity yields to two-line units of thought. Briefly sketched personifications common in didactic verse, such as Reason as the enemy of Love and Discretion bearing the sway, do not sustain the more extended treatment of the personification of love in the first six lines. The second half works by direct address rather than by metaphor. These lines show a poet able to write according to the aesthetic of Sidney and the courtly sonneteers actively discarding it for the aesthetic of Googe. Refusing to use the courtly poetic to appeal to the reader's passions, this poet chooses instead the drab mid-century aesthetic to appeal to the reader's reason.

Unlike Sidney's unrevised version of his romance, which ends in a state of pleasing irresolution with the restoration of Basilius to save the protagonists from Euarchus's judgements, this poem presents no witty conclusion to modify the perspective of reason. The concluding couplet of this poem sides with "discretion," to represent courtly love as "vanity." The clash of the two aesthetics in this poem perhaps accounts for the final couplet's lack of conformity to any declared Renaissance standard. Its metrics chaotic, the syntax of its final line unclear, its content self-contradictory (how can vanity first vanish and then decay?), the couplet seems unfinished for a poet who has demonstrated such control of both drab and courtly poetics. The final image of discretion bearing the "sway" suggests the insuperability of the problem posed by the gendered poetic of her day as this poet attempted to write a courtly lyric. By representing the "sway" of "discretion" (so inimical to the "vanity" of Petrarchan love) as beneficent rather than tyrannical, this poet endorsed a patriarchal discourse that, finally, denied her a role as a courtly poet.

Philomela Loud and Sweetly Cries

Like the first and third holograph poems, the second holograph poem does not appear to be careful copy meant for circulation, for the writing itself is somewhat loose, especially near the end, and some words in the third stanza and some revisions in all three stanzas are written with an unusually thick quill. The second line of the third stanza, with its several false starts, indicates that the poem was in the process of composition, rather than a complete poem with revisions added later. The hand, the inking, the poem's placement in a blank space in the first gathering, all point to its composition at approximately the same period of time as the first and third holograph poems.

The second holograph is as follows:

The breath all <   >ldeth fourthe
                                        stes
Comfortes the flowers <   >~~hich the Coold~~ did kylle
                                                chillyng
And Phebus beames beate~~s~~ backe the ~~stormye~~ northe
        nature<s>
whose   raeffs ~~regard~~ the earth wth

~~Which euery place wth quakyng~~ stormes did fille
Nowe Philomela sweetly doeth bewaylle
That faulshood Cowld on treu loue so preuaylle

The buddes bownde in by harde and massy barke
safftly breake fourth to blossomes and to leaues
longe lyghtes
The chearfulle day ~~drives bake~~ the drowsy darke
receaues
whoe tooke most Care most Comfort nowe ~~Conceaues~~
Nowe in eache bushe sweet Phylomela synges
~~wille~~ lastes sweet when sower
Treu love ~~is best aboue al~~ other thynges

The fealdes doe fealle noe more the byttyng froste~~s~~
vnto there
The blossomes grow~~ne are to~~ ~~the a~~ knotted frutte
sweet suguered
~~Boeth~~ syghtes, and smelles, are ~~sweeted~~ of free Coste~~s~~
All
This ~~good~~ geaues Nature wthout Charge, or sutte
lowde and sweetly
Nowe Phylomela ~~sweetly and doeth~~ Cryes
whoe byedes liues stille and
~~lyue stille~~ in love ~~and thou shalt~~ neuer dyes.

My edited version of the second holograph:

The breath all < >ldeth forth
Comforts the flowers <which the bla>sts did kill,
And Phoebus' beams beat back the chilling north
Whose nature<'s> riefs the earth with storms did fill.
Now Philomela sweetly doth bewail
That falsehood could on true love so prevail.

The buds bound in by hard and massy bark
Softly break forth to blossoms and to leaves.
The cheerful day long lights the drowsy dark;
Who took most care most comfort now receives.
Now in each bush sweet Philomela sings,
True love lasts sweet when sour other things.

The fields do feel no more the biting frost,
The blossoms grow unto their knotted fruit.

Sweet sights, and smells, are sugared of free cost:
All this gives Nature without charge, or suit.
Now Philomela loud and sweetly cries,
Who bides in love lives still and never dies.

This poem is probably more accessible to modern readers than the other two poems. Its images are fresh and forceful: "Phoebus' beams" beating back the "chilling north," the buds "bound in by hard and massy bark," the blossoms growing into their "knotted fruit." While these images create vivid visual impressions, other phrases appeal to other senses: Philomela's changing song appeals to the sense of hearing; the "biting frost" once penetrating the fields appeals to the sense of feeling; and Nature sweetens not only sights, but smells. In addition to offering an abundance of sense impressions, the poem shows impressive control of technique. Regular but not rigid, its graceful pentameter accommodates occasional trochees, such as "comforts" and "softly" in the second lines of stanzas 1 and 2, respectively. The short *e* and the long *o* sounds provide an effective contrast between gaiety and languor in the line "The cheerful day long lights the drowsy dark." The alliterative *s* contributes to the sweet sound of the line "Sweet sights, and smells, are sugared of free cost." Structured on a seasonal cycle, the poem's organization is clear; and the final stage of Philomela's changing song ends the poem on a firm note of resolution.

The subject matter of this second poem no doubt accounts in part for the poem's success. By writing about nature, this poet evaded some of the problems posed by the subject matter of the other poems. While the discourse of the first poem required the alienation of the poet from her body, nature's very immanence in flowers, fruits, birds, and seasonal movement draws upon the sense of fertility and cyclicity abundantly present in the female body. The fading flowers rejected for the transience of their beauty in the first poem grow into "knotted fruit" in the fertile world of the second. Similarly, while the sensuous imagery of the first half of the third poem implicated the poet in a passionate discourse of courtly love rejected in the second half, the sensuous imagery in this second poem conveys no such connotations of guilty love. In Nature, love and even sexual attraction are necessary and free from the judgements of human morality. While a woman wooer may incur the censure of a moral reader, a nightingale will not; for nightingales, unlike women, are empowered to sing sweet songs of love.

With its passionate yet guiltless song, the nightingale lends itself as a convenient vehicle for a woman poet. The extension of the figure of Philomela, whose name means "lover of sweetness," beyond the image of the nightingale to provide a version of authorship for the poem is suggested by this poem's otherwise peculiar emphasis upon sweetness, in the word "sweet" used three times in the space of five lines (lines 11, 12, and 15), " 'sweetly" used twice (lines 5 and 17), and "sugared" (line 15, changed from "sweeted"). The use of the nightingale, often called Philomela, as a figure for the poet or as analogous to the poet was already conventional by the end of the sixteenth century, having appeared in poems by Petrarch, Spenser, and Shakespeare, as well as in the writings of Sir Philip Sidney and Lady Mary Wroth. Thus, the nightingale Philomela offered an authorial role already endorsed by the Renaissance patriarchy which yet accommodated the gender of a woman poet.

The viability of the nightingale as a vehicle for a woman poet solved various problems facing women's authorship. First, as a reclusive bird who shunned the presence of men, the nightingale/poet could not be accused of seeking to impress, influence, or seduce an audience. This Renaissance perception of the nightingale as figure for the solitary poet was easily accessible in Georg Schuler's influential allegorization of Ovid's myth of Philomela, first published in 1555 and still influential in the late sixteenth century. In contrast to the more urban swallow Progne, who represented Oratory, the nightingale confined herself to "arbusta & siluas . . . & loca non ab hominibus, sed a Musis & diis celebrata," to arbors and forests, to places frequented by muses and by gods rather than by men.[21] In Sidney's *New Arcadia,* solitude created the nightingale as an authorial role appropriate for Philoclea, enabling her poem of grief over Pyrocles' supposed infidelities with her mother: "[Pyrocles] was met with the latter end of a song which Philoclea (like a solitary nightingale bewailing her guiltless punishment and helpless misfortune) had newly delivered over, meaning none should be judge of her passion but her own conscience."[22]

In addition to eliminating the problem of audience, the nightingale also offered a viable authorial role for a woman poet by representing her poem as a natural, untutored effusion from the heart rather than a complex work of art demonstrating skill and learning. In Renaissance poems, the nightingale/poet was, in fact, sometimes conflated with another group of spontaneous, untutored female poet figures—the same nymphs and other mourners populating Renaissance pastorals that prepared the way for the countess of Pembroke's version of authorship. Like elegiac nymphs, the nightingale, often called Philomela, performed the passionate and therefore womanly function of grieving and of helping the poet to grieve. Spenser used the nightingale this way in various poems. In *The Shepheardes Calender,* the shepherd Colin portrays Philomele, whose "song with teares doth steepe," as one pastoral mourner for Dido; in *Daphnaida* the poet laments Daphne's death with the intent to "wake and sorrow all the night / with *Philumene,* my fortune to deplore, / With *Philumene,* the partner of my plight"; in *The Teares of the Muses,* the muse Euterpe bewails the state of poetry by comparing herself to *Philomele,* who "all comfortless doth hide her chearlesse head / During the time of her widowhead."[23] In this last poem, Philomela appears to be mourning her deceased husband, rather than her rape. Some sense of her past history of wrongs emerges in Sidney's *New Arcadia,* when an Arcadian shepherd mourns Basilius's apparent death:

> O Philomela with thy breast oppressed
> By shame and grief, help, help me to lament
> Such cursed harms as cannot be redressed.
>
> (777)

Perceiving Philomela as a version of a woman poet creates of this poem a narrative of woman's authorship. Set against the backdrop of the changing seasons, Philomela's developing song structures the poem. In all three stanzas, Philomela embodies the constant female lover. While Philomela's commitment to love never changes, her song is transformed by a dramatic change of mood. In the first stanza, she has presumably been deceived by a lover, for in the late winter or early spring, her song is sad, as she "sweetly doth bewail / That falsehood could on true love so prevail." Like the constant heroines present, for example, in the writings of Lady Mary Wroth, Philomela's song denies the presence of anger to remain "sweet" in her grief. In the second stanza, her situation as a lover is not as clear. The line "Who took most care most comfort now receives" suggests that by midspring, the happiness of Philomela and others generally reaches the level of the sadness of the previous time. Is this change in mood motivated by her beloved's return of her affections or by her growing self-sufficiency? This question is still not answered by the last stanza, when Philomela's song takes on a new strength, as she "loud and sweetly cries / Who bides in love lives still and never dies." Is this confidence in love born of her success with the object of her love or merely of her growing inner faith? Perhaps Philomela's love situation is not important to the poem, which focuses instead upon the change in her song itself, its developing volume and power.

The transformation in Philomela's song seems to be caused, if anything, by the changing seasons. The marked gendering of the forces controlling these seasons contains evocative implications for the conditions conducive to a woman's authorship. In the first stanza, the late winter or early spring is not only cold; the forces dominating it are personified as male. It seems most probable, in fact, that these lines characterizing the "chilling north" wind drew from Ovid's version of the Boreas myth, which following directly upon the narrative of Philomela, was shaped by her rape. The Thracian origin of Philomela's rapist caused Erechtheus, Athenian successor to Philomela's father, to deny the Thracian Boreas his daughter's hand; the boorish Boreas's response was to raise up a violent storm to abduct and, presumably, rape his beloved, since twins were born to her soon after their wedding. The successive revisions of the fourth line, which apparently went through the following stages, vividly characterizes the "chilling north" wind and its relationship with the earth:

1. Which eury place wth quakyng stormes did fille

A straightforward reading of the crossouts in the line, this version suggests the presence of fear in the storms in the word "quakyng." This word perhaps loosely resonates with Golding's translation of Boreas's claim to "make the verie world to quake," together with the forceful description of the violent storms he raised up in his abduction of Orithya from the Athenian king.[24]

2. Whose ruff regard the earth wth stormes did fille

"Whose raeffs regard the earth wth stormes did fille" does not make sense. Close inspection reveals that the *ae* on "raeffs" conceals something underneath; the *s* on "raeffs" could well have been added later. "Ruff" would seem the logical word. Developing more explicitly the cause for the earth's storms as its fearful response to the "ruff regard" of the North Wind, this characterization corresponds to the "boystous wrath" (6.867) typical of Ovid's cloddish Boreas.

3. Whose nature⟨s⟩ raeffs the earth wth stormes did fille

Since the end of "nature" is obscured by the *ff* of "raeffs" below it, and since its placement on the page indicates that it should go before "raeffs," an *-s* ending (*-'s* in a modern edition) makes the most sense of the phrase: "Whose natures raeffs." *Raeff* is an alternative spelling of the Renaissance word *reif*, now obsolete, which means "plunder" or "the act or practice of robbery" (*OED*). Thus, "Whose natures raeffs," or "Whose raeffs of nature," depicts the North Wind as plundering the nature whose bounty is stressed in the last stanza. The North Wind's intimidation of the earth in the second version has evolved into outright aggression by the third.

This use of "raeffs" is a bold decision, depicting the North Wind as a plundering barbarian or an outlaw in a single word. What was stolen? While the poem, oddly enough, omits a description of the actual theft, the underlying myth suggests the abduction of Boreas's beloved, which filled the earth with storms, and her rape. The embattled masculinity of the world of this first stanza is further evident in the North Wind's contest with Phoebus, who must stalwartly beat it back with his beams. It is, presumably, Phoebus's victory over the barbaric North Wind which enabled Philomela's song, sad as it was.

In the second stanza, open conflict has given way to transformation of a milder sort. The restriction of the "hard and massy bark," once binding in the buds, is now overcome not by force, but by an inner expansion, its gentleness emphasized by the trochee, "softly," that opens the second line. In contrast to the battles of the first stanza, the relationship between the "cheerful day" and the "drowsy night" appears to be complementary rather than antagonistic. The blossoms which bloom in the second stanza achieve fruition in the third in an uncommonly nurturing environment created by a very maternal Nature, who, like an ideal mother, requires no fee or "suit" as she sugars sights and smells. It is presumably this generous, maternal influence that allows blossoms to reach fruition and Philomela's song to become loud and sweet.

How far can the implications of this highly gendered narrative be taken? Can we read the widespread antagonism of patriarchy to authorship by women in the chilling, fear-inducing, thieving north wind which must be beaten back before Philomela can sing even a sad song? Whether or not the first stanza criticizes the force of patriarchy, the confidence of Philomela's concluding song, so linked with the fruition of the blossoms and the fecundity of the natural world, thrives only within a nurturing environment, overseen by a Nature so generous and so beneficent that she fulfills the fantasy, as common as it is powerful, of the undemanding and all-providing mother of infancy. This very female environment, so full of sensuous pleasures and free from tensions of any sort, seems to recall that time, or the fantasy of that time, enjoyed between mothers and infants, before the demands of the adult world disrupted this primal sense of union. The poet represents this time, or the fantasy of this time, as offering the conditions necessary for the full development of women's authorship.[25] From this abundance provided by an all-giving Mother Nature, Philomela creates a kind of women's verse, a verse not of sad bewailing but of loud confidence.

The Silent Ground

Even as the third stanza represents the nightingale's newly confident song, it elicits an awareness of this vision as a hollow fantasy. Within the very terms in which the poem presents the developing song of the nightingale, it also evokes a sense of the limitations of that song and, finally, of its impossibility. Perhaps the most striking accomplishment of this poem lies, in fact, in its evocation of the not-said, of the spaces surrounding its words, of the silences shaping its speech. The poem draws attention to these silences in three ways: first, in the creation of two competing narrative structures, one of which limits the nightingale's optimism as subject to time and seasonal change; second, in its contradiction of contemporary received knowledge about nightingales, who were not thought to sing loudly in the summer; and third, in its creation of a happy Philomela, confident in love, from a mythological figure whose rape and mutilation propelled her on a course of bloody revenge. In this last strategy, the poem makes visible the cultural dislocations organizing other Renaissance poems which deny Philomela's anger to create of her a figure of sweet pathos. These dislocutions, which could not allow a direct expression of a woman's justified rage, created a formidable barrier to women's authorship in the Renaissance. It is to this barrier that the silences, the not-saids, of this poem point.

The first means through which the poem evokes an awareness of what it has not said is through its structure, composed of two competing narratives which coexist in direct and unresolved contradiction. The nightingale's song follows a narrative of progress as it moves from grief, to increased optimism in love, and finally to its loud cry of faith. But the very sense of resolution achieved in the poem's final line also elicits a sense of dissonance; for this triumphant conclusion of the narrative of progress represents only a stage in the alternative narrative of seasonal cyclicity. Unlike conventional seasonal poems, such as Spenser's *Shepherd's Calendar,* which completed their annual movement, this poem ends in midcycle. Beginning with the thaws of early spring in its first stanza, the poem has moved to midspring, when the buds blossom and leaves emerge, and finally to summer, when the blossoms become fruit. This seasonal movement elicits a consciousness of the subsequent stages: of autumn, when leaves fall and fruit decays, and finally of frigid winter, when, presumably, the nightingale will fall silent once more. The poem's unusual refusal to complete this cycle evokes a reader's awareness of the not-said. The creation of meaning from the white spaces of the page through the absence of the expected stanzas on autumn and winter is aided by the poem's repetition of "now" in the fifth line of each stanza. By emphasizing the conditionality of the nightingale's song, this repetition of "now" reminds the reader of a past or future time which is not-now. In these areas of silence, the poem eloquently presents the nightingale's optimism, tied as it is to seasonal cycle, as a fleeting sensation subject to the passage of time.

Philomela's confident song is further exposed as a fantasy by the conventional lore of nightingales. Nightingales were not supposed to sing in the summer, when "blossoms grow unto their knotted fruit." Pliny's *Naturall Historie,* the standard Renaissance reference work on this subject, is absolutely explicit on this point. It was during the time of the second stanza, when the buds "break forth to blossoms and to leaves," that nightingales achieved eloquence as well as volume; then, said Pliny, "the Nightingale for fifteene daies and nights together, never giveth over but chaunteth continually, namely, at that time as the trees begin to put out their leaves thicke . . . for is it not a woonder that so lowd and cleere a voice should come from so little a bodie?" After this fifteen days, nightingales' song began to "abate and slake." By summer, they had lost their virtuosity altogether: "For some time after, when the weather groweth hotter, their voice is cleane altered: for neither are they musicall and tuneable in their measures with variety as before, but onely sing plaine-song and keepe them to one tune."[26]

This awareness of spring as the time of the nightingale's song seems to have been common knowledge among Renaissance poets, who usually set their nightingale poems explicitly in that season. Sir Philip Sidney's nightingale sings, for example, "as soone as Aprill bringeth / Unto her rested sense a perfect waking"; while Lady Mary Wroth's nightingale also sings in the "merry spring."[27] Shakespeare specifically uses this diminution of the nightingale's song as the basis of the poetic conceit in sonnet 102.

Our love was new, and then but in the spring,
When I was wont to greet it with my lays,
As Philomel in summer's front doth sing,
And stops her pipe in growth of riper days.[28]

This nightingale lore created a silent subtext in the second holograph poem, which existed in absolute contradiction to its manifest text. The poem's portrayal of Philomela's summer song as "loud" undoubtedly created a sense of dissonance for an audience educated on Pliny and well-read in nightingale poems. The presence of this silent subtext represented the nightingale's emerging confidence, her ability to "loud and sweetly" cry, as an impossibility in nature.

The Philomela of the third stanza defies tradition in one final respect. Expressing confidence in the power of love, her song is optimistic. This Philomela appears to be happy; and in her happiness, she is, I believe, unique among Philomelas. Her happy confidence in love contrasts dramatically with the anger of the Philomela of classical myth, the raped and mutilated virgin who, with her sister, exacts a horrible revenge. This Ovidian narrative, together with its Renaissance redactions, provides important insights into the cultural anxieties about women's speech that shaped the second holograph poem and exerted formative pressures upon women's authorship in the Sidney circle and, no doubt, in the Renaissance in general.

Ovid's Philomela and Her Tongue

The classical myth of Philomela is a forceful narrative of a woman's silencing, conveying considerable dread over the violence possible to women's revenge. According to Ovid's much-read *Metamorphoses,* the nightingale was once a young virgin named Philomela savagely raped by her brother-in-law Tereus, who cut out her tongue to prevent her from identifying him as the rapist.[29] Weaving her story in a tapestry, Philomela informed her sister Procne of her husband's crime. In vengeance, both women murdered the son of Procne and Tereus, and together they baked him in a dish which Tereus greedily consumed. Discovering that he had just eaten his son, Tereus drew his sword on the two women; and at that moment all three, the pursuing and the pursued, turned into birds.

The attempted silencing of Philomela receives special emphasis in Ovid's myth, and the excision of Philomela's tongue remains memorable in a scene which is gory even by Ovidian standards. William Golding, a popular Renaissance translator of Ovid's *Metamorphoses,* translates the passage in this way:

> The cruel tyrant came,
> And with a paire of pinsons fast did catch hir by the tung,
> And with his sword did cut it off. The stumpe whereon it hung

Did patter still. The tip fell downe, and quivering on the ground
As though that it had murmured it made a certaine sound,
And as an Adders tayle cut off doth skip a while: even so
The tip of *Philomelaas* tongue did wriggle to and fro,
And nearer to hir mistresseward in dying still did go.

(708–15)

The description comes close to ascribing to Philomela's tongue a life and a consciousness of its own, as it moves and even makes "a certaine sound" independent of Philomela herself. But the character that it for a moment becomes is not consistent; and the conflicting attitudes shaping the tongue's representation also reveal conflicting attitudes towards women's speech. On the one hand, the comparison of the tongue's wriggling to an "Adders tayle" suggests that her tongue also possesses the lethal venom of that serpent. On the other hand, the comparison of the tongue to a servant invests it with a grisly pathos. Awarded the feminine pronoun, Philomela's tongue proves her mettle in the manner of other classical heroines by dying well, loyally attempting to move "hir mistresseward" in death.

These conflicting attitudes towards Philomela's tongue parallel the conflicting attitudes towards Philomela which organize the myth. The pathos elicited by the mute Philomela is finally lethal in its consequences as she changes from sympathetic victim to brutal revenger. The silencing of Philomela plays a crucial role in this transformation, for it is Philomela's inability to speak that motivates Procne's role in the horrible murder of her own son:

She turned to hir sisters face from *Itys,* and behelde
Now tone, no tother earnestly and said, why tattles he,
And she sittes dumbe bereft of tongue? As well why calles not she
Me sister, as this boy doth call me mother?

(798–801)

After Procne stabs her son, Philomela slits his throat; perhaps the excision of Philomela's tongue determines the specific form of her revenge, for cutting Ithys's throat also represents a form of silencing. Thoroughly caught up in revenge, the two women tear the boy's body apart "while some life and soule was in his members yit" (8.14) to prepare him for cooking in a horrible parody of domesticity. When Tereus calls for his son, it is Philomela who eagerly assumes the ghastly duty of informing Tereus of the content of his meal:

Out
Lept *Philomele* with scattred haire aflaight like one that fled
Had from some fray where slaughter was, and threw the bloody head
Of *Itys* in his fathers face.

(831–34)

By the end of the myth, Philomela's character is far from pathetic. According to the myth, her speech, if she had it, would express not grief or regret, but horrible joy over her unnatural revenge upon Tereus:

And never more was shee
Desirous to have had hir speache, that able she might be
Hir inward joy with worthie wordes to witnesse franke and free.

(834–36)

By the end of the myth, Philomela is not a grieving victim but an angry murderer. In their metamorphoses into birds, the guilt of the two sisters is actually encoded upon their bodies:

And of their murther from their brestes not yet the token goth,
For even still yet are stainde with bloud the fethers of them both.

(847–48)

Renaissance Philomelas

This understanding of Philomela as an angry revenger was available in the Renaissance. Ovid's *Metamorphoses* was immensely popular at this time, both in the original and in translation.[30] In the epistle prefacing his translation of Ovid's myths, William Golding explicitly describes the Philomela myth as demonstrating "the cruell wreake of women in their wrath" (139). The striking absence of this straightforward interpretation of the myth from most Renaissance versions of Philomela, however, suggests the anxiety elicited by women's anger within Renaissance culture.

Most readings of Philomela in Renaissance emblem books and in allegorical commentaries on the *Metamorphoses* swerve from acknowledging the power of her anger. While Philomela appeared by name in emblem books, for example, few of them even alluded to her anger or to her rape. Camerarius describes how "philomela" teaches her young ones to sing to render them "pius." Another emblem writer repeats Georg Schuler's allegory of Philomela as poetry and Procne as oratory. One emblem compiler, alluding only indirectly to Philomela by including her in his picture but not in his text, interprets Procne under the heading "Impotentis Vindictae Foemina."[31] Surely this interpretation of the impotence of women's revenge contrasts oddly with the accompanying picture, which portrays the sisters' preparations of Ithys's body for cooking. Among allegorists of the *Metamorphoses* besides Schuler, Pierre Bersuire reveals anxiety about women's malice, particularly as revealed in their speech, in his interpretation of the nightingale Philomela as resembling evil women, always occupied with the concerns of others.[32] This stereotype of the woman gossip functions, however, to allay anxiety about women's anger by rendering it inappropriate.

In the context of this allegorical background, Shakespeare's treatment of Lavinia as a Philomela figure in *Titus Andronicus* seems unusually direct; and for this reason, Shakespeare's representation of Lavinia deserves particular attention. Lavinia, whose rape and mutilation is repeatedly compared to Philomela's, becomes a revenge heroine. A comparison with Shakespeare's Ovidian source, however, reveals the extent to which even Shakespeare's play consistently softens Lavinia's role to portray her more as a figure of pathos than of anger. The wrongs committed upon Lavinia's body exceed those committed upon Philomela's, for not only is Lavinia raped and muted, but her hands are cut off as well. Despite the excess of these atrocities, Lavinia's participation in revenge is less lethal and more justified than Philomela's. The guilty rapists, not an innocent child, become the victims of grisly revenge. It is her father, not Lavinia, who slits the victims' throats; and as she holds a basin between her stumps to catch the spurting blood, Lavinia is acting the role of dutiful daughter as well as of revenger. When the rapists' mother consumes the dish made of her sons' bodies, Lavinia observes without protest and does not, like Philomela, throw their heads before their parent. Lavinia is finally flawed not from her participation in revenge, but from the loss of her virginity, for which her father, modelling himself upon the Roman story of Appius and Virginia, kills her. The text's lack of cues at this point implies her passive acquiescence even in her own murder-execution. While the potential for an angry Lavinia no doubt exists for an individual production of the play, Shakespeare's text never provides an explicit cue for her to express anger.

However much Lavinia has become a figure of pathos rather than of rage, she literally points to the wrongs suffered by Philomela by opening a copy of Ovid's *Metamorphoses* to the Philomela myth. Several allusions to Philomela in Spenser's verse, however, dissociate her name from her myth. Spenser repeatedly appropriates Philomela's sadness for the purposes of elegy, as "Philomele" mourns the death of Dido in the November eclogue in his *Shepheards Calender* and "Philumene" acts as the "partner" of the narrator's grief for Daphne in *Daphnaida*. One allusion directly contradicts an essential detail of the mythical history of this woman, who was never married or, given Roman attitudes towards even involuntary lapses from virginity, eligible for marriage. As mentioned above, the muse Euterpe in Spenser's *Teares of the Muses* represents "Philomele" as a widow whose complaint expresses grief only over her deceased husband, as she hides her "chearlesse head / During the time of that her widowhead" (lines 239–40). Finally, the single Spenser allusion that acknowledges her rape, however indirectly, still requires the obliging reader to forget her rage. Spenser's August eclogue represents the nightingale as singing "plaintive pleas, the more taugment / The memory of his misdeade, that bred her woe" (lines 185–86).

The representation of Philomela in Spenser's August eclogue is characteristic of most Renaissance versions of Philomela. The transformation of the vengeful Philomela of Ovid to the grieving Philomela of the Renaissance authors is perhaps as remarkable as her original transformation from woman to nightingale. Like the raped and mutilated Lavinia in Shakespeare's *Titus Andronicus,* Renaissance Philomelas almost universally become figures of pathos rather than of rage; and even those allusions which acknowledged her rape omitted any suggestion of the anger that was so forcefully present in her myth of origin. In *Arcadia,* for example, Sir Philip Sidney repeatedly represents Philomela as grieving, rather than raging, over her undeserved wrongs. When Philoclea is led to believe that Cecropia has executed Pamela, the narrator compares her laments to Philomela's in their capacity to inspire pity in an audience less hardened by its crimes: "And so, like lamentable Philomela, [Philoclea] complained she the horrible wrong done to her sister, which, if it strived not in the wickedly closed minds of her tormentors a pity of her sorrow, yet bred it a weariness of her sorrow" (559).

When Philoclea's grief over Pyrocles' supposed sexual interest in her mother leads her to sing like "a solitary nightingale bewailing her guiltless punishment and helpless misfortune" (681), her song expresses her inability to remain angry at Pyrocles: while at first his "unkindness kindled noble rage . . . Ah, (in vain) my sight Doth his face shun; For no time can quench Mine embraced fire" (681–82, following the words marked "2"). When Sidney appropriates Philomela for elegaic purposes, he alludes to her rape as her "shame" in the Arcadian shepherds's elegy for Basilius, who has apparently been murdered:

O Philomela with thy breast oppressed
  By shame and grief, help, help me to lament
Such cursed harms as cannot be redressed.
(777)

In all of these examples, the response of anger, which is at least as appropriate as grief, is notably absent. The consistency with which anger is absent from these portrayals of characters who, like Philomela, lament rather than rage over undeserved wrongs, strongly implies that this omission is more than coincidental. Like other Renaissance writers, Sidney used Philomela to signify the absence of ugly, raw anger, which is transformed instead into graceful, artistic expressions of grief which in no way jeopardize the beauty of heroines or of pastoral shepherds. Unlike anger, pathos, in fact, only increases their appeal.

Anger is especially absent from Sidney's most developed representation of Philomela, in *Certain Sonnets*, number 4, which deprives Philomela even of sufficient cause for grief:

The Nightingale, as soone as Aprill bringeth
Unto her rested sense a perfect waking,
While late bare earth, proud of new clothing springeth,
Sings out her woes, a thorne her song-booke making:
  And mournfully bewailing,
  Her throate in tunes expresseth
  What griefe her breast oppresseth,
  For *Thereus'* force on her chaste will prevailing.
    O *Philomela* faire, o take some gladnesse,
    That here is juster cause of plaintfull sadnesse:
    Thine earth now springs, mine fadeth,
    Thy thorne without, my thorne my heart invadeth.

Alas she hath no other cause of anguish
But *Thereus'* love, on her by strong hand wrokne,
Wherein she suffring all her spirits' languish,
Full womanlike complaines her will was brokne.
  But I who dayly craving,

Cannot have to content me,
Have more cause to lament me,
Since wanting is more woe then too much having.
  O *Philomela* faire, o take some gladnesse,
  That here is juster cause of plaintfull sadnesse:
  Thine earth now springs, mine fadeth:
  Thy thorne without, my thorne my heart invadeth.

Certain Sonnets, number 4, takes the denial of Philomela's anger a step further than other representations of Philomela. Even though the poem alludes explicitly to "*Thereus'* force," this Philomela, like other Renaissance Philomela's, is portrayed as sad, as "mournfully bewailing," rather than as angry. Yet even this response to her rape is deprived of dignity; for the narrator describes her complaint as "full womanlike," inappropriately verbose and exaggerated, especially when compared to his allegedly more justified complaint of unrequited love. Essential to this representation is the perception of Tereus's rape as a form of love rather than of aggression, for the narrator claims that Philomela should feel "gladnesse" because her plight, the "too much having" of love, is preferable to the "wanting," the unfulfilled desires of an unrequited lover. Even though it was "on her by strong hand wrokne," "*Thereus'* love" is represented as a positive emotion, differing in extent but not in kind from the response the narrator desires from his own beloved.

The suppressed sense of the aggression of rape returns, however, in the description of the thorn pressing against Philomela's breast. According to tradition, this thorn supposedly functioned to keep Philomela awake to sing all night long.[33] But an awareness of the Philomela myth evokes another function. The thorn's penetration of Philomela's breast is a transparent displacement of Tereus's original rape. The thorn pressing against Philomela's breast creates her rape as continually and distressingly present, and her song as a cry in response to painful penetration.

This evocation of the thorn's penetration of Philomela's breast was no means unique to Sidney; other nightingale poems also represented the song of mournful Philomela as prompted by the pressure of a thorn.[34] Taken together, these poems suggest an imaginative merging of the singing nightingale and the woman in the process of being raped. This conflation renders visible the cultural dislocutions through which the gracefully melodious lament of the nightingale, so unlike an agonized scream, represents a denial of the anger and pain produced by the painful penetration of an undesired penis. With the other nightingale sonnets, *Certain Sonnets,* number 4 demonstrates the effort, and the ultimate futility of that effort, of denying the validity of Philomela's grief, and by extension, the grief of other women who would voice their distress.

Lady Mary Wroth's nightingale poem, "Come merry spring delight us," represents the nightingale's song as a common delight occurring in spring without denying the song's painful source. The first two stanzas of her poem portray the "mirthe" of spring, and the third stanza concludes the poem with this representation of Philomela's song:

Philomeale in this arbour
Makes now her loving harbour
Yett of her state complaining
Her notes in mildnes straining
  Which though sweet
  Yett doe meete
Her former luckles payning.
(*PMW,* pp. 136–37)

Like the song of most Philomelas, the song of Wroth's "Philomeale" is sweet. Like most Renaissance versions of Philomela, Wroth's poem portrays Philomela's grief rather than her anger. Yet Wroth's nightingale poem differs from the others in its acknowledgment of the paradox in the sweetness of Philomela's song. Her use of the words "though" and "yett" suggest that songs of "luckles payning" do not usually yield "sweet" notes and that the mildness of Philomela's complaint exists in spite of, not because of, her distress. In this recognition, Wroth's nightingale poem avoids the suppression of rage common to other nightingale poems in the Renaissance and begins to expose the dislocutions through which other authors denied, or attempted to deny, the anger of Philomela and of other women.

Wroth's other nightingale poem, "O! that I might but now as senceles bee" (*PMW,* pp. 171–72), composed in her romance by the stately queen of Naples, mother of Amphilanthus and Urania, in the company of her women, reveals this same sense of paradox in the sweetness of the nightingale's song:

Yett contrary wee doe owr passions move
Since in sweet notes thou doest thy sorrowes prove.

Later lines in the poem develop this analogy between the nightingale's song and Wroth's own attempt to write poetry to provide perhaps the most explicit statement of the problem facing women authors in the Renaissance:

I, butt in sighs and teares can show I grieve
And those best spent, if worth doe them beeleeve;
Yett thy sweet pleasure makes mee ever finde
That hapines to mee, as love is blinde,
And these thy wrongs in sweetnes to attire
Throwse down my hopes, to make my woes aspire,
Beesids of mee th'advantage thou has gott
Thy griefe thou utterest, mine I utter nott,
Yett thus att last wee may agree in one
I mourne for what still is, thou what is gone.

In this poem, the queen expresses succinctly the ways in which the figure of Philomela represents the quandaries posed by women's authorship. Like the nightingale, the queen of Naples is mourning. Unlike the nightingale, she cannot transmute her grief to art. The queen is constrained by the requirement that women's "wrongs" can only be expressed in songs that are sweet. Expressing her grief in "sighs and teares," the queen of Naples cannot, like the nightingale, "attire" her wrongs in "sweetnes"; her woes cannot "aspire" so high. But her grief requires some expression; and poetry provides consolation for those who can, like the nightingale, use it to express their feelings. The queen claims that she cannot, that the pleasure the nightingale takes in her own sweet song is a happiness that is unavailable, as "blinde" as love, to the queen. The nightingale has the "advantage" of her in expressing her suffering at all: "Thy grief thou utterest, mine I utter nott." But of course she has. While she has never revealed the reasons for her grief, the queen has pointed to its presence. In contrasting her condition with the nightingale's, the queen of Naples has attired her "wrongs in sweetnes"; she has written a "sweet" and accomplished poem. In the very writing of a poem on the impossibility of authorship, she has demonstrated its possibility.

Pointing to Absence

Perhaps in part in response to Wroth's poem, the anonymous poet of the Bright manuscript has taken the opposite ploy. She has demonstrated the impossibility of women's authorship, or at least of women's "loud" and confident authorship, by claiming its possibility only under conditions that can never exist: Philomela's song can be loud and happy only when nightingales sing in the summer. Similarly, by connecting Philomela's optimism about love to the still uncompleted seasonal cycle, the poem points to the next stage, not present in the poem, in which, presumably, the nightingale's faith will decline with the cold breezes of autumn. In both of these poetic strategies, the poem is pointing to absences: first, to conditions that do not exist, and second, to a stage in the seasonal cycle which is not described in the poem.

In the context of these two strategies, the poem's concluding portrayal of Philomela as happy can easily be read as a third way of pointing to absence. Perhaps prompted by the Sidney's advice in *Certain Sonnets,* number 4, to "take some gladnesse," this Philomela exists in absolute contradiction to the sweetly mournful Philomela of Renaissance tradition. Yet this apparent submission functions as subversion. Through the assertion of difference from the conventionally sorrowful Philomela, this anonymous poem renders visible the mechanisms necessary for the operation of this Renaissance tradition of Philomela. By requiring even more forgetfulness of the classical Philomela than do other Renaissance poems, this poem points to the presence of this forgetfulness, and, by extension, to the absence of the anger of Ovid's virgin. This strategy appears to render self-conscious a phenomenon that often operates within the unconscious: the return of the repressed. In Renaissance poems, as in the human unconscious in general, the repressed almost always returns in some form. This mechanism is amply demonstrated by the narrator of the fourth of Sidney's *Certain Sonnets,* who, demanding that the obliging reader forget the pain of rape, renders that pain palpable in the image of the penetrating thorn. Through the image of the thorn, the very material that the reader was required to forget returns to betray the primary text of the poem.

This anonymous poet requires the obliging reader to forget even more of this myth from the much-read Ovid's *Metamorphoses*. Her creation of a happy Philomela, confident about love, requires a suppression of the Philomela myth so absolute that the poem seems to point to its own strategy. In her representation of Philomela, this anonymous poet has strained the connection between the nightingale and the raped virgin to the breaking point. One significant difference between her poem and the others is the greater extent of the gap between her Philomela and Ovid's. Since her poem functions by pointing to other absences, as well, another crucial difference separating her nightingale poem from those of Shakespeare, Spenser, and Sidney is the probability that her suppression of Ovid's Philomela operates as a self-conscious strategy. Unlike most Renaissance nightingale poems, which operate as fragments of a larger cultural discourse prohibiting women's anger, this anonymous nightingale poem points to the repressions lying within that discourse. Cultural repressions, like any others, can never be complete. The words that are repressed always return, sometimes in ghostly forms, to haunt the texts that silenced them.

It seems unlikely that Renaissance authors created their version of Philomela as an embodiment of the problem of women's authorship. They used it, instead, to expand their own versions of authorship to permit them to express sorrow, a feeling often associated with women. But in the process of representing Philomela as sorrowful, in the process of stripping the classical Philomela of her horrible rage, Renaissance poets made visible the restrictions placed upon women's anger within the Renaissance culture. The same figure which permitted men to write poems of mourning prohibited women from writing poems of rage.

Through these Renaissance versions of Philomela, otherwise hidden barriers to women's authorship become visible. Raped and mutilated, Philomela wished to speak her rage and to accuse her rapists. But within the culture of the Renaissance, as within the mouth of the mutilated Philomela, the means to speak that rage effectively was absent. As a nightingale, she could only use her tongue to mourn. Women writers were also left with a gap, the same gap that remained in the mouth of Philomela. From this gap issued most of the writings of all three women in the Sidney circle. All three of them—the nightingale poet, the countess of Pembroke, and Lady Mary Wroth—wrote of an anger that was continually present in order to be made continually absent. For all three of them, women's anger, as present/absent as Philomela's tongue, constituted an essential part of their authorship. Nowhere was this presence/absence of anger so apparent as in their common creation of the constant heroine. Like the optimistic Philomela in the Bright manuscript poem, the constant heroines created in the writings of Mary Sidney and Mary Wroth base their heroism on the simultaneous expressions and denials of rage.

Tongues in the Trees

What is the relationship of these versions of authorship to versions of the self constructed by these women in the Sidney circle? Did they use this heroine as a rhetorical strategy, as the only viable means available to them at least to indicate an anger, however obscured, to find expression within their culture? Or did they sometimes use this presence/absence of anger to construct themselves as constant heroines, denying anger at personal cost like the "vertuous Octavia"? Of course, not all women in any culture or even in any family react in identical ways to the same cultural forces. Despite the discourses which dismissed their words as shrill and their anger as mere shrewishness, some Renaissance women undoubtedly expressed their anger directly and eloquently. In fact, one woman even took an undisguised expression of anger as her version of authorship. Just as Lady Mary Wroth's romance admitted women's sexuality to vindicate it as a form of heroism, so a Renaissance woman apparently took on the name Jane Anger to justify rather than to deny women's anger.

Considering the cultural pressure exerted at least upon the women of the Sidney circle to deny the very anger which their works elicited, Jane Anger's *Protection of Women* (1589) is a revolutionary work. Anticipating criticism even from women for her "choleric vein," she nevertheless stretches "the veins of her brains, the strings of her fingers, and the lists of her modesty" to defend women against a "surfeiting lover" who slandered women for their "kindness."[35] In the early seventeenth century, other women, sometimes under pseudonyms, entered the fray to write pamphlets: Rachel Speght, *A Mouzell for Melastomus* (1617); Ester Sowernam, *Ester hath hang'd Haman* (1617); Constantia Munda, *The Worming of a mad Dogge* (1617); Mary Tattlewell and Joan Hit-him-home, *The Women's Sharpe Revenge* (1640).[36] As direct expressions of anger against men for the way women were treated, these sometimes crude pamphlets perhaps did as much as the more sophisticated works of the Sidney women to prepare the way for women's authorship in subsequent centuries.

As Renaissance versions of Philomela have demonstrated, no suppressions are complete. The occasional success of some women in expressing anger directly in no way negates the attempts of the patriarchal culture of the Renaissance to dismiss or to silence women's rage. While these attempts shaped the kinds of writing that women in the Sidney family could accomplish and certainly prevented many women from writing at all, the project to suppress women's anger exacted a cost from men as well as from women. Living with a constant heroine was probably not much more pleasant than living with a shrew. While it was possible to silence many women authors and perhaps even many women, anxiety about women's anger continued to exert pressure upon the very patriarchal discourses which attempted to contain that anger. By dismissing angry women as shrews, by burning troublesome women as witches, the Renaissance culture created categories for unruly women which invested women's anger with more emotional threat than would be possible in a culture which admitted women's anger as a normal response. The opening stanza of Patrick Hannay's translation of Ovid's Philomela myth provides a particularly grotesque if perhaps not altogether conscious expression of this apprehension about even inarticulate expressions of women's rage:

The quaking Aspine light and thinne
To th'ayre light passage gives:
  Resembling still
  The trembling ill
Of tongues of womankinde,
  Which never rest,
  But still are prest
To wave with every winde.[37]

Hannay's image of women's tongues in the trees suggests the destructive effects of the suppression of women's public speech, oral or written, on men as well as upon women. The very attempt to silence women granted their speech enormous power, worthy of the considerable cultural work necessary for its suppression. This suppression was considered necessary, I have argued, to contain women's sexuality and especially women's rage. But often the voicing of anger leads to a clearing of the air, to a recognition of a problem requiring attention. Allowing women public expressions of anger may indeed have led to social changes judged undesirable in a patriarchal society. But the alternative presented its own difficulty, in the form of a strong undercurrent of hostility all the more enduring and vehement for its lack of clear and public expression. For Philomela's tongue had a life of its own. Its excision did not provide peace of mind to women or to men. Cut out, it multiplied a thousandfold to whisper its anger in the leaves of the trees.

Appendix

Notes

Bibliography

Index

Appendix

Two Narrative Strands in *The Countess of Montgomery's Urania*

To demonstrate the complexity of Wroth's romance, this appendix will confine itself to a narration of the two major plots: the relationship between Pamphilia and Amphilanthus, and Urania's discovery of her parentage.

Pamphilia and Amphilanthus

Folio Portion

At the beginning of the romance, Amphilanthus (son of the king of Naples) loves Antissia (daughter of the king of Romania), while Pamphilia (daughter of the king of Morea) hides her passion for him. Antissia, following Pamphilia into a wood, reads Pamphilia's love sonnet carved on a tree, but Pamphilia continues to deny her passion, assuring Antissia of her friendship to her. Later, mistaking Pamphilia's brother Rosindy for Amphilanthus as he embraces Pamphilia in a garden, Antissia becomes terribly jealous until she discovers her mistake.

Meanwhile, Amphilanthus writes a poem in which he alludes to his love for someone besides Antissia. He visits the sage Melissea, who warns him that while his lady loves him, he will lose her if he does not beware of a treacherous servant; she also warns him that he will be wounded by a woman. She orders him to Cyprus to end the enchantment of the towers (see below). Amphilanthus finds many men and women from court encamped outside the towers; Pamphilia arrives to join them. Amphilanthus enters the towers with Pamphilia to release the enclosed lovers, including Urania (see below), from their enchantments.

The court party, including Pamphilia, Amphilanthus, and Urania, goes to ask the wise Melissea their fortunes. She tells Pamphilia that fear will hinder her marriage and that she will endure many afflictions, especially from women. Returning to Italy, Pamphilia continues to express her tormented love for Amphilanthus in verse. On the death of his father, Amphilanthus becomes king of Naples. Arriving in Italy after adventures, he asks to read Pamphilia's verses. Blushing, she obliges, revealing her love for him, which he thoroughly reciprocates. In a fit of jealous grief, Antissia carves a seat at the top of a willow tree, later sending her nephew to murder Amphilanthus. He kills an imposter by mistake. Antissia repents her attempt to have Amphilanthus murdered.

Boarding a ship to join Pamphilia's aged father, Pamphilia and Urania are shipwrecked in the Adriatic, where they find a beautiful round building with a throne and four rich chairs of marble. With other ladies, they sit in these thrones and are locked inside until two conditions are met: "the man most loving, and most beloved" should also be enclosed with them, and then, second, until the entrance of "the sweetest and loveliest creature, that poore habits had disguised greatnesse in" (RR4v). In this building, they imagine that they see their loves. Various women disguise themselves and go to the Theater, as it is called, but the doors do not open to them. The doors of the Theater do open, however, to admit Amphilanthus, who fulfills the first of the conditions. He is now in love with a woman named Musalina, whom Pamphilia sees at the entrance of the Theater. All are rescued by an alleged shepherdess Veralinda. As the doors open to admit her, she touches the lovers with Apollo's rod. A pillar of gold appears with a book hanging on it. Only Urania can get the book, and she needs Veralinda's help to open it. It reveals both the story of Urania's infant kidnapping and Veralinda's actual identity as a princess (the daughter of king of Phrygia).

Later, Pamphilia walks alone, grieving and constant to the now false Amphilanthus, for whom she writes sonnets. "Against her owne minde" (CCC3), Urania advises Pamphilia against constancy because her extreme melancholy seems to threaten her life. Urania finally succeeds in getting Pamphilia to appear in court to comfort her parents. Meanwhile, Amphilanthus feels remorse over his infidelity to Pamphilia and renounces Musalina, who still loves him. Pamphilia continues to write sad verses and a complaint of Lindamira, whom others suspect as a version of her own sad self.

A refused wooer of Pamphilia, the king of Celicia, mounts an invasion against Pamphilia's realm. Amphilanthus arrives to rescue her by jousting with the king of Celicia. He is reunited with the astonished and gratified Pamphilia. Soon, however, they go hunting, and Amphilanthus disappears. Pamphilia swoons when she finds Amphilanthus's broken and bloody armor. Then a stone opens into a burning hell-like place where she sees Musalina crowned, with another woman named Lucenia (also jilted by Amphilanthus), holding a sword about to raze the name Pamphilia from Amphilanthus's exposed heart. The opening to the stone shuts to Pamphilia, for only false lovers can enter. Pamphilia returns to court to lead a life more like a religious convert than a court lady. Various knights set off to rescue Amphilanthus.

Much later, Amphilanthus is found. He had rushed after thieves who appeared to be stealing someone who looked like Pamphilia and had killed their leader. This figure of Pamphilia was carried invisibly into a group of stones. Amphilanthus pulled a ring of iron in the midst of these stones, to find "Pamphilia" dead, her breast open and his name written in burning letters on her heart. He is prevented from joining her by magic. He hears Musalina and Lucenia call for help, for Lucenia is being carried away by a savage man. He runs distracted all night, until he catches up with them. Lucenia is being thrown into a boat, while Musalina cries for help on shore. Musalina has, as it turns out, staged all of this by magic. He goes to live with them in Tenedos. Informed of Pamphilia's continuing love for him, Amphilanthus resolves to see her as he returns to Germany (where he is now also king). Coming upon Pamphilia weeping into a stream, he embraces her and she forgives him. He claims that drinking this water filled with her tears has infused constancy in him. Amphilanthus invites Pamphilia to come to Italy with him to visit his mother.

Manuscript Continuation

Amphilanthus and Pamphilia visit Amphilanthus's mother in Naples, and then they proceed to visit Pamphilia's father in Morea, where Urania is also visiting. At Morea, there ensues a long discussion among those present (including various reappearing characters) concerning Amphilanthus's infidelity; Amphilanthus vows constancy. They all enjoy listening to Pamphilia sing. Sitting on the grass, they exchange gossip, especially about Antissia. Pamphilia feels sorry for her.

The young and darkly handsome Rodomandro (king of Tartaria) falls in love with Pamphilia. Feeling jealous, Amphilanthus asks Pamphilia to marry him, and she does so the next day, although the contract is not yet legally binding. The king of Tartaria presents a magnificent masque for the occasion.

An ambassador from Candia arrives at Morea to invite knights, including Amphilanthus, to participate in games. Knowing the beauty of the Candian queen, Pamphilia fears that Amphilanthus will be unfaithful. After his departure, she dreams that Amphilanthus is about to be married to another woman. Meanwhile, Amphilanthus rescues a courtly group from a dreaded giant. Later, Amphilanthus's squire tells of Amphilanthus's desperate melancholy, which has moved him to ship himself off in a small boat. Pamphilia fears that a new love is the reason for his melancholy. In fact, the evil Candian queen has enlisted the aid of his old tutor, learned in enchantments, to help her to marry Amphilanthus to the princess of Slavonia. Misinformed that Pamphilia has married the king of Tartaria, Amphilanthus marries this princess, but he does not feel good about it. He sends his new wife to her father and departs with one squire on a boat bound for anywhere.

Amphilanthus lands by chance near the court of his sister Urania, who finds him and tells him to have hope. He joins two knights to search for the lost princesses, rumored to be enchanted at Lesbos under the care of Melissea. Amphilanthus, his sister, and others, are shipwrecked on a Melissea's island through her magic. Melissea also reassures Amphilanthus, who berates himself for his infidelity to Pamphilia. Amphilanthus gets on a boat again, and rescues women and children, including Urania's daughter Claribella, from one hundred giants. He proceeds to further self-lacerations and to Prague. On the way, he meets a boat containing Pamphilia. While their reunion is tender, she asks him to see her as seldom as possible and vows never to speak to him. Amphilanthus vanquishes yet another giant, attempts to help Parselius search for lost children (including Parselius's daughter Candiana), and is visibly impressed by two shepherds, Belario and his extremely well-read sister Clorina.

Earlier, Pamphilia had gathered together friends (including the exceedingly chivalric king of Tartaria) and allies to defend her from the fierce Sophie of Persia, who has usurped his throne from Sophia, his niece. Now Pamphilia's father approves of the king of Tartaria's attentions. Amphilanthus and the king of Tartaria join in the fight against the evil Sophie. They win, but the rightful heir, Sophia, is whisked away in a chariot drawn by dragons. The king of Tartaria proposes marriage to Pamphilia, who accepts "against her own minde, yett nott constrain'd" (II, 11Br). She wears black to her wedding, presumably in mourning for her brother, killed in battle, but actually because of her feelings for Amphilanthus. Amphilanthus is suitably distraught on her wedding day. On the request of Amphilanthus's mother, Pamphilia breaks her vow of silence to him to exchange courtesies. Her new husband leaves on a trip. Amphilanthus and his mother discover her with red eyes and guess that the reason is her continuing love for Amphilanthus. Pamphilia and Amphilanthus gaze into each other's eyes. Only a little later, Amphilanthus stops by her chamber before his own departure to attempt the "adventure of the unaccessible rock" (II, 12Bv). They kiss passionately.

On his adventures, Amphilanthus is strangely moved by a young knight of no discernable parentage, called "Faire Design" after the cipher on his chest; he will know his parentage when he meets a woman with the same cipher on her chest.

Staying with her friend Urania, Pamphilia befriends a nymph named Leutissia who lives in a fountain, hiding there from all mankind after a traumatic episode. Leutissia had witnessed a scene in which her evil guardian had forced his wife to hold their daughter while he raped her, and then had killed his wife, their daughter, and their son (the beloved of Leutissia). When he attempted to kill her, she fled to the fountain to save her life. He then killed himself. Pamphilia draws her out a little.

The parents of Amphilanthus's wife send ambassadors to request consummation of their marriage. He invites them to his court, solemnizing their marriage with a scarcely described second wedding. Amphilanthus settles her in Vienna before returning to see his sister Urania in Italy. Still feeling tormented by his love for Pamphilia, he pauses by a fountain, which opens up to reveal Leutissia and Pamphilia. Leutissia understands the chastity of their love and approves their reunion. Pamphilia forgives Amphilanthus. In remorse, he considers suicide. Soon thereafter, Pamphilia and Urania meet a dying conjurer who confesses that he had deceived Amphilanthus into believing that Pamphilia had already married the king of Tartaria; he had also withheld her letters. Pamphilia does not grant him her forgiveness.

Having sprained her ankle, Pamphilia is confined to bed. Urania and Amphilanthus visit her; Amphilanthus kisses her hand, and they are happy for many days. An ambassador from the king of Tartaria arrives to request their presence; Amphilanthus is to help him with problems he is having with his subjects. The king of Tartaria, Pamphilia, Amphilanthus, Urania, and Steriamus all remain happily together enjoying pastimes, particularly hunting.

The concluding section of the romance is sketchy and inconsistent. The king of Tartaria dies, leaving Pamphilia the mother of a boy who also soon dies. Pamphilia goes to her native country with Amphilanthus on a ship on which the king of Tartaria is suddenly again present without explanation, magical or otherwise. The king does not seem to be present in the last gathering of the court party surrounding Pamphilia and Amphilanthus. The romance ends mid-sentence with news of Faire Design, who is seeking them because Melissea has informed him that a great enchantment will not be ended without their help.

Urania

Folio Portion

Wroth's romance opens with the shepherdess Urania's complaint over her ignorance of her own estate or birth. Going into a cave, she finds a knight weeping for his lost love, apparently dead after her unwilling marriage to a cruel husband. Urania sympathizes. Leaving the cave, she is saved from a wolf by two shepherds who introduce her to their father (actually the king of Albania) and their guest Amphilanthus, who is searching for his lost sister. Amphilanthus notes Urania's striking resemblance to his youngest brother. Urania falls in love with Amphilanthus's traveling companion Parselius (son of the king of Morea), who, returning her love, hopes she is the lost princess but vows to make her a princess if she is not. (Later it evolves, of course, that she is.) As the party boards a ship to rescue the king's cousin, who is imprisoned in a tower by a usurping king, they are captured by pirates. The captain of the pirates kneels to her, mistaking her for Antissia, whom he had been charged to deliver to Prince Leandrus. Another group of pirates attack the ship, led by this same Leandrus.

Many stories later, the ship is blown to Cyprus, where the group finds the three Towers of Desire, of Love, and of Constancy, the latter of which will end the enchantment of those enclosed in all three when entered by "the valientest Knight and loyallest Lady" (F4v). Drinking of water that inflames them with passions, the men of the party are dispersed, while the women enter the towers. Urania is locked in the Tower of Love. Parselius dreams that Urania has forsaken him. On his travels, he meets the lovely Dalinea (princess of Achaya), whom he marries. In a dream, Urania reproaches Parselius, who, leaving Dalinea to search for Urania, gets on a boat bound for anywhere, ending up in a hermit's cell.

Freed from the Tower of Love by Pamphilia and Amphilanthus (see above), Urania is informed by the wise Melissa that she is the sister of Amphilanthus, who is then instructed to throw her into the sea at St. Maura in order to free her of her love for Parselius. Leaping in to the sea to save her, Parselius is delivered from his love for Urania but not for Dalinea, whom he now longs to see. Later in Italy, an old pilgrim reveals that he had stolen Urania as a baby and that robbers had stolen Urania from him. Having given birth to Parselius's child, Dalinea arrives at court to seek justice. Parselius confesses and pledges his love to his wife Dalinea. Steriamus (king of Albania) successfully pledges his love to a wary Urania, exchanging a diamond bracelet for a bracelet of her hair. Urania worries that Steriamus will not value her love because she loved Parselius first, but he does. Imprisoned in the Theater with Pamphilia, she finally reads the story of her royal birth with the help of Veralinda (see above).

Manuscript Continuation

Married to Steriamus, Urania is happy. They have five children, including a son also named Steriamus. Her primary plot function is to serve as friend to Pamphilia and to worry over her missing daughter, whom she had sent by boat, along with other aristocratic children, to visit the queen of Naples. The boat moves off course, and children are confined by magic within the Inaccessible Rock, where they are eventually freed by Faire Design, whose own parentage remains somewhat of a mystery.

Notes

INTRODUCTION

1. Sir Philip Sidney, *The Countess of Pembroke's Arcadia,* ed. Maurice Evans (New York: Penguin, 1977), p. 376. I have chosen the Evans edition because it uses as its copytext the 1593 edition, produced under the auspices of the countess of Pembroke, rather than Fulke Greville's 1590 edition, which serves as the copytext for Victor Skretkowicz's excellent 1987 edition. The countess's edition would have been more widely read in the Sidney family.

2. Ibid., pp. 241–42.

3. This introduction represents an application to gender of the theories of sexuality in Michel Foucault's *History of Sexuality,* vol. 1, *An Introduction,* trans. Robert Hurley (New York: Vintage Books, 1980). Another critic who has extended Foucault's concepts to apply to gender is Teresa de Lauretis, "The Technology of Gender," in *Technologies of Gender* (Bloomington: Indiana Univ. Press, 1987), pp. 1–30; the sexualization of women's knowledge, especially in Shakespeare's plays, is discussed in Lisa Jardine, "Cultural Confusion and Shakespeare's Learned Heroines: 'These are old paradoxes,'" *Shakespeare Quarterly* 38 (1987): 1–18. An excellent historical perspective is presented in Susan Dwyer Amussen, *An Ordered Society: Gender and Class in Early Modern England* (Oxford: Blackwell, 1988). Foucault has been well applied in Jonathan Dollimore, "Transgression and Surveillance in *Measure for Measure,*" in *Political Shakespeare: New Essays in Cultural Materialism,* ed. Jonathan Dollimore and Alan Sinfield (Ithaca: Cornell Univ. Press, 1985), pp. 72–87. The phrase "the discourse of gender difference" is adapted from the title *Rewriting the Renaissance: The Discourses of Sexual Difference in Early Modern Europe,* ed. Margaret W. Ferguson, Maureen Quilligan, and Nancy J. Vickers (Chicago: Univ. of Chicago Press, 1986).

4. For issues facing male Renaissance authors see Jacqueline T. Miller, *Poetic License: Authority and Authorship in Medieval and Renaissance Contexts* (Oxford: Oxford Univ. Press, 1986), pp. 3–33; John Guillory, *Poetic Authority: Spenser, Milton, and Literary History* (Columbia Univ. Press, 1983), pp. vii–xiii; and David Quint, *Origin and Originality in Renaissance Literature* (New Haven: Yale Univ. Press, 1983). For issues facing women Renaissance authors, see Tilde Sankovitch, "Inventing Authority of Origin: *The*

Difficult Enterprise," in *Women in the Middle Ages and the Renaissance: Literary and Historical Perspectives,* ed. Mary Beth Rose (Syracuse: Syracuse Univ. Press, 1986), pp. 227–44; Ann Rosalind Jones, "Assimilation with a Difference: Renaissance Women Poets and Literary Influence,' *Yale French Studies* 62 (1981): 135–53; Margaret L. King, "Book-lined Cells: Women and Humanism in the Early Italian Renaissance," in *Beyond Their Sex: Learned Women of the European Past,* ed. Patricia H. Labalme (New York: New York Univ. Press, 1980), pp. 66–90; Gary Waller, "Struggling into Discourse: The Emergence of Renaissance Women's Writing," in *Silent But for the Word,* ed. Margaret P. Hannay (Kent, Ohio: Kent State Univ. Press, 1985), pp. 238–56; and Waller, "The Countess of Pembroke and Gendered Reading," forthcoming.

5. Margaret J. M. Ezell, *The Patriarch's Wife* (Chapel Hill: Univ. of North Carolina Press, 1987), esp. pp. 62–126 and 161–63. Ezell's description of the gaps between repressive patriarchal theory and its looser implementation should not, however, be overgeneralized to apply to the sixteenth and early seventeenth centuries, which were more repressive to women writers. See also Amussen, pp. 61–63 for gaps between ideology and practice.

6. Recent anthologies of women's writings include Betty Travitsky, comp. and ed., *The Paradise of Women: Writings by Englishwomen of the Renaissance* (Westport, Conn.: Greenwood Press, 1981); Moira Ferguson, ed., *First Feminists: British Women Writers, 1578–1799* (Bloomington: Indiana Univ. Press, 1985); Katherine Usher Henderson and Barbara F. McManus, eds., *Half Humankind: Contexts and Texts of the Controversy about Women in England, 1540–1640,* (Urbana: Univ. of Illinois Press, 1985); Simon Shepherd, ed., *The Women's Sharp Revenge: Five Women's Pamphlets from the Renaissance* (London: Fourth Estate, 1985); Katherina M. Wilson, ed., *Women of the Renaissance and Reformation* (Athens: Univ. of Georgia Press, 1987).

7. See, among many others, Louis Althusser, "Ideology and Ideological State Apparatuses (Notes towards an Investigation)," in *Essays on Ideology* (Thetford, Norfolk: Verso, 1984), pp. 1–60; Raymond Williams, *Culture* (Glasgow: Fontana, 1981); Dollimore, foreword and intro. to *Political Shakespeare,* pp. vii–viii, 2–17; and Catherine Belsey, *The Subject of Tragedy: Identity and Difference in Renaissance Drama* (London: Methuen, 1985).

8. See, for example, Foucault's *History of Sexuality,* 1:92–102.

9. Suzanne W. Hull, *Chaste, Silent, and Obedient: English Books for Women, 1475–1640* (San Marino, Calif.: Huntington Library, 1982), p. 142. The collapse of these terms is acutely noted by Peter Stallybrass, "Patriarchal Territories: The Body Enclosed," in Ferguson et al., *Rewriting the Renaissance,* p. 127. See also Belsey, "Silence and Speech," in *The Subject of Tragedy,* pp. 149–91.

10. William Whately, *The Bride-Bush* (London, 1619), CC3, discussed in

Lisa Jardine, *Still Harping on Daughters: Women and Drama in the Age of Shakespeare* (New Jersey: Barnes and Noble, 1983), p. 106.

11. Ralph Houlbrooke, *Church Courts and the People during the English Reformation, 1520–1570* (Oxford: Oxford Univ. Press, 1979), p. 80, cited in Stallybrass, "Patriarchal Territories," p. 126.

12. Jardine, *Still Harping on Daughters,* p. 121.

13. Margaret W. Ferguson, "A Room Not Their Own: Renaissance Women as Readers and Writers," in *The Comparative Perspective on Literature: Approaches to Theory and Practice,* ed. Clayton Koelb and Susan Noakes (Ithaca: Cornell Univ. Press, 1988), pp. 93–116.

14. See, for example, Luis Vives, *Instruction of a Christen Woman* (London, 1557), D1; Suzanne Hull, *Chaste, Silent, and Obedient,* p. 141, notes the misquotation of this verse in Thomas Bentley, *Monument of Matrones* (London, 1582), to claim even more power for patriarchy.

15. Whately, *The Bride-Bush,* CC4v, generalized this verse to advocate women's silence within the house as well as outside it. This use of this verse is discussed also by Jardine, *Still Harping on Daughters,* p. 106, and Labalme, intro. to *Beyond their Sex,* pp. 2–3.

16. Stallybrass, "Patriarchal Territories," pp. 126–27; Ann Rosalind Jones, "Nets and Bridles: Early Modern Conduct Books and Sixteenth-Century Women's Lyrics," in *The Ideology of Conduct: Essays on Literature and the History of Sexuality,* ed. Nancy Armstrong and Leonard Tennenhouse (New York: Methuen, 1987), pp. 39–72; Belsey, *The Subject of Tragedy,* pp. 192–221; D. E. Underdown, "The Taming of the Scold: the Enforcement of Patriarchal Authority in Early Modern England," in *Order and Disorder in Early Modern England,* ed. A. J. Fletcher and J. Stevenson (Cambridge: Cambridge Univ. Press, 1985), p. 122. See also Amussen, pp. 122–23.

17. A number of these are cited in Ruth Kelso, *Doctrine for the Lady of the Renaissance* (Urbana: Univ. of Illinios Press, 1956).

18. Thomas Becon, "A new catechisme," in *Worckes* (London, 1564), Bbbii; discussed in Kelso, *Doctrine,* p. 50, and Jardine, *Still Harping on Daughters,* p. 107.

19. *Sermons of Bernadine Ochyne . . . concerning the predestination and election of god,* trans. A[nne] C[ooke] (London, c. 1570), A3.

20. For the Renaissance perception of reading as a form of listening "set in motion by sight," see Walter Ong, *Orality and Literacy* (New York: Methuen, 1982), p. 121; also his *Rhetoric, Romance, and Technology* (Ithaca: Cornell Univ. Press, 1971), pp. 23–47.

21. [George Puttenham], *Arte of English Poesie* (1589), ed. Gladys D. Willcock and Alice Walker (Cambridge: Cambridge Univ. Press, 1936), p. 249.

22. I have begun a project dealing with three Renaissance women

readers. Two of several excellent recent resources on women readers are Elizabeth A. Flynn and Patrocinio P. Schweickart, eds., *Gender and Reading: Essays on Readers, Texts, and Contexts* (Baltimore: Johns Hopkins Univ. Press, 1986), and Mary Jacobus, *Reading Women: Essays in Feminist Criticism* (New York: Columbia Univ. Press, 1986).

23. David Cressy, *Literacy and the Social Order: Reading and Writing in Tudor and Stuart England* (Cambridge: Cambridge Univ. Press, 1980), pp. 20–25; his figures are questioned by Margaret Spufford, *Small Books and Pleasant Histories: Popular Fiction and Its Readership in Seventeenth-Century England* (Athens: Univ. of Georgia Press, 1981), pp. 22, 34–37, who notes that because reading and writing were taught as separate activities, many women who could read may well not have been able to sign their names.

24. Luis Vives, *Instruction of a Christen Woman* (London, 1557), D3.

25. Susan Noakes, "On the Superficiality of Women," in Koelb and Noakes, *The Comparative Perspective on Literature*, pp. 339–55.

26. Giovanni Boccaccio, *The Decameron* (London, 1620), A4.

27. Richard Hyrde, dedication of Desiderius Erasmus, *Devout Treatise Upon the Pater Noster*, trans. Margaret Roper (London, c. 1526), A4. For powerfully ambivalent connections between writing and spinning, see Sankovitch, "Inventing Authority of Origin," pp. 237–42; for a discussion of real women workers in cloth, see Merry E. Wiesner, "Spinsters and Seamstresses: Women in Cloth and Clothing Production," in Ferguson et al., *Rewriting the Renaissance*, pp. 191–205.

28. A range of these is presented in Kelso, *Doctrine*, pp. 58–77.

29. Rosemary Radford Ruether, "Misogynism and Virginal Feminism in the Fathers of the Church," in *Religion and Sexism*, ed. Rosemary Radford Reuther (New York: Simon and Schuster, 1974), pp. 150–83, discusses attitudes of the church fathers towards women.

30. Belsey, *The Subject of Tragedy*, pp. 4–6, 149–60, discusses discontinuities within subject positions offered Renaissance women in society, as well.

31. See anthologies and discussions by Travitsky, Ferguson, Henderson, and Shepherd (see note 6, above).

32. Lady Anne Clifford, for example, did both; see George C. Williamson, *Lady Anne Clifford, Countess of Dorset, Pembroke, and Montgomery, 1590–1676: Her Life, Letters, and Work.* (East Ardsley, Yorkshire: S. R. Publ., 1922).

33. See Merry E. Wiesner, *Women in the Sixteenth Century: A Bibliography* (Saint Louis: Center for Reformation Research, 1983); for the late Renaissance, Patricia Crawford, "A Provisional Checklist of Women's Published Writings, 1600–1700," in *Women in English Society, 1500–1800*, ed. Mary Prior (New York: Methuen, 1985), pp. 211–32.

34. J. W. Saunders, "The Stigma of Print: A Note on the Social Bases of Tudor Poetry," *Essays in Criticism* 1 (1951): 139–64; Arthur Marotti, *John Donne, Coterie Poet* (Madison: Univ. of Wisconsin Press, 1986), pp. 3–24; and esp. Ezell, *The Patriarch's Wife*, pp. 64–100, who stresses the early perception of publication as an author's loss of control of the work.

35. "M. C. to the Ladie A. B.," in *An Apologie or answere in defence of the Church of Englande*, trans. Anne Bacon (London, 1564), A2v. The first edition (1562) did not contain this prefatory material. Discussed in Mary Ellen Lamb, "The Cooke Sisters: Attitudes towards Learned Women in the Renaissance," in Hannay, *Silent But for the Word*, p. 117.

36. Discussed in Lamb, "The Cooke Sisters," p. 114.

37. A[nne] C[ooke], dedication, *Sermons of Barnadine Ochine*, A4–A4v.

38. Lamb, "The Cooke Sisters," p. 110.

39. Margaret P. Hannay, "'Doo What Men May Sing': Mary Sidney and the Tradition of Admonitory Dedication," in Hannay, *Silent But for the Word*, pp. 149–65.

40. Anne Lake Prescott, "The Pearl of the Valois and Elizabeth I: Marguerite de Navarre's *Miroir* and Tudor England," in Hannay, *Silent But for the Word*, pp. 61–76.

41. Lady Jane Lumley, *Iphigeneia at Aulis*, ed. Harold H. Child (London: Chiswick Press for Malone Society Reprints, 1909); discussed in Nancy Cotton, *Women Playwrights in England, c. 1363–1750* (Lewisburg, Pa.: Bucknell Univ. Press, 1980), p. 28; Elaine V. Beilin, *Redeeming Eve: Women Writers of the English Renaissance* (Princeton: Princeton Univ. Press, 1987), pp. 153–57.

42. John Florio, trans., *Essays*, by Montaigne (London, 1603), A2; discussed in Lamb, "The Cooke Sisters," pp. 115–17. The representation of intellectual endeavors as masculine "births" possibly derived in part from Plato's *Symposium*.

43. Excerpted in *The Paradise of Women*, Travitsky, pp. 38–41, and discussed in Beilin, *Redeeming Eve*, pp. 72–73, respectively.

44. *The first examinacyon of Anne Askewe, lately martyred in Smythfelde* (Wesel, 1546) and *The lattre examinacyon of the worthye servaunt of God mastres Anne Askewe* (Wesel, 1547), discussed in Beilin, *Redeeming Eve*, pp. 29–47.

45. Belsey, *The Subject of Tragedy*, pp. 185–91.

46. Travitsky, *The Paradise of Women*, pp. 156–57; Ezell, *The Patriarch's Wife*, p. 92.

47. The effect of the civil wars upon women's speech within the English church is discussed in Phyllis Mack, "Women as Prophets during the English Civil War," *Feminist Studies* 8 (1982): 19–46; Keith Thomas, "Women and the Civil War Sects," *Past and Present* 13 (1958): 42–62; and

Antonia Fraser, "When Women Preach," in *The Weaker Vessel* (New York: Knopf, 1984), pp. 244–66. Also see Ezell, *The Patriarch's Wife*, pp. 92–94.

48. Jones, "Nets and Bridles," pp. 40–48.

49. Ezell, *The Patriarch's Wife*, pp. 62–100.

50. Sidney Lee, "Penelope Rich," *Dictionary of National Biography*, 16:1006–8. Rich and her lover experienced censure at the court of James I only when they married. See also Clark Hulse, "Stella's Wit: Penelope Rich as Reader of Sidney's Sonnets," in Ferguson et al., *Rewriting the Renaissance*, pp. 272–86.

51. Josephine Roberts, "The Imaginary Epistles of Sir Philip Sidney and Lady Penelope Rich," *English Literary Renaissance* 15 (1985): 63–73.

52. Spufford, *Small Books and Pleasant Histories*, pp. 63–75, 156–58. The popularity of these books in the seventeenth century also proceeds from some loosening of the restraints of this discourse of gender difference from the sixteenth century. For a discussion of seventeenth-century feminism, see Hilda Smith, *Reason's Disciples: Seventeenth-Century English Feminists* (Urbana: Univ. of Illinois Press, 1982).

53. The servant's description of this song as "without bawdry" is humorous in this context; Perdita's anxiety about the possibility of "scurrilous words" represents, I believe, an upper-class overlay on a lower-class tradition, her concern revealing her innate aristocratic taste. Class is interrogated for French women writers in Ann Rosalind Jones, "City Women and Their Audiences: Louise Labe and Veronica Franco," in Ferguson et al., *Rewriting the Renaissance*, pp. 299–316.

54. Henderson and McManus, *Half Humankind*, pp. 21–23, argue against critics who suggest "Anger" may have been a pseudonym adopted by a male writer; and Shepherd, *The Women's Sharp Revenge*, p. 30, locates a "handful of women at the right age at the right time" by that name. Anger's tract is excerpted in *Half Humankind* (pp. 173–88) and printed in Shepherd (pp. 29–52). See also discussions in Linda Woodbridge, *Women and the English Renaissance: Literature and the Nature of Womankind, 1540–1620* (Urbana: Univ. of Illinois Press, 1984), pp. 63–65; and Beilin, *Redeeming Eve*, pp. 250–53.

55. Shepherd, *The Women's Sharp Revenge*, p. 58, quoting from Speght's contemporary Ester Sowernam. Speght wrote *A Mouzzell for Malestomus* (London, 1617), printed in Shepherd, pp. 57–84. See also discussions in Woodbridge, *Women and the English Renaissasnce*, pp. 87–92, and Beilin, *Redeeming Eve*, pp. 253–57.

56. Carolyn G. Heilbrun, *Writing a Woman's Life* (London: Norton, 1988), has superbly demonstrated that the writing of much later women was enabled by the transformation of their lives by some event from "a conventional to an eccentric story" (p. 48).

57. Leah Marcus, *Puzzling Shakespeare: Local Reading and Its Discontents*

(Berkeley and Los Angeles: Univ. of California Press, 1989). For Elizabeth's poems, see *The Poems of Queen Elizabeth I*, ed. Leicester Bradner (Providence: Brown Univ. Press, 1964), esp. "On Monsieur's Departure," p. 5; see also Travitsky, *The Paradise of Women*, pp. 187–207.

58. Sandra K. Fischer, "Elizabeth Cary and Tyranny, Domestic and Religious," in Hannay, *Silent But for the Word*, pp. 225–37; Beilin, *Redeeming Eve*, pp. 157–76; and Cotton, *Women Playwrights in England*, pp. 31–37. Other writings are excerpted in Travistky, *The Paradise of Women*, pp. 209–33.

59. Belsey, *The Subject of Tragedy*, pp. 171–75.

60. Heilbrun, *Writing a Woman's Life*, pp. 48–52, notes a similar phenomenon in the sexual activities of George Eliot and Dorothy Sayers.

61. Historical Manuscripts Commission (HMC), *De L'Isle*, 5:305, cited in Josephine Roberts, *The Poems of Mary Wroth* (Baton Rouge: Louisiana State Univ. Press, 1983), p. 25. For a range of attitudes towards illegitimacy in the seventeenth century see Keith Wrightson, "The Nadir of English Illegitimacy in the English Seventeenth Century," in *Bastardy and Its Comparative History*, ed. Peter Laslett et al. (Cambridge: Harvard Univ. Press, 1980), pp. 176–91.

62. These entries from Forman's diary are cited and discussed in A. L. Rowse, intro. to *The Poems of Shakespeare's Dark Lady: Salve Deus Rex Judaeorum by Emilia Lanier* (London: Cape, 1978), pp. 9–16; see also Barbara K. Lewalski, "Of God and Good Women: The Poems of Aemilia Lanyer," in Hannay, *Silent But for the Word*, pp. 203–24. In this context, see Ann Rosalind Jones's discussion of the French courtesan-poet Veronica Franco in "City Women and Their Audiences," in Ferguson et al., *Rewriting the Renaissance*, pp. 299–316.

63. Foucault, *The History of Sexuality*, 1:101–2.

64. Jones, "Nets and Bridles," pp. 63–68; see also Travitsky, " 'The Wyll and Testament' of Isabella Whitney," *English Literary Renaissance* 10 (1980): 76–95.

65. Ben Jonson, "Conversations with William Drummond of Hawthornden," *Works*, ed. C. H. Herford and Percy and Evelyn Simpson (Oxford: Clarendon Press, 1947), 1:138.

66. These poems, discussed in Chapter 5, have been published in Mary Ellen Lamb, "Three Unpublished Holograph Poems in the Bright Manuscript: A New Poet in the Sidney Circle?" *Review of English Studies*, n.s., 35 (1984): 301–15.

67. Michael Brennan, *Literary Patronage in the Renaissance: The Pembroke Family* (London: Routledge, 1988), p. 54, perceptively suggests that Sidney's funeral may have also been designed to divert attention from the beheading of Mary Stuart eight days before.

68. Alan Hager, "The Exemplary Mirage: Fabrication of Sir Philip Sid-

ney's Biographical Image and the Sidney Reader," *ELH* 48 (1981): 1–16, reprinted in *Essential Articles for the Study of Sir Philip Sidney,* ed. Arthur Kinney (Hamden, Conn.: Archon, 1986), pp. 15–30.

69. Gary Waller, "The Rewriting of Petrarch: Sidney and the Languages of Sixteenth-Century Poetry," in *Sir Philip Sidney and the Interpretation of Renaissance Culture,* ed. Gary Waller and Michael D. Moore (Totowa, N.J.: Barnes and Noble, 1984), pp. 69–83; Richard C. McCoy, *Sir Philip Sidney: Rebellion in Arcadia* (New Brunswick: Rutgers Univ. Press, 1979); Andrew Weiner, *Sir Philip Sidney and the Poetics of Protestantism: A Study of Contexts* (Minneapolis: Univ. of Minnesota Press, 1978); Gary Waller, "'This Matching of Contraries': Calvinism and Courtly Philosophy in the Sidney Psalms," *English Studies* 55 (1974): 22–31.

70. Sir Philip Sidney, "To my dear lady and sister, the Countess of Pembroke," *The Countess of Pembroke's Arcadia,* p. 57; Sidney, *Miscellaneous Prose,* ed. Katherine Duncan-Jones and Jan Van Dorsten (Oxford: Clarendon, 1973), p. 121; Katherine Duncan-Jones, "Philip Sidney's Toys," *Proceedings of the British Academy* 66 (1980): 161–78; Annabel Patterson, *Censorship and Interpretation: The Conditions of Writing and Reading in Early Modern England* (Madison: Univ. of Wisconsin Press, 1984), pp. 24–43; Ann Rosalind Jones and Peter Stallybrass, "Courtship and Courtiership: The Politics of *Astrophil and Stella,*" *Studies in English Literature* 24 (1984): 53–68.

71. A discussion of the growing Renaissance "heroics of marriage" is included in Mary Beth Rose, *The Expense of Spirit: Love and Sexuality in English Renaissance Drama* (Ithaca: Cornell Univ. Press, 1988).

72. Pertinent to this discussion is a statement concerning modern women writers in Heilbrun, *Writing a Woman's Life,* p. 15: "If one is not permitted to express anger or even to recognize it within oneself, one is, by simple extension, refused both power and control." Groundbreaking work on the cultural conditions surrounding emotions, including anger, is currently being undertaken by anthropologists such as Catherine A. Lutz, *Unnatural Emotions* (Chicago: Univ. of Chicago Press, 1988).

73. Elaine Showalter, "The Other Bostonians: Gender and Literary Study," *Yale Journal of Criticism* 1 (1988): 182.

CHAPTER 1. Pembrokiana and the Bear Whelps: Inscriptions of the Countess of Pembroke

1. Some of the information and discussion of texts in this chapter originally appeared in my essay "The Countess of Pembroke's Patronage," *English Literary Renaissance* 12 (1982): 162–79.

2. Richard Hyrde, dedication of Desiderius Erasmus, *Devout Treatise upon the Pater Noster,* A4, discussed above in the Introduction.

3. These dedications are conveniently indexed in Franklin Williams, *Index to Dedications and Commendatory Verses in English Books before 1641* (London: Bibliographical Society, 1962).

4. Mary Sidney, *The Triumph of Death and Other Unpublished and Uncollected Poems*, ed. G. R. Waller (Salzburg: Institut für Englische Sprache und Literatur, 1977), pp. 181–83. According to *The Progresses and Processions of Queen Elizabeth*, ed. John Nichols, 3 vols. (London: Nichols, 1788–1805), 2:2, 3:167–68, the queen had planned a progress to North Wiltshire in 1600 but had cancelled for reasons of health. Nichols records no actual visit to Wilton or to other Pembroke estates while Mary was countess of Pembroke.

5. Mary Sidney, *The Triumph of Death*, pp. 88–95. One of these verses is particularly discussed in Margaret P. Hannay, "'Doo What Men May Sing': Mary Sidney and the Tradition of Admonitory Dedication," in *Silent But for the Word*, ed. Margaret P. Hannay (Kent, Ohio: Kent State Univ. Press, 1985), pp. 149–65.

6. "Mornay," *Short-Title Catalogue of Books Printed in England, Scotland, and Ireland, 1425–1600*, comp. A. W. Pollard and G. R. Redgrave, rev. W. A. Jackson and F. S. Ferguson (London: Bibliographical Society, 1976), 2:163.

7. Henry Harington, ed., *Nugae Antiquae* (London: J. Dodsley, 1779), 1:149–50.

8. Abraham Conham, prefatory letter to Gervase Babington, *A Very Fruitful Exposition of the Commandements by Way of Questions and Answers* (London, 1583), 2v.

9. Thomas Moffett, *Silkwormes and Their Flies* (London, 1599), dedication.

10. HMC, *Salisbury*, 22:161, reproduced in Josephine Roberts, *The Poems of Mary Wroth* (Baton Rouge: Louisiana State University Press, 1983), pp. 238–39.

11. John Aubrey, *Brief Lives*, ed. Oliver Lawson Dick (London: Secker and Warburg, 1950), p. 139. All citations are to this edition.

12. Moffett, *Silkwormes and Their Flies*, L1.

13. BL, Harleian MS 6995, fol. 35; this letter is quoted by G. C. Moore-Smith in his edition of Abraham Fraunce, *Victoria*, in *Materialien zur Kunde des alteren Englishcen Dramas* (Louvain: A Uystpruyst, 1906), xxxv. In the 1580s, Fraunce dedicated various manuscript works on logic to Sir Philip Sidney, and after Sidney's death, Fraunce's prefatory letter to *Lawyers Logike* (1588) states that his interest in logic began in Sidney's company. Fraunce concludes a manuscript of emblems with a verse addressed to Philip Sidney, whose similar interest is amply demonstrated in *The Countess of Pembroke's Arcadia (The New Arcadia)*. After Sidney's death, Fraunce

dedicated the published version of this manuscript to Philip's brother Robert Sidney under the title, *Insignium, Armorum, Emblematum, Hieroglyphicorum, et Symbolorum quae ab Italis Imprese nominatur, explicatio* (1588). Fraunce's later tendency to present translated work as his original compositions began in his dedication to Philip Sidney of a play *Victoria*, an unacknowledged Latin translation of Luigi Pasqualigo's Italian *Il Fedele* (1579).

14. Abraham Fraunce, *The Lamentations of Amyntas (1587)*, ed. Franklin M. Dickey (Chicago: Univ. of Chicago Press, 1967), p. 8.

15. Thomas Watson, *Melibeous* (London, 1590), dedication. Fraunce gave Watson credit for his original poem when he republished his translation in 1591.

16. BL, Harleian MS 6995, fols. 35, 51; BL, Lansdowne MSS 63, 77. Also see Moore-Smith, Intro. to Fraunce, *Victoria*, pp. xxxiii, xxxviii.

17. This prose epistle to a manuscript epithalamium (1633), addressed to a daughter of the earl of Bridgewater, was recorded in Joseph Hunter's *Chorus Vatum;* see Moore-Smith, Intro. to Fraunce, *Victoria*, pp. xxxix, xl. This manuscript has since disappeared. One critic doubts Hunter's discovery entirely, claiming that Fraunce died before 1595: see Harry Morris, "Thomas Watson and Abraham Fraunce," *PMLA* 76 (1961): 152–53.

18. All citations from Fraunce's text are taken from *The Countess of Pembroke's Ivychurch* (London, 1591).

19. In Tasso's *Aminta*, the heroine's arrow strikes the wolf "a sommo 'l capo" (line 1392) (ed. C. E. J. Griffiths [Manchester: Manchester Univ. Press, 1972], p. 64).

20. S. N. Eisenstadt and Louis Roniger, "Patron-Client Relations as a Model of Structuring Social Exchange," *Comparative Studies in Society and History* 22 (1980): 42–77; for a general framework, see Marcel Mauss, *The Gift: Forms and Functions of Exchange in Archaic Societies* (Glencoe, Ill.: Free Press, 1954), esp. p. 63.

21. Ovid, *Metamorphoses*, trans. R. Humphries (Bloomington, Ind.: Indiana Univ. Press, 1955), p. 376; P. Ovidii Nasoniis, *Metamorphoses . . . cum commentarius Regii* (Basil, 1543), p. 339. Regius's commentary cites Pliny, bk. 8, chap. 36, as an authority for the phenomenon.

22. Two useful surveys are Arthur Henkel and Albrecht Schone, eds., *Emblemata: Handbuch zur Sinnbildkunst des XVI und XVII Jahrhunderts* (Stuttgart: J. B. Metzlersche, 1967), p. 441, and Mario Praz, *Studies in Seventeenth-Century Imagery* (Rome: Edizioni di storia e letteratura, 1964), p. 106.

23. Guillaume de la Perriere, *Le Theatre des bons engines* (Paris: Denis Janot, 1539), N8.

sance Studies for Dame Helen Gardner in Honor of Her Seventieth Birthday, ed. John Carey (Oxford: Clarendon Press, 1980), pp. 10–11.

25. This anecdote, reported in "Vita Donati," in *Vitae Vergilianae Antiquae,* ed. Colinus Hardie (Oxford: Clarendon Press, 1954), p. 22, is ascribed to Suetonius in the English translation: "The Lives of Illustrious Men," in Suetonius, *Works,* trans. J. C. Rolfe (1914: London: Heinemann, 1979), 2:471–72. My gratitude to John B. Dillon, librarian at the University of Wisconsin—Madison, for a wealth of information on this topic.

26. Robert Greene, *Philomela The Lady Fitzwaters Nightingale* (London, 1592), dedication.

27. Gregorio Bersmano and John Camerarius, *Phile sapientissimi versus iambici, De Animalium propietate* (Leipzig, 1575), G2, "De Ursa."

28. James M. Osborn, *Young Philip Sidney: 1572–1577* (New Haven: Yale Univ. Press, 1972), p. 79n.

29. This work has been published as *Thomas Watson's Latin "Amyntas" (1585) and Abraham Fraunce's Translation "The Lamentations of Amyntas" (1587),* ed. Walter F. Staton, Jr., and Franklin M. Dickey (Chicago: Univ. of Chicago Press, 1967).

30. All citations to Fraunce's text are taken from *The Third Part of the Countess of Pembrokes Ivychurch* (London, 1592).

31. Interestingly enough, Ovid himself came to be perceived by at least one writer as addressing women readers. In a prefatory poem, "To Ladies and Gentlewomen," in Wye Saltonstall's *Ovids Heroicall Epistles* (1636), the author concludes:

> Yet this his comfort was in Banishment,
> His Loves, and Lines, did yeeld your sex content.
> Let English Gentlewomen as kind appeare
> To Ovid, as the Roman Ladies were.
>
> (Blv)

32. Lucan, *Works,* trans. A. M. Harmon, Loeb Classical Library (London: Heinemann, 1953), 2:268–323. Menippus tells a friend how, with the use of wings from an eagle and a vulture, he flew up to the moon to find out about heavenly bodies for himself. From that vantage point, he observed the follies of men, and particularly of philosophers, before he traveled on to Olympus to visit Zeus, whose daily activities he recorded. My thanks to Peter Travis for his observation that the *Anticlaudianus* by Alain de Lille also includes a journey to heaven, in this case by Prudence, to request a soul for the body of a perfect man.

33. Abraham Fraunce, *Lawyers Logike* (London, 1588), M1v.

34. "The Countesse of Penbrookes Love," in Nicholas Breton, *Works,*

ed. Alexander Grosart, 2 vols. (Edinburgh: Edinburgh Univ. Press, 1879), 1:21–28, discussed briefly by Jean Robertson, ed., *Poems by Nicholas Breton* (Liverpool: Liverpool Univ. Press, 1952), p. liii. Citations in the text are to pages of this poem in vol. 1 of Grosart's edition. Breton also dedicated other works to the countess which do not inscribe her as a character. In addition to *The Pilgrimage to Paradise,* joined with "The Countesse of Penbrookes Love," he dedicated to her *Apiscante Jehova; Maries Exercise* (1597), a series of thirteen prose prayer-meditations; and *A Divine Poeme, divided into Partes: The Ravisht Soule, and the Blessed Weeper* (1601).

35. I am using quotation marks around "Countess of Penbrooke" and "Countess" to refer to the countess as Breton represents her.

36. The poem has this title in Sloane MS 1303, published as "The Countesse of Penbrooks Passion," in Breton, *Works,* 1:3–15, discussed by Robertson, *Poems by Nicholas Breton,* pp. lv–lxi, under "Passions of the Spirit." It was apparently written by 1594, when a variant, *The Passions of the Spirit,* published in 1599, was entered in the Stationer's Register.

37. Facsimile edition of Nicholas Breton, *Brittons Bowre of Delights,* ed. Hyder Rollins (Cambridge: Harvard Univ. Press, 1933), Al, line 16.

38. Robertson, *Poems by Nicholas Breton,* p. xxiii. This possibly autobiographical passage is discussed by Ursula Kentish-Wright, eds., *A Mad World My Masters and Other Prose Works,* by Nicholas Breton (London: Cresset Press, 1929), l:xxx; but see Robertson, pp. ciii–civ, for doubts concerning the autobiographical nature of the letter.

39. BL, Harleian MS 6995, fol. 35, from Ivychurch, dated 25 August 1590. "St. David Without" is listed as a "civil parish" in the "rural district of Brecknockshire, Wales," in Melville Richards, *Welsh Administrative and Territorial Units* (Cardiff: Univ. of Wales Press, 1969), p. 19.

40. See Robertson, *Poems by Nicholas Breton,* p. lvii, and Jean Robertson, "'The Passions of the Spirit' (1599) and Nicholas Breton," *Huntington Library Quarterly* 3 (1939): 69.

41. Grosart, ed., *Works,* 1:xxvii; Robertson, *Poems by Nicholas Breton,* p. xxv.

42. Michael G. Brennen, "Nicholas Breton's *The Passions of the Spirit* and the Countess of Pembroke," *Review of English Studies* 38 (1987):221–24.

43. Thomas Moffett, *Silkewormes and Their Flies,* B1 and G1. A facsimile of this work, edited by Victor Houliston, will soon be available through the Early English Text Society.

44. The will is preserved at Somerset House; much of it is quoted by Frances Young in *Mary Sidney, Countess of Pembroke* (London: David Nutt, 1912), p. 81.

45. John Aubrey, *The Natural History of Wiltshire,* ed. John Britton (London: J. B. Nichols for the Wiltshire Topographical Society, 1847), p. 89;

"Thomas Muffet, gent.," in Great Britain, Parliament, House of Commons: Members of Parliament (Ordered by the House of Commons to be printed, March 1878), 1:435; William Oldys, "Extract of the Church Register at Wilton," included in Moffett's *Health's Improvement* (London, 1746), a12, b2v.

46. Dwight L. Durling, *Georgic Tradition in English Poetry* (New York: Columbia University Press, 1935), p. 33.

47. James I was later to encourage strongly this industry: see John Laurence, *A New System of Agriculture* (London, 1726), pp. 161–67. Anne Clifford, later to marry Mary Sidney's second son and become a countess of Pembroke herself, raised silkworms: V. Sackville-West, intro. to *The Diary of the Lady Anne Clifford* (London: William Heinemann, 1923), p. xxvii.

48. Ian Maclean, *The Renaissance Notion of Woman* (Cambridge: Cambridge Univ. Press, 1980), p. 42.

49. Council Register (Elizabeth), IX, 508, cited in *Acts of the Privy Council*, 21:409.

50. *Calendar of State Papers, Domestic (Elizabeth)*, 244:42. The full version of this examination is entertaining. Apparently, Jane Shelley asked an astrologer to tell her if she would find her goods again. He foresaw, wisely enough, that Baxter would pawn them.

51. According to *Spenser Allusions in the Sixteenth and Seventeenth Centuries*, ed. William Wells (Chapel Hill: Univ. of North Carolina Press, 1972), p. 102, Baxter's description of Cynthia's Amazonian attire derives from Spenser's Belphoebe and Radigund.

52. The "Ourania" in Baxter's title also suggests the influence of Saluste Du Bartas's reworking of the Endymion myth in his poem *L'Uranie*, in which the moon takes her lover high above the earth to learn the secrets of the heavens; Baxter's poem was probably also influenced by Michael Drayton's *Endimion and Phoebe*, for the moon also inspires Drayton's Endymion with occult secrets of nature. For a discussion of these Renaissance versions of the Endymion myth, see Douglas Bush, *Mythology and the Renaissance Tradition in English Poetry* (1932; New York: Norton, 1963), pp. 158–59.

53. Alexander Grosart, "Nathaniel Baxter," *Dictionary of National Biography*, 1:1348.

54. Poems of mourning written by women are listed in *The Paradise of Women: Writings by Englishwomen of the Renaissance*, ed. Betty Travitsky (Westport, Conn.: Greenwood Press, 1981), pp. 23, 34; see particularly *Four Epitaphes made by the Countes of Oxenford after the death of her young sonne the Lord Bulbecke, etc.* (London, 1584).

55. Edmund Spenser, "Astrophel," *Poetical Works*, ed. J. C. Smith and

E. de Selincourt (London: Oxford Univ. Press, 1912), p. 549, line 216. All citations to this poem are from this edition.

56. *The Works of Edmund Spenser: A Variorum Edition*, ed. Edwin Greenlaw et al. (Baltimore: Johns Hopkins Press, 1943), pp. 500–507, provides a useful summary of the evidence of authorship; see also Gary Waller, *Mary Sidney, Countess of Pembroke: A Critical Study of Her Writings and Literary Milieu* (Salzburg: Institut für Anglistik und Amerikanistik, 1979), pp. 91–93. A recent voice favoring Spenser as the author is Michael G. Brennan, *Literary Patronage in the English Renaissance: The Pembroke Family* (London: Routledge, 1988), p. 62.

57. Fraunce might have obtained the manuscript from Spenser directly rather than from the countess; see William Nelson, *The Poetry of Edmund Spenser: A Study* (New York: Columbia Univ. Press, 1965), p. 5, and Katherine Koller, "Abraham Fraunce and Edmund Spenser," *ELH* 7 (1940): 117.

58. "Dedicatory Sonnets," *Faerie Queene*, in Spenser, *Poetical Works*, p. 413.

59. "The Ruines of Time," ibid., p. 471.

60. "Colin Clout's Come Home Again," ibid., p. 541.

61. Other authors include Lodowick Bryskett, Matthew Roydon, and Sir Walter Raleigh; see *Works: A Variorum Edition*, ed. Greenlaw et al., pp. 500–507.

62. Claude Lévi-Strauss, *The Elementary Structures of Kinship* and *The Raw and the Cooked*, together with other sources cited in Sherry B. Ortner, "Is Female to Male as Nature Is to Culture?" in *Woman, Culture, and Society*, ed. Michelle Zimbalist Rosaldo and Louise Lamphere (Stanford: Stanford Univ. Press, 1974), pp. 67–87.

63. A good source for conventions of pastoral elegy is *The Pastoral Elegy*, ed. Thomas Perrin Harrison (Austin: Univ. of Texas Press, 1939).

64. Attributed to Hugh Sanford, cited in Sir Philip Sidney, *The Countess of Pembroke's Arcadia (The Old Arcadia)*, ed. Jean Robertson (Oxford: Clarendon Press, 1973), p. xlix.

65. Gary Waller, *Mary Sidney, Countess of Pembroke: A Critical Study of Her Writings and Literary Milieu*, pays serious attention to the countess's translation of the psalms; Waller's edition of her work *The Triumph of Death* provides an especially detailed and interesting discussion of her Psalms, also edited and discussed in J. A. C. Rathmell, *The Psalms of Sir Philip Sidney and the Countess of Pembroke* (New York: New York Univ. Press, 1963). See also Hannay, "'Doo What Men May Sing,'" pp. 149–65, Beth Wynne Fisken, "Mary Sidney's *Psalmes:* Education and Wisdom," in *Silent But for the Word*, pp. 166–83; and Margaret Hannay, "'Princes you as men must dy': Genevan Advice to Monarchs in the *Psalms* of Mary Sidney," *English Literary Renaissance* 19 (1989): 22–41.

66. Some or all of this view is included in T. S. Eliot, "Seneca in Eliza-

bethan Translation," in *Selected Essays* (London: Faber and Faber, 1932), pp. 92–94, and his "Apology for the Countess of Pembroke," in *The Use of Poetry and the Use of Criticism* (London: Faber and Faber, 1933), pp. 37–52; D. Nichol Smith, "Authors and Patrons," in *Shakespeare's England* (Oxford: Clarendon Press, 1917), pp. 197–99; Alexander Witherspoon, *The Influence of Robert Garnier on Elizabethan Drama*, Yale Studies in Drama, 65 (New Haven: Yale Univ. Press, 1924); Felix Schelling, "Sidney's Sister, Pembroke's Mother," *Shakespeare and the Demi-Science* (Philadelphia: Univ. of Pennsylvania Press, 1927), pp. 100–125; Frances Young, *Mary Sidney, Countess of Pembroke* (London: Nutt, 1912); Tucker Brooke and Matthias A. Shaaber, *The Renaissance*, vol. 2 of *A Literary History of England*, ed. Albert C. Baugh (New York: Appleton-Century-Crofts, 1967), pp. 473–74; Rolf Soellner, "The Garnier-Pembroke Connection," *Shakespeare Studies* 15 (1982): 2–3; and esp. John Buxton, "The Countess of Pembroke," in *Sir Philip Sidney and the English Renaissance* (London: Macmillan, 1964), pp. 173–204. Waller, *Mary Sidney*, pp. 107–28, shows the influence of this tradition, although his conclusions are broader and he stresses her own writing as well.

67. Such authors include Henry Lok, Richard Barnfield, Gabriel Harvey, Ben Jonson, John Florio, and Philip Massinger. Discussions of these authors and the critics who claim them for Mary Sidney's circle are included in Lamb, "The Countess of Pembroke's Patronage," pp. 162–79.

68. Schelling, "Sidney's Sister," pp. 124–25.

69. Ibid., p. 122.

70. Waller, *Mary Sidney*, p. 100; also see pp. 69–70.

71. Mention of Mary Sidney's influence over Spenser has been quietly dropping out of Spenser studies; see for example the entry by A. Kent Hieatt, "Edmund Spenser," in *New Encyclopedia Britannica*, 15th ed., 17:493–96, which does not mention the countess at all.

72. See discussion and critics cited in Mary Ellen Lamb, "The Myth of the Countess of Pembroke," *Yearbook of English Studies* 11 (1981): 194–202, and in Rolf Soellner, "Shakespeare's *Lucrece* and the Garnier-Pembroke Connection," *Shakespeare Studies* 15 (1982): 3.

73. Brooke and Shaaber, *The Renaissance*, p. 473.

74. Eliot, "Apology for the Countess of Pembroke," p. 41.

CHAPTER 2. *The Countess of Pembroke's Arcadia* and Its (Com)Passionate Women Readers

1. Sir Philip Sidney, *The Countess of Pembroke's Arcadia (The Old Arcadia)*, ed. Jean Robertson (Oxford: Clarendon Press, 1973), p. 3; page citations in the text to the *Old Arcadia* are taken from this edition.

2. Sidney, *The Countess of Pembroke's Arcadia (The Old Arcadia)*, ed. Robertson, pp. 27, 29, 38, 39, 40, 45, 49, 51, 54, 55 (twice), 108 (to "sweet Philoclea"), 227, 242, 243. One reference to "fair ladies" appears in a passage added from the *Old Arcadia* in the countess's attempt to provide an ending for the unfinished *New Arcadia*; see Sidney, *The Countess of Pembroke's Arcadia*, ed. Maurice Evans (New York: Penguin Books, 1977), p. 679.

3. Ariosto's addresses to his "cortesi donne" are discussed in Robert M. Durling, *The Figure of the Poet in Renaissance Epic* (Cambridge: Harvard Univ. Press, 1965), pp. 112–81; he views these unstable attitudes towards women, however, as dramatizing "the problem of man's understanding the *varium et mutabile* of experience" (p. 175). For Sidney's use of Ariosto, see Freda Townsend, "Sidney and Ariosto," *PMLA* 61 (1946): 97–108.

After instructing men not to dote on their wives, but to use them as "necessary evils," George Pettie's narrator resolves to join the character Alexius, who has gone on pilgrimage to escape his wife, whose beauty hindered his "heavenly cogitations." George Pettie, *A petite Pallace of Pettie his pleasure*, ed. Herbert Hartman (London: Oxford University Press, 1938), p. 270. Richard Helgerson, *The Elizabethan Prodigals* (Berkeley and Los Angeles: Univ. of California Press, 1976), p. 4, suggests the seriousness of this resolve, for Pettie writes "no more of love" after this collection. Helgerson's brilliant book has been very influential on my thinking on this issue. Sidney's narrator is linked to Pettie's in Paul Salzman, *English Prose Fiction, 1558–1700: A Critical History* (Oxford: Clarendon Press, 1985), p. 50.

4. Notable among a large body of criticisms are Alan Sinfield, "Power and Ideology: An Outline Theory and Sidney's *Arcadia*," *ELH* 52 (1985): 259–78; David Norbrook, *Poetry and Politics in the English Renaissance* (London: Routledge and Kegan Paul, 1984), pp. 91–108; Annabel Patterson, *Censorship and Interpretation: The Conditions of Writing and Reading in Early Modern England* (Madison: Univ. of Wisconsin Press, 1984), pp. 24–43; Martin Ratiere, *Faire Bitts: Sir Philip Sidney and Renaissance Political Theory* (Pittsburgh: Duquesne Univ. Press, 1984); Richard C. McCoy, *Sir Philip Sidney: Rebellion in Arcadia* (New Brunswick: Rutgers Univ. Press, 1979); and Andrew Weiner, *Sir Philip Sidney and the Poetics of Protestantism: A Study of Contexts* (Minneapolis: Univ. of Minnesota Press, 1978). McCoy combines political and biographical approaches.

5. Some of the excellent work being done on this project includes Dympna Callaghan's analysis of the analogy king is to subject as husband is to wife in *Women and Gender in Renaissance Tragedy* (Atlantic Highlands, N.J.: Humanities Press International, 1989), pp. 9–33; Leah Marcus's demonstration of the anxieties caused by a female monarch, most recently in *Puzzling Shakespeare: Local Reading and Its Discontents* (Berkeley and Los

Angeles: Univ. of California Press, 1988), pp. 51–105; Margaret Olofson Thickstun's exploration of the "distrust of flesh and an identification of the flesh with women" (p. 7) within the Puritan church in *Fictions of the Feminine: Puritan Doctrine and the Representation of Women* (Ithaca: Cornell Univ. Press, 1988), esp. pp. 7–15; and Amussen's acute analysis of the use of family hierarchy to reinforce class hierarchy (esp. pp. 33, 182–83).

6. Helgerson, *The Elizabethan Prodigals*, pp. 32, 35.

7. Ben Jonson, *Epicoene*, 3.3.120, in *The Complete Works*, ed. C. H. Herford and Percy Simpson (Oxford: Clarendon Press, 1937), 5:186.

8. Mary Astell, "Sidney's Didactic Method in the *Old Arcadia*," *Studies in English Literature* 24 (1984): 50–51; Helgerson, *The Elizabethan Prodigals*, p. 136; Stephen Greenblatt, "Sidney's *Arcadia* and the Mixed Mode," *Studies in Philology* 7 (1973): 277; Richard A. Lanham, "The *Old Arcadia*," in *Sidney's Arcadia* (New Haven: Yale Univ. Press, 1965), pp. 316–24.

9. Ronald Levao, *Renaissance Minds and Their Fictions: Cusanus, Sidney, Shakespeare* (Berkeley and Los Angeles: Univ. of California Press, 1985), p. 196. Salzman, *English Prose Fiction*, pp. 50–51; Margaret E. Dana, "The Providential Plot of the *Old Arcadia*," *Studies in English Literature* 17 (1977): 39–57; and Lanham, "The *Old Arcadia*," pp. 320–21, discuss the narrator well.

10. See Ann Rosalind Jones, "Nets and Bridles: Early Modern Conduct Books and Sixteenth-Century Women's Lyrics," in *The Ideology of Conduct: Essays on Literature and the History of Sexuality*, ed. Nancy Armstrong and Leonard Tennenhouse (New York: Methuen, 1987), pp. 39–72.

11. Lanham, "The *Old Arcadia*," p. 234; Walter Davis, *A Map of Arcadia: Sidney's Romance and Its Tradition* (New Haven: Yale Univ. Press, 1965), p. 161; Helgerson, *The Elizabethan Prodigals*, pp. 138–39; Mark Rose, *Heroic Love* (Cambridge: Harvard Univ. Press, 1968), p. 59.

12. Helgerson, *The Elizabethan Prodigals*, p. 154. Helgerson's statement of the Elizabethan fear that "art is sex" (p. 130) is expanded brilliantly in the parallel between the princes' defense in the *Old Arcadia* and poetry's defense in the *Defence of Poetry*; see Margaret W. Ferguson, *Trials of Desire: Renaissance Defenses of Poetry* (New Haven: Yale Univ. Press, 1983), pp. 137–38, 146.

13. Foremost among these is Richard C. McCoy, *Sir Philip Sidney*, pp. 52, 132–37; see also Helgerson, *The Elizabethan Prodigals*, p. 138.

14. My gratitude to Constance Jordan for sharing with me her paper "Gender and Politics in Sidney's *New Arcadia*," delivered at the Renaissance Society of America Conference at Tempe, Arizona (November 1987). Pertinent to any discussion of Renaissance views of equity is the careful distinction made in Sir Thomas Elyot between "mercye," which is a "temperaunce of the mynde . . . always joyned with reason," and the "vayne pitie" for those who "for every little occasion" are "moved with

compasion." This latter emotion is "a sicknesse of the mynde where with at this daye the more parte of men be diseased." See *The Book Named the Governor* (1531), a facsimile edited by R. C. Alston (Menston, England: Scolar Press, 1970), fols. 127v, 128. According to John W. Dickinson, "Renaissance Equity and *Measure for Measure*," *Shakespeare Quarterly* 13 (1962): 289, Elyot's distinction is drawn from Seneca's *Moral Essays*, which associates pity (*misericordia*) specifically with "old women and wretched females" (see p. 439 of John W. Basore's translation [London: Heinemann, 1958]).

15. McCoy, *Sir Philip Sidney*, p. 132.

16. Logocentric assumptions governing such binary oppositions are critiqued in Hélène Cixous, "Sorties," in *The Newly Born Woman*, trans. Betsy Wing (Minneapolis: Univ. of Minnesota Press, 1986), pp. 63–65.

17. Aristotle, *Politics*, trans. Harris Rackham (London: Heinneman, 1932), p. 63; see also Aristotle's *Ethics*, book 8. Both are discussed with religious, medical, political, and legal implications in Ian Maclean, *The Renaissance Notion of Woman* (Cambridge: Cambridge University Press, 1980). For a fascinating study of the continued use of this binary opposition between reason and passion to construct gender, see Catherine Lutz, "Emotion, Thought, and Estrangement: Emotion as a Cultural Category," *Cultural Anthropology* 1 (1986): 287–309.

18. Cited by Lawrence Stone, *The Family, Sex, and Marriage in England, 1500–1800* (New York: Harper and Row, 1977), p. 198.

19. This phrase recurs in *De regulis juris antiqui* and in Renaissance legal texts as cited by Maclean, *Renaissance Notion of Woman*, p. 78.

20. These representations are commonplace. See, for example, Roger Ascham's praise of the formidable mind of the sixteen-year-old Elizabeth as containing "no womanly weakness" in a letter to Johannes Sturm, in *The Whole Works*, ed. J. A. Giles (London, 1865), vol. 1, pt. 1, lxii–lxiv, as cited in Pearl Hogrefe, *Women of Action in Tudor England* (Ames: Iowa State Univ. Press, 1977), p. 218. Macduff's representation of crying for his murdered wife and child in *Macbeth*, 4.3.230, is another example.

21. Callaghan, *Women and Gender*, p. 19, describes this "concealment of analogical reasoning under the assertion of identity" as a "primary ideological ploy." Amussen, pp. 55–60, adds to this analogy between family and state the complex nature of marital power.

22. Stone, *The Family, Sex, and Marriage*, pp. 195–204; Natalie Zemon Davis, "Women on Top," in *Society and Culture in Early Modern France* (Stanford: Stanford Univ. Press, 1975), pp. 127, 150; Maclean, *Renaissance Notion of Woman*, p. 49; Jonathan Goldberg, *James I and the Politics of Literature* (Baltimore: Johns Hopkins Univ. Press, 1981), pp. 85–87. For a religious application see Thickstun, *Fictions of the Feminine*, p. 7.

23. John Morgan, *Godly Learning: Puritan Attitudes towards Reason, Learning, and Education, 1560–1640* (Cambridge: Cambridge Univ. Press, 1986), pp. 43–48; Weiner, *Sidney and the Poetics of Protestantism*, pp. 9–10.

24. Stone, *The Family, Sex and Marriage*, pp. 195–204; Goldberg, *James I*, pp. 85–87. Amussen notes that this power was by no means total despite the strength of the analogical model (pp. 61–66).

25. In the *New Arcadia*, three of Gynecia's soliloquies take place on pp. 213, 377–78, and 799; her dreams are recorded on pp. 376 and 799.

26. William Healey, *An Apologie for Women* (Oxford, 1608), cites the *New Arcadia* on C2v, C3, D1, and E4v. My thanks to James Turner for alerting me to this source.

27. Mark Rose, "Sidney's Womanish Man," *Review of English Studies*, n.s., 15 (1964): 356–57; Lanham, "The *Old Arcadia*," p. 206. William Craft, "Heroic Self in the *New Arcadia*," *Studies in English Literature* 25 (1985): 59, denies that the princes' "folly in love" is critiqued in Sidney's work, claiming "Sidney wishes us to see that perfection in love is more . . . exacting than even the high classical virtue that the princes embody."

28. See Walter R. Davis, "Actaeon in *Arcadia*," *Studies in English Literature* 2 (1962): 97, for discussions of Pyrocles' discovery that "his most hated enemy is a mirror image of himself."

29. The identification of the pen as a "metaphorical penis" in Sandra M. Gilbert and Susan Gubar, *The Madwoman in the Attic* (New Haven: Yale Univ. Press, 1979), p. 7, may imply an even more explicit connection between Basilius's authorship, his "long idle pen," and his defective masculinity.

30. James M. Osborn, *Young Philip Sidney, 1572–1577* (New Haven: Yale Univ. Press, 1972), p. 537.

31. Sidney, *The Countess of Pembroke's Arcadia*, ed. Evans, pp. 70, 71. All citations to the *New Arcadia* are taken from the Evans edition, which, as indicated in note 1 of the Introduction, I have chosen to use rather than the impressive and more recent edition by Victor Skretkowicz because Evans relies on the 1593 edition prepared by the countess of Pembroke, rather than the 1590 *New Arcadia* text prepared by Fulke Greville.

32. See, e.g., Norbrook, *Poetry and Politics*, pp. 95–96.

33. See, e.g., A. C. Hamilton, *Sir Philip Sidney: A Study of His Life and Works* (Cambridge: Cambridge Univ. Press, 1977), p. 27. Mona Wilson, *Sir Philip Sidney* (Oxford: Oxford Univ. Press, 1932), p. 108, attributes Sidney's retirement from court to money problems.

34. Dedication reprinted in *The Countess of Pembroke's Arcadia (The Old Arcadia)*, ed. Robertson, p. 3. See also Katherine Duncan Jones, "Philip Sidney's Toys," The Chatterton Lectures, *Proceedings of the British Academy* 66 (1980): 161–78.

35. *The Correspondence of Sir Philip Sidney and Hubert Languet*, ed. Stuart A. Pears (London: Pickering, 1845), p. 143. This letter is discussed by Louis Adrian Montrose, "Celebration and Insinuation: Sir Philip Sidney and the Motives of Elizabethan Courtiership," *Renaissance Drama*, n.s., 8 (1977): 7–13.

36. Quoted in Osborn, *Young Philip Sidney*, p. 505.

37. This sexualization even of women's silence shows the flexibility of gender ideology to render even chastity a sexual trait, complicating the association between women's silence and their bodily purity discussed so well in Margaret Ferguson, "A Room Not Their Own: Renaissance Women as Readers and Writers," in *The Comparative Perspective on Literature: Approaches to Theory and Practice*, ed. Clayton Koelb and Susan Noakes (Ithaca: Cornell Univ. Press, 1988), pp. 93–116.

38. The way Queen Elizabeth's role as ruler confuses the issue of gender so as to allow speech is aptly discussed in Leah Marcus, "Shakespeare's Comic Heroines, Elizabeth I, and the Political Uses of Androgeny," in *Women in the Middle Ages and the Renaissance*, ed. Mary Beth Rose (Syracuse: Syracuse Univ. Press, 1986), pp. 135–44. Helen identified as a representation of Elizabeth in Shelley Thrasher-Smith, *The Luminous Globe: Methods of Characterization in Sidney's "New Arcadia,"* Salzburg Studies in English Literature, 94 (Salzburg: Institut für Anglistik und Amerikanistik, 1982), p. 145.

39. Discussed by Thrasher-Smith, *The Luminous Globe*, p. 109.

40. Winifred Schleiner, "Differences of Theme and Structure of the Erona Episodes in the *Old* and *New Arcadia*," *Studies in Philology* 70 (1973): 382–88.

41. Dicus's poem is discussed in Levao, *Renaissance Minds*, pp. 232–39.

42. Walter R. Davis, "Actaeon in *Arcadia*," *Studies in English Literature* 2 (1962): 95–110, discusses the way the cave signifies sexual passion for both Gynecia and Pyrocles.

43. The shift from the princes to the princesses as the heroes of the *New Arcadia* is discussed in Myron Turner, "The Heroic Ideal in Sidney's Revised *Arcadia*," *Studies in English Literature* 10 (1970): 63–82, and McCoy, *Sir Philip Sidney*, pp. 205–8.

44. See my discussion of Foxe's *Actes and Monuments* as enabling the public speech of women martyrs in the Introduction, above. William Haller, *Foxe's "Book of Martyrs" and the Elect Nation* (London: Jonathan Cape, 1963), p. 14, claims that this work was "accepted as an expression of the national faith second in authority only to the Bible."

45. For book-length discussions of Renaissance Stoicism, see Gordon Braden, *Renaissance Tragedy and the Senecan Tradition: Anger's Privilege* (New

Haven: Yale Univ. Press, 1985); Jason Lewis Saunders, *Justius Lipsius: The Philosophy of Renaissance Stoicism* (New York: Liberal Arts Press, 1955); and Guillaume du Vair, *The Moral Philosophy of the Stoicks,* trans. Thomas James (1598), ed. Rudolf Kirk (New Brunswick: Rutgers Univ. Press, 1951). Maclean, *The Renaissance Notion of Woman,* pp. 51, 55, cites the Renaissance understanding of the particular pertinence of Stoic virtues for women; see also Michel Foucault, *The History of Sexuality,* vol. 3, *The Care of the Self,* trans. Robert Hurley (New York: Pantheon Books, 1986), p. 161, who says that the "Stoics . . . granted both sexes, if not identical aptitudes, at least an equal capacity for virtue." See also my discussion of women and Stoicism in Chapter 3, below. The term *Stoicism* has been used somewhat broadly by Robert E. Stillman, *Sidney's Poetic Justice* (Lewisburg, Pa.: Bucknell Univ. Press, 1986), who perceives the *Old Arcadia* as a "Stoic pastoral" (p. 71) because it advocates the "Stoic virtues of the quiet life" (p. 73).

46. Saunders, *Justius Lipsius,* pp. 71–73, 79–80. Alan Sinfield, *Literature in Protestant England, 1560–1660* (Totowa, N.J.: Barnes and Noble, 1983), p. 113, relates the Calvinist concept of predestination and Stoic fatalism in the Renaissance. For the popularity of Stoicism at this time, see Ralph Graham Palmer, *Seneca's "De Remediis Fortuitorum" and the Elizabethans,* Institute of Elizabethan Studies (Kendal, England: Titus Wilson and Son, 1953).

47. For Mornay's combination of Christian and Stoic doctrine, see Diane Bornstein, *The Countess of Pembroke's Translation of Philippe de Mornay's "Discourse of Life and Death"* (Detroit: Michigan Consortium for Medieval and Early Modern Studies, 1983), p. 6. The friendship between Sidney and Mornay is documented in Wilson, *Sir Philip Sidney,* pp. 55, 80, 145; Sidney also translated part of Mornay's *Verite de la religion chretienne.*

48. Michael McCanles, "The Rhetoric of Character Portrayal in Sidney's *New Arcadia,*" *Criticism* 25 (1983): 127–28, discusses the way Sidney differentiates yet balances the sisters between the extremes of "sweetness and majesty."

49. Ronald B. Levinson, "The 'Godlesse Minde' in Sidney's *Arcadia,*" *Modern Philology* 29 (1931): 21–26; Constance Miriam Syford, "The Direct Source of the Pamela-Cecropia Episode in the *Arcadia,*" *PMLA* 49 (1934): 472–89; D. P. Walker, "Ways of Dealing with Aetheists," *Bibliotheque d'humanism et de la renaissance,* 17 (1955): 252–77.

50. William Anderson, introduction to *Boethius: The Consolation of Philosophy* (Carbondale: Southern Illinois Univ. Press, 1963), pp. 10–13. While Boethius was created Saint Severinus, it is not positive that he was in fact a Christian; his consolations are taken from philosophic rather than Christian sources (ibid., p. 10).

51. McCoy, *Sir Philip Sidney*, pp. 205–7.

52. Josephine Roberts, *Archetectonic Knowledge in the New Arcadia (1590): Sidney's Use of the Heroic Journey*, Elizabethan and Renaissance Studies, 69 (Salzburg: Institut für Englische Sprache und Literatur, 1978), pp. 260–65; discussed as ambivalence in McCoy, *Sir Philip Sidney*, p. 183. William Craft, "Heroic Self," p. 66, perceives that both forms of heroism are combined into a "new heroism of selfless love" that includes "both passive endurance and active valor."

53. Seventeenth-century copies of the epitaph for Argalus and Parthenia, "His being was in her alone," are recorded in Peter Beal, *Index of Literary Manuscripts*, vol. 1, *1450–1625* (London: Mansell, 1980), pt. 2, 474–75.

54. Noted by Levao, *Renaissance Minds*, p. 219.

55. This manner of seeing through the "spectacles of pity" unites the sadistic and the fetishistic forms of scopophilia described as common for spectators of cinema by Laura Mulvey, "Visual Pleasure and Narrative Cinema," *Screen* 16 (1975): 8–14.

56. The phrase I have used for the subheading to this section, and much of my thinking on this subject, is derived from Kenneth Burke, "Literature as Equipment for Living," in *The Philosophy of Literary Form* (1941; Baton Rouge: Louisiana State Univ. Press, 1967), pp. 293–304.

57. Josephine Roberts, "The Imaginary Epistles of Sir Philip Sidney and Lady Penelope Rich," *English Literary Renaissance* 15 (1985): 73; D. Tyndale, discussed in Roberts, "The Imaginary Epistles," p. 65. See also Thrasher-Smith, *The Luminous Globe*, p. 145.

58. Roberts, "The Imaginary Epistles," pp. 69, 71, 73–74.

59. Laurence Stone, *Crisis of the Aristocracy, 1558–1641* (Oxford: Clarendon Press, 1965), pp. 661–62 speaks eloquently about the crisis in forced marriages especially from 1595 to 1620, when "something like one-third of the older peers were estranged from or actually separated from their wives," presumably in part because of the pressure exerted on children to marry against their wishes. The perception of seventeenth-century romantic fiction as a response to this issue, as "both an influence upon actual behavior and a reflection of it," is discussed in Sara Heller Mendelson, "Debate, The Weightiest Business. Marriage in an Upper-Gentry Family in Seventeenth-Century England," *Past and Present* 85 (1979): 129–30.

60. Cited in Antonia Fraser, *The Weaker Vessel* (New York: Knopf, 1984), p. 15; Stone, *Crisis*, p. 597, expressed doubts about the factuality of this event.

61. Tania Modleski, in *Loving with a Vengeance: Mass-Produced Fantasies*

for Women (New York: Methuen, 1982), pp. 59–84 convincingly argues that the gothic novel, which often has episodes bearing striking resemblance to this captivity episode, is a response to marital situations encountered by women. See also Janice Radway, *Reading the Romance: Women, Patriarchy, and Popular Tradition* (Chapel Hill: Univ. of North Carolina Press, 1982), pp. 45–86.

62. Cited in Salzman, *English Prose Fiction*, p. 135. We have few if any descriptions by women of women's reading of the *New Arcadia*. When they are made public, Anne Clifford's notations in her volume of the *New Arcadia* will provide provocative evidence for her reading; see also the list of passages extracted from the *New Arcadia* as writing practice by Katherine Manners, the niece of Philip Sidney's daughter Elizabeth, described in Josephine Roberts, "Extracts from the *Arcadia* in the MS Notebook of Lady Katherine Manners," *Notes and Queries*, n.s., 28 (1981): 35–36.

63. McCoy, *Sir Philip Sidney*, p. 206.

64. Fulke Greville, *The Life of Sir Philip Sidney* (1652; Oxford: Clarendon Press, 1907), pp. 15, 223.

65. John Buxton, "A Draught of Sir Phillip Sidney's *Arcadia*," in *Historical Essays (1600–1750) Presented to David Ogg*, ed. H. E. Bell and R. L. Ollard (London: Adam and Charles Black, 1963), p. 77.

66. Cited in John Buxton, *Elizabethan Taste* (New York: St. Martins Press, 1964), p. 252.

67. Trans. of Achilles Tatius, *Loves of Clitophon and Leucippe* (Oxford, 1638), A2, cited in Suzanne Hull, *Chaste, Silent, and Obedient: English Books for Women, 1475–1640* (San Marino, Calif.: Huntington Library, 1982), p. 14.

68. Wye Saltonstall, *Picturae Loquentes; or, Pictures Drawne forth in Characters with a Poeme of a Maide* (London: 1631), E6v; also discussed in Louis Wright, "Reading of Renaissance Englishwomen," *Studies in Philology* 28 (1931): 684.

69. H. S. Bennett, *English Books and Readers, 1558 to 1603* (Cambridge: Cambridge Univ. Press, 1965), p. 254.

70. Thomas Powell, *Tom of All Trades* (1631), ed. Frederick J. Furnivall, New Shakespeare Society, ser. 6 (London: Trubner, 1876), 2:173; discussed in Buxton, *Elizabethan Taste*, p. 252.

71. The meaning of the act of reading itself, beyond the content of the material read, is interestingly discussed for modern women in Radway, *Reading the Romance*, p. 118.

72. Dying still ranks as a prominent possibility among the limited opportunities for women's heroism in modern literature, as discussed in Joanna Russ, "What Can a Heroine Do? or, Why Women Can't Write," in

Images of Women in Fiction, ed. Susan Koppelman Cornillon (Bowling Green: Ohio Univ. Press, 1972), pp. 3–20.

CHAPTER 3. The Countess of Pembroke and the Art of Dying

1. This chapter expands upon an earlier version, "The Countess of Pembroke and the Art of Dying," in *Women in the Middle Ages and the Renaissance,* ed. Mary Beth Rose (Syracuse: Syracuse Univ. Press, 1986), pp. 207–26.

2. Translating Psalms was often undertaken for the good of the soul, according to Lily B. Campbell, *Divine Poetry and Drama in Sixteenth-Century England* (Cambridge: Cambridge Univ. Press, 1959), p. 54. In Nicholas Breton's "An Olde Mans Lesson and a Young Mans Love," in *The Works in Verse and Prose of Nicholas Breton,* comp. Alexander B. Grosart (1879; New York: AMS Press, 1966), 2:14, a young man is advised in ways of contenting his wife: "If she be learned and studious, perswade her to translation, it will keepe her from Idlenes, & it is a cunninge kinde taske: if shee be unlearned, commend her huswifery." For translations by women in the Renaissance, see Patricia Gartenberg and Nena Thames Whittemore, "A Checklist of English Women in Print, 1475–1640," *Bulletin of Bibliography* 34 (1977): 1–13.

3. Mary Sidney, Countess of Pembroke, *The Triumph of Death and Other Unpublished and Uncollected Poems,* ed. Gary F. Waller, Salzburg Studies in English Literature, 65 (Salzburg: Institut für Englische Sprache und Literatur, 1977), pp. 88–94. All citations from these poems are taken from this work.

4. Margaret P. Hannay, "'Doo What Men May Sing': Mary Sidney and the Tradition of Admonitory Dedication," in *Silent But for the Word,* ed. Margaret P. Hannay (Kent, Ohio: Kent State Univ. Press, 1985), pp. 149–65; Margaret P. Hannay, "'Princes You as Men Must Dy': Genevan Advice to Monarchs in the *Psalms* of Mary Sidney," *English Literary Renaissance* 19 (1989): 22–41. This latter essay also reveals advice to Elizabeth in the translations of the Psalms themselves.

5. Beth Wynne Fisken, "Mary Sidney's *Psalmes:* Education and Wisdom," in Hannay, *Silent But for the Word,* p. 167; Hannay, "'Doo What Men May Sing,'" p. 149; Waller, introduction to *The Triumph of Death,* by Mary Sidney, p. 40.

6. These views are included singly or in combination in Virginia Beauchamp, "Sidney's Sister as a Translator of Garnier," *Renaissance News* 10 (1957): 12–13; Frances Young, *Mary Sidney, Countess of Pembroke* (London: David Nutt, 1912), p. 140; Gary F. Waller, *Mary Sidney, Countess of*

Pembroke: A Critical Study of Her Writings and Literary Milieu (Salzburg: Institut für Anglistik and Amerikanistik, 1979), p. 100. See also the section "Modern Constructions of the Countess of Pembroke" in Chapter 1, above.

7. Baldassare Castiglione, *The Book of the Courtier,* trans. Sir Thomas Hoby (1561; New York: AMS Press, 1967), p. 258.

8. Luis Vives, *The Instruction of a Christian Woman* (London, 1592), H5v.

9. Thomas Salter, *A Mirrhor mete for all Mothers . . . intitlued the Mirrhor of Modestie* (London, 1579), C4. Ruth Kelso, *Doctrine for the Lady of the Renaissance* (1956; rpt. Urbana: Univ. of Illinois Press, 1978), pp. 41–45, has shown this work to be a translation of a 1555 Italian treatise by Giovanni Bruto; see also Janis Butler Holm, "The Myth of a Feminist Humanism: Thomas Salter's *The Mirrhor of Modestie,*" *Soundings* 67 (1984): 443–52.

10. Nancy Lee Beaty, *The Craft of Dying: A Study in the Literary Tradition of the Ars Moriendi in England,* Yale Studies in English, 175 (New Haven: Yale Univ. Press, 1970); Louis B. Wright, *Middle-Class Culture in Elizabethan England* (Chapel Hill: Univ. of North Carolina Press, 1935), pp. 248–51.

11. Diane Bornstein, ed., *The Countess of Pembroke's Translation of Philippe de Mornay's "Discourse of Life and Death"* (Detroit: Michigan Consortium for Medieval and Early Modern Studies, 1983), p. 6.

12. W. B., *The Maner to Dye Well* (London, 1578), C5.

13. I. S., *A christian exhortation taken oute of the holy Scriptures, for the great comfort of every person being in the agonie of deathe* (London, 1579).

14. William Perkins, *A Salve for a Sicke man; or, The right manner of dying* (London, 1595). For other exemplary deaths of women see the lives of Katherine Evans and Sarah Chevers (1662), Mary Simpson (1649), Elizabeth Wilkinson (1659), and others listed in Owen C. Watkins, *The Puritan Experience* (London: Routledge and Kegan Paul, 1972), pp. 241–60. Central to this development is the increasing publication of funeral sermons as examples to the faithful.

15. Raphael Holinshed, *The Third Volume of Chronicles . . . Now newlie recognised, augmented, and continued . . . to the year 1586* (London, 1587), L1111112.

16. Henry Herbert to Sir Francis Hastings, 24 December 1595, described and quoted in HMC, *Hastings,* 2:43–44.

17. Rowland Whyte to Robert Sidney, 5 December 1595, quoted in Arthur Collins, *Letters and Memorials of State . . . Memoirs of the Lives and actions of the Sydneys* (London, 1746), 1:372.

18. Seneca, *Ad Lucilium Epistulae Morales,* trans. Richard M. Gummere (Cambridge: Harvard Univ. Press, 1953), p. 131.

19. Ralph Graham Palmer, *Seneca's "De Remediis Fortuitorum" and the*

Elizabethans, Institute of Elizabethan Studies (Kendal, England: Titus Wilson, 1953), p. 18. Reasons for the compatibility of Seneca's ideas in the Renaissance are ably discussed in Gordon Braden, *Renaissance Tragedy and the Senecan Tradition: Anger's Privilege* (New Haven: Yale Univ. Press, 1985), 63–98.

20. Frederick Kiefer, "Seneca's Influence on Elizabethan Tragedy," *Research Opportunities in Renaissance Drama* 21 (1978): 17–34; Geroge L. Geckle, *John Marston's Drama: Themes, Images, Sources* (Rutherford: Fairleigh Dickinson University Press, 1980), pp. 58–88, 115–20; Nicholas Brooke, Introduction and Appendix to George Chapman, *Bussy D'Ambois* (London: Methuen, 1964), pp. xxii–xxiii, lx, 149–53; Braden, *Renaissance Tragedy*, pp. 153–223.

21. Rudolf Kirk, Introduction to Guillaume du Vair, *The Moral Philosophie of the Stoicks*, trans. Thomas James (New Brunswick: Rutgers Univ. Press, 1951), pp. 4–6.

22. Ian Maclean, *The Renaissance Notion of Woman* (Cambridge: Cambridge Univ. Press, 1980), p. 85.

23. G. C. Williamson, *Lady Anne Clifford* (East Ardsley, Yorkshire: S. R. Publ., 1967), p. 339.

24. Vives, *Instruction of a Christian Woman*, 4v; Kelso, *Doctrine for the Lady of the Renaissance*, pp. 70–73.

25. Leicester Bradner attributes this translation from Seneca to Queen Elizabeth but lists his "many doubts" in his introduction and notes to *The Poems of Queen Elizabeth I* (Providence, R.I.: Brown Univ. Press, 1964), pp. xiv, 80–81. Elizabeth Cary translated portions of Seneca in the early seventeenth century; see *The Lady Falkland: Her Life, from a MS in the Imperial Archives at Lille* (London: Catholic Publishing and Bookselling Co., 1861), p. 4.

26. Maclean, *The Renaissance Notion of Woman*, pp. 51 and 20.

27. Braden, *Renaissance Tragedy*, pp. 17 and 227, cites conflicting scholarship on this point.

28. Philippe du Plessis Mornay, *Discourse de la vie et de la mort* (La Rochelle, 1581), A4.

29. Mary Sidney, trans., *Antonius, A Tragedie written also in French by Ro. Garnier* (London, 1592), G1. All citations are taken from this edition, which was bound with the tract by Mornay. It is commonly referred to as *Antonie*.

30. Du Vair, *Moral Philosophie of the Stoicks*, pp. 73–75.

31. Samuel Daniel, *Tragedie of Cleopatra* (London, 1594), A2.

32. This description is translated from Pierre Spriet, *Samuel Daniel (1563–1619): Sa Vie, son oeuvre* (Paris: Didier, 1968), p. 375.

33. Daniel, *Tragedie of Cleopatra*, 3.485–88, 495–96. All citations are

taken from the 1599 edition available in Geoffrey Bullough, *Narrative and Dramatic Sources of Shakespeare* (New York: Columbia Univ. Press, 1964), 5:406–49. The 1595 edition of Mary Sidney's *Antonie* is also available in this volume.

34. A conflict between self-assertion and self-effacement is present in several seventeenth-century autobiographies by women; see Mary Beth Rose, "Gender, Genre, and History: Seventeenth-Century English Women and the Art of Autobiography," in Rose, *Women in the Middle Ages and the Renaissance,* pp. 245–78.

35. Braden, *Renaissance Tragedy,* pp. 30, 36.

36. Samuel Daniel, "A Letter from Octavia to Marcus Antonius," *The Complete Works,* ed. Alexander B. Grosart (London: Hazell, Watson, and Viney, 1885), 1:121–22.

37. Williamson, *Lady Anne Clifford,* pp. 31–33, 38.

38. Ibid., p. 339.

39. Daniel, "Certaine Epistles," lines 76–83, *The Complete Works,* 1:203–7.

40. I am using quotation marks around "countess of Cumberland" to distinguish Daniel's representation from the actual countess, whom Daniel's character may or may not have resembled.

41. Braden, *Renaissance Tragedy,* p. 20.

42. Ruth Hughey discusses parallels between *The vertuous Octavia* and Daniel's "Letter from Octavia," in *The Arundel Harington Manuscript of Tudor Poetry* (Columbus: Ohio State Univ. Press, 1966), 2:383; see also R. B. McKerrow, introduction to Samuel Brandon, *The vertuous Octavia* (Oxford: Oxford Univ. Press for the Malone Society, 1909), p. v.

43. Arthur Collins, *The Peerage of England* (London: T. Bensley, 1812), 6:554, and *The Visitation of Wiltshire, 1623,* ed. George W. Marshall (London: Bell and Sons, 1882), p. 60.

44. Mary Sidney, *The Triumph of Death,* 1.52–54, ed. Waller, p. 68. All citations are taken from this edition.

45. Ernest Hatch Wilkins, Introduction to *The Triumphs of Petrarch* (Chicago: Univ. of Chicago Press, 1962), p. v.

46. Thomas M. Greene, *The Light in Troy: Imitation and Discovery in Renaissance Poetry* (New Haven: Yale Univ. Press, 1982), pp. 104–26; Guiseppe Mazzotta, "The *Canzoniere* and the Language of the Self," *Studies in Philology* 75 (1978): 271–96.

47. For discussion of the role of these models, see Lisa Jardine, *Still Harping on Daughters* (New York: Barnes and Noble, 1983), pp. 169–98.

48. Anne Bacon, trans., *An apologie or answere in defence of the Church of Englande* (London, 1564), A2v. The first edition (1562) did not contain this prefatory material.

CHAPTER 4. The Heroics of Constancy in Mary Wroth's *Countess of Montgomery's Urania*

1. Josephine A. Roberts, ed., *The Poems of Mary Wroth* (Baton Rouge: Louisiana State Univ. Press, 1983), p. 31; hereafter cited as *PMW*. Roberts is currently editing both portions of the romance, to be published through the Early English Text Society. Citations to the manuscript continuation, which falls into two parts, are designated I or II; it is paginated according to folio gatherings, each including four pages (Ar, Ab, Br, Bv). Citations to the printed folio are to signature numbers.

2. For Lord Edward Denny's recognition of Pamphilia as Wroth, and congruent details between Pamphilia's life and Wroth's, see *PMW*, pp. 30–31, and Paul Salzman, *English Prose Fiction, 1558–1700: A Critical History* (Oxford: Clarendon Press, 1985), p. 140. For the implications of Pamphilia as "all loving" as well as a possible precedent in a historian named Pamphilia writing in the reign of Nero, see *PMW*, p. 42. See also Josephine A. Roberts, "The Biographical Problem of *Pamphilia to Amphilanthus*," *Tulsa Studies in Women's Literature* 1 (1982): 44.

3. Mary Wroth to William Feilding, first earl of Denbigh, in which she requests his aid in a reconciliation between her and "his Majesty" (HMC, *Denbigh*, 5:3), cited in *PMW*, p. 35.

4. Roberts, in *PMW*, pp. 43–44, remains cautious about the identification of Amphilanthus as William Herbert, despite her excellent evidence, including Amphilanthus's recitation of a poem of his composition dependably ascribed to William Herbert; see also Roberts, "Biographical Problem," pp. 48–49.

5. A description of Wroth's romance is also provided in Salzman, *English Prose Fiction*, pp. 140–44, and Elaine V. Beilin, *Redeeming Eve: Women Writers of the English Renaissance* (Princeton: Princeton Univ. Press, 1987), pp. 214–32. Particularly good on the manuscript continuation is Margaret A. Witten-Hannah, "Lady Mary Wroth's *Urania:* The Work and the Tradition" (Ph.D. diss., Univ. of Auckland, 1978), pp. 196–215.

6. HMC, *De L'Isle*, 5:305, cited in *PMW*, p. 25; for Roberts's meticulous research into obscurely documented information on Worth's illegitimate children, see also pp. 24–25. For attitudes towards illegitimacy in the seventeenth century, see Keith Wrightson, "The Nadir of English Illegitimacy in the English Seventeenth Century," in *Bastardy and Its Comparative History*, ed. Peter Laslett et al. (Cambridge: Harvard Univ. Press, 1980), pp. 176–91.

7. HMC, *Seventh Report*, 434b–435, cited in *PMW*, p. 25.

8. See also *PMW*, pp. 37, 70.

9. See, for example, Elizabeth Dipple, "The Captivity Episode in the *New Arcadia*," *Journal of English and Germanic Philology* 70 (1971): 418–31.

Richard C. McCoy, *Sir Philip Sidney: Rebellion in Arcadia* (New Brunswick: Rutgers Univ. Press, 1979), pp. 213–16, links Sidney's inclusive ending to other patterns of ambivalence and evasion in his life and art deriving from a conflict between obedience and autonomy.

10. For details of Wroth's life, see Sidney Lee, "Mary Wroth," *Dictionary of National Biography,* 20:1076–77; Gary Waller, ed., Introduction to Mary Wroth, *Pamphilia to Amphilanthus,* Salzburg Studies in English Literature, 64 (Salzburg: Institut für Englische Sprache und Literatur, 1977), pp. 4–5; and *PMW,* pp. 3–27.

11. For a range of attitudes on the bearing of illegitimate children in the seventeenth century, see Wrightson, "Nadir of English Illegitimacy," pp. 176–91.

12. The possibility that Wroth was named for her aunt is raised by Roberts, *PMW,* p. 15.

13. *PMW,* pp. 47–48.

14. Title page reproduced in *PMW,* p. 76.

15. Ben Jonson, "Conversations with William Drummond of Hawthornden," in *Works,* ed. C. H. Herford and Percy and Evelyn Simpson (Oxford: Clarendon Press, 1947), 1:138

16. HMC, *Rutland,* 1:418, and HMC, *De L'Isle,* 4:234, 236, 243, and 245, cited in *PMW,* p. 19.

17. *PMW,* p. 44, reproduced on pp. 217–18.

18. These epitaphs are printed in John Soowthern, *Pandora, the musyque of the beautie; or, His Mistresse Diana* (London, 1584), C3v–4v; Soowthern's dedication of this work to Anne Cecil's husband, Edward Vere, increases the trustworthiness of his ascription of these epitaphs to her.

19. Visits are recorded in HMC, *De L'Isle,* 3:412, 421, and 4:45, 276, 282, cited in *PMW,* p. 27; see also John Nichols, ed., *The Progresses, Processions, and Magnificent Festivities of King James the First* (London, J. B. Nichols, 1828), 1:489, n.5.

20. *PMW,* pp. 42–44.

21. Roberts, *PMW,* pp. 43–45, is cautious concerning the evidence she provides for this identification.

22. Jonson, "Conversations with William Drummond," p. 142.

23. William Prynne, *Historiomastix* (London, 1633), index under "women actors"; for discussion, see Annabel Patterson, *Censorship and Interpretation: The Conditions of Writing and Reading in Early Modern England* (Madison: Univ. of Wisconsin Press, 1984), pp. 105–6.

24. Josephine A. Roberts, "The Huntington Manuscript of Lady Mary Wroth's Play, *Loves Victorie,*" *Huntington Library Quarterly* 46 (1983): 163–66; *PMW,* pp. 37–38, 56. Roberts remains cautious about the possibility that Wroth's play was acted by the Dering group.

25. *PMW,* p. 17; Ben Jonson, "A Sonnet, To the noble Lady, the Lady

Mary Wroth," line 3, in *Works,* 8:182. Jonson's sonnet is quoted in full in the text, below.

26. For the inclusion of masques in Wroth's romance see *PMW,* p. 13, and especially Witten-Hannah, "Lady Mary Wroth's *Urania,*" pp. 171–79.

27. Margaret A. Witten-Hannah, "Sleeping with Monsters: Lady Mary Wroth's Complete *Urania,* The Book and Manuscript Continuation," *Aulla XX: Proceedings and Papers of the Twentieth Congress of the Australasian Universities Language and Literature Association* (1980), p. 329, believes the folio was pirated; Carolyn Ruth Swift, "Feminine Identity in Lady Mary Wroth's Romance *Urania,*" *English Literary Renaissance* 14 (1984): 329–40, seems not to; Roberts, *PMW,* p. 70, believes it is "unclear to what extent, if any, the author participated in the publication of her work."

28. Bodleian Library MS Add.D.111, fols. 173r–v is printed in full in *PMW,* p. 236, and discussed on p. 35.

29. Early responses to Wroth and her work are discussed in *PMW,* pp. 17–22, 32–35, 59–60.

30. Jonson, *Works,* 1:182–83; also reproduced in *PMW,* pp. 59–60.

31. See Waller, Introduction to Wroth, *Pamphilia to Amphilanthus,* p. 8, for comments on the old-fashionedness of Wroth's use of Petrarchan conventions. Important discussions of the sonnet sequence include *PMW,* pp. 41–49, and Beilin, *Redeeming Eve,* p. 232–43; see also Beilin, "'The Onely Perfect Vertue': Constancy in Mary Wroth's *Pamphilia to Amphilanthus,*" *Spenser Studies* 2 (1981): 229–45, and Swift, "Feminine Identity," pp. 328–46.

32. *Chapman's Homer,* lines 181–83, ed. Allardyce Nicoll, Bollingen Series, 41 (New York: Pantheon Books, 1956), 1:285–86.

33. Jonson, "Hymenaei," *Works,* 7:224.

34. Jonson, "Volpone," *Works,* 5:112.

35. Poem printed in Josephine A. Roberts, "An Unpublished Literary Quarrel Concerning the Suppression of Mary Wroth's *Urania* (1621)," *Notes and Queries* 222 (1977): 532–35. The background of Denny's poem is discussed in Paul Salzman, "Contemporary References in Mary Wroth's *Urania,*" *Review of English Studies* 29 (1978): 178–81, and in *PMW,* pp. 31–35. Wroth's reply to Denny is published in Roberts, "An Unpublished Literary Quarrel," p. 534, and *PMW,* pp. 34–35.

36. Roberts, "An Unpublished Literary Quarrel," p. 533, n. 11.

37. *The Historie of the World: Commonly Called the Naturall Historie of C. Plinius Secundus,* trans. Philemon Holland (London, 1601), bk. 9, chap. 35, "Of Pearles: how, and where they be found," Z1v; my italics. On Z2, the oyster is explicitly referred to as "she" in a warning to fishermen to protect their fingers: "Assoone as it perceiveth and feeleth a mans hand within it, by and by she shutteth; and, by that meanes hideth and covereth her riches within: for well woteth she that therefore, she is sought for."

38. Eric Partridge, *Shakespeare's Bawdy* (New York: E. P. Dutton, 1969), p. 62.

39. HMC, *Salisbury*, 22:161, reproduced in *PMW*, pp. 238–39.

40. Antissia is discussed in Salzman, *English Prose Fiction*, p. 144.

41. Roberts, *PMW*, p. 48, discusses Wroth's debt to Ovid in her sonnets.

42. The function of lightning rod corresponds to the Renaissance use of the stage misogynist to defend women, discussed interestingly by Linda Woodbridge, *Women and the English Renaissance: Literature and the Nature of Womankind, 1540–1620* (Urbana: Univ. of Illinois Press, 1984), p. 297.

43. Constancy emerges as a central topic in almost all discussions of Wroth's romance or poetry; see especially Roberts, *PMW*, p. 49; Beilin, *Redeeming Eve*, pp. 214–42; Swift, "Feminine Identity," pp. 336–37. My viewpoint differs from these.

44. Notable exceptions include Antissius's wife (G2–G3v) and Polidorus's wife, who dies on hearing the news of her husband's death, "by curious art . . . dying as though the word dead had kild her; excellent griefe, and most excellent strength of passion, that can bring so resolute, and brave an end" (PP3–PP4).

45. Swift's discussion of Allarina's self-sufficiency does not note her subsequent marriage.

46. Discussions of Urania's advice to Pamphilia do not note that Urania was arguing "against her owne minde" to save Pamphilia's life: see Swift, "Feminine Identity," p. 337, and Witten-Hannah, "Sleeping with Monsters," p. 326.

47. Beilin, "'The Onely Perfect Vertue,'" p. 232; see also Beilin's *Redeeming Eve*, p. 219. I do not concur, however, with Beilin's sense of the religious thrust of Pamphilia's love.

48. Labyrinth discussed in Beilin, "'The Onely Perfect Vertue,'" pp. 236–38.

49. Swift, "Feminine Identity," pp. 341–43, where she discusses the contradiction the institution of marriage presented to Renaissance women.

50. Discussed by Salzman, *English Prose Fiction*, pp. 142–43.

51. For this confusion, see also Walter Ong, *Orality and Literacy* (New York: Methuen, 1982), p. 121, and his *Rhetoric, Romance, and Technology* (Ithaca: Cornell University Press, 1971), pp. 23–47, both discussed above in the Introduction.

52. Wroth to the duke of Buckingham, in *PMW*, p. 236.

53. *The Letters of John Chamberlain*, ed. Norman Egbert McClure (Philadelphia: American Philosophical Society, 1939), 2:427. In addition to Denny's outraged poem, another contemporary acknowledgment of the topi-

cality of Wroth's romance is implied in a 1640 letter by George Manners, seventh earl of Rutland, apparently to Mary Wroth, in which he requests a key to the persons signified by the characters; see *PMW*, p. 29.

54. Edward Le Comte, *The Notorious Lady Essex* (New York: Dial Press, 1969), p. 213.

55. Torquato Tasso, *Discourses on the Heroic Poem*, trans. Mariella Cavalchini and Irene Samuel (Oxford, 1973), pp. 27, 40, and 58, cited by Patterson, *Censorship and Interpretation*, p. 161.

56. John Barclay, *Argenis* (London, 1629), pp. 130–31 and 469, discussed in Patterson, *Censorship and Interpretation*, pp. 180–85, and Roberts, *PMW*, p. 28.

57. Patterson, *Censorship and Interpretation*, p. 182.

58. Roberts, *PMW*, p. 30, urges caution in the identification of Bellamira with Mary Wroth in light of the sensational history of Bellamira's father, which does not reflect the life of Wroth's father. For an argument that Renaissance topicality was often not consistent in its details, see Mary Ellen Lamb, "The Nature of Topicality in *Love's Labour's Lost*," *Shakespeare Survey* 38 (1985): 49–60.

59. *PMW*, pp. 10–12; letter reproduced on pp. 233–34.

60. Ben Jonson, "To Sir Robert Wroth," *The Forrest*, in *Works*, 8:96–100.

61. *PMW*, p. 30; Salzman, *English Prose Fiction*, p. 140.

62. *PMW*, p. 44; Roberts, "Biographical Problem," p. 48.

63. Edward, Earl of Clarendon, *The History of the Rebellion*, re-edited by W. Dunn Macray (Oxford: Clarendon Press, 1888), 1:72.

64. Swift, "Feminine Identity," p. 336, and Beilin, *Redeeming Eve*, p. 220, provide good discussions of this episode.

65. Phrase taken from Stephen Orgel, *The Illusion of Power* (Berkeley and Los Angeles: Univ. of California Press, 1975); see esp. Orgel's epilogue, pp. 88–89.

66. For an indication of the appeal of romances to women in the early seventeenth century, see Suzanne Hull, *Chaste, Silent, and Obedient: English Books for Women, 1475–1640* (San Marino, Calif.: Huntington Library, 1982), p. 79.

67. Scenes of reading will be discussed in my sequel, "Women Readers in Mary Wroth's *Countess of Montgomery's Urania*," in *Essays on Mary Wroth*, ed. Naomi Miller and Gary Waller (Knoxville: Univ. of Tennessee Press, forthcoming).

CHAPTER 5. Singing with the (Tongue) of a Nightingale

1. This manuscript is described in some detail in William Ringler, ed., *The Poems of Sir Philip Sidney* (Oxford: Clarendon Press, 1962), pp. 538–39,

and in Mary Ellen Lamb, "Three Unpublished Holograph Poems in the Bright Manuscript: A New Poet in the Sidney Circle?" *Review of English Studies*, n.s., 35 (1984): 301–15.

2. Ringler, *Poems of Sir Philip Sidney*, pp. 447–49.

3. These corroborations took place in interviews in the summer of 1979; see also Peter J. Croft, ed., *The Poems of Robert Sidney* (Oxford: Clarendon Press, 1984), pp. 5–6.

4. Martin Billingsley, *The Pens Excellencie* (London, c. 1617), C2v. The texts of poems from *Astrophel and Stella* were also copied into the Bright manuscript in an italic hand.

5. David Cressy, *Literacy and the Social Order: Reading and Writing in Tudor and Stuart England* (Cambridge: Cambridge Univ. Press, 1980), pp. 20–25; but see also Margaret Spufford, *Small Books and Pleasant Histories* (Athens: Univ. of Georgia Press, 1981), pp. 22, 34–37.

6. My description of this hand owes much to Peter J. Croft.

7. Ringler, *Poems of Sir Philip Sidney*, pp. 449, 539.

8. "In a greene woode thicke of shade" (fol. 11) imitates Song 8 from *Astrophel and Stella*, "In a grove most rich of shade"; "All mi sensees weare bereaved" (fol. 14) resembles *Certain Sonnets*, number 27, "Al my sense thy sweetnesse gained."

9. Viscount de L'Isle to Lady de L'Isle, 28 September 1612, HMC, *De L'Isle*, 5:63.

10. For technical information identifying the arms stamped on the calf binding of the mansucript as those of the first Baron Halifax between 1700 and 1714, see Lamb, "Three Unpublished Holograph Poems," p. 302.

11. Arthur Collins, ed., *Letters and Memorials of State . . . Memoirs of the Lives and actions of the Sydneys* (London, 1746), 2:454, 472, 489; HMC, *De L'Isle and Dudley*, 6:75, 106, 121; Kent Archives Office MS U1475 C108. Walter Montague wrote a pastoral comedy, *The Shepherd's Paradise*, that evidently was influenced by Sidney's *Arcadia*. See also Croft, *Poems of Sir Robert Sidney*, p. 6, and Lamb, "Three Unpublished Holograph Poems," pp. 303–6.

12. Ben Jonson, "Conversations with William Drummond of Hawthornden," in *Works*, ed. C. H. Herford and Percy and Evelyn Simpson (Oxford: Clarendon Press, 1947), 1:138. Manuscripts used to compare handwriting samples include the following: Mary (Sidney) Herbert, countess of Pembroke, letter in BL, Add. MS 15,232; Mary (Sidney) Wroth, Folger MS VA104; Elizabeth (Sidney) Manners, countess of Rutland, letter at Belvoir Castle (described in HMC, *Rutland*, 1:417). My thanks to the duke of Rutland for his permission to see the letter by Elizabeth Manners. My thanks also to Peter Beal of Sotheby's for the use of his extensive collection of facsimiles of manuscripts accumulated for his

Index of English Literary Manuscripts, Vol. 1, *1450–1625* (London: Mansell, 1980).

13. The Sidney Psalter, quoted in Frances Berkeley Young, *Mary Sidney, Countess of Pembroke* (London: Nutt, 1912), p. 42. The last mention of Anne is not the 1603 reference Young cites on p. 100; Anne is mentioned in a 1604 letter quoted in HMC, *De L'Isle and Dudley*, 3:134. Robert Sidney's children are listed, with known dates, in Collins, ed., *Letters and Memorials of State*, 1:120. The third daughter, Elizabeth, died in her midteens, and the youngest surviving daughters would probably have written in a later hand.

14. For visits actual or anticipated, see HMC, *De L'Isle and Dudley*, 3:189; 4:283, 289; 5:307, 320.

15. See, for example, the primarily "drab" verse of the Mary Sidney's retainer Thomas Howell, *Howell His Devises* (London, 1581), included in *Occasional Issues of Unique or Very Rare Books*, ed. Alexander Grosart, vol. 8 (Manchester: Charles E. Simms, 1879). (On drab verse, see note 17, below.) For an analogous poem, see "The frailtie and hurtfulness of beautie," in *Tottel's Miscellany*, ed. Hyder Edward Rollins (Cambridge: Harvard Univ. Press, 1965), 1:9.

16. This passage from the unpublished journal of Lady Mildmay is cited by Rachel Weigall in "An Elizabethan Gentlewoman: The Journal of Lady Mildmay, circa 1570–1617," *Quarterly Review* 215 (1911): 121.

17. I am adopting the admittedly controversial term "drab" from C. S. Lewis, *English Literature in the Sixteenth Century*, Oxford History of English Literature, 3 (Oxford: Clarendon Press, 1965), pp. 222–71. The characteristics of drab poetry are discussed especially well in G. K. Hunter, "Drab and Golden Lyrics of the Renaissance," in *Forms of Lyric: Selected Papers from the English Institute*, ed. Reuben A. Brower (New York: Columbia Univ. Press, 1970), pp. 1–18; the late circulation of the form is discussed by Douglas L. Peterson, *The English Lyric from Wyatt to Donne: A History of Plain and Eloquent Styles* (Princeton: Princeton Univ. Press, 1967), pp. 39–48.

18. Howell, *Howell His Devises*, H1v–H2.

19. Sherod M. Cooper, *The Sonnets of Astrophel and Stella: A Stylistic Study* (The Hague: Mouton, 1968),p. 79.

20. A useful summary of Petrarchan characteristics and Sidney's relation to them is included in David Kalstone, "The Petrarchan Vision," in *Sidney's Poetry: Contexts and Interpretations* (New York: Norton, 1965), pp. 105–32.

21. Ovid, *Metamorphosis seu Fabulae Poeticae: Earumque Interpretatio . . . Georgii Sabini* (New York: Garland, 1955, from the 1589 Frankfort ed.), pp. 214–15. George Schuler published under the name Sabinus.

22. Sir Philip Sidney, *The Countess of Pembroke's Arcadia*, ed. Maurice Evans (New York: Penguin Books, 1977), cited by page numbers in the text.

23. Edmund Spenser, *Poetical Works*, ed. J. C. Smith and E. de Selincourt (London: Oxford Univ. Press, 1966), pp. 462, 533, and 482. A useful survey of the Renaissance use of the nightingale Philomela is included in H. W. Garrod, "The Nightingale in Poetry," in *Profession of Poetry and Other Lectures* (Oxford: Clarendon Press, 1929), pp. 131–59. The analysis in this chapter may explain in part Garrod's observations of the Renaissance nightingale: "In no period is he more vocal. But in no period so wailful" (p. 133), and "In general the nightingale poetry of the Elizabethans sticks in triviality and convention" (p. 154).

24. Ovid, *Metamorphoses* 6.881, in *Shakespeare's Ovid*, trans. Arthur Golding, ed. W. H. D. Rouse (Carbondale: Southern Illinois Univ. Press, 1961). *Metamorphoses* is cited by book and line numbers in the text.

25. This fantasy takes on special interest as the time before the child is absorbed into the symbolic order: see Jacques Lacan, *Ecrits: A Selection*, trans. Alan Sheridan (New York: Norton, 1977), and Julia Kristeva, *Desire in Language: A Semiotic Approach to Literature and Art*, trans. Thomas Gora, Alice Jardine, and Leon S. Roudiez, ed. Leon S. Roudiez (New York: Columbia Univ. Press, 1980).

26. Pliny, *The Historie of the World: Commonly Called the Naturall Historie of C. Plinius Secundus*, trans. Philemon Holland (London, 1601), BB5.

27. Sir Philip Sidney, *Certain Sonnets*, number 4 (quoted in full on pp. 221–22, below), in Ringler, *Poems of Sir Philip Sidney*; Roberts, *PMW*, p. 136.

28. *The Riverside Shakespeare* (Boston: Houghton Mifflin, 1974).

29. This tale occurs in 6.530–853 of Golding's translation.

30. See, for example, L. P. Wilkinson, *Ovid Recalled* (Cambridge: Cambridge Univ. Press, 1955), pp. 399–438.

31. These three emblem writers are quoted in Arthur Henkel and Albrecht Schone, eds., *Emblemata: Handbuch zur Sinnbildkunst dest XVI und XVII Jahrhunderts* (Stuttgart: Metzlersche, 1967), pp. 872, 1597, and 1599; for English emblems of nightingales see Huston Diehl, ed., *An Index of Icons in English Emblem Books, 1500–1700* (Norman: Univ. of Oklahoma Press, 1986), pp. 105, 153, and 162.

32. Pierre Bersuire, commentator, *Metamorphosis Ovidiana Moraliter . . . Explanata* (New York: Garland, 1979, from the 1509 Paris ed.), fol. 53.

33. Ringler, *Poems of Sir Philip Sidney*, p. 427.

34. These are cited ibid., and in Garrod, "The Nightingale in Poetry," p. 154.

35. Jane Anger, *Her Protection of Women* (London, 1589), in Katherine

Usher Henderson and Barbara F. McManus, eds., *Half Humankind: Contexts and Texts of the Controversy about Women in England, 1540–1640* (Urbana: Univ. of Illinois Press, 1985), pp. 172–88 (quotes from pp. 173–74). This work is also printed in Simon Shepherd, *The Women's Sharp Revenge* (London: Fourth Estate, 1985), pp. 29–52. Henderson and McManus, pp. 21–23, argue against critics who suggest that Anger may have been a pseudonym adopted by a male writer: and Shepherd, p. 30, locates some women by that name at the appropriate period of time.

36. All of these pamphlets are included in Shepherd, *Women's Sharp Revenge*.

37. Patrick Hannay, *The Poetical Works* (1722; New York: Johnson Reprint Co., 1966), B2.

Bibliography

Primary Sources

Acts of the Privy Council of England. Vol. 9.

Aristotle. *Politics.* Trans. Harris Rackham. London: Heinemann, 1932.

Ascham, Roger. *The Whole Works.* Ed. J. A. Giles. London, 1865.

Askewe, Anne. *The first examinacyon of Anne Askewe, lately martyred in Smythfelde.* Wesel, 1546.

Askewe, Anne. *The lattre examinacyon of the worthye servaunt of God mistres Anne Askewe.* Wesel, 1547.

Aubrey, John. *Brief Lives.* Ed. Oliver Lawson Dick. London: Secker and Warburg, 1950.

Aubrey, John. *The Natural History of Wiltshire.* Ed. John Britton. London: J. B. Nichols for the Wiltshire Topographical Society, 1847.

B., W. *The Maner to Dye Well.* London, 1578.

Bacon, Anne, trans. *An apologie or answere in defence of the Church of Englande.* London, 1564. (See also Anne Cooke.)

Barclay, John. *Argenis.* London, 1629.

Baxter, Nathaniel. *Sir Philip Sidneys Ourania.* London, 1606.

Becon, Thomas. "A new catechisme." In *Worckes.* London, 1564.

Bentley, Thomas. *Monument of Matrones.* London, 1582.

Bersmano, Gregorio, and John Camerarius. *Phile sapientissimi versus iambici: De Animalium proprietate.* Leipzig, 1575.

Billingsley, Martin. *The Pens Excellencie.* London, c. 1617.

Boccaccio, Giovanni. *The Decameron.* London, 1620.

Boethius. *The Consolation of Philosophy.* Ed. William Anderson. Carbondale: Southern Illinois Univ. Press, 1963.

Brandon, Samuel. *The vertuous Octavia.* Oxford: Oxford Univ. Press for the Malone Society, 1909.

Breton, Nicholas. *Brittons Bowre of Delights.* Ed. Hyder Rollins. Cambridge: Harvard Univ. Press, 1933.

Breton, Nicholas. *A Mad World My Masters.* Ed. Ursula Kentish-Wright. 2 vols. London: Cresset Press, 1929.

Breton, Nicholas. *Poems.* Ed. Jean Robertson. Liverpool: Liverpool Univ. Press, 1952.

Breton, Nicholas. *Works in Verse and Prose.* Ed. Alexander Grosart. 2 vols. 1879; New York: AMS Press, 1966.

British Library. Additional MS 15, 232. (The Bright Manuscript.)

British Library. Harleian MS 6,995.

British Library. Lansdowne MSS 63, 77.

Calendar of State Papers, Domestic, of the Reigns of Edward, Mary, Elizabeth and James.

Cary, Elizabeth. *The Lady Falkland: Her Life, from a MS in the Imperial Archives at Lille.* London: Catholic Publishing and Bookselling Co., 1861.

Castiglione, Baldassare. *The Book of the Courtier (1561).* Trans. Sir Thomas Hoby. New York: AMS Press, 1967.

Cecil, Anne. "Four Epitaphes made by the Countes of Oxenford after the death of her young sonne the Lord Bulbecke, etc." In *Pandora, the musyque of the beautie; or, His Mistresse Diana.* Comp. John Soowthern. London, 1584.

Chamberlain, John. *Letters of John Chamberlain.* Ed. Norman Egbert McClure. Philadelphia: American Philosophical Society, 1939.

Clifford, Anne. *Diary.* Ed. Vita Sackville-West. London: William Heinemann, 1923.

Collins, Arthur, ed. *Letters and Memorials of State . . . Memoirs of the Lives and actions of the Sydneys.* London, 1746.

Collins, Arthur. *The Peerage of England.* London: T. Bensley, 1812.

Conham, Abraham. Prefatory letter to Gervase Babington, *A Very Fruitful Exposition of the Commandements by Way of Questions and Answers.* London, 1583.

C[ooke], A[nne], trans. *Sermons of Bernadine Ochyne . . . concerning the predestination and election of god.* London, c. 1570. (See also Anne Bacon.)

Cotton, Charles. "The Surprize." *The Poems of Charles Cotton.* Ed. John Buxton. Cambridge: Harvard Univ. Press, 1958.

Daniel, Samuel. *The Complete Works.* Ed. Alexander B. Grosart. London: Hazell, Watson and Viney, 1885.

Daniel, Samuel. *Tragedie of Cleopatra.* London, 1594.

Daniel, Samuel. *Tragedie of Cleopatra* (1599). In *Narrative and Dramatic Sources of Shakespeare,* ed. Geoffrey Bullough, 5:406–49. New York: Columbia Univ. Press, 1964.

du Vair, Guillaume. *The Moral Philosophy of the Stoicks.* Trans. Thomas James. London, 1598. Ed. Rudolf Kirk. New Brunswick: Rutgers Univ. Press, 1951.

Elizabeth I. *The Poems of Queen Elizabeth I.* Ed. Leicester Bradner. Providence: Brown Univ. Press, 1964.

Elyot, Thomas. *The Book Named the Governor* (1531). Ed. R. C. Alston. Menston, England: Scholar Press, 1970.

Florio, John, trans. *Essays,* by Montaigne. London, 1603.

Foxe, John. *The Acts and Monuments of John Foxe*. New York: AMS Press, 1965. (Also known as *The Book of Martyrs*.)

Fraunce, Abraham. *Arcadian Rhetorike*. London, 1588.

Fraunce, Abraham. *The Countess of Pembrokes Ivychurch*. London, 1591.

Fraunce, Abraham. *Insignium, Armorum, Emblematum, Hieroglyphicorum, et Symbolorum quae ab Italis Imprese nominatur, explicatio*. London, 1588.

Fraunce, Abraham. *Lamentations of Amyntas for the Death of Phyllis*. London, 1587. See Watson, Thomas.

Fraunce, Abraham. *Lawyers Logike*. London, 1588.

Fraunce, Abraham. *The Second Part of the Countess of Pembrokes Ivychurch*. London, 1591.

Fraunce, Abraham. *The Third Part of the Countess of Pembrokes Ivychurch. Entituled Amintas Dale*. London, 1592.

Fraunce, Abraham. *Victoria*. Ed. G. C. Moore-Smith. In *Materialien zur Kunde des Alteren Englischen Dramas*. Louvain: A. Uystpruyst, 1906.

Garnier, Robert. See Sidney, Mary, trans. *Antonius*.

Great Britain, Parliament, House of Commons. *Members of Parliament*. London: By Order of House of Commons, 1878.

Greene, Robert. *Philomela The Lady Fitzwaters Nightingale*. London, 1592.

Greville, Fulke. *The Life of Sir Philip Sidney*. 1652; Oxford: Clarendon Press, 1907.

Hannay, Patrick. *The Poetical Works* (1722). New York: Johnson Reprint Co., 1966.

Harington, Henry, ed. *Nugae Antiquae*. London: J. Dodsley, 1779.

Healey, William. *An Apologie for Women*. Oxford, 1608.

Henderson, Katherine Usher, and Barbara F. McManus, eds. *Half Humankind: Contexts and Texts of the Controversy about Women in England, 1540–1640*. Urbana: Univ. of Illinois Press, 1985.

Historical Manuscripts Commission (HMC). *Report on the Manuscripts of the Duke of Rutland*. Vol. 1.

Historical Manuscripts Commission (HMC). *Report on the Manuscripts of the Late Reginald Hastings*. Vol. 2.

Historical Manuscripts Commission (HMC). *Report on the Manuscripts of Lord de L'Isle and Dudley*. Vols. 3–6.

Holinshed, Raphael. *The Third Volume of Chronicles . . . Now newlie recognised, augmented, and continued . . . to the year 1586*. London, 1587.

Homer. *Chapman's Homer*. Ed. Allardyce Nicholl. Bollingen Series, 41. New York: Pantheon Books, 1956.

Howell, Thomas. *Howell His Devises*. London, 1581. (Also included in *Occasional Issues of Unique or Very Rare Books*. ed. Alexander Grosart. Manchester: Charles E. Simms, 1879. Vol 8.)

Hughey, Ruth, ed. *The Arundel Harington Manuscript of Tudor Poetry.* Columbus: Ohio Univ. Press, 1966.

Hyde, Edward (first earl of Clarendon). *History of the Rebellion.* Re-edited by W. Dunn Macray. Oxford: Clarendon Press, 1988.

Hyrde, Richard. Dedication to Desiderius Erasmus. *Devout Treatise Upon the Pater Noster.* Trans. Margaret Roper. London, c. 1526.

Jonson, Ben. *Complete Works.* Ed. C. H. Herford and Percy and Evelyn Simpson. Oxford: Clarendon Press, 1947.

Laurence, John. *A New System of Agriculture.* London, 1726.

Lucan. *Works.* Trans. A. M. Harmon. Loeb Classical Library. London: Heinemann, 1953.

Lumley, Lady Jane. *Iphigeneia at Aulis.* Ed. Harold H. Child. London: Chiswick Press for Malone Society Reprints, 1909.

Marshall, George W., ed. *The Visitation of Wiltshire, 1623.* London: Bell and Sons, 1882.

Moffett, Thomas. *Health's Improvement.* London, 1746.

Moffett, Thomas. *Silkwormes and Their Flies.* London, 1599.

Mornay, Philippe du Plessis. *Discours de la vie et de la mort.* La Rochelle, 1581.

Mornay, Philippe du Plessis. See Sidney, Mary, trans.

Nichols, John, ed. *Progresses and Processions of Queen Elizabeth.* 3 vols. London: J. B. Nichols, 1788–1805.

Nichols, John, ed. *Progresses, Processions, and Magnificent Festivities of King James the First.* 4 vols. London: J. B. Nichols, 1828.

Ovid. *Metamorphoses.* Trans. R. Humphries. Bloomington: Indiana Univ. Press, 1955.

Ovid. *Metamorphoses . . . cum commentarius Regii.* Basil, 1543.

Ovid. *Metamorphosis Ovidiana Moraliter . . . Explanata.* Commentary by Pierre Bersuire. Paris, 1509. New York: Garland, 1979.

Ovid. *Metamorphosis seu Fabulae Poeticae: Earumque Interpretatio . . . Georgii Sabini.* Frankfurt, 1589; New York: Garland, 1955.

Ovid. *Shakespeare's Ovid.* Trans. Arthur Golding. Ed. W. H. D. Rouse. Carbondale: Southern Illinois Univ. Press, 1961.

Pears, Stuart A., ed. *The Correspondence of Sir Philip Sidney and Hubert Languet.* London: Pickering, 1845.

Perkins, William. *A Salve for a Sicke man; or, The right manner of dying.* London, 1595.

Perriere, Guillaume de la. *Le Theatre des bons engines.* Paris: Denis Janot, 1539.

Petrarch. *The Triumphs of Petrarch.* Trans. and ed. Ernest Hatch Wilkins. Chicago: Univ. of Chicago Press, 1962.

Petrarch. See Sidney, Mary. *The Triumph of Death.*

Pettie, George. *A petite Pallace of Pettie his pleasure.* Ed. Herbert Hartman. London: Oxford Univ. Press, 1938.

Pliny. *The Historie of the World: Commonly Called the Naturall Historie of C. Plinius Secundus.* Trans. Philemon Holland. London, 1601.

Powell, Thomas. *Tom of All Trades (1631).* Ed. Frederick J. Furnivall. New Shakespeare Society, ser. 6. London: Trubner, 1876.

Prynne, William. *Historiomastix.* London, 1633.

[Puttenham, George.] *Arte of English Poesie* (1589). Ed. Gladys D. Willcock and Alice Walker. Cambridge: Cambridge Univ. Press, 1936.

S., I. *A christian exhortation taken oute of the holy Scriptures, for the great comfort of every person being in the agonie of deathe.* London, 1579.

Salter, Thomas. *A Mirrhor mete for all Mothers . . . intitlued the Mirrhor of Modestie.* London, 1579.

Saltonstall, Wye. *Picturae Loquentes; or, Pictures Drawne forth in Characters with a Poeme of a Maide.* London, 1631.

Saltonstall, Wye. "To Ladies and Gentlewomen." In *Ovid's Heroicall Epistles.* London, 1636.

Seneca. *Ad Lucilium Epistulae Morales.* Trans. Richard M. Gummere. Cambridge: Harvard Univ. Press, 1953.

Seneca. *Moral Essays.* Trans. John W. Basore. London: Heinemann, 1958.

Shakespeare, William. *The Riverside Shakespeare.* Boston: Houghton Mifflin, 1974.

Shepherd, Simon, ed. *Woman's Sharp Revenge: Five Women's Pamphlets from the Renaissance.* London: Fourth Estate, 1985.

Sidney, Mary. *Psalms.* See Sidney, Sir Philip. *The Psalms.*

Sidney, Mary. *The Triumph of Death and Other Unpublished and Uncollected Poems.* Ed. Gary F. Waller. Salzburg Studies in English Literature, 65. Salzburg, Institut für Englische Sprache und Literatur, 1977.

Sidney, Mary, trans. *Antonius, A Tragedie written also in French by Ro. Garnier.* London, 1592. Also published in Geoffrey Bullough. *The Narrative and Dramatic Sources of Shakespeare.* Vol. 5. New York: Columbia Univ. Press, 1964.

Sidney, Mary, trans. *The Countess of Pembroke's Translation of Philippe de Mornay's "Discourse of Life and Death."* Ed. Diane Bornstein. Detroit: Michigan Consortium for Medieval and Early Modern Studies, 1983.

Sidney, Sir Philip. *The Countess of Pembroke's Arcadia (The Old Arcadia).* Ed. Jean Robertson. Oxford: Clarendon Press, 1973.

Sidney, Sir Philip. *The Countess of Pembroke's Arcadia.* Ed. Maurice Evans. New York: Penguin, 1977.

Sidney, Sir Philip. *The Countess of Pembroke's Arcadia.* Ed. Victor Skretkowicz. Oxford: Clarendon Press, 1987.

Sidney, Sir Philip. *Miscellaneous Prose.* Ed. Katherine Duncan-Jones and Jan Van Dorsten. Oxford: Clarendon Press, 1973.

Sidney, Sir Philip. *The Poems of Sir Philip Sidney.* Ed. William Ringler. Oxford: Clarendon Press, 1962.

Sidney, Sir Philip. *The Psalms of Sir Philip Sidney and the Countess of Pembroke.* Ed. J. A. C. Rathmell. New York: New York Univ. Press, 1963.

Sidney, Sir Philip. See Pears, Stuart A.

Sidney, Robert. *The Poems of Robert Sidney.* Ed. Peter J. Croft. Oxford: Clarendon Press, 1984.

Speght, Rachel. *A Mouzzell for Malestomus.* London, 1617.

Spenser, Edmund. *Poetical Works.* Ed. J. C. Smith and E. de Selincourt. 1912; London: Oxford UP, 1966.

Spenser, Edmund. *Works: A Variorum Edition.* Ed. Edwin Greenlaw et al. Baltimore: Johns Hopkins Press, 1943.

Suetonius. "The Lives of Illustrious Men." In *Works,* trans. J. C. Rolfe, 2:471–72. 1914; London: Heinemann, 1979.

Tasso, Torquato. *Aminta.* Ed. C. E. J. Griffiths. Manchester: Manchester Univ. Press, 1972.

Tasso, Torquato. *Discourses on the Heroic Poem.* Trans. Mariella Cavalchini and Irene Samuel. Oxford: Clarendon, 1937.

Tatius, Achilles. *Loves of Clitophon and Leucippe.* Oxford, 1638.

Tottel's Miscellany. Ed. Hyder Rollins. Cambridge: Harvard Univ. Press, 1965.

Travitsky, Betty, ed. *The Paradise of Women: Writings by Englishwomen of the Renaissance.* Westport, Conn.: Greenwood Press, 1981.

Vergil. "Vita Donati." *Vitae Vergilianae Antiquae.* Ed. Colinus Hardie. Oxford: Clarendon Press, 1954.

Vives, Luis. *Instruction of a Christen Woman.* London, 1557.

Vives, Luis. *Instruction of a Christian Woman.* London, 1592.

Watson, Thomas. *Meliboeus.* London, 1590.

Watson, Thomas. *Thomas Watson's Latin "Amyntas" (1585) and Abraham Fraunce's Translation "The Lamentations of Amyntas" (1587).* Ed. Walter F. Staton, Jr., and Franklin M. Dickey. Chicago: Univ. of Chicago Press, 1967. See Fraunce, Abraham. *Lamentations.*

Wells, William, ed. *Spenser Allusions in the Sixteenth and Seventeenth Centuries.* Chapel Hill: Univ. of North Carolina Press, 1972.

Whately, William. *The Bride-Bush.* London, 1619.

Wroth, Lady Mary. *Pamphilia to Amphilanthus.* Ed. Gary F. Waller. Salzburg Studies in English Literature, 64. Salzburg: Institut für Englische Sprache und Literatur, 1977.

Wroth, Lady Mary. *The Poems of Mary Wroth.* Ed. Josephine A. Roberts. Baton Rouge: Louisiana State Univ. Press, 1983.

Secondary Works

Althusser, Louis. "Ideology and Ideological State Apparatuses (Notes towards an Investigation)." In *Essays on Ideology,* pp. 1–60. Thetford, Norfolk: Verso, 1984.

Amussen, Susan Dwyer. *An Ordered Society: Gender and Class in Early Modern England.* Oxford: Blackwell, 1988.

Astell, Mary. "Sidney's Didactic Method in the *Old Arcadia.*" *Studies in English Literature* 24 (1984): 45–53.

Beal, Peter. *Index of Literary Manuscripts.* Vol. 1, *1450–1625.* London: Mansell, 1980.

Beaty, Nancy Lee. *The Craft of Dying: A Study in the Literary Tradition of the Ars Moriendi in England.* Yale Studies in English, 175. New Haven: Yale Univ. Press, 1970.

Beauchamp, Virginia. "Sidney's Sister as a Translator of Garnier." *Renaissance News* 10 (1957): 8–13.

Beilin, Elaine V. "'The Onely Perfect Vertue': Constancy in Mary Wroth's *Pamphilia to Amphilanthus.*" *Spenser Studies* 2 (1981): 229–45.

Beilin, Elaine V. *Redeeming Eve: Women Writers of the English Renaissance.* Princeton: Princeton Univ. Press, 1987.

Belsey, Catherine. *The Subject of Tragedy: Identity and Difference in Renaissance Drama.* London: Methuen, 1985.

Bennett, H. S. *English Books and Readers, 1558–1603.* Cambridge: Cambridge Univ. Press, 1965.

Braden, Gordon. *Renaissance Tragedy and the Senecan Tradition: Anger's Privilege.* New Haven: Yale Univ. Press, 1985.

Brennan, Michael. *Literary Patronage in the Renaissance: The Pembroke Family.* London: Routledge, 1988.

Brennan, Michael. "Nicholas Breton's *The Passions of the Spirit* and the Countess of Pembroke." *Review of English Studies* 38 (1987): 221–25.

Brooke, Nicholas. Introduction to *Bussy D'Ambois,* by George Chapman. London: Methuen, 1964.

Brooke, Tucker, and Matthias Shaaber. *The Renaissance.* Vol. 2 of *A Literary History of England.* Ed. Albert C. Baugh. New York: Appleton-Century-Crofts, 1967.

Bullough, Geoffrey. *The Narrative and Dramatic Sources of Shakespeare.* New York: Columbia Univ. Press, 1964.

Burke, Kenneth. "Literature as Equipment for Living." In *The Philosophy of Literary Form,* pp. 293–304. 1941; Baton Rouge: Louisiana State Univ. Press, 1967.

Bush, Douglas. *Mythology and the Renaissance Tradition in English Poetry.* 1932; New York: W. W. Norton, 1963.

Buxton, John. "A Draught of Sir Philip Sidney's *Arcadia.*" In *Historical Es-*

says (1600–1750) Presented to David Ogg, ed. H. E. Bell and R. L. Ollard, pp. 60–77. London: Adam and Charles Black, 1963.

Buxton, John. *Elizabethan Taste*. New York: St. Martins Press, 1964.

Buxton, John. *Sir Philip Sidney and the English Renaissance*. 1954; London: Macmillan, 1964.

Callaghan, Dympna. *Women and Gender in Renaissance Tragedy*. Atlantic Highlands, N.J.: Humanities Press International, 1989.

Campbell, Lily B. *Divine Poetry and Drama in Sixteenth-Century England*. Cambridge: Cambridge Univ. Press, 1959.

Cixous, Hélène. "Sorties." *The Newly Born Woman*. Trans. Betsy Wing. Minneapolis: Univ. of Minnesota Press, 1986.

Cooper, Sherod M. *The Sonnets of Astrophel and Stella: A Stylistic Study*. The Hague: Mouton, 1968.

Cotton, Nancy. *Women Playwrights in England, c. 1363–1750*. Lewisburg, Pa.: Bucknell Univ. Press, 1980.

Craft, William. "Heroic Self in the *New Arcadia*." *Studies in English Literature* 25 (1985): 45–67.

Crawford, Patricia. "A Provisional Checklist of Women's Published Writings, 1600–1700." In *Women in English Society, 1500–1800*, ed. Mary Prior, pp. 211–32. New York: Methuen, 1985.

Cressy, David. *Literacy and the Social Order: Reading and Writing in Tudor and Stuart England*. Cambridge: Cambridge Univ. Press, 1980.

Croft, Peter. See Sidney, Robert. *Poems*. (Primary Sources)

Dana, Margaret E. "The Providential Plot of the *Old Arcadia*." *Studies in English Literature* 17 (1977): 39–57.

Davis, Natalie Zemon. "Women on Top." *Society and Culture in Early Modern France*. Stanford: Stanford Univ. Press, 1975.

Davis, Walter. "Actaeon in *Arcadia*." *Studies in English Literature* 2 (1962): 95–110.

Davis, Walter. *A Map of Arcadia: Sidney's Romance and Its Tradition*. In Walter Davis and R. A. Lanham, *Sidney's Arcadia*. New Haven: Yale Univ. Press, 1965.

De Lauretis, Teresa. "The Technology of Gender." In *Technologies of Gender*, pp. 1–30. Bloomington: Indiana Univ. Press, 1987.

Dickinson, John W. "Renaissance Equity and *Measure for Measure*." *Shakespeare Quarterly* 13 (1962): 287–97.

Diehl, Huston, ed. *An Index of Icons in English Emblem Books, 1500–1700*. Norman: Univ. of Oklahoma Press, 1986.

Dipple, Elizabeth. "The Captivity Episode in the *New Arcadia*." *Journal of English and Germanic Philology* 70 (1971): 418–31.

Dollimore, Jonathan. "Transgression and Surveillance in *Measure for Measure*." In *Political Shakespeare: New Essays in Cultural Materialism*, ed. Jonathan Dollimore and Alan Sinfield, pp. 72–87. Ithaca: Cornell Univ. Press, 1985.

Dollimore, Jonathan, and Alan Sinfield. *Political Shakespeare: New Essays in Cultural Materialism*. Ithaca: Cornell Univ. Press, 1985.

Duncan-Jones, Katherine. "Philip Sidney's Toys." *Proceedings of the British Academy* 66 (1980): 161–78.

Duncan-Jones, Katherine. "Sidney and Titian." In *English Renaissance Studies for Dame Helen Gardner in Honor of Her Seventieth Birthday*, ed. John Carey, pp. 1–11. Oxford: Clarendon Press, 1980.

Durling, Dwight L. *Georgic Tradition in English Poetry*. New York: Columbia Univ. Press, 1935.

Durling, Robert M. *The Figure of the Poet in Renaissance Epic*. Cambridge: Harvard Univ. Press, 1965.

Eisenstadt, S. N., and Louis Roniger. "Patron-Client Relations as a Model of Structuring Social Exchange." *Comparative Studies in Society and History* 22 (1980): 42–77.

Eliot, T. S. "Apology for the Countess of Pembroke." In *The Use of Poetry and the Use of Criticism*, pp. 29–44. London: Faber and Faber, 1933.

Eliot, T. S. "Seneca in Elizabethan Translation." In *Selected Essays*, pp. 51–88. London: Faber and Faber, 1932.

Ezell, Margaret J. M. *The Patriarch's Wife*. Chapel Hill: Univ. of North Carolina Press, 1987.

Ferguson, Margaret W. "A Room Not Their Own: Renaissance Women as Readers and Writers." In *The Comparative Perspective on Literature: Approaches to Theory and Practice*, ed. Clayton Koelb and Susan Noakes, pp. 93–116. Ithaca: Cornell Univ. Press, 1988.

Ferguson, Margaret W. *Trials of Desire: Renaissance Defenses of Poetry*. New Haven: Yale Univ. Press, 1983.

Ferguson, Margaret W., Maureen Quilligan, and Nancy J. Vickers, eds. *Rewriting the Renaissance: The Discourses of Sexual Difference in Early Modern Europe*. Chicago: Univ. of Chicago Press, 1986.

Ferguson, Moira, ed. *First Feminists: British Women Writers, 1578–1799*. Bloomington: Indiana Univ. Press, 1985.

Fischer, Sandra K. "Elizabeth Cary and Tyranny, Domestic and Religious." In Hannay, *Silent But for the Word*, pp. 225–37.

Fisken, Beth Wynne. "Mary Sidney's *Psalmes:* Education and Wisdom." In Hannay, *Silent But for the Word*, pp. 166–83.

Flynn, Elizabeth A., and Patrocinio P. Schweickart, eds. *Gender and Reading: Essays on Readers, Texts, and Contexts*. Baltimore: Johns Hopkins Univ. Press, 1986.

Foucault, Michel. *History of Sexuality*. Vol. 1, *An Introduction*. Trans. Robert Hurley. New York: Vintage Books, 1980.

Foucault, Michel. *History of Sexuality.* Vol. 3, *Care of the Self.* Trans. Robert Hurley. New York: Pantheon, 1986.

Fraser, Antonia. *The Weaker Vessel.* New York: Knopf, 1984.

Garrod, H. W. "The Nightingale in Poetry." In *Profession of Poetry and Other Lectures,* pp. 131–59. Oxford: Clarendon Press, 1929.

Gartenberg, Patricia, and Nena Thames Whittemore. "A Checklist of English Women in Print, 1475–1640." *Bulletin of Bibliography* 34 (1977): 1–13.

Geckle, George L. *John Marston's Drama: Themes, Images, Sources.* Rutherford: Fairleigh Dickinson Univ. Press, 1980.

Gilbert, Sandra M., and Susan Gubar. *The Madwoman in the Attic.* New Haven: Yale Univ. Press, 1979.

Goldberg, Jonathan. *James I and the Politics of Literature.* Baltimore: Johns Hopkins Univ. Press, 1981.

Greenblatt, Stephen. "Sidney's *Arcadia* and the Mixed Mode." *Studies in Philology* 70 (1973): 269–78.

Greene, Thomas. *The Light in Troy: Imitation and Discovery in Renaissance Poetry.* New Haven: Yale Univ. Press, 1982.

Guillory, John. *Poetic Authority: Spenser, Milton, and Literary History.* New York: Columbia Univ. Press, 1983.

Hager, Alan. "The Exemplary Mirage: Fabrication of Sir Philip Sidney's Biographical Image and the Sidney Reader." *ELH* 48 (1981): 1–16. Reprinted in *Essential Articles for the Study of Sir Philip Sidney,* ed. Arthur Kinney, pp. 15–30. Hamden, Conn.: Archon, 1986.

Haller, William. *Foxe's "Book of Martyrs" and the Elect Nation.* London: Jonathan Cape, 1963.

Hamilton, A. C. *Sir Philip Sidney: A Study of His Life and Works.* Cambridge: Cambridge Univ. Press, 1977.

Hannay, Margaret P. "'Doo What Men May Sing': Mary Sidney and the Tradition of Admonitory Dedication." In Hannay, *Silent But for the Word,* pp. 149–65.

Hannay, Margaret P. "'Princes You as Men Must Dy': Genevan Advice to Monarchs in the *Psalms* of Mary Sidney." *English Literary Renaissance* 19 (1989): 22–41.

Hannay, Margaret P., ed. *Silent But for the Word.* Kent, Ohio: Kent State Univ. Press, 1985.

Harrison, Thomas Perrin, ed. *The Pastoral Elegy.* Austin: Univ. of Texas Press, 1939.

Heilbrun, Carolyn G. *Writing a Woman's Life.* London: W. W. Norton, 1988.

Helgerson, Richard. *The Elizabethan Prodigals.* Berkeley and Los Angeles: Univ. of California Press, 1976.

Henderson, Katherine Usher, and Barbara F. McManus. *Half Humankind.* See Primary Sources.

Henkel, Arthur, and Albrecht Schone, ed. *Emblemata: Handbuch zur Sinnbildkunst des XVI und XVII Jahrhunderts.* Stuttgart: J. B. Metzlersche, 1967.

Hieatt, A. Kent. "Edmund Spenser." *New Encylopedia Britannica,* 15th ed. (1974), 17:493–96.

Hogrefe, Pearl. *Women of Action in Tudor England.* Ames: Iowa State Univ. Press, 1977.

Holm, Janis Butler. "The Myth of a Feminist Humanism: Thomas Salter's *The Mirrhor of Modestie.*" *Soundings* 67 (1984): 443–52.

Hull, Suzanne W. *Chaste, Silent, and Obedient: English Books for Women, 1475–1640.* San Marino, Calif.: Huntington Library, 1982.

Hulse, Clark. "Stella's Wit: Penelope Rich as Reader of Sidney's Sonnets." In Ferguson et al., *Rewriting the Renaissance,* pp. 272–86.

Hunter, G. K. "Drab and Golden Lyrics of the Renaissance." In *Forms of Lyric: Selected Papers from the English Institute,* ed. Reuben A. Brower, pp. 1–18. New York: Columbia Univ. Press, 1970.

Jacobus, Mary. *Reading Women: Essays in Feminist Criticism.* New York: Columbia Univ. Press, 1986.

Jardine, Lisa. "Cultural Confusion and Shakespeare's Learned Heroines: 'These Are Old Paradoxes.'" *Shakespeare Quarterly* 38 (1987): 1–18.

Jardine, Lisa. *Still Harping on Daughters: Women and Drama in the Age of Shakespeare.* Totowa, N.J.: Barnes and Noble, 1983.

Jones, Ann Rosalind. "Assimilation with a Difference: Renaissance Women Poets and Literary Influence." *Yale French Studies* 62 (1981): 135–53.

Jones, Ann Rosalind. "City Women and Their Audiences: Louise Labe and Veronica Franco." In Ferguson et al., *Rewriting the Renaissance,* pp. 299–316.

Jones, Ann Rosalind. "Nets and Bridles: Early Modern Conduct Books and Sixteenth-Century Women's Lyrics." In *The Ideology of Conduct: Essays on Literature and the History of Sexuality,* ed. Nancy Armstrong and Leonard Tennenhouse. pp. 39–72. New York: Methuen, 1987.

Jones, Ann Rosalind, and Peter Stallybrass. "Courtship and Courtiership: The Politics of *Astrophil and Stella.*" *Studies in English Literature* 24 (1984): 53–68.

Jordan, Constance. "Gender and Politics in Sidney's *New Arcadia.*" Paper presented at the Renaissance Society of America Conference, Tempe, Arizona, November 1987.

Kalstone, David. *Sidney's Poetry: Contexts and Interpretations.* New York: Norton, 1965.

Kelso, Ruth. *Doctrine for the Lady of the Renaissance.* Urbana: Univ. of Illinois Press, 1956.

Kiefer, Frederick. "Seneca's Influence on Elizabethan Tragedy." *Research Opportunities in Renaissance Drama* 21 (1978): 17–34.

King, Margaret L. "Book-Lined Cells: Women and Humanism in the Early Italian Renaissance." In Labalme, *Beyond Their Sex,* pp. 66–90.

Kirk, Rudolf. See du Vair. (Primary Sources)

Koller, Katherine. "Abraham Fraunce and Edmund Spenser." *ELH* 7 (1940): 108–20.

Kristeva, Julia. *Desire in Language: A Semiotic Approach to Literature and Art.* Trans. Thomas Gora, Alice Jardine, and Leon S. Roudiez. Ed. Leon S. Roudiez. New York: Columbia Univ. Press, 1980.

Labalme, Patricia, ed. *Beyond their Sex: Learned Women of the English Renaissance.* New York: New York Univ. Press, 1980.

Lacan, Jacques. *Ecrits: A Selection.* Trans. Alan Sheridan. New York: Norton, 1977.

Lamb, Mary Ellen. "The Cooke Sisters: Attitudes towards Learned Women in the Renaissance." In Hannay, *Silent But for the Word,* pp. 107–25.

Lamb, Mary Ellen. "The Countess of Pembroke and the Art of Dying." In Rose, *Women in the Middle Ages and the Renaissance,* pp. 207–26.

Lamb, Mary Ellen. "The Countess of Pembroke's Patronage." *English Literary Renaissance* 12 (1982): 162–79.

Lamb, Mary Ellen. "The Myth of the Countess of Pembroke." *Yearbook of English Studies* 11 (1981): 194–202.

Lamb, Mary Ellen. "The Nature of Topicality in *Love's Labour's Lost.*" *Shakespeare Survey* 38 (1985): 49–60.

Lamb, Mary Ellen. "Three Unpublished Holograph Poems in the Bright Manuscript: A New Sidney Poet?" *Review of English Studies* 35 (1984): 301–15.

Lanham, Richard A. *The Old Arcadia.* In Walter Davis and R. A. Lanham, *Sidney's Arcadia.* New Haven: Yale Univ. Press, 1965.

Le Comte, Edward. *The Notorious Lady Essex.* New York: Dial, 1969.

Lee, Sidney. "Penelope Rich." *Dictionary of National Biography,* 16:1006–8.

Levao, Ronald. *Renaissance Minds and Their Fictions: Cusanus, Sidney, Shakespeare.* Berkeley and Los Angeles: Univ. of California Press, 1985.

Levinson, Ronald B. "The 'Godlesse Minde' in Sidney's *Arcadia.*" *Modern Philology* 29 (1931): 21–26.

Lewalski, Barbara K. "Of God and Good Women: The Poems of Aemilia Lanyer." In Hannay, *Silent But for the Word,* pp. 203–24.

Lewis, C. S. *English Literature in the Sixteenth Century.* Oxford History of English Literature, 3. Oxford: Clarendon Press, 1965.

Lutz, Catherine A. "Emotion, Thought, and Estrangement: Emotion as a Cultural Category." *Cultural Anthropology* 1 (1986): 287–309.

Lutz, Catherine A. *Unnatural Emotions.* Chicago: Univ. of Chicago Press, 1988.

McCanles, Michael. "The Rhetoric of Character Portrayal in Sidney's *New Arcadia.*" *Criticism* 25 (1983): 123–39.

McCoy, Richard C. *Sir Philip Sidney: Rebellion in Arcadia.* New Brunswick: Rutgers Univ. Press, 1979.

Mack, Phyllis. "Women as Prophets during the English Civil War." *Feminist Studies* 8 (1982): 19–46.

Maclean, Ian. *The Renaissance Notion of Woman.* Cambridge: Cambridge Univ. Press, 1980.

Marcus, Leah. *Puzzling Shakespeare: Local Reading and Its Discontents.* Berkeley and Los Angeles: Univ. of California Press, 1989.

Marcus, Leah. "Shakespeare's Comic Heroines, Elizabeth I, and the Uses of Androgeny." In Rose, *Women in the Middle Ages and the Renaissance,* pp. 135–54.

Marotti, Arthur. *John Donne, Coterie Poet.* Madison: Univ. of Wisconsin Press, 1986.

Mazzotta, Guiseppe. "The *Canzoniere* and the Language of the Self." *Studies in Philology* 75 (1978): 271–96.

Mauss, Michael. *The Gift: Forms and Functions of Exchange in Archaic Societies.* Glencoe, Ill.: Free Press, 1954.

Mendelson, Sara Heller. "Debate, The Weightiest Business: Marriage in an Upper-Gentry Family in Seventeenth-Century England." *Past and Present* 85 (1979): 126–35.

Miller, Jacqueline T. *Poetic License: Authority and Authorship in Medieval and Renaissance Contexts.* Oxford: Oxford Univ. Press, 1986.

Modleski, Tania. *Loving with a Vengeance: Mass-Produced Fantasies for Women.* New York: Methuen, 1982.

Montrose, Louis Adrian. "Celebration and Insinuation: Sir Philip Sidney and the Motives of Elizabethan Courtiership." *Renaissance Drama,* n.s., 8 (1977): 3–35.

Moore-Smith, G. C. See Abraham Fraunce. *Victoria.* (Primary Sources)

Morgan, John. *Godly Learning: Puritan Attitudes towards Reason, Learning, and Education, 1560–1640.* Cambridge: Cambridge Univ. Press, 1986.

Morris, Harry. "Thomas Watson and Abraham Fraunce." *PMLA* 76 (1961): 152–53.

Mulvey, Laura. "Visual Pleasure and Narrative Cinema." *Screen* 16 (1975): 6–18.

Nelson, William. *The Poetry of Edmund Spenser: A Study.* New York: Columbia Univ. Press, 1965.

Noakes, Susan. "On the Superficiality of Women." In *The Comparative Perspective on Literature: Approaches to Theory and Practice*, ed. Clayton Koelb and Susan Noakes, pp. 339–55. Ithaca: Cornell Univ. Press, 1988.

Norbrook, David. *Poetry and Politics in the English Renaissance*. London: Routledge and Kegan Paul, 1984.

Ong, Walter. *Orality and Literacy*. New York: Methuen, 1982.

Ong, Walter. *Rhetoric, Romance, and Technology*. Ithaca: Cornell Univ. Press, 1971.

Orgel, Stephen. *The Illusion of Power*. Berkeley and Los Angeles: Univ. of California Press, 1975.

Ortner, Sherry B. "Is Female to Male as Nature Is to Culture?" In *Women, Culture, and Society*, ed. Michelle Zimbalist Rosaldo and Louise Lamphere, pp. 67–87. Stanford: Stanford Univ. Press, 1974.

Osborn, James M. *Young Philip Sidney, 1572–1577*. New Haven: Yale Univ. Press, 1972.

Palmer, Ralph Graham. *Seneca's "De Remediis Fortuitorum" and the Elizabethans*. Institute of Elizabethan Studies. Kendal, England: Titus Wilson, 1953.

Partridge, Eric. *Shakespeare's Bawdy*. New York: E. P. Dutton, 1969.

Patterson, Annabel. *Censorship and Interpretation: The Conditions of Writing and Reading in Early Modern England*. Madison: Univ. of Wisconsin Press, 1984.

Peterson, Douglas L. *The English Lyric from Wyatt to Donne: A History of Plain and Eloquent Styles*. Princeton: Princeton Univ. Press, 1967.

Praz, Mario. *Studies in Seventeenth-Century Imagery*. Rome: Edizioni di storia e letteratura, 1964.

Prescott, Anne Lake. "The Pearl of the Valois and Elizabeth I: Marguerite de Navarre's *Miroir* and Tudor England." In Hannay, *Silent But for the Word*, pp. 61–76.

Quint, David. *Origin and Originality in Renaissance Literature*. New Haven: Yale Univ. Press, 1983.

Radway, Janice. *Reading the Romance: Women, Patriarchy, and Popular Tradition*. Chapel Hill: Univ. of North Carolina Press, 1982.

Ratiere, Martin. *Faire Bitts: Sir Philip Sidney and Renaissance Political Theory*. Pittsburgh: Duquesne Univ. Press, 1984.

Richards, Melville. *Welsh Administrative and Territorial Units*. Cardiff: Univ. of Wales Press, 1969.

Ringler, William. See Sidney, Sir Philip. *Poems*. (Primary Sources)

Roberts, Josephine. *Architectonic Knowledge in the New Arcadia (1590): Sidney's Use of the Heroic Journey*. Elizabethan and Renaissance Studies, 69. Salzburg: Institut für Englische Sprache und Literatur, 1978.

Roberts, Josephine. "The Biographical Problem of *Pamphilia to Amphilanthus*." *Tulsa Studies in Women's Literature* 1 (1982): 43–53.

Roberts, Josephine. "Extracts from the *Arcadia* in the MS Notebook of Lady Katherine Manners." *Notes and Queries*, n.s., 28 (1981): 35–36.

Roberts, Josephine. "The Huntington Manuscript of Lady Mary Wroth's Play, *Loves Victorie*." *Huntington Library Quarterly* 46 (1983): 156–74.

Roberts, Josephine. "The Imaginary Epistles of Sir Philip Sidney and Lady Penelope Rich." *English Literary Renaissance* 15 (1985): 59–77.

Roberts, Josephine. "An Unpublished Literary Quarrel Concerning the Suppression of Mary Wroth's *Urania* (1621)." *Notes and Queries* 222 (1977): 532–35.

Roberts, Josephine. See Wroth, Lady Mary. *Poems*. (Primary Sources)

Robertson, Jean. "*The Passions of the Spirit* (1599) and Nicholas Breton." *Huntington Library Quarterly* 3 (1939): 69–73.

Rose, Mark. *Heroic Love*. Cambridge: Harvard Univ. Press, 1968.

Rose, Mark. "Sidney's Womanish Man." *Review of English Studies*, n.s., 15 (1964): 353–63.

Rose, Mary Beth. *The Expense of Spirit: Love and Sexuality in English Renaissance Drama*. Ithaca: Cornell Univ. Press, 1988.

Rose, Mary Beth. "Gender, Genre, and History: Seventeenth-Century English Women and the Art of Autobiography." In Rose, *Women in the Middle Ages and the Renaissance*, pp. 245–78.

Rose, Mary Beth, ed. *Women in the Middle Ages and the Renaissance: Literary and Historical Perspectives*. Syracuse: Syracuse Univ. Press, 1986.

Rowse, A. L., ed. *The Poems of Shakespeare's Dark Lady: Salve Deus Rex Judaeorum by Emilia Lanier*. London: Cape, 1978.

Ruether, Rosemary Radford. "Misogynism and Virginal Feminism in the Fathers of the Church." In *Religion and Sexism*, ed. Rosemary Radford Reuther, pp. 150–83. New York: Simon and Schuster, 1974.

Russ, Joanna. "What Can a Heroine Do? or, Why Women Can't Write." In *Images of Women in Fiction*, ed. Susan Koppelman Cornillon. Bowling Green: Ohio Univ. Press, 1972.

Salzman, Paul. "Contemporary References in Mary Wroth's *Urania*." *Review of English Studies* 29 (1978): 178–81.

Salzman, Paul. *English Prose Fiction, 1558–1700: A Critical History*. Oxford: Clarendon Press, 1985.

Sankovitch, Tilde. "Inventing Authority of Origin: *The Difficult Enterprise*." In Rose, *Women in the Middle Ages and the Renaissance*, pp. 227–44.

Saunders, Jason Lewis. *Justius Lipsius: The Philosophy of Renaissance Stoicism*. New York: Liberal Arts Press, 1955.

Saunders, J. W. "The Stigma of Print: A Note on the Social Bases of Tudor Poetry." *Essays in Criticism* 1 (1951): 139–64.

Schelling, Felix. "Sidney's Sister, Pembroke's Mother." In *Shakespeare and the Demi-Science*, pp. 100–125. Philadelphia: Univ. of Pennsylvania Press, 1927.

Schleiner, Winifred. "Differences of Theme and Structure of the Erona Episodes in the *Old* and *New Arcadia*." *Studies in Philology* 70 (1973): 377–91.

Showalter, Elaine. "The Other Bostonians: Gender and Literary Study." *Yale Journal of Criticism* 1 (1988): 179–87.

Sinfield, Alan. *Literature in Protestant England, 1560–1660*. Totowa, N.J.: Barnes and Noble, 1983.

Sinfield, Alan. "Power and Ideology: An Outline Theory and Sidney's *Arcadia*." *ELH* 52 (1985): 259–78.

Smith, D. Nichol. "Authors and Patrons." In *Shakespeare's England*, 2:182–211. Oxford: Clarendon Press, 1917.

Smith, Hilda. *Reason's Disciples: Seventeenth-Century English Feminists*. Urbana: Univ. of Illinois Press, 1982.

Soellner, Rolf. "Shakespeare's *Lucrece* and the Garnier-Pembroke Connection." *Shakespeare Studies* 15 (1982): 1–20.

Spriet, Pierre. *Samuel Daniel (1563–1619): Sa Vie, son oeuvre*. Paris: Didier, 1968.

Spufford, Margaret. *Small Books and Pleasant Histories: Popular Fiction and Its Readership in Seventeenth-Century England*. Athens: Univ. of Georgia Press, 1981.

Stallybrass, Peter. "Patriarchal Territories: The Body Enclosed." In Ferguson et al., *Rewriting the Renaissance*, pp. 123–44.

Stillman, Robert E. *Sidney's Poetic Justice*. Lewisburg, Pa.: Bucknell Univ. Press, 1986.

Stone, Laurence. *The Crisis of the Aristocracy, 1558–1641*. Oxford: Clarendon Press, 1965.

Stone, Laurence. *The Family, Sex, and Marriage in England, 1500–1800*. New York: Harper and Row, 1977.

Swift, Carolyn Ruth. "Feminine Identity in Lady Mary Wroth's Romance *Urania*." *English Literary Renaissance* 14 (1984): 328–46.

Syford, Constance Miriam. "The Direct Source of the Pamela-Cecropia Episode in the *Arcadia*." *PMLA* 49 (1934): 472–89.

Thickstun, Margaret Olofson. *Fictions of the Feminine: Puritan Doctrine and the Representation of Women*. Ithaca: Cornell Univ. Press, 1988.

Thomas, Keith. "Women and the Civil War Sects." *Past and Present* 13 (1958): 42–62.

Thrasher-Smith, Shelley. *The Luminous Globe: Methods of Characterization in Sidney's New Arcadia*. Salzburg Studies in English Literature, 94. Salzburg: Institut für Anglistik und Amerikanistik, 1982.

Townsend, Freda. "Sidney and Ariosto." *PMLA* 61 (1946): 97–108.

Travitsky, Betty. "'The Wyll and Testament' of Isabella Whitney." *English Literary Renaissance* 10 (1980): 76–95.

Travitsky, Betty. *The Paradise of Women*. See Primary Sources.

Turner, Myron. "The Heroic Ideal in Sidney's Revised *Arcadia*." *Studies in English Literature* 10 (1970): 63–82.

Underdown, D. E. "The Taming of the Scold: The Enforcement of Patriarchal Authority in Early Modern England." In *Order and Disorder in Early Modern England*, ed. A. J. Fletcher and J. Stevenson, pp. 116–36. Cambridge: Cambridge Univ. Press, 1985.

Walker, D. P. "Ways of Dealing with Atheists." *Bibliotheque d'Humanism et de la Renaissance* 17 (1955): 252–77.

Wallace, Malcolm. *The Life of Sir Philip Sidney*. Cambridge: Cambridge Univ. Press, 1915.

Waller, Gary F. "The Countess of Pembroke and Gendered Reading." Forthcoming.

Waller, Gary F. *Mary Sidney, Countess of Pembroke: A Critical Study of Her Writings and Literary Milieu*. Salzburg: Institut für Anglistik und Amerikanistik, 1979.

Waller, Gary F. "The Rewriting of Petrarch: Sidney and the Languages of Sixteenth-Century Poetry." In *Sir Philip Sidney and the Interpretation of Renaissance Culture*, ed. Gary F. Waller and Michael D. Moore, pp. 69–83. Totowa, N.J.: Barnes and Noble, 1984.

Waller, Gary F. "Struggling into Discourse: The Emergence of Renaissance Women's Writing." In Hannay, *Silent But for the Word*, pp. 238–56.

Waller, Gary F. "'This Matching of Contraries': Calvinism and Courtly Philosophy in the Sidney Psalms." *English Studies* 55 (1974): 22–31.

Waller, Gary F., ed. *Pamphilia to Amphilanthus*. See Wroth, Mary. (Primary Sources)

Waller, Gary F., ed. *The Triumph of Death*. See Sidney, Mary. (Primary Sources)

Watkins, Owen C. *The Puritan Experience*. London: Routledge and Kegan Paul, 1972.

Weigall, Rachel. "An Elizabethan Gentlewoman: The Journal of Lady Mildmay, circa 1570–1617." *Quarterly Review* 215 (1911): 119–38.

Weiner, Andrew. *Sir Philip Sidney and the Poetics of Protestantism: A Study of Contexts*. Minneapolis: Univ. of Minnesota Press, 1978.

Wiesner, Merry E. *Women in the Sixteenth Century: A Bibliography.* St. Louis: Center for Reformation Research, 1983.

Wiesner, Merry E. "Spinsters and Seamstresses: Women in Cloth and Clothing Production." In Ferguson et al., *Rewriting the Renaissance,* pp. 191–205.

Wilkins, Ernest Hatch. See Petrarch. (Primary Source)

Wilkinson, L. P. *Ovid Recalled.* Cambridge: Cambridge Univ. Press, 1955.

Williams, Franklin. *Index to Dedications and Commendatory Verse in English Books before 1641.* London: Bibliographical Society, 1962.

Williams, Raymond. *Culture.* Glasgow: Fontana, 1981.

Williamson, George C. *Lady Anne Clifford, Countess of Dorset, Pembroke, and Montgomery, 1590–1676: Her Life, Letters, and Work.* East Ardsley, Yorkshire: S. R. Publ., 1967.

Wilson, Katherina M., ed. *Women of the Renaissance and Reformation.* Athens: Univ. of Georgia Press, 1987.

Wilson, Mona. *Sir Philip Sidney.* Oxford: Oxford Univ. Press, 1932.

Witherspoon, Alexander. *The Influence of Robert Garnier on Elizabethan Drama.* Yale Studies in Drama, 65. New Haven: Yale Univ. Press, 1924.

Witten-Hannah, Margaret A. "Lady Mary Wroth's *Urania:* The Work and the Tradition." Ph.D. dissertation, Univ. of Auckland, 1978.

Witten-Hannah, Margaret A. "Sleeping with Monsters: Lady Mary Wroth's Complete *Urania,* the Book and Manuscript Continuation." *Aulla XX: Proceedings and Papers of the Twentieth Congress of the Australasian Universities Language and Literature Association.* Canberra: Australasian Univ. Language and Literature Assoc., 1980.

Woodbridge, Linda. *Women and the English Renaissance: Literature and the Nature of Womankind, 1540–1620.* Urbana: Univ. of Illinois Press, 1984.

Woolf, Virginia. *"The Countess of Pembroke's Arcadia."* In *The Common Reader: Second Series,* pp. 39–49. New York: Harcourt Brace, 1948.

Wright, Louis. *Middle-Class Culture in Elizabethan England.* Chapel Hill: Univ. of North Carolina Press, 1935.

Wright, Louis. "Reading of Renaissance Englishwomen." *Studies in Philology* 28 (1931): 671–88.

Wrightson, Keith. "The Nadir of English Illegitimacy in the English Seventeenth Century." In *Bastardy and Its Comparative History,* ed. Peter Laslett et al., pp. 176–91. Cambridge: Harvard Univ. Press, 1980.

Young, Frances. *Mary Sidney, Countess of Pembroke.* London: David Nutt, 1912.

Index